FORGOTTEN
VOICES

This book is dedicated to the late Jack Sharpe, whose courage and tenacity in the face of the enemy overcame the most appalling of circumstances.

His spirit, and the spirit of so many like him, is embodied in this book.

FORGOTTEN VOICES

OF THE
SECOND WORLD WAR

IN ASSOCIATION WITH THE
IMPERIAL WAR MUSEUM

MAX ARTHUR

EBURY
PRESS

First published in Great Britain in 2004

10 9 8 7 6 5 4 3 2 1

First published by
Ebury Press
Random House, 20 Vauxhall Bridge Road, London SW1V 2SA

Random House Australia (Pty) Limited
20 Alfred Street, Milsons Point, Sydney, New South Wales 2061, Australia

Random House New Zealand Limited
18 Poland Road, Glenfield, Auckland 10, New Zealand

Random House South Africa (Pty) Limited
Endulini, 5A Jubilee Road, Parktown 2193, South Africa

The Random House Group Limited Reg. No. 954009

www.randomhouse.co.uk

A CIP catalogue record for this book is available from the British Library.

Cover Design by Two Associates
Text design and typesetting by Textype

ISBN 0091897343

Papers used by Ebury Press are natural, recyclable products made from wood
grown in sustainable forests

Printed and bound in Great Britain by Clays Ltd, St Ives plc

Contents

Acknowledgements

Within the Imperial War Museum I am indebted to Margaret Brooks, the Keeper of the Sound Archive, and her excellent staff, John Stopford-Pickering and Richard McDonough. I am also most grateful to Peter Hart, the Museum's distinguished oral historian, for his advice on particular accounts. Members of the Photographic Department of the Museum could not have been more helpful with the location of photographs amidst their vast collection. Terry Charman, the Museum's historian, read through the manuscript for historical accuracy and suggested changes, which have been incorporated. I am grateful to him for his attention to detail.

At my publishers Ebury Press, I would like to thank Jake Lingwood, my editor, who has put maximum energy behind both books. He has been ably supported by the most helpful and patient Claire Kingston, as assistant editor. I must also pay tribute to the Sales and Marketing force of Ebury Press and particularly thank them for their continued enthusiasm and commitment for both books. Martin Noble did a tremendous job in editing the final draft and Steve Cox proofread the manuscript with his usual diligent eye. My agent Barbara Levy, who is also the agent for the Imperial War Museum, helped create the project and has been a hundred per cent behind it throughout and I thank her.

The initial research and transcription of the tapes for the book was carried out most methodically by Jo Coombes, ably supported by her brother Tim. Vicky Thomas not only transcribed additional tapes and organised the transcripts but also researched the historical aspects of the book. I am in great debt to her for her professionalism and tenacity. Joshua Levine, who worked on my previous book, brought considerable flair and imagination to his research for this book and I profoundly thank him.

My brother Adrian, an expert on the British Army, always came up with the correct title for each regiment and offered sound advice. Don and Liz McClen, who have supported me through all my work over the last twenty years, were a constant source of encouragement, as was my friend Susan Jeffreys. This work has been enriched by the loyal and loving support of Ruth Cowen.

During the writing of this book my good friend Sir Martin Gilbert has given me sound advice and made a number of suggestions, all of which have enhanced the book. I am most grateful to him and in particular for his fine Introduction.

Any errors in this book are entirely the responsibility of the author.

Max Arthur
July 2004

Author's Preface

Forgotten Voices of the Second World War is a sequel to *Forgotten Voices of the Great War* and has been created from the remarkable collection of taped interviews held by the Sound Archive of the Imperial War Museum. It is an archive of extraordinary depth, containing thousands of recordings of men and women who have served or witnessed the wars and campaigns from the First World War to the present.

The Second World War archive contains several thousand taped interviews recorded over the last thirty years. I have drawn extensively from this archive and listened to hundred of hours of taped interviews and read countless transcripts of people's experiences of the war.

Apart from a number of French and German accounts, the Imperial War Museum interviews primarily cover British and Commonwealth participants, so I have concentrated on the campaigns where they have been involved. The exception is the Salerno landings, where the personal accounts are of American troops. These accounts come from a collection presented to the Sound Archive some years ago.

I have arranged the accounts, wherever possible, in chronological order. However I have made an exception with the accounts of the Far East, which I have placed at the end of each year. Because these are personal accounts, not cold histories, the order in which I have placed them may sometimes seem imperfect. Wherever possible I have checked for historical accuracy. The length of these accounts varies – some take many pages, whereas others select the most affecting moments. In some cases, contributors appear several times to tell of different actions in which they were involved. To place the accounts in an historical context, I have included a short history of each year from 1939 to 1945, and where necessary have given further background to the campaign within the particular year.

What I have sought to do is capture the experiences and atmosphere of the Second World War: the waiting, the preparation, the action and the consequences of those actions. Some of these accounts are raw and horrific, others more matter-of-fact or reflective. They all have their place in the tapestry of war.

Recalling experiences forty or fifty years after the event can lead to occasional inaccuracies, but what cannot be taken away is the feeling that comes from these interviews, and I have tried to capture the intensity of these feelings. It has been a privilege to listen to these men and women, many long dead, and to bring to life again their vivid memories. These are their words – I have been but a catalyst.

Max Arthur
July 2004

Introduction by Sir Martin Gilbert

Max Arthur put all students of war in his debt with his book on the First World War, *Forgotten Voices*. This book revived long-hidden archival recollections of those who had fought in what became known as 'the war to end war'. Had that been the case, this second volume would not have been needed, or indeed possible. When war broke out again in 1939, many of those who had fought twenty years earlier, and millions of new faces, entered an even longer conflict.

This new volume covers almost six years of fighting on land, sea and air between 1939 and 1945. It spans all the war fronts on which British troops, sailors and airmen were to be found. Civilian voices are also heard in these pages.

Max Arthur has a sensitive ear for the nuances as well as the hammer blows of war. He has found space for the young evacuees who were taken away from their homes in the threatened cities and into the countryside, or across the Atlantic. Many little-recorded episodes of the war, such as the Norwegian campaign on 1940, the convoy run to Malta and the Chindit expeditions behind Japanese lines, find a place in these pages.

Although German bombs had dropped on London in the First World War – from Zeppelin and aircraft – and many hundreds of civilians killed, it was during the Blitz in 1940–1 that the full intensity and horror of civilian bombing became apparent, long before Hamburg or Dresden. The voices of those grim months in Britain are powerful and evocative.

The campaigns and battles of the war are illuminated by the voices assembled here. They include the Dunkirk evacuation, the raids on St Nazaire and Dieppe, the war in North Africa, the battles in Italy, the bombing of Germany, the preparations for the Normandy landings, the Normandy landings themselves (an extraordinarily graphic set of recollections), the war in Burma and on the Indian frontier, Arnhem, the Ardennes, crossing the Rhine in March 1945, Victory-in-Europe Day, the terrifying battles against the Japanese, and the Nuremberg Trials. Taken together they form a varied and vivid tapestry, emotionally draining, heroic in its portrait of men and women at war.

While the voices are predominantly British, they include, among others, a German schoolgirl in Dresden, a Japanese officer in Burma, New Zealand pilots, Australian infantrymen, a Rajput major, a French cavalryman, a Polish parachutist and a French resistance fighter. Commonwealth troops are well represented, as they are also well represented in the war cemeteries of Europe, North Africa, the Far East and the Pacific.

The variety of contributors is remarkable: they include a fourteen-year-old telegram delivery boy delivering 'death telegrams' to those who had lost a loved one, British medical students entering a liberated Belsen concentration camp, a British prisoner of war in Nagasaki when the atom bomb was dropped, merchant seamen, submariners, snipers, commandos, clerks, buglers, war correspondents, wireless operators, firemen and nurses, parachutists, prisoners of war. These were the fortunate survivors of more than two thousand days of war. The millions of men who killed are forever silent.

Those who recorded the stories that Max Arthur has chosen for this book – from the remarkable Imperial War Museum collection – will live on, in the printed word, with all its emotional power, for as long as books continue to be read.

Martin Gilbert,
Honorary Fellow,
Merton College, Oxford,
3 August 2004

1939

The day war was declared, the admiral called us together in the wardroom and gave us champagne and gave us a toast – 'Damnation to Hitler'.

No one wanted to admit that another European conflict was inevitable – the horror of the last war was such that, to some, almost any compromise would be acceptable to avoid conflict again. In 1938, however, Hitler's foreign policy became more aggressive and he made plans to annexe parts of Czechoslovakia. The British Prime Minister Neville Chamberlain flew to Germany to discuss Czechoslovakia with the German, French and Italian leaders, and returned having agreed to cede the disputed Sudetenland area to Germany, with a promise of 'Peace for our time'.

However, as 1939 dawned, the Allies began to prepare for war in earnest. Hitler continued his steady drive to take over Europe, unperturbed by any signed agreements, and his troops invaded Czechoslovakia in March. By mid-May, Hitler had joined with Italy in 'The Pact of Steel', and revoked the non-aggression pact with Poland, reaching an agreement with Stalin in August as to how they would partition Poland. The Polish Army mobilised as Hitler's sent a force of some 750,000 men into Poland on 1 September. Britain and France honoured their obligation to their ally, and declared war on Germany on 3 September.

Britain's army at the outbreak of war had been boosted by the introduction of conscription for the first time during peace – but it was still an under-manned, under-equipped British Expeditionary Force that sailed for France on 9 September.

On land there was no full-scale fighting. There were naval confrontations when on the night of 3 September U-30 sank the British passenger liner *Athenia*, and the navy sank U-39 in the Atlantic. As 1939 drew to a close, Poland had been divided between Germany and Russia, and Soviet forces had invaded Finland, but Europe seemed to hold its breath. A strange sense of anticlimax reigned.

THE OUTBREAK OF WAR

Young men joined up, many before conscription reached them – and women too embraced a new life in the forces. Those who remembered the previous conflict, however, saw bleak times ahead. Gas had proved a deadly weapon in the trenches – and the prospect now was that it could be inflicted on the civilian population. Gas masks were issued to the public, air-raid sirens were tested, Air Raid Precautions demanded that full black-out be achieved during hours of darkness, and people dug up their gardens to erect air-raid shelters. After a flurry of sand-bagging and bomb-proofing, there was an atmosphere of fearful anticipation. Western Europe waited for the first action, and hoped fervently that the troops would be home before Christmas.

Evelyn White
Civilian in Birmingham
I remember vividly 'peace in our time' – Neville Chamberlain coming back from Munich. We thought, 'Thank God, it's going to be peace. It's not going to be war.' But of course, events proved wrong. I began thinking, 'Is it going to be like the First World War?' when thousands of men were killed. In a way, they were human fodder. I thought, 'Is it going to be a repeat? What's going to happen to my brothers?'

Muriel Tucker
Civilian, aged 13, in London
I remember the bother with Czechoslovakia, and we thought there was going to be a war. My father certainly did – and we were quite prepared for it. Then of course it all blew over temporarily, and I remember Dad bought us a dolly each to celebrate, because it seemed as if it was going to be all right – and of course, it wasn't.

Frederick Winterbotham
Secret Intelligence Service
We had an agreement with our man in Warsaw that he would let us know the moment hostilities started. And I think it was when the first bomb dropped on Warsaw that he got through to us at once – and I had the signal brought in to me and I was sleeping in the office, of course, at the time. I had the pleasure of ringing up the Secretary to the Cabinet, who was sleeping at that time, and happened to be a friend of mine. I said, 'I've got a job for you. War has broken

War becomes a reality, 3 September 1939.
Grim faces greet the news on a London street.

On 3 September. Crowds in Downing Street, are restrained by police in tin helmets, as the news is released that war has been declared.

out and I think you'd better advise the cabinet.' I won't repeat his language at the other end, because he didn't get another wink of sleep that night. But we were now at war. Chamberlain talked about the subject on the radio a few days later.

Dorothy Williams
Teenager at outbreak of war
It was a very anxious time. My parents followed the events very closely, so when we knew that war could break out – I think it was 11 o'clock in the morning – we were really keyed up. I was frightened. We didn't know what was ahead. We had relatives who had been badly gassed. Father said if the Germans ever landed, he would kill us all rather than us ever fall into their hands. That frightened us a little bit too – we didn't know which was going to be the worse of the two. Oh yes, he meant it. He had been right through the previous war and he had seen a lot.

We had to go to a hall in the village and collect our gas masks. I never found mine very comfortable. For babies there were the big gas masks in which the child lay. I know my baby sister was absolutely terrified of it. I don't know what would have happened if she had remained in it for a long time because she was so frightened. She screamed the place down and went quite blue in the face. Of course we had to carry them everywhere we went in those little cardboard boxes with a piece of string attached. We never moved without them. I took mine with me until I joined up.

Doris Scott
Civilian from Canning Town, East London
I was terrified of what would happen, since I had been through the First World War, and had had to take shelter in a chapel on the corner of the street where we lived. The air power of the First World War wasn't anything like that of 1939, but those raids were frightening enough. The possibility of war was really frightening, especially with two young children.

We were told that we all had to go to the local town hall and receive gas masks. My baby had to be issued with a sort of diving helmet with horizontal wires, totally encasing her. My other daughter was three, and had this Mickey Mouse gas mask which wouldn't scare her. My mother, being asthmatic, was given another contraption, which was right for her breathing – and I had the normal mask that everyone else did. So we had four different types of gas mask in one family.

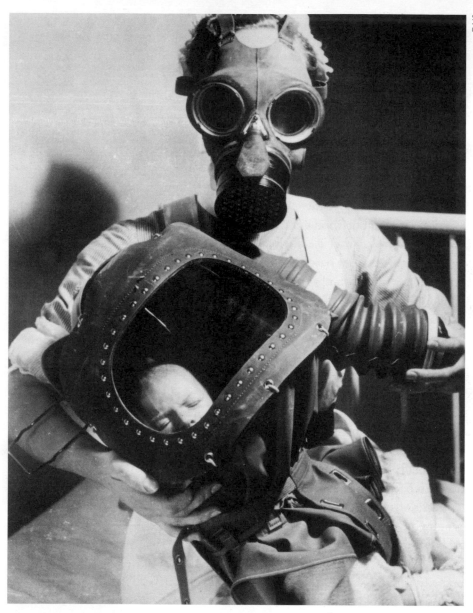

Fully kitted out to face a gas attack, a nurse shows how to fit a special baby's gas mask.

Ronald McGill
Evacuee from Vauxhall, South London – nine at the outbreak of war
The week prior to the outbreak of war, everybody seemed to know it was going to happen – and my parents were worried. They thought that our part of London would be devastated by bombs the first moment that the war was declared. Although now we know it's ridiculous, when you look back, it wasn't. These people round there that lived in the Vauxhall area – they weren't too well educated, the parents. The children were gradually getting better than the parents who were very working-class. They had a very real fear.

My mother had seen the Zeppelins come down over Elstree in the First World War, and she thought that was going to happen again. I heard her telling another lady that if Germany did attack, she would rather kill her own children than let them be taken. I just couldn't believe it – I couldn't imagine Germans in my house. It didn't make sense. They issued gas masks in Walworth Road before the outbreak of war, and that was the last straw. They thought about gas, and that frightened all these average working-class ladies. It was a fear which was generated by our own air-raid precautions, if you like.

Jutta Buder
Jewish girl living in Germany
We were on vacation in September 1939 and we were playing on the beach – and our parents came running down to the beach and told us war had broken out, and that we had to go home immediately. I thought it was very exciting, even though I didn't want to leave the beach – and we all pushed into trains and everybody had to go home.

Mysterious things were beginning to happen. We lived in a duplex, and the radio used to be on the wall facing us – and my parents moved the radio to an inside wall of the house and away from our neighbours, and they would keep it very low, because they were listening to foreign stations – which was, of course, forbidden. Sometimes my mother listened from under a blanket so that nobody could hear outside – and we were told not to talk about that outside our home.

Edward Doe
Former soldier who had fought in the Spanish Civil War
Looking round, I could see that we were quite unprepared to enter a war of any magnitude – we just weren't ready. We never had the kit and we never had the men. We never had anything – we had so far lagged behind.

Us chaps who had been in the service were under no illusion as to what the word 'war' itself meant. We had no illusions on that score. However, I answered the call the same as many thousands of others and reported myself at Winchester, and we were there a total of two days. Everything was in chaos because the barracks not only housed the King's Royal Rifle Corps, it also housed the Rifle Brigade and also the Hampshire Regiment. You can imagine the chaos as literally hundreds and hundreds were pouring through the gates those first three days – all reserves answering the call.

Lieutenant Dick Caldwell
Lieutenant-surgeon, Royal Navy
As war approached, I think the thought of going to war was exciting. The day war was declared, the admiral called us together in the wardroom and gave us champagne and gave us a toast – 'Damnation to Hitler'.

Pilot Officer Douglas Grice
32 Squadron, RAF
On September 3rd 1939, I seem to remember listening to the wireless, as it was called – hearing the announcement that we were at war with Germany. And there was, I mean a suppressed cheer – the thought that at long last we would earn our keep was really quite exhilarating. We didn't know quite what was going to follow. But at the time, we were all fully trained – well, as trained as we could have been for fighting. I mean we didn't know then that our tactics were all wrong – but anyway, we could fly our aeroplanes rather well.

Our tactics had never been tested in warfare – unlike the Germans, who had the Spanish Civil War to practise in. We had a set series of attacks – they were number one, two, three, four, five and six. And there were various manoeuvres you had to go through, like going from flying in Vic formation to flying in line astern. Attacking bombers from above, behind – the side – none of which was the slightest bit of use when you came to the point of actually finding the enemy and wanting to fire your gun.

Lady Anne Chichester
Civilian voluntary worker in Hampshire
Although the war hadn't reached England, it had very much reached the Continent, and two or three days before war broke out, 46 children arrived from Portsmouth with some of their teachers. They came in buses from Beaulieu Road Station, and the Red Cross detachment all greeted them in the village and in the WI hut we had tea for them and gave them buns and biscuits before we sorted out

which house they should go to. Each of them was given a bag of rations. The sad thing was that whoever had organised the departure of the children from Portsmouth had forgotten to tell the children to bring knives and forks and spoons, so we all had to rush round and borrow from everybody.

On that fateful day of Sunday, 3rd September at 11 in the morning, we all sat round the radio and we heard Neville Chamberlain's speech with the horrific news that we were actually, from that moment, at war with Germany. Everybody was extremely shattered, and by an extraordinary coincidence, within ten minutes of the announcement, all the sirens went off. And we really did think that at that very moment the bombers were about to arrive. But it was only a false alarm, and the all-clear went – but it was a very strange time. We really thought that we were going to be bombed. By about six o'clock in the evening, King George VI spoke to the nation. It was a very amazing time to live through. We spent most of the day just talking about the horror of it all, and trying to plan what we could do in the immediate future to get all of the organisation moving that we had been planning for some time.

Lady Isabel Napier
Civilian living in London
We had a butler – four staff, I think. But the moment, of course, the war broke out, everything dissolved around me. The butler went off to join up. The cook left – she was frightened she might be bombed. The nursery governess left to help evacuate the LCC children – the London children. All the kids were evacuated as quickly as possible, and anyone living in the country with a spare room was liable to have these evacuees sent to them. And some of them, of course, had never seen the country – never seen the sea or farm animals and all the rest of it. I don't think, really, it was a great success.

Ronald McGill
Evacuee from Vauxhall, South London
I'd been convalescent in 1938 – I could see more country, as far as I was concerned. Bigger and bigger Vauxhall parks. For children it was extremely exciting. I don't think this had come over enough – it was a great adventure . . . but when it came to the moment when we lined up, and your mum and dad were on one side of the road, and you were on the other – then we all just burst in tears, the lot of us.

The teachers told their own classes they were going, and we were all told to be packed and to have our little bags. We were given a list we had to give our mother and father, which they had to return within two days – so they knew the children were prepared. The ones they didn't get them back from, they went visiting them in the evenings to make sure what was happening and why – because a lot of the mothers were working-class and weren't going to let their children go. They were going to refuse. If their children were going to die, they were going to die with them. My mother was one of those – she didn't want us to go. It was only our father who made us go. My family was completely split, and there were terrible rows over it. In our area there were no children who didn't go – the teachers literally forced them. The fact that some were back within a week was immaterial, but they did make everyone go at first. Some parents were moving away anyway – there was a voluntary evacuation as well. Some were leaving and going to relatives. Everybody knew that our part of London – near Waterloo – was going to be an immediate target.

There was help for those who couldn't get together their things – hygiene things were got for them – soap, flannels and toothbrushes were got – but nothing else. Some just walked along there with just a paper bag and everything they had in it. I had a model Bren-gun carrier which I wasn't going to lose. My sister took a doll with her – we were allowed small things which we carried in our bag.

All we were told was we were going to the countryside. In the week prior to going we did things like drawing cows – how much we knew about trees – we were geared up for the countryside. Some little children had never been to the country – never seen cattle. We were told we would be following the Thames – and that was it. All the boys had loved fishing – which at the time was just the ponds of Clapham Common – and suddenly they were transported and couldn't wait to enjoy the Thames life.

'Be all over by Christmas,' some were saying – but the teacher said, 'You allow for a year.' I've no idea how we were supposed to manage for a year with a toothbrush and one change of socks.

Doris Scott
Civilian from Canning Town, East London

I thought it was awfully funny – although I suppose I shouldn't say that in a war – but when the warning went, there was a chappie who lived at the end of the street. He was under the impression that as soon as the warning went, that he had to put his gas mask on. He did this over and over again, running through the streets with it on. We had been told only to use the gas mask if we heard rattles, and that the normal warning was for getting into your shelter. It was very funny.

Ronald McGill
Evacuee from Vauxhall, South London

We waved goodbye. The parents stayed on one side of the road and they all cried their eyes out – it was terrible, but we were all happy and joking by then. We'd had our apple, bagged our gasmask and we'd said our goodbyes.

We got into Vauxhall Station, and it was like entering a tomb – all tiled and dark. We had to wait down there until the train came in. It was a Southern Railway train that went round the loop line to Reading.

It really was packed! What I remember is the noise – ten carriages of children, and half of them were hanging out the windows. A lot of police there. It was just bedlam. I felt the teachers were very, very harassed, and in retrospect, they did a marvellous job. They shepherded us all there, looked after us – and they were worried themselves – some of their own children were with us.

Mum said that after we left it was like a cathedral, it was so quiet, the whole area. In the evenings, she said, it was unbelievable. They didn't realise 'til then the noise of children playing. The streets had been our playgrounds.

On the train we were all happy – thrilled, adventurous. We whizzed under funny old archways at Clapham Junction and Wandsworth Town; we could see people lined up above it all, waving to us, and that cheered us up no end. We were joyful for them. We went through Richmond, across the Thames, and you knew we were in the countryside. It wasn't long before we saw cows – we were thrilled. It was a tremendous adventure for us.

When we got to Reading we were taken into a big hall. People came in and sat at desks, then they walked down the line and tried to take pairs and families. I was taken by a local council man. The house was super. We went by car – I just couldn't believe it. My sister and I were just earmarked. 'We wanted a boy and a girl. You'll do.'

We were handed over to a maid. We hardly saw the husband and wife that took us. We had two small beds. I remember crying a lot at first – we used to sob and sob and sob. I was nine and she was seven, and we probably spent an hour crying. After that we'd eat an apple or read something, and go to bed. Teachers came round occasionally to see us in the evening, but we felt very cut off.

Joan Reed
Schoolgirl in Woodford, Essex, evacuated to nearby Ongar

I don't recall anything apart from the blackout, and having these black curtains, and the windows with sticky tape in case they got shattered. Some houses had boards that you put up to completely block out the light. I remember a warden shouting, 'Put out that light!' You heard that quite often, because they patrolled the streets. And the food shortages – my sister didn't know what a banana was until after the war, and oranges were kept for pregnant women and small children under five.

I don't remember my mother saying, 'This is it – you're going.' We were in the playground and my young sister was crying – lots of little children were crying. This was mainly because mothers were left outside the gate, and we were ushered into the school. We all walked to the station with our gas masks round our necks, in a long crocodile from Leytonstone High Road. When we arrived at Ongar Station we walked into the local school hall, where we stood around – and in the centre were the prospective foster mothers, but they walked around as if we were cattle.

John Brasier
Evacuee from Hastings, aged eight at the outbreak of war
We ate our sandwiches, laughed and joked. Having left at nine that morning and arriving at about five or six o'clock, we were pretty tired. We were then taken to the local school, and it was upsetting because it was near the end before anyone claimed us.

Sylvia Taylor
Evacuee from Hook, Surrey, to Leeds, aged four at the outbreak of war
We arrived and were introduced. We were very, very shy. Then they said tea was ready, and we were taken into the dining room – and there was a table, groaning with food. Our eyes nearly popped out of our heads. We'd never seen so much food.

Gwendoline Stewart
Schoolgirl evacuated from Birmingham to Ashby-de-la-Zouch
Helen started to cry when she saw my mother, and asked, 'Mum, why can't we come home?' My mother asked if she could speak privately to her children, and she was shown into another room. I said, 'Mum, we can't sit down to eat – we have to stand at the table. They don't give us chairs, and we have to eat sardines – and we don't like sardines.' Jack said, 'Look, Mum,' and took down his little trousers and showed his bottom – which was red and raw. Helen said, 'And me!' They had been so hungry that they had broken into the food larder and opened a jar of strawberry jam and taken it to bed with them to eat – and the father had found out and had whipped them. My mother was incensed at

the injustice of this – we were just being used for the extra money coming into the house.

Henry Metelmann
German youth apprenticed to the railway
Germany had invaded Poland, and to us it was something great. With shame I express this feeling now, because I had no idea what it really meant to the people there, to be invaded by a foreign army – and anyway, to be honest, I didn't care. I thought of the German greatness and I thought, 'Well, anyway, the Poles are second-rate and they have treated our German people living there very badly. It serves them right.' And also, to think that Germany now could occupy Poland, then surely we would be a powerful state in central Europe – that appealed to me.

People in general did not like it, because many of the neighbours, they remembered the First World War. My father had been a soldier. He said, 'I remember at first it was all great, the colours and all this and fighting for the Kaiser and the Empire. But then later on, things turned and changed, and it could well happen again, because it could be a long war.'

The Blitzkrieg was a great idea. With our superior technology in warfare, we would smash that little lot – yet within a few days France and England came in. We made a point of it, that it was not Germany who had declared war on England or France – but it was the ultimatum they sent to us, saying 'If you are not out of Poland by so and so, we consider ourselves to be at war with you.' That was a strong propaganda line. 'We have not declared war on the western democracies – they have declared war on us!' and they should have kept out of our arrangement we had with the Poles – that was our business.

I thought a war was a great thing. We were being told it cleanses the nation, and a war is necessary in order to get the rubbishy element out of our blood – and I believed it.

Francis Codd
Civilian working in City of London for a printer
I had foreseen that with Hitler's advance across Europe and his latest move that war was both inevitable and necessary. That evening of the invasion, I was too numbed with tiredness and sadness really to feel much except misery that all my past life would be changed from now on. And funny enough, it wasn't till the Saturday morning that I got up in my own flat, that I felt an intolerable weight of sadness.

I had worked all my life in the family printing business in the City, within two minutes' walk of the Bank of England. At that time I was thirty years old and I'd had a very pleasant bachelor life – and now I felt it was coming to an end.

Mike Sherwood
Apprentice in the Merchant Navy

On our way out to Australia war was declared. I remember being on the bridge with the Second Officer, called Ring. He always had a bit of a sardonic twist to him. He said, 'Well, Sherwood, this will be something for you to write home about: it's war.' I wondered what the hell he was talking about. To me war being declared meant nothing.

When we reached Australia we had to go and be fitted with a 6-inch gun. The gun's crew was made up from us apprentices and various members of the crew. We had to go over to the naval base at Rushcutter's Bay and learn all about guns. When the time came for us to sail they put on board a DEMS (Defensively Equipped Merchant Ship) gunner, a Royal Navy fellow to look after the gun and see that we knew what we were doing. We steamed out to give this gun a trial, out through Sydney Harbour. I was the sight setter. I used to stand at the side of the gun and say, 'Range so-and-so.' We loaded it up, the gunner said 'Fire,' and there was such a clatter. I was knocked flat to the ground. Everyone else was flat around me. There was a great roar and commotion from below in the deck house where all the stewards and cooks lived because nobody had told them we were firing and all the bunks and everything fell down. We didn't feel that we were at war.

Sub-Lieutenant John Roxburgh
Aboard HMS Walpole

Come August 1939 it was obvious the war was coming. Convoys for merchant shipping had already started. At eleven o'clock on a Sunday morning, 3rd September we were at war, our depth-charges were primed and we were ready to go. A quarter of an hour after war had been declared we found a submarine echo which we attacked and dropped eleven charges. We were never credited with a submarine and I should think it was quite likely a shoal of fish or a rock, but it really got one's mind racing. There was I, a young chap of twenty, actually dropping things to kill people. It was quite exciting.

Gunther Rall
Luftwaffe fighter pilot

There was a big, depressed mood throughout the country, 'What is going on?' But as a fighter pilot I also felt, if there is a war, then I want to be successful and be a fighter pilot and do my duty. But the population as such was very much shocked by the war, there's no doubt.

Ordinary Seaman Douglas Stevens
Signaller aboard HMS Saon

I was called up by the RNVR – people seemed to cheer you on your way and wish you all the best. People at the bus-stop, when I caught the bus to the Embankment with my kitbag. People seemed to want to pat you on the back as you went.

Midshipman Ian McIntosh
Aboard HMS Sussex

When war was declared, we'd had a bit of patrolling off the Spanish coast during the Civil War on the Mediterranean side, then around June the whole fleet moved to Alexandria. We were in fact in Alexandria when war was declared. One of the preparations for war, apart from fusing all the shells, was to sharpen the cutlasses for the boarding party. As this was likely to be led by midshipmen, the idea of sailors behind you with sharp cutlasses wasn't a very cheerful thought!

Gwendoline Saunders
Civilian in Weymouth

On Monday I went back to the library. There was a fair stir about, and by the end of that week, this other girl had already been scouting round, apparently, to find what she could do. She'd been up to this air force station. She said, 'It's rather exciting. I think I shall like this. I've signed for a plotter.' So I said, 'What is that?' 'Well,' she said, 'I think we shall plot the operations, but I'll have to go for training. I had to sign a form. It was either for the duration or for four years.' So I said, 'What did you do?' She said, 'I signed for the duration. It can't go on longer than four years, can it?'

Aircraftwoman Elsie Bartlett
An early recruit to the WAAF

All types turned up at Hallam Street to enlist – short, fat, thin, small, dowdy, glamorous – typists and shop-girls, married and single, from all walks of life. They were fussy about who they took at the beginning, and I hadn't a lot going for me – what with spinal curvature and bad eyes. However, I slipped in as a grade C3 and, by that evening, was in Harrogate with the King's shilling and a sore arm from injections.

When I got my posting, I opened it and read 'RAF Dunkirk'. Well, I nearly had heart failure! 'My God', I thought, 'things must be dodgy.'

My Dunkirk turned out to be a village in Kent. So there I was, a small WAAF weighed down in a heavy greatcoat, hat pulled down tight, carrying a gas mask, a tin hat, a case, a kitbag almost as big as me, and clutching my orders and a packet of sandwiches. Off I staggered to Kent.

Ordinary Seaman Vernon Coles
Stoker 2nd Class, Royal Navy, aboard HMS **Faulknor**
I saw my first real action on the 14th September. We were exercising with *Ark Royal* and three destroyers off St Kilda. Suddenly, during the mid-afternoon, there were two terrific explosions – we went to action stations immediately. We learnt that a German U-boat had fired two torpedoes at *Ark Royal*. Their torpedoes had magnetic heads on, so when they came within the magnetic field of *Ark Royal*, they both exploded. Otherwise she would have been hit.

We sailed straight down the torpedo tracks, dropped a full pattern of depth-charges and up she came. It was *U-39*. We took them all prisoner; we rescued the men in the whalers and then brought them on board. They were badly shaken, as anybody would have been on the receiving end of a couple of depth-charges.

I talked to some of the German prisoners. They thought they were going to be shot and they were actually surprised at the way they were treated. We had to communicate with them in sign language, but we gave them cigarettes and things. They were rather wet, so they were supplied with blankets while all their clothes and underwear were taken down to the boiler room to dry off. Their vests all had the German swastika on, so off they came during the night – they were taken as souvenirs. The Germans were most upset about that.

We off-loaded them in Scapa Flow. That was the first U-boat of the war to go down and they were the first naval prisoners-of-war.

Ordinary Seaman Stanley Allen
Recruit, Royal Navy
I went up to Skegness with a small suitcase, taking what I was told to take – which was very little – met other people at the railway station on the way up, and when we got to Skegness, we came out and it was raining. A little man in a blue Burberry and a badge on his cap, who I later found was a petty officer, he says, 'Here, you long bastard.' I was the tallest one amongst them. 'You come and stand here.' I was brought up in a church home, and of course he must have seen my face, and he said, 'Oh, don't take any notice, Lofty. If we

calls you a bastard, we loves you.' And of course, as I was the tallest, he was putting me as right-hand man from which the others could fall in.

Lieutenant-Colonel Alexander Stanier
1st Battalion, Welsh Guards

I think we rather thought that it would be very like the First War – there'd be the rush forward by the Germans – we'd hold them. Then trench warfare would come about as it was. We did realise that there'd be much more bombing from the air – in fact, we thought that it would be much greater than it was to start off with. Gas – so everybody had gas masks.

Evelyn Fee
Civilian mother

We had the blackout. All the streetlamps went out and, oh, it was awful. Pitch black out there. And then we had the barrage balloons all up overhead. Yes, I think that was the worst part – waiting for it, you know.

We heard about the evacuation from the school. I wanted to stay in London with my little ones, but we had a friend living with us, who kept on at me. He said that it would be best if I did go away, because, he said, 'Once this lot starts, it's really going to start.'

I can remember the little girl catching hold of my coat. My little girl – she looked so beautiful – she really did. I can always remember Jean that morning – and Teddy, the boy – because he was a lovely little boy too.

Captain Anthony Rhodes
253 Field Company, Royal Engineers

One of the things we were told – the sort of rumour that was going round – was that the Germans couldn't possibly have built up an army since 1933, in six years. People even said that, when the Germans paraded their tanks through the cities of northern Germany, some of them were made of cardboard. That is the sort of rumour one heard.

Bugler Edward Watson
8th Battalion, King's Royal Rifle Corps

The boat was just going out – very leisurely out of Dover Harbour. I was still convinced that they were going to take us out and bring us back again.

We were all laughing and joking. This fellow Day, and another fellow, Corporal West, started flashing away with this signal lamp, up to the top of the cliffs of Dover. Lights are flashing back from there to the boat. I said to

Packed up and labelled like parcels, bewildered London evacuees prepare to board the train, which will take them to new homes with unfamiliar foster parents. It is hardly surprising that many were desperately unhappy.

Day, 'What are they doing?' He said, 'He's wishing us good luck and hope you come back soon.' So I said, 'What are you saying?' 'I'm thanking him very much.' I said, 'We're not going, are we?' He said, 'Oh yes.' And that was the first time I realised. I said, 'But I can't – I haven't told my mum.' It was all quite different then. This was the real thing – it wasn't an exercise.

I went and stood at the edge of the boat and started thinking, because it was going on. 'What am I going to do?' I was a bugler. I had a gun with a Bren tripod – and a bugle as well. We had silver bugles. I thought to myself, 'What am I going to do with this bugle? Supposing they ask me to play it over there – or blow it? There's Germans there – they'll hear me. They'll shoot me.' I took the bugle off and threw it in the Channel.

Charles 'Bertie' Nash
Civilian, living in London

On my wedding day, which was 12th October 1939, at four o'clock in the afternoon I received a little buff envelope asking me, in reference to my volunteering, I should report to the Acton Town Recruiting Office and get myself sworn in and attested. I must admit I was rather shattered at receiving this on my wedding day.

THE PHONEY WAR

War had been declared – Christmas came as troops bided their time in Britain and France. There was a deep feeling of unease. But only one thing was certain – sooner or later in 1940 the war would begin in earnest.

Ronald McGill
Evacuee from Vauxhall, London, to Reading

We were in a very grand house – but I can't remember walking over it. I think we must have been told to stay in our sort of area, or the garden – and that's the only parts I can remember of the house, except for sitting down for meals. I think we were there, tucked away; somebody was looking after us and they were giving us a good home. We were away from anything that was going to happen – and as the weeks went by, nothing was going to happen. Perhaps they began to feel, 'We've taken them in for nothing.' A very real feeling.

Our parents visited us after three weeks – and they came by bus. The lady looking after us took us into Reading, and we waited by the cinema. I remember my mum and dad getting off the bus. They took us round the town to a café and bought us sweets and made a fuss – then they were straight back on the bus after a couple of hours. I can't remember my mum and dad coming back to the house. I don't know why, but they didn't come to see our billet – which is unusual when you think about it. Dad had to go back to work, so we were just collected again and they went back to London. But we said we weren't happy then.

The week after Mum had gone back, I sent a card – and on the bottom of it I'd written, 'Dear Mum, we want to come home.' Within a week they were down and took us back. We were really only away for seven weeks at the most. They must have seen the difference in us, and I don't know why. We were well fed, we were being looked after – but it didn't work. Mum's thoughts of whatever was going to happen to her and Dad would include us. The people didn't demur – they just accepted it. I think, quite frankly, they were glad to see the back of us.

Nancy Bazin
Civilian in Devon, working as a supply teacher

I have very strong memories of the first evacuee children coming to the West Country. The obvious place to send a great number of the London borough children was to the West Country, and all the families were being asked to take in their homes one, two, according to the number of rooms they had. Children were being billeted and I was involved with friends who were billeting officers. I have a very keen recollection of these little things with their gasmask box and a little suitcase in their hands, looking very, in many cases, dejected – very small children in particular – and of taking them to homes with people speaking in, to their way, a very curious accent. The Devonian is a kind-hearted person, but on the other hand, not very used to the Cockney child. They were an odd mixture. In most cases they settled in very well. I was to see the next side when I was actually teaching in mixed classrooms. They settled down remarkably well, particularly in the completely rural areas, because there the farm children had a great plus in that they knew everything about the animals and the livestock and the general countryside, and there was a lot of interest for the town children. Though they felt lost, they were pleased to be surrounded by a lot of animals, and children who could teach them so much. I think it was a good blending.

During that period, known as the Phoney War, there was a lot of feeling that it was an unnecessary exercise, and that they really might as well be at home with their parents, who were missing them very much. And of course, there was no doubt that I think the families in Devon probably were quite relieved to have a period without them – so some went back.

Joan Reed
Schoolgirl evacuee in Ongar
I couldn't understand why we'd been sent. Nothing had happened, because there didn't seem to be any war. It seemed very premature. Mother was at home – everything was perfect at home.

Doris Scott
Civilian from Canning Town, East London, evacuated to Wallingford, Berkshire
I really did fear invasion – because we knew that they had just marched into Poland, just like that. A Polish refugee was in our billet, and she used to get into hysterics about what she had gone through. We had to calm her down. I felt, 'God, if that happens here, what would it be like?'

Lilias Walker
Schoolgirl evacuated from Hull to Scarborough
I thought it was a great joke. You get into these school stories and you think, 'Oh it's just like a boarding school.' We were evacuated to a hotel, the Astoria, which overlooked the Italian gardens at Scarborough. There were two girls to a bed and we were six to a bedroom. It was a very cold winter and everything froze up and there was no hot water in the place. One of my first memories is of the first meal that we had at the hotel. For dessert we got bread and butter pudding, but we didn't like the lettuce and the meat that was floating about in it. We went to school in the morning and did nothing in the afternoon. It was just a beautiful summer, we just went swimming and things like that.

Sergeant Raymond Trivass
Drum-Major, 1st Battalion, Coldstream Guards
There was a football match between us and a French Army unit, and they had a French band there and we had my Corps of Drums. And at the end we were both together on the football field and the French bandmaster conducted the British National Anthem and then I was called upon to conduct the French National Anthem. When it had finished, they turned about and saluted the top brass and I saw the brigadier coming out from the saluting box with the French general. I had a nasty idea what was going to happen – and it did, of

In Muswell Hill, North London, railway vehicles have been commandeered to deliver the corrugated steel panels for the residents to construct Anderson bomb shelters in their gardens.

course. When he approached, I saluted him and he then kissed me on both cheeks. A huge great roar came from the Coldstreams in the stands. Somebody sent a report to London, which was put in the Brigade magazine – which I never saw. It took a bit of living down once we got back. I was in the sergeants' mess and the sergeant-major came in and said, 'Do I have to kiss you, Drum-Major?' I said, 'No you certainly do not,' or words to that effect.

Captain Derek Boileau Lang
Adjutant, 4th Battalion, Cameron Highlanders

There was never any question of us anticipating and pre-empting a German attack. We were always on the defensive. Apart from anything else, the Maginot Line itself was designed, wrongly as it turned out, to be a bastion of defence which nobody would get through. In fact, the cry was 'On ne passera pas'.

They had done nothing, really, to prepare their defences. There's a good example of this down in the Maginot Line. The Maginot Line defences consisted of four lines, but only one was the concrete line with all the built-in heavy armament. There was one defence line in front of it and two behind, known as the Ligne de Contact, the one in front the Ligne de Recueil, and the one immediately behind, and behind that was the Ligne d'Arrêt – the line of stopping.

When our general, General Victor Fortune, went down to the Ligne d'Arrêt a number of the French *poilus* came along with picks and shovels and started to dig fences around him. He asked, 'What are they doing? What's going on?' and they said, 'Oh, we were told that a British general was coming down to look at the defences and we thought we'd better dig them and make a start.' That really presents the picture of those three lines, other than the Maginot.

Captain Paul Hawkins
Royal Norfolk Regiment

Our duties were in fact to guard ammunition dumps which were laid out along the sides of a network of roads about seven or eight miles from Arras, and also to try and dig fresh emplacements by the side of the road to put in shells and ammunition. I always remember that time of digging out one particular piece by the side of the road, which would only come away in large chunks because the frost was in the ground to a couple of feet deep. We found the skeleton of a First World War German soldier whose jackboots were still reasonably intact, and a Canadian soldier whose identification disc was still there. They were taken away and buried elsewhere.

Sergeant William Harding
Royal Artillery, attached to Queen Victoria's Rifles

We had dugouts only. We dug our own holes in the ground, covered them over with sandbags and corrugated iron. But there was no provision for water. Nobody ever dreamed that water was going to come down like it did, because it flooded down. We dug channels in the ground, but it went to terrible gooey mud, just like a lot of porridge. Your boots got twice the size and squelched as you walked along – and you ended up with wet feet. Nothing was dry – nothing at all was dry because it just rained, day in, day out. Eventually the officers arranged a rum issue at night to keep the cold out.

The meals were bully beef stew, day in, day out. That's all they had to offer. Sometimes they fried it in flour and water and made fritters – other times we had sandwiches of bully beef, but bully beef it was. We got to the situation where officers were buying food out of their own pocket. Things got so bad that the cook sergeant asked for six volunteers – and I went. We went in a three-ton lorry without the officers knowing, and raided farms round about and stealing everything we could lay our hands on – cabbages – anything.

There seemed to be a complete lack of interest at that time from the people at home about the BEF. I think, with the long drag from September onwards with nothing really happening, their interest had died. And I think they got the impression we were all having a marvellous time, living it up – Gay Paree, sort of thing.

We were short of water, so the habit caught on of shaving in the last drop of tea in the mug. We just existed that way. Eventually it got so bad that, just before Christmas, we were moved. It was just untenable. Men were going into hospital and things were showing themselves in a very bad way with health generally.

Flight Lieutenant Peter Brothers
32 Squadron, RAF

I was sent to Uxbridge first, for ground training, getting kitted out and so on. At Uxbridge there was this splendid First World War pilot, Ira Taffy Jones, who stuttered terribly. One day he stood up and said, 'There is going to be a b-b-bloody wa-wa-war and you ch-chaps are going to be in it. I'll give you one piece of advice – wh-wh-when you fir-first get into a co-combat, you will be fu-fu-fucking fr-frightened. No never forget the ch-chap in the other each cockpit is tw-twice as fu-fucking fr-frightened as you are.' I reckon he saved my life with that piece of advice. In my first combat over France, I suddenly thought, 'My God, the chap in that other cockpit must be having hysterics,' and shot him down. But I give all credit to Taffy.

The first hint of war came into my life with the Munich crisis, when I began to think, yes, this is deadly serious. Then came the so-called 'phoney war', convoy patrols and constant scrambles, but you never saw the enemy.

Gunther Rall
Luftwaffe fighter pilot
The Versailles Treaty had ruined the German economy, and there was much bitterness, particularly against France. We had to pay and pay and pay – and there were restrictions everywhere.

I heard Hitler on the radio. He said from now on we are fighting back. As a soldier and as a pilot, we were all feeling, 'Come on now, we are ready.' I mean, there was a great anxiety about what was coming, but that did not mean that you were not willing to show that we were capable fighter pilots. You wanted to prove that you had mastered what you had learned.

Josephine Pearce
In Paris, en route to join Ambulance unit 282 in Alsace
When I eventually got to Sarraguemines, where the unit was, I was inundated with questions from the nurses. They were asking me, 'Was Paris behaving itself?' And at first I thought, 'What do they mean?' I realised what they meant, because we'd been at war for three months – and they were behaving as though there was no war. They were doing nothing, nothing to protect the people, nothing to protect themselves.

THE BATTLE OF THE RIVER PLATE

In August, before war was declared, Hitler put the pocket battleships *Graf Spee* and *Deutschland* to sea, before the Allies could blockade them in their home ports. When war was declared, he issued a directive for German naval vessels above and below the water to attack Allied shipping. In the course of two-and-a-half months, *Graf Spee* sank nine British ships, including the *Doric Star*, before heading for South American waters. On 13 December, three British cruisers – one of the eight hunting groups formed to protect Allied shipping – spotted *Graf Spee* off Montevideo. Although the German vessel managed to inflict heavy damage on HMS *Exeter*, she sustained such serious damage herself that she took refuge in the mouth of the River Plate where, on Hitler's orders, Captain Langsdorff scuttled her to avoid the disgrace of being sunk by the enemy. At last there was positive news in the naval war – a much-needed boost for British morale.

Peter Brothers flew with 32 Squadron, based at Hawkinge in Kent during the Battle of Britain, then in September joined 257 Squadron at Debden. He was credited with ten 'kills' during the course of the Battle of Britain.

Lieutenant-Commander Richard Jennings
Gunnery officer aboard HMS **Exeter**

On the 8th December the commodore told us to patrol around the Falkland Islands in case the Germans were planning a comeback to mark the anniversary of the Battle of the Falkland Islands in 1914. But nothing happened, so we headed north and joined the commodore in the Plate estuary on the evening of 12th December. We did some steam tactics on arrival, and Commodore Harwood sent for the captains of the *Exeter, Ajax* and *Achilles* to inform them of his intentions, should we encounter the pocket battleship. No one else knew what tactics he was going to pursue.

I had the middle watch that night of 12th December. When I was relieved I went aft, shaved and decided against turning in as dawn action stations was due at 0440. After some more steam tactics we reverted to third degree of readiness. I got into my pyjamas, arranged for a call by the sentry (just outside my cabin door) and turned in, only to be called ten minutes later. I hustled up to my action station in the Director Control Tower. As I was crossing the compass platform the captain hailed me – not with the usual sort of rigmarole of 'Enemy in sight, bearing etc', but with 'There's the fucking *Scheer!* Open fire at her!' Throughout the battle the crew of the *Exeter* thought they were fighting the *Admiral von Scheer*. But the name of the enemy ship was, of course, the *Graf Spee*.

So the fight was on. It was about 0612. In the DC Tower I was in telephonic touch with the Transmitting Station which, in turn, was in touch with all main armament quarters. I ordered 'Open fire'. The range was then about 20,000 yards and the *Graf Spee* was as large as life on the horizon. Our 8-inch guns could hit any target up to 30,000 yards away.

At 0624, while loading for the ninth broadside, B turret received a direct hit, knocking it out of action. Not only that, but fragments peppered the compass platform, leaving only the captain and two others standing. The captain, with his eyes full of grit, decided to fight the ship from the after conning position. We in the DC tower – less that 15 feet above the compass platform – were quite unaware of all this upset. Another round entered the fore superstructure, ran along the deck of the Remote Control W/T office, passed out through my office and burst over the starboard AA guns, starting fires in the area of the ready-use ammunition lockers. In the meantime, A turret, when loading for our 32nd broadside, was put out of action by a direct hit on the right gun.

It was perhaps the last hit that came in by the Petty Officer's mess and burst in the Chief Petty Officer's locker flat that caused the most worry. The flat was above three magazines and a diesel generator was put out of action. The transmitting station was rendered useless, as visibility was nil due to white powder used for insulating the space around the transmitting station. Breathing was also difficult. The crew was ordered out to join up with the damage-control parties. I left the DC tower, finding, to my surprise, that the compass platform had been abandoned. I went aft to the after control and, with the control officer, decided to put Y turret into local control, with me standing on the gun house roof to help with the spotting. While talking to the After Control Officer, I failed to notice we had altered course a few degrees, and that the guns of Y turret were only a few feet away. When the guns spoke, I remember looking down and seeing that my legs were still there!

After perhaps two salvos in local control, Y turret lost all power due to flooding – and the flooding in the ship grew worse. At this stage, Harwood told us to drop out of action and head for Port Stanley. There was nothing we could do, for now the *Graf Spee* was too far away to ram.

Able Seaman Reginald Fogwill
Aboard HMS Exeter

Although the *Exeter* was now on only two guns, we steamed into action with the guns firing on the foremost bearing. The control of the tower was taken on by the gunnery officer Richard Jennings, with utter disregard for his own safety, he stood on top of the turret, shouting directions down into the front of the guns.

By now we were in a sinking condition and slowly listing to port. When it became apparent to the commodore that we were in a dangerous condition, we were ordered to withdraw from the action and make our way to Port Stanley. But we weren't in any great hurry to retreat. The captain had mentioned to the ship's doctor that he intended to ram the *Graf Spee*, so we were all ready to rig up the Lewis guns – but in the end, we didn't have to. Nobody felt particularly relieved that we were out of action. The general feeling was that we hadn't done enough. It made you kind of bloodthirsty. You felt so isolated from the real activity, because it's shells from the ship which are doing the job, not you. I never experienced fear, not even in retrospect.

We stopped for lunch and everybody was given a tot or rum. It was my first, because I was only 18 and under age. The shock of what we had been through sank into us in the form of hunger. At that time there was no means of getting a meal, and the only thing we could get our hands on was raw cabbage. We had this and enjoyed it.

Then we set to work to clear away the damage. Some of this work was ghastly, because as the debris was cleared away, the great number of dead and wounded was brought to light. I was put on lookout on the wings of the bridge on the flag deck. It was pretty grim because there were still some bodies around. The shell which had passed from port to starboard had sliced right through the deck and chopped off the legs of all the telegraphers who were lined up on a bench. They were all killed instantly. There were over 60 killed and over 120 wounded. During the afternoon, our fallen comrades were buried at sea with full naval honours. I know that every survivor thinks with pride of those who were lost, and will never forget them.

1940

Once, as I was leaving the park shelter and coming back to my house,
those all around were bomb blasted, and I saw this woman cleaning the front
doorstep of her demolished house as if it were business as usual.

With the German invasion of Denmark and Norway in April 1940 and the sudden sweeping assault of *Blitzkrieg* – lightning war – across Western Europe launched on 10 May, the Phoney War was over, and Hitler's actions left no doubt as to his ambitions. The Prime Minister Neville Chamberlain, already discredited for his appeasement of Hitler at the Munich conference, resigned to be replaced by Winston Churchill. The British Expeditionary Force, woefully outnumbered and under-equipped, fought a rearguard action back to Dunkirk, where it was successfully evacuated. The Germans were poised to invade.

Wanting to strike while Britain's armed forces were still in disarray, Hitler needed only air superiority over the Channel to launch an invasion – and on 11 July Luftwaffe commander Hermann Goering promised that his pilots could destroy the RAF in a month. Britain's defence against the coming onslaught was in the hands of Air Chief Marshal Dowding – to him fell the task of directing and garnering the RAF's resources to defend Britain from invasion during the summer of 1940 – the Battle of Britain. Despite heavy losses of men and aircraft during the battle, the tide was turned by the end of September. It became apparent that Operation Sealion – the invasion – could not go ahead. The Luftwaffe then turned to Britain's cities – initially London and then to industrial centres and ports – to destroy production and terrorise the civilian population. By the end of 1940, Britain stood alone, and it was her citizens who were on the front line, weathering the attrition of the Blitz.

Following the evacuation of the BEF from Dunkirk in June, Italy declared war on Britain and France on 10 June. Across Europe, around the Mediterranean, the Axis alliance of Germany and Italy launched actions to protect the supply routes from Africa to mainland Europe. In June, Italian bombers attacked Malta and the following month, Italian troops entered Egypt from Libya and on 28 October invaded Greece and Albania, effectively opening up two new fronts. British forces were sent to the defence of Greece, landing on 2 November. On 9 December the British attacked the Italians in the deserts of western Egypt – these actions were a prelude to the all-out warfare which would open up the following year.

NORWAY

The first major strike which broke the artificial calm of the Phoney War came on 9 April 1940, as the German fleet engaged with British warships sent to lay mines in the waters off neutral Norway to disrupt the routes used for supplying iron ore to Germany. The Royal Navy suffered some losses – and the German fleet continued on its mission to land invasion forces. On 9 April, German troops landed at Narvik, Trondheim, Bergen, Kristiansand and Oslo. Although the Norwegians defended bravely and inflicted significant damage on the invaders, they were eventually overwhelmed.

Despite efforts by the Royal Navy to come to Norway's aid during the period from 10 April to the beginning of June, and their success in sinking ten German destroyers off Narvik, the German invaders still held the town of Narvik itself and had little trouble repulsing a British attempt to land troops at Trondheim. Although the Allies retook Narvik on 28 May, the sheer weight of German numbers prevailed, and Norway came under German rule as the last Allied troops were evacuated on 8 June.

Leading Seaman Donald Auffret
Wireless operator, Royal Navy, aboard HMS **Warspite**
When the Norwegian campaign broke out, we were patrolling off Norway, and one evening, Captain Crutchley came on the public address and told us that a flotilla of H-Class destroyers had entered Narvik Fjord and attacked the merchant shipping in there. They had been attacked by some German Maas-Class destroyers, and had come off worse, because they weren't as heavily armed as the H boats. Captain Warburton-Lee had been killed, and received the VC on the *Hardy*, and, in his words, we were going in the next day to clear the mess up.

It was very sombre, and I can remember as we came to the entrance of the fjord, we could see the mountains on either side, all grey, topped with snow, and it looked a very, very grim place. The sea was the colour of lead – it looked very forbidding.

We closed up for action stations round about one o'clock or twelve o'clock. My action station was the bridge wireless office, which gave access to the flag deck. Nothing happened for about three-quarters of an hour – and then it was all hell let loose, as our main armament was firing.

We were getting reports from our Swordfish aircraft, which had been catapulted off. He was pinpointing where the German destroyers were, because Narvik Fjord has fjordlets off it, and we were firing directly over the bow. The turrets were trained almost fore and aft, and consequently all the blast was coming back aboard. One of the forward hatches was blown off, and all the blast was actually going down into the cable deck. It caused quite a considerable amount of self-inflicted damage.

The first view of any of the action I had was when I went out on to the flag deck. At that moment we came abreast of one of these little side fjords. A German destroyer had dodged down there, obviously waiting for us to come around the headland – and when we did, she appeared to fire torpedoes, and these passed under the ship. They were set too deep. At the same time, *Warspite* fired a broadside, and she was literally lifted out of the water, up on to the beach – and then slid down again. She must have been hit by about six 15-inch shells simultaneously.

The next thing I saw was another German destroyer on our starboard bow, blazing furiously and people jumping into the water. Then one of the Tribal-class destroyers – the *Cossack* – went past and as they did, they cheered us. They were probably glad that we were there to give the heavier fire-power.

I then went back on watch, and the next signal I remember seeing was from the Swordfish aircraft to say that she'd bombed a U-boat. Then there was another signal to say that one of the German destroyers was hiding in Rombaks Fjord, at the end past Narvik town. One of the Tribals, the *Eskimo* – poked her bow round and promptly had it blown off, but she managed to get her A and B turrets around, and she dealt with that particular destroyer.

We then anchored off Narvik and had some German prisoners from one of the destroyers transferred to us, because we could accommodate them more than the Tribal-class destroyers could. They looked at the damage and by the look on their faces, they thought they had inflicted it. They were very cocky. The feedback we got from the people who were detailed to be sentries over them was that this was only a very temporary thing, and that Germany would have won in the next six months anyway, so they weren't too bothered about being taken prisoner. I heard this with amazement, because it did not ever occur to me that we would lose the war. I wouldn't even consider the fact.

We on the *Warspite* felt that it had been a victory at Narvik. As far as we were told, there were eight German Maas-class destroyers sunk, which was the whole of the German navy that was in Narvik at the time.

Lieutenant Robert Wynter
York and Lancaster Regiment

We were told the plan – and we drew stores – extra ammunition and maps. These maps covered the area of our objective. The plan was that the brigade should capture Trondheim. My platoon was given the task of an assault landing to capture an outpost which had guns on the outskirts of Trondheim. It was to be a mad dash in and seize the post to cover the advance of the rest of the brigade. We practised this on a bleak Scottish hilltop.

We were issued with really splendid reversed-hide sheepskin coats, similar to an Afghan poshteen, only sweeter smelling. They were lovely – ankle length – they saved our lives in Norway.

We landed at Aandalsnes in the dark – in the early morning – and embarked on a Norwegian train of mixed stock. I, being slow getting aboard, found myself in an open coal truck. I was intrigued to notice that the staff captain from the brigade was standing on the footplate of the engine, brandishing a pistol to ensure that the driver took the train.

We rode in this train for some number of hours – as far as Dombaas, where we detrained and bivouacked in the woods outside the town. This was lucky, because shortly after arrival, it now being daylight, I witnessed an air raid for the first time – German planes bombed the little town of Dombaas. The planes appeared to come so slowly and drop their bombs, which came down and caused considerable damage. This went on throughout the day, including the strafing of anything that moved – civilian or military. To my undying surprise, the company brought down three German aeroplanes with small-arms fire. I've never seen that happen since. I think the Germans were unused to having opposition – and we were unused to air raids. It was a combination of the two – the carelessness on the part of the Germans, who were low, slow and unworried – and extreme enthusiasm on the part of the British soldiers.

We went to a small village south of Otta – and here the battalion sent one company forward to assist the King's Own Yorkshire Light Infantry. The remainder of the battalion took up a defensive position across the valley. We set about digging in in the normal way, but quickly discovered that the topsoil was only a matter of six to twelve inches deep – thereafter it was solid rock. This was a distinct blow. The company commander reminded us that if you couldn't dig in, you built up, so we chopped small trees to form sangars – trees reinforced by rocks and filled in with bits of earth.

During the night we were told that the KOYLI would be withdrawing, and we would be a front line. This was successfully achieved with no alarm or excursion. The following morning we were still completing our sangars and defences, when we came under artillery fire. This wasn't particularly harassing, because they were some way back and they were merely firing on the hills and not on individual targets. We had the odd air raid again, then, about late morning we started seeing the Germans approaching, coming gradually nearer and nearer.

When the tanks came within range, we tried out our Boyes anti-tank rifles. This was extremely accurate – but completely ineffective. The projectile simply bounced off the front of the tank.

Fortunately the anti-tank two-pounders were quite effective. In fact, they were the only supporting weapon we had. As the advance got nearer, they started firing incendiary shells.

We were not taking many casualties until we had to relinquish our posts. The company commander, Major Walters – a very dashing officer and a first-class chap – led a counter attack, but unfortunately was killed. We managed to delay the advance until dark, and although we'd lost a portion of our front, the platoon nearest the road managed to hold on. We then got the order to withdraw behind the Green Howards, who were then behind us. This battle was taking place in a long valley with each battalion behind the other, so we were to withdraw during the night. Having issued those orders to my platoon, it was then discovered that the enemy had got round the flank of the fire of our company and established a post across the middle of the road. So a platoon was sent from one of the other companies to eject it.

When our turn came to withdraw, we left the road and went round in a circle up the side of the hill, getting round behind the Germans. The Germans were terribly keen on incendiary bullets, and they had a much higher percentage of tracer in their ammunition than we had. But they were using so much tracer, that my platoon – or what was left of it – managed to crawl safely underneath the line of the projectiles and get round the enemy and back on the road again.

That night we were to withdraw back to Dombaas by train, which my platoon accomplished successfully. The company second-in-command was not so fortunate. He was relying on a company of another battalion to his right to tell him when to withdraw, and in the confusion, he wasn't warned. When he eventually discovered he was alone, and that the rest of the brigade had left, he'd missed the train. Undeterred, he started to walk down the railway line, and he came upon one of those four-wheeled trucks with a lever to propel the vehicle – the sort of truck you see in a cartoon – and between them they managed to propel this thing and eventually arrived some three or four hours later in Dombaas.

By the time I arrived in Aandalsnes it was dark, and we moved down to the quay just in time for a really splendid sight of a naval cruiser coming in to the jetty in a wonderful flourish, all engines hard astern, rudder far over and landing with a bang against the quay. It was the quickest and slickest docking I've ever seen. This was the *Galatea* – and on we trooped to sail for home.

Captain Desmond Gordon
1st Battalion, Green Howards
We were fighting a losing battle from the time that we arrived in Norway, so morale was not high – it couldn't be expected to be – though discipline was remarkably good. Most of the men in my company were recalled army reservists who'd served in India with me until being demobilised – so they were seasoned soldiers, and they behaved magnificently.

The Germans had about a dozen tanks which could only be deployed one behind another on the road. They had come up against almost no opposition until they met the leading elements of the 15th Infantry Brigade near a village called Kvam. There the 10th Company commander had deployed forward four of his anti-tank guns, and concealed them astride the road, hidden in the gardens of the houses. That company destroyed the first German tank of the war, and that had a remarkable effect in slowing down the German advance. Not only did it block the road – and everything hinged on road movement – but it was an indication to the Germans that they were up against a force better equipped than what they had experienced so far.

Unknown to me, the higher command had decided that we had got to be evacuated back to Aandalsnes. A train had been assembled in the tunnel at Dombaas which was to take the battalion back. By that time, the Germans had caught up with us, and we were told to hold our position until I got the signal that the rest of the battalion had entrained in the tunnel. For the first and only time in this short-lived campaign, my company was given the support of a troop of Norwegian 25-pounder guns. The effect on morale of having these shells going over our heads in the direction of the enemy was incredible. With their help, we literally ran to the train and I staggered into the very last carriage, completely exhausted. By that time it was late evening. We came to a halt when the engine hit a bomb crater. We at the back of the

April 1940. British troops march into captivity under German guard, following the unsuccessful Allied campaign to turn back the German invasion of Norway.

train were ordered to get out and get on to the road which ran parallel with the railway line.

The commanding officer got hold of the intelligence officer – who'd got a bicycle from somewhere – and said, 'Go to the nearest village and find out if there is a tunnel where we can hide.' His one thought was that we must get some protection from German air attack when daylight arrived. He came back and reported that there was one 18 miles away. We marched through the night and we had just about reached it when the first German aircraft spotted us. We had about 700 men in the tunnel – and there was also a bloody train, which had to keep steam up – so we were practically suffocated. All that day we sat there, with the Germans air-bombing us, trying to hit the tunnel – which they failed to do. We stayed there until darkness appeared, then we got into this train and finally ended up in Aandalsnes – which by this time was virtually an inferno. The whole of the fjords around us were just lit up with flames of this little town burning. It was an unforgettable sight. Those aircraft that were bombing us in the tunnel went on to bomb Aandalsnes.

I found myself on a cruiser – the *Calcutta* – who hadn't got a single shell left to fire. She'd tucked herself in under one of the fjords throughout that day, and had fired every single round of ammunition she had to protect herself. I shall always be very grateful for the way the crew received us on board and looked after us during our trip back to Scotland.

We weren't in frightfully good shape by that time. We got very little sleep and we were very, very tired from being continually on the move and withdrawing. You can sustain yourself when you're advancing and achieving success – you can sustain yourself on short rations – but that's not so easy when you are retreating.

Stoker Reginald Reading
Aboard *Tribal-class destroyer* HMS Sikh

When Germany invaded Norway, we were at sea, and we quickly went across to Namsos. At that time the Navy sent half of the ship's company of various battleships straight ashore – even before the army had gone in there. We went back and escorted the *Empress of Britain* to Namsos as they took the Green Howards in. All the time the Germans were bombing us.

Then we went back again with other destroyers to fetch the troops in and it was the first time the Green Howards had been in any sort of action at all. Again, all the way up the fjord we were being bombed and our guns were firing. At Namsos, the whole of the jetty was on fire – all their stores and ammunition was being blown up, but we got them off.

We went in again about a fortnight afterwards and evacuated all those that we possibly could, together with other destroyers. There were very few people that had survived that lot. We did pick up the naval lads – most of them did get back. But as far as the troops were concerned, they had been really harrowed by the Germans. Anything that was burdening them in any way, shape or form, was just left. As we were pulling away from the quay, we could see the German tanks coming over the top of the hills – down towards the fjord. We were getting out just in front of the German troops.

Wing Commander Kenneth Cross
46 Squadron, RAF

We were told we would be ferried to Norway by the aircraft carrier *Glorious* – but that it wasn't possible to land on the carrier, because tests had indicated that the deck was not long enough for the Hurricanes to land and come to a stop. They had no hooks as the Fleet Air Arm aircraft had.

We taxied the aeroplanes through fields to jetty, put them on a lighter and went down the Clyde, to where the *Glorious* was anchored. We got all 18 aircraft hoisted aboard the *Glorious* with her cranes, and the next day we set forth for Norway.

I had some difficulty with the plan which we received from the shore as to how the squadron should fly into Skaanland. It was proposed that we should go in in dribs and drabs. From experience, I thought this would be fatal, as we could easily be bombed without being able to defend ourselves. We wanted to go in in three formations of six. The first one would go in. When it landed, the second one would stay overhead and guard them while they were being refuelled and coming to readiness on the ground. Then, the second formation would land. They would be covered by the third six. In that way we would always be ready for action with at least two-thirds of the squadron.

This conflicted with instructions I got from the shore, but Commander Heath on the *Glorious* agreed that my plan would be adopted.

With our variable-pitch air screws and the full power of the Merlin engine, our Hurricanes leapt off the deck without any difficulty at all, and we reached Skaanland – which was a muddy strip on the edge of the fjord, covered with coconut matting and somerfelt tracking. I landed first and as I came to a stop, the wheels sank in. The aeroplane tipped gently forward and I bent about two inches of my air screw. I was furious, because it was apparent that the airfield was unfit for landing on.

Two days later the attack on Narvik started. We patrolled Narvik alternately with 263 Squadron in Gladiators. The whole of the time the assault was taking place, no German air opposition was successful – the odd German aircraft – Ju 88s or Heinkel 111s appeared – and we shot down several during this period.

We were in Norway for about two weeks – then the attack on France started. We listened to the news of the German advance. It was a great disappointment to us when the commander told us that the government had decided to evacuate from north Norway, because we'd captured Narvik and pushed the Germans right back to the Swedish border. In another two weeks the whole of north Norway would have been ours. But we understood that the amount of shipping required to sustain an expedition at that distance up at Narvik was impossible with the major commitment now being in France. So we were to evacuate.

We were told, 'We want you to cover the evacuation of the troops from the various fjords by destroyers, and then, when the evacuation is complete, you can either destroy your aeroplanes or you can fly them up to the extreme north or Norway to Lakselv, where you can dismantle your aeroplanes yourselves, and we will endeavour to get a tramp steamer there. You can load them aboard that way.'

I declined that course straight away – as I did the proposal to burn the aeroplanes – as we thought they would be needed at home anyway. I asked if we could make an attempt to land on the *Glorious*.

I did the first landing – and in fact it turned out to be a relatively simple operation. My Hurricane stopped a little over two-thirds up the deck. All seven aircraft came on successfully. We fell into the bunks which were allocated to us. Nobody woke up until mid-afternoon the next day, which was 8th June.

I woke up about half-past three, I went along to the wardroom, and was having a cup of tea when the action stations was sounded. I assumed this was another practice. I went along to my cabin and put on my padded Irvine jacket. For some unknown reason I put the squadron funds, amounting to £200–£300, in an envelope in my inner pocket.

I reported to the bridge, as the CO of the squadron. For the next thirty to forty minutes, the ship was steadily hit. After about an hour or perhaps a little less, the ship began to list very badly, but we were still doing quite a good forward speed, some 12–15 knots. We were zigzagging. I thought she would roll over, she had such a list on. Then eventually the order was given to abandon ship.

Carley floats were thrown over the side for the crew and us passengers to swim to when we'd jumped over the side. I asked a naval pilot what was the form on abandoning ship. He said, 'When they drop these floats, we're still doing quite a considerable speed, so you want to go pretty quickly afterwards, otherwise you'll have a very long way to swim.' So when they dropped a float from the quarter deck, I had my Mae West on and I went over the side, came up like a cork, swam about ten yards and scrambled aboard the Carley float.

Very soon we had twenty or thirty people in the ship. To my great delight Flight Lieutenant Jameson, my number two in the squadron, came swimming along and scrambled aboard the Carley float with me. We sat side by side. Eventually the *Glorious* came to a halt about half a mile away from us. One moment she was there. Then we looked round again and she was gone.

It was rough and very cold. Within a short time some of the sailors began to die. Within three hours the first died. We had between twenty and thirty aboard our float. But within a few hours there were only seven of us left.

BLITZKRIEG

On 10 May German paratroops landed on the roof of the 'impregnable' Belgian fortress of Eben Emael in the first strike in Western Europe. The roller-coaster of *Blitzkrieg* now swept through the Low Countries of Holland and Belgium towards the British Expeditionary Force in northern France. The sheer speed, scale and violence of the invasion by heavily armed motorised columns of tanks and vehicles took the Allies by surprise, and they could offer little resistance as German troops cut a swathe through towards the Channel coast. The Belgian Army surrendered on 28 May. The French forces and the BEF fought a forceful rearguard action but soon they were in retreat towards the Channel.

Captain Francis Barclay
Royal Norfolk Regiment
On the 9th May, the first thing that happened was the Phantom Reconnaissance Forces of our own which were largely composed of light armoured cars from the 17th/21st Lancers – whose job it was to get early information of the approaching enemy   started to withdraw. They'd come back through our positions, over the bridge which was planned for blowing. They told us that Namur had ceased to hold out and that Liège would fall jolly soon, and that the Germans would probably arrive on the River Dyle the evening of the following day. So we dug in our positions – in fact, the Germans appeared the following day. The vanguard of

their advance guard consisted of motor bikes and sidecars mounted with machine guns. We knocked out about five of these, and then of course there was a build-up which one could see in the distance, and eventually I got the order to pull back over the river.

Father Charles-Roux Jean
Officer with French cavalry

When the German attack came on the 10th May 1940, I was in bed at three in the morning, and there was a frightful noise, and I didn't know what it meant. It sounded like a storm and an earthquake all at the same time. Then I realised that it was an artillery bombardment.

Hans Heinrich von Bittenfeld
German officer in 1st Cavalry

For the campaign in France we first had to go through Holland. Dutch resistance was courageous and brave, but they were outnumbered, so there was nothing they could do. In France, the French Army was already beaten, and we only had to do the cleaning up. We ended up south of Bordeaux, where relations with the local population were normal. We had a wonderful time. We would have only two hours a day of duty a day, and then we would go swimming.

I remember there was a famous textile industrialist who owned some famous racing horses. We politely asked if we could ride them. He said if we could find some food for the horses, then we would be allowed to, so this was something we were delighted to do, and we had a great time riding the horses until some SS came and tried to take them away.

Flight Lieutenant Peter Brothers
32 Squadron, RAF

When we went into action for the first time, on the 10th May 1940, we were told to ground-strafe an airfield in Holland, which had been captured by the Germans. I was leading the squadron because the commanding officer was new, and flying number two to me. We left 'A' flight up above to protect us whilst we went down to ground-strafe, but to my surprise the airfield was covered with Junkers 52s, troop transport aircraft. They were all burnt out in the middle, but the nose, tail and wing tips were still there. We thought this was very odd, so we didn't fire at them because it was a waste of time. Then we found one undamaged aircraft parked between some hangars. We set that on fire and came back to base. It was some months later before we discovered that the

Dutch had recaptured the airfield just before our arrival. They'd destroyed those aircraft on the ground, leaving one in which to escape to England. And that was the one we'd set on fire.

Gunther Rall
Luftwaffe pilot

There was another quiet period of time until our attack into the Netherlands, Belgium and France. This was my first confrontation with the French air force – it was 12th May 1940. My squadron had a mission to locate a German reconnaissance plane which had been deep in France, and escort it back to Germany. We took off with ten aircraft and we saw the plane we were looking for. But behind we saw ten dots chasing our plane. These were twelve P46s. Our reconnaissance plane escaped, but we were engaged in this dog-fight. This was a tremendous excitement, especially as it was the first time I had come that close to the enemy – I could see his head and his eyes in the cockpit.

I chased one who turned and turned, and he got right in front of me, so I shot him down. But I also took a lot of bullets into my aeroplane, because there was a plane on my tail. When I got back to base, I realised that he had hit my aeroplane seriously, but I was conscious and confident. This was my first victory, which had a very important psychological effect. You have proved that you can do the job.

Pilot Officer Douglas Grice
32 Squadron, RAF

We were sent on fighter sweeps over France. Patrol St Omer at 12,000 feet was a typical sort of order. And I suppose it was very early on, May 13th or 14th, that we actually met the enemy for the first time. Frightening experience it was, for me.

There we were – it was a lovely day. The sun was shining with lots of cumulus clouds around, and we just skirted one big lump of it, when there, in the distance, was a sight I shall never forget. The sky was full of aircraft, and in the space of a split second, a Hurricane had flown past me in flames. Out of the corner of my eye I saw a Me 110 climbing with a parachute wrapped round its tail, and a poor unfortunate airman, still attached to it. Then suddenly I saw a Me 110 only 300 yards ahead. I had already switched the gun button to fire, so I eagerly started pointing towards him and I thought, 'Well, I had better have one quick look behind' – which I did, and horror of horrors – there was another Me 110 three hundred yards behind me. He was panning gently to the left, obviously about to fire at me. Well, you don't hesitate in those circumstances – it was a case of the stick hard over, full right rudder, and I was into a screaming dive in about a fifth of a second. And by the time I'd pulled out, there wasn't an aircraft to be seen in the sky.

Anyway, seeing no friend or foe in the sky, and feeling very frightened and out of breath, I dived into the nearest cumulus cloud and came out the other side – still nothing to be seen – and flew home. At least I'd survived.

Flight Lieutenant Frank Carey
3 Squadron, RAF

Once I was commissioned, I went straight to France from Kenley. We patrolled the front line, wherever it happened to be at the time. The Hun aircraft were all over the place – you just took off and there they were. If you flew anywhere in the Pas de Calais or east over Belgium, there were lashings of them, absolutely asking for it. They had very few fighters about at that time, and over the first four days after my arrival, I must have had about twenty engagements. I shot down what I think was about fourteen aircraft in that period. I didn't get out of my clothes because we had nowhere except the floor to sleep. We had nowhere to eat. We used to ask the ground crew to get bits and pieces from the local village and bring it out to us. On my fourth day there, I was finally given a billet. So I picked up my kit – which was still on a big pile at the edge of the airfield – and took it to this place. I was on the dawn shift the next morning, so I couldn't sleep there, and I thought – tomorrow night I'll have a bath and I'll have a sleep.

On one attack I was ably assisted by an Me 109. Going in to attack some Ju 88s one day, we could see the fighters above, but we thought we would get a nice burst in before they got near us. I got behind this Ju 88 and pressed the button, and to my utter amazement bits flew off and the damage was astonishing! Our .303 guns weren't heavy enough to do so much damage. Then I saw fire over my head. There was a 109 trying to hit *me* but shooting high and we were both knocking the hell out of this poor old Ju 88! It went down. Really I shouldn't claim that one. I should have given it to the 109!

The trouble with the .303 on the Hurricane was that one had to learn to conserve one's ammunition: we only had fifteen seconds of fire and then you were finished. Chaps used to put on long bursts, and then they would only have half a burst left and that was it. An unarmed fighter is pretty useless. It was always a worry, that shortage of ammunition. I don't think the Spitfire was much better.

John Wheeler
Teenage son of evacuee host in Purton, Wiltshire
People were asked to join the Local Defence Volunteers. A pal and I went to the local police sergeant and we were the first two people to enlist that night. My mother was worried to death. My friend Nelson and I sat on a farm cart with Mr Lloyd and waited for the Germans until daylight. It seems so ridiculous now – what could we have done with a farm cart and no weapons? But that was the spirit of the time.

Nancy Bazin
Teacher in the West Country, aged 18
We were told that we had to mobilise all our civilian force in Exmouth to resist the invasion that was likely to come across the Channel. Our local battalion of Devons which were organising this were going round with microphones and loudspeakers, calling us to come to the beach with spades and shovels – anything we could lay our hands on. And I went with several friends. I remember particularly the stretch of sand allotted – it was very near where our lifeboat station was. We were told to dig, and we dug a trench in the sand, and we were, at the same time as digging and getting blisters on our hands, and working for hours on this, we were looking out to sea, expecting to see these flotillas of German invading troops come. On this whole two-mile stretch of beach we were digging this trench, and it was so obviously hopeless because, with the wind and the rain and the high tide, all our work would disappear. But we did it, in this extraordinary way, believing that somehow we were defending. That was a futile operation. There was a sergeant or an officer every hundred yards, saying, 'Keep digging!'

THE FALL OF FRANCE

Realising the extent of the German advance, civilian populations in threatened towns and villages in France gathered their personal possessions and took to the roads in any transport they could find – or on foot – to escape the German occupation. Such was the totality of the German invasion that, after the armistice, finding nowhere to go, many refugees were forced to return to their homes, only to find them occupied and under German control. Paris was soon under threat, and on 10 June the government fled the capital for Tours. Paris fell on 14 June, and three days later, after German troops had crossed the Maginot Line, France sued for an armistice. By 22 June the surrender was official.

Spring 1940. The Belgian Army, still widely using horse-drawn transport, makes a weary retreat on the Louvain–Brussels road.

Captain Stewart Carter
Sherwood Foresters (Nottinghamshire and Derbyshire Regiment)
We had dug in near the River Lasne when my company commander sent me to get in touch with the Belgian Army on our left. I found them lined up on the road, not far from our position. I was somewhat surprised to see this, as it rather looked like the end of an exercise in England. So, I said to an officer, 'Where are your positions going to be?' as he obviously had none. And he just said they were 'finis'. So I said, in my best schoolboy French, 'Well, what do you mean by that?' And he repeated, 'We are finished.' I thought this was the most extraordinary remark. So I said, 'Do you mean to say you've surrendered?' He said, 'That is it. We have finished the war.' So I was thunderstruck and went back to my major and reported that the Belgian Army had surrendered. The major said, 'Don't be so damn silly. Go back and see them again. I never heard such nonsense.'

So I went back again, knowing full well that they had – and a more senior Belgian officer confirmed this.

The Belgians – well, they were in a very bad way, quite exhausted. But then, of course, we were pretty rough by that time ourselves. But their whole attitude was one of complete dejection, and looking at them more closely, I could see they really had finished.

Sergeant William Harding
Royal Artillery
The roads were absolutely jammed solid with civilians of all ages – mostly very young and very old. The old people I shall never forget because it's something I've never seen before – never thought I'd see. Some of them must have been in their eighties, with huge bundles on their backs, bowed right over, walking along these hot roads.

There were mothers pulling prams piled up with belongings, little children hanging on their skirts crying. They weren't walking – they were just trudging along in the heat, virtually worn out. We all responded straight away. All the lads rummaged in their pockets, everywhere. The cookhouse – it was just the field kitchens – started making loads of tea with what water we had, and dishing it out. We felt so sorry for them. I was so fagged out, my legs felt like lead. So all I could do, shells or no shells, was just amble along. I just trudged along, carrying this old Bren gun and all this ammunition stuck in my blouse, in the boiling hot sun. Sweat was pouring off me.

On the 23rd the Germans must have got nearer, because this is where the mortars really took hold of the situation. The mortars came over thick and fast. Nearby there was a Vickers pom-pom on blocks of wood, manned by three gunners. A mortar bomb hit it and the three blokes were just shattered. I ran over to them, and I looked at one poor fellow – his face – his eyes staring up at me. And I thought, 'Well, I can't do anything for him.' I ran back again, and there was this chap, dragging himself on his elbows. He was sobbing, and there were two lines in the sand from his legs – but there was no feet on the end of his legs. I thought. 'God what a terrible thing to happen to anybody!' I looked away because there were more explosions all around us. Then I saw this rifleman running in front of me. One minute he was there – there was a terrific explosion – next minute he was in bits. How can a man, fully clothed in webbing, uniform, a belt round his waist, gas mask, boots and everything else, within seconds be lying there without a stitch of clothing on him? He was totally in pieces with his head lying on his neck, eyes open. The skin of his belly was taken right off – and there was his intestines, just like you see in a medical book, undisturbed. How can something like this happen?

Then a rifleman next to me shot an old woman that ran out of a house – and I cursed him for what he'd done. I thought it was unnecessary to shoot an old lady – but he said, 'I'm sorry, that was my orders. Anybody dressed as old women, nuns or priest or civilians running about, gets shot. Five of my company have been shot by Germans dressed as nuns'.

Private Denis Hoy
7th Battalion, King's Royal Rifle Corps

At one stage, with members of the headquarters platoon, I was sent off in a van with rifles and a Bren gun. We were told that three tanks would be coming up the road, and we were to stop them.

It was all quite an Arabian Nights fantasy! I got really past caring about it. I thought, 'I'm going to get killed now, but if I see any Germans I'll shoot them.' I thought, 'This is the end of me – let's just go along with it.' We were soon captured. They made us put our hands over our heads and get into line, and then they went round and searched us to see if we'd got any weapons.

We were marched off until nightfall. Then they just told us to stop, and I just sort of laid down wherever I was. In the morning I found I'd been lying on a pile of sharp stones that they put on roads – and I had no idea. I'd just gone down there, absolutely exhausted, and slept the night through.

On the march, we went into this field, where we were given some watery soup. We got nothing to have it in, so we had it in our tin helmets.

At odd times on this march, the French put out buckets of water for us, and very often the Germans kicked them over as we went by.

Weary men of the 4th Battalion, Border Regiment, who were with a group cut off for five days from the main body of the BEF in the Somme area, travel in a lorry they have commandeered.

Corporal Edgar Rabbets
Sniper with 5th Battalion, Northamptonshire Regiment
I'd been out for quite a long time, and very tired, so I'd dropped down in the bottom of a ditch, where I was well protected from casual view. When I woke up, there was a lot of noise going on and the Germans had set up a little artillery field gun group. I was able to put two gun crews out of action before I decided that was enough. They were too busy looking the other way, and with the noise of the artillery my rifle fire just got lost. I was able to get in a few quick shots and then make myself scarce.

There were some Belgians – but they may have been Germans, who were ploughing a field down two sides so that the corner pointed towards our headquarters. This was for the benefit of enemy aircraft, who duly arrived and plastered our headquarters out of existence. We lost our first colonel through that. It was somewhere between the Oudenaarde and Ypres areas. The ground had been ploughed in the form of an arrow, aiming straight at our headquarters. No farmer ploughs his land that way. After that, when I noticed anybody ploughing wrongly, he got shot. I shot two of them who were doing that. They knew what they were doing – I knew what they were doing – so there was no need to say anything.

Lieutenant-Commander Alexander Stanier
Commanding 1st Battalion, Welsh Guards
The civilian population of Boulogne weren't at all helpful, I'm sorry to say. I had moved headquarters to the local water board, where the adjutant said, 'The Frenchman wishes to see you.' I said, 'I want my supper – I've had nothing to eat all day.' He said, 'He won't keep quiet until he's seen you.' I went to see him and he said, 'I won't have your soldiers moving across my flowerbeds.'

Just as I was about to tell him what to do with his flowerbeds, there was a most appalling explosion, and the place blew up. I thought it was a shell, but actually it was my supper, which had been on a primus stove, overheating and blowing up. My quartermaster, with great presence of mind, threw a mattress full of feathers on the top of it to put out the fire, but it made the most awful smoke – we all had to put on our gas masks. I'm pleased to say the Frenchman hadn't got one – so he went away choking.

The following day we caught a priest with a Bible in his cassock, which had an awful lot of notes in it. My Intelligence Officer said, 'These seem to be extraordinary notes for a priest to have.' Whether he was a proper priest or not, I don't know, but he was dressed as one. The troops threw him into the

Near Louvain, Belgium, May 1940. Belgian civilian refugees including one child with a wooden leg – take to the road with scant possessions, in hope of finding safety.

drink – I should think he was drowned. It's the sort of thing you don't ask about.

Private William Tilley
Clerk with Base Depot, Royal Army Service Corps
Some of the refugees were pushing little handcarts, some had got cars. The cars were all grossly overloaded, both with people and with whatever they could take with them. The other thing I can remember is the smell. Obviously, many of them had not had an opportunity to wash for quite a while, so whenever we got near a lot of refugees, the smell made us realise that they'd been living fairly roughly for a long time. An extremely sad sight, that.

Private Edward Watson
Bugler, 8th Battalion, King's Royal Rifle Corps
As we were going along, walking along the road, I remember seeing English tanks blown to pieces. These lovely English tanks. We'd been told that the Germans only had cardboard tanks, and I couldn't believe it.

We shared the food out, with some wine that we had found. I don't think I'd ever drunk wine before – I didn't like it very much, this red stuff – tasted very bitter, but some of the fellows were really gushing it. Banbury, the officer, said that if he found anyone drunk he would shoot them. 'You can drink as much as you like', he said, 'but if you're drunk, then I'm going to kill you.'

We were finally taken prisoner. They were outside and throwing hand-grenades into this house and calling – what was the phrase? 'Tommy, for you the war is over.' They could all say this – they must have been taught to say this.

I remember being very impressed with these German soldiers at the time – how bloody tough they looked. How efficient they seemed, relative to us. They were so businesslike and how very smart the officers seemed by comparison. Everything seemed so much better than what we had. They were professionals by comparison to us. I'd never seen anything like them.

Evelyn Jaulmes
Daughter of former British intelligence officer, living in Paris
We saw the Belgians and the Dutch fleeing with anything they could bring. We knew this was a dangerous period and so we left on the 11th June and two days later the Germans entered Paris. There were thousands and thousands of us with all the cherished things we could bring, mattresses on the tops of cars. Miles and miles of us and we hindered the French army a lot because all the roads were completely blocked by refugees and the army couldn't get their

tanks and troops through to the front to fight the Germans. There was such a panic – we all knew the Germans were coming and we had to go.

Marika Phillips
Civilian living in Paris
I realised that I must say goodbye to my mother, so we went to see her and she was delighted to see us. We later heard that she'd spat at a German officer and she was put to punishment with some other old lady to clean German boots. Poor old girl. Then we went to the Boulevard St Michel where we were stopped by a young policeman. He said, 'Where are you going? Your car is sending out black fumes.' I told him it was running on a strange recipe. 'I've never seen that before,' he said. I asked him if he'd like to have some food so we took the saucepan out of the car but he said, 'It's no good taking all that. You should leave it here. All of it. I'm not saying this because I want it for myself. You should leave it here.' So we left the silver, the bed linen, everything. He said, 'You should take the road to Orléans. You must hurry up. There's not much time left. Very little time.'

At some point, we stopped at a bistro. Inside we saw a mother and her children crying. She was shouting and when I looked in the kitchen, I saw two men fighting over a piece of meat while outside the children were crying from hunger. I went up to the two men, took the piece of meat, took a knife and went to the table with the mother and the children, gave them the meat and said, 'Here you are.' It was like a surrealist dream.

After we moved off again, we came across packed lines of people going to Orléans, coming back from Orléans, soldiers who were lost. It was impossible. We couldn't move. And then to my horror, I heard a German plane overhead firing its machine guns. And then another one. I said to Paul, 'Listen, let's leave the car, let's walk.' Paul said 'No, we'll push the car.' So we pushed the car across a field in the general direction of Orléans, but the sky that way was red and black with smoke so I said, 'We can't go there.' And we went instead to a little village named Gange, where the people cultivated vineyards. Nearby was Roquefort so we had cheese to eat and wine to drink. We stayed there for three months.

DUNKIRK

The British Expeditionary Force was in retreat, in a degree of disarray and haste that demanded that the men abandon much of their equipment in order to save themselves. The last week of May saw the retreating British and French armies assembling on the beaches at Dunkirk. The first priority was to save the men to fight another day – to transport them back to Britain to regroup. It was a seemingly impossible undertaking, but with the massed efforts of the Royal Navy and private vessels of every description, large and small, a total of 338,226 British and French troops were brought back to British shores between 26 May and 4 June. Hitler's troops failed to press home their obvious advantage and did not annihilate the retreating British. One of the last lifts of troops took place on 17 June, from St Nazaire by the *Lancastria*, which was sunk by German bombs. Churchill was at pains to remind the nation that wars are not won by evacuations – however, most of the army had been rescued. There was something to build on for the forthcoming conflict.

Squadron Leader Al Deere
New Zealander, 54 Squadron, RAF

Station Commander 'Boy' Bouchier assembled all the pilots in the billiards room in the officers' mess, to tell us we had been assigned to take part in the protection of the British troops over Dunkirk. For fourteen days we went non-stop. I did something like thirty-seven hours in ten days. We just kept flying. We had no reserve pilots.

Ordinary Seaman Dick Coppeard
Royal Navy

At Portland we were given a night's leave, so we went ashore, picked up a couple of WAAFs and took them to the pictures. While we were there they flashed on the screen for all personnel of the ships in harbour to return to their ships immediately.

Eventually we found out that we were going over to France to pick up the troops. We were told to carry on to Fécamp and embark as many people from the jetties as we could. Most of them were stretcher-cases and walking wounded. They looked like a beaten army – they weren't really, but they looked it. Some were from the 51st Highland Division, a few French, and a regiment from the Midlands.

We cleared the mess decks to make room for the stretchers. The walking cases were pushed into corners. There were two or three hundred of them on board, plus about sixty of us crew. We tried to feed them but ran out of food. At one point we had to take bread off some French soldiers who didn't want to share it around. They seemed shocked and were very, very quiet. I don't think they realised what was happening to them. A lot of them had never seen warfare. We got the chaps off at Portsmouth. Those that could walk marched off the jetty, heads up and shoulders back.

Corporal Elizabeth Quayle
WAAF, on liaison duties, running the phone line into Dunkirk

I'd be rather ashamed to say it, but it put the fear of God into me! We knew where the Huns were – we had maps with pins in – and they seemed to be advancing very fast. The Dunkirk crisis itself was unbelievable. A lot of people coming back had jettisoned their guns and vehicles. They were just pouring through. I think the officers at the other end of the phone were largely confined to their building, but they could see very clearly what was going on. It was absolute mayhem.

Dunkirk was full of people who had mostly walked there, not in any form or order. They had just got there as fast as they could. Some had hitched lifts wherever possible. There were lots of refugees coming in. It had been bombed. We knew that a lot of the troops were sheltering in the buildings along the shore. We had no idea they were going to be rescued – it seemed the whole army was going to be captured.

I was extremely upset, because it never occurred to me that we would survive. I thought we were defeated, and quite frankly thought we would surrender and sue for peace.

Lieutenant Bruce Junor
On leave from HMS **Ajax**

The Commander rang me up to report at once with my boots and gaiters on and prepare to go overseas. I dashed back to Chatham where I and another officer went in an Admiralty car to Ramsgate and boarded an old destroyer, HMS *Wolfhound*.

We crossed the Channel under heavy attack by bombers but we landed on the jetty at Dunkirk. A British naval officer was giving the orders but Captain Tennant was in overall charge from a dugout at the landward each of the jetty or mole which was roughly 400 yards long.

For the first 48 hours I was never off my feet. Soldiers came from scattered units and in small groups under command, all disarmed and dispirited from fighting and marching with no food or rest. Montgomery, the Divisional Commander, marched the troops by night and handled the Division so well to manage to evacuate so very many soldiers.

The Admiralty got hold of Dutch schoots which were robust, petrol-powered, large, open barges with powerful engines designed to carry cargo in the Dutch inland waterways. For the evacuation they were manned by British naval personnel and of course were so useful because of their very shallow draft which enabled them to get up to the root of the pier. The destroyers could only safely reach the end of the jetty and then only at high water.

The evacuation of the beaches was a magnificent bit of organisation but it has gone down in history that the whole of the British Expeditionary Force came off on Dunkirk beaches which is nonsense. Thirty to forty thousand men were evacuated from the beaches by the 'little ships' which was a magnificent effort. It was however, a drop in the ocean compared to the evacuation, by the Royal and Merchant Navy from the jetty, of some 220,000 men.

Francis Codd
Auxiliary Fire Service in London, aboard the Massey Shaw, *a shallow-draft fire-fighting ship based on the Thames*
From about a mile away, still no aeroplanes, no bombs, no menace – then we could see it was a flat beach, a sandy beach, and then we saw the silhouette of houses against this sky, the setting sun. We couldn't see what was on the beach. We gradually saw reflections on the calm water, and I though I could see a wrecked small craft, and then a bigger craft. Gradually we could see dark shapes against the sand – and then we saw that there were hundreds – thousands – of people on this sand, and stretching up to the line of houses which stood, presumably, on the road that ran along the coast.

It was an extraordinary sight. Nothing seemed to be happening. They didn't seem to be moving in any organised way – not marching. They were standing or sitting, but mainly we noticed that they were columns of men stretching down into the sea. We didn't really understand what this was at first – and then it suddenly occurred to us that these were columns of men waiting to be picked up. The first man in the sea was the next man to be picked up.

One of our auxiliaries, Shiner Wright, was a good swimmer, and he went from the *Massey Shaw* some fifty to a hundred yards to a wrecked boat which was right inshore in about two or three feet of water. He swam with what we called the 'grass line', which is a rope that floats on water, and he tied it to the wreck so that we had a fixed line into shallow water. Now there were lots of little rowing boats in the water, mainly sunk or not being used. So they got a rowing boat that would hold very few people, a light rowing boat, and worked it along the line, pulling hand over hand. When we got organised, this worked very well. Whoever was in charge of the column of men lined up near the shore end of the line, detailed six men into the rowing boat to pull along the line 'til they reached the *Massey Shaw*, climb out on board and send their rowing boat back for another half-dozen. In that way I think we took aboard 36 soldiers out of the water that night.

Ordinary Seaman Stanley Allen
Aboard HMS Windsor

A megaphone asked if there was anyone who would volunteer to crew up a fishing boat, where some of the crew had been machine-gunned. This boy of 17– who'd been sunk twice that day – volunteered immediately. He got cheered by the sailors and the soldiers who were on board.

One old, three-badge able seaman – which meant he'd had thirteen years of undetected crime – said to me, 'With youngsters like that, how can we effing-well lose?' And really it was something. It did us the world of good. It was a real tonic that this boy who had gone down twice in that morning, instead of coming back to England to his family – volunteered again.

What I couldn't help marvelling about as well, was how the soldiers, who were very tired and very hungry – were squatting down sending rapid fire up at the aircraft. I took my hat off to them – everybody did.

Some Spitfires appeared, and a couple of Stukas got shot down. They were cheered into the sea. But our first-lieutenant – after the incident was over, he appealed to the soldiers, 'Please don't fire, because you are putting our machine-gunners on the bridge in jeopardy in your enthusiasm.' He said it so calmly and nicely that all the soldiers laughed.

As we were going out with these boats, it came to me – and came to a lot of us – that we'd had a heck of a pasting the day before and today – we must be untouchable. Nothing could hit us. It was rather a strange feeling – that we'd got through, and we were going to get through it again.

When we got alongside at Dunkirk and secured, a file of Scottish soldiers who were wearing khaki aprons over their kilts, came along led by an officer who'd got his arm in a sling. He called out to the bridge, 'What part of France are you taking us to?' One of our officers called back, 'We're taking you back to Dover,' So he said, 'Well, we're not bloody well coming.' They turned round and went back to continue their war with the Germans on their own. It was something remarkable.

The Crested Eagle – the old London pleasure ship which used to go between Tower Bridge down to Clacton – was a hospital ship, painted up with red crosses. She'd been bombed and settled in the water. But the German aircraft

Dunkirk evacuees – one with a captured German helmet – have a pie (courtesy of Telfer), a cuppa, and laugh with a friendly ATS girl as their train fills up at Dover.

were still machine-gunning her. That wasn't cricket. There was no real hatred about the Germans, really, except they just weren't playing the game. That wasn't the right way to win a war – to have a go at wounded people.

There was a little dog, a terrier-type mongrel, who came on board with some of the soldiers. He had a harness on him with pouches. He only understood French. When I spoke to him he wouldn't leave me. That little dog came back with us on the other two trips that we made. He didn't understand any English, which rather tickled some of the soldiers. One of our sub-lieutenants felt that Kirk, as we called him, should not be destroyed to keep to the necessary anti-rabies laws, so after Dunkirk was all over, Kirk was collected by a PDSA van to go into quarantine for six months before, as the sub-lieutenant put it, 'being taken on the staff of the parish where his father was vicar'. All of us cheered the old dog off. It was a very nice human touch amongst all that carnage of Dunkirk – as though people, in spite of all, were still caring.

The other thing was seeing all the soldiers coming back without their equipment. We began to think it was sort of the end of our way of life. We didn't know how long we'd be able to hold Jerry off in England. We knew we had the Navy, and that we would fight – but we didn't know what the soldiers would be able to do if Jerry had landed – because they had nothing.

Ordinary Seaman Douglas Stevens
Signaller aboard HMS *Saon*

I think it was on the 24th May, round about midnight, I was called to the bridge as there was a flashing light coming from Cap Gris Nez. It turned out to be an SOS. We waited for daylight, and then we could see there was a lot of troops all clustered around Cap Gris Nez, up the cliffs and on the beach. We could see someone was trying to semaphore with flags to us, asking if we could send a boat to take off troops as they were trapped. There were German tanks in the woods behind Cap Gris Nez and they were shelling them.

We saw quite a lot of bodies – mainly French troops. They appeared to have their tin hats and full pack on when they drowned in the water. I know it's a bit gruesome, because they were in a very bloated condition, and we had orders to stick boat hooks in them and sink them – which is what we did.

On one occasion, the whole convoy was attacked by about 70 Stukas. I got wounded in the left arm, and the gun layer got badly wounded in his leg. The skipper was killed right alongside me – we heard afterwards it was a cannon shell from one of the Stukas. We were in sinking condition, and the tugs came out from Dover and tied themselves alongside us and dragged us back into Dover Harbour.

Sergeant Edward Doe
2nd Battalion, King's Royal Rifle Corps
On the 24th May we were advancing in open formation up a main road when, all of a sudden, a machine gun opened up and the left and the right of the formation simply disappeared. They were down. It was awful. It was plain murder, and by God, I was scared. It was devastating. We in the centre got away with it. My goodness me, I shall remember that to my dying day.

When the German soldiers came towards us, he just had his jackboots on, a belt round his waist, a canister on the side of him and a water bottle. He wasn't lumbered down, he wasn't tied down with packs and equipment like we were – and furthermore, he was armed with a Tommy gun. We had to fire one shot and then eject the cartridge and reload again. It was an awful situation to be in. We were not only outnumbered, we were out-armed in every way. It was, quite frankly a bloodbath.

By the 25th they were closing in all the time – gradually eliminating, mopping up pockets here and there. We were desperately short of ammunition. There were chaps pleading for ammunition and being told, 'I'm sorry, you can't have none of mine – I might need what I've got.' That was the situation.

The Germans had brought the tanks in and they were blasting. They knew when they brought those damned great big tanks in, that was it. I actually fired the Boyes anti-tank rifle for the first time in my life – a terrifying weapon. To even fire, you had to hang on to it, like grim death, because it would dislocate your shoulder if you didn't. I fired at a tank coming over the bridge that wasn't blown – and I couldn't miss it from about 50 yards away. An officer was right beside me, and I saw this hit the tank and all it had done was to just about knock the paintwork off. It made a noise like a ping-pong ball. The officer who was beside me said to me, 'Leave the blasted thing there, Doe – get the hell out of it!' And we did – and only just in time. We scarpered – quick! We just disappeared off the other side of the bridge only just in time, because this fellow opened up and he blew half the coping of the bridge off with this terrible big gun on the front of the tank.

I finished up with a group of about eight chaps in a railway shed, which was more than half full of women and children – mainly French – huddled there. All of a sudden everything went quiet, and we heard a voice somewhere at the back of the shed say to us, 'Come out' – perfect English, too – 'You haven't got a chance. If you're not out within five minutes, we'll blow you to pieces.' So we just walked out, a dozen of us. Just left our rifles where they were. I had the sense to remove the bolt from the rifle, and chucked it. We went out with our hands up in the air – and there they were. The chap that had called us up was a young German officer. He called us 'the swine', 'the pigs' – and why didn't we give in, we were foolish, oh dear, oh dear.

The first thing they did was to take our rings and watches off us. My watch was a wedding present. I also lost a gold wedding ring. We were assured, when they were taken off us, that we'd get them back at the end of the war – but we knew darned well we wouldn't.

I even had some family pictures taken off me, and the German looked at them and tore them up and chucked them on the floor at his feet. I could have annihilated him. Just tore them up – just contempt.

Sergeant Leonard Howard
210 Field Company, Royal Engineers

We were making our way from the brewery at Flêtre to Dunkirk, when we had to cross a road open to enfilade by the Germans. We could only cross one at a time. You had to pick your spot and take your chance. I crossed this road behind a driver, Wheeler, who was some eight feet in front of me when he was hit in the stomach by a machine gun. As I got almost up to him, a further burst of fire took the top of his head off, literally in front of me. Had it not been for him, I would have had that burst. So in many ways, I always think that poor Wheeler, who'd bought it anyway, saved my life.

On the night of 29th/30th May we left Flêtre and then started our forty-mile trek to Dunkirk. We walked and ran throughout that night, and indeed, all the next day. One was continually making diversions to miss the enemy.

I remember, there was a Captain Whitty, who had been shot through the chest – an amazingly brave man. He was leading quite a sizeable group of infantry, and for a while we tagged on. It was a case of every man for himself. It was chaotic. The Germans were very close, and people were being killed. At 21 years old, one hadn't experienced death and people being killed. So it was a bit frightening.

Survival, of course, was the main object in everyone's mind. I saw an RSM walking down the road. He was in his knee breeches and his service dress jacket and cap – and the tears were streaming down his face. He said, 'I never thought that I would see the British Army like this.' And I always remember him. Poor man was absolutely shattered. He was a regular soldier, and the tears were streaming down his face.

We got into Dunkirk around five o'clock in the evening – we hadn't eaten and it was really chaos. The sand was littered with bodies and crowds of chaps all hoping to get off.

I was exhausted, and I went to sleep. I lay in the sand in the dunes, and I slept, because I was really completely exhausted. The next morning, my mate Bill Baldry was still around, and he and I went into the water, hoping to get picked up. But there was no hope. They tried to organise queues, but it was very difficult. People were not only being Stuka-ed, but there was also panic on the beaches themselves.

I saw British men shoot British troops. On one occasion, a small boat came in – and they piled aboard it to such a degree that it was in danger of capsizing. The chap in charge of this boat decided he must take some action. He ordered one man who was hanging on the side to get away – but he didn't, so he shot him through the head. From the people around there was no reaction at all. There was such chaos on the beach that that didn't seem to be out of keeping. There were chaps who were going round the bend. I saw chaps run into the water screaming, because mentally it had got too much for them.

I was wearing a battledress blouse and slacks, and it was bitterly cold at night. I came out of the water and I removed a corporal's overcoat from a corpse on the beach.

They landed some beachmasters, who were in service dress, and they had red bands on their arms – trying to organise the evacuation. They'd come over from the UK to try and organise the queues on the beach. Well, frankly, the chaps who'd made it to Dunkirk, didn't want chaps with service dress and Sam Browns and red bands round their arm trying to organise them into queues.

There was a very flimsy canoe, and two chaps paddled out in this canoe. A Stuka had come down and machine-gunned them, and they both leaned the same way – and they were both drowned. The canoe was upside-down, and it was floating some way off the beach. Bill swam out to this canoe and pulled it ashore, and we emptied it of water, got a couple of spades off an abandoned lorry, and we paddled out. HMS *Whitehall* came past us with its gun blazing away at these Stukas, threw us a line and we were pulled aboard.

Flying Officer Geoffrey Page
56 Squadron, RAF

Our operations over Dunkirk fell into two main categories. One was that we would do a fighter sweep. We would sweep all the way round, behind the beaches and try and intercept any German aircraft coming up to attack the soldiers on the ground. In the other role, we would escort a bomber called the Blenheim, and be their fighter escort when they went to bomb targets that were related to the evacuation from Dunkirk.

I think our ground crews were the people who got into more fisticuffs in local pubs, because after a few beers, the soldiers would say, 'Where were you?' and our ground crews knew very well that we'd gone over there.

Corporal Henry Palmer
1/7th Battalion, Queen's Royal Regiment
The beach was one vast sea of bodies. I had never seen so much dejection. Soldiers felt that they had been left there. Some seemed to have given up, but personally I didn't. There was one place I was going, and that was back to England.

There was panicking, but most of us managed to keep our heads. One chap scrounged a tin of bully beef and laid it out like a picnic, tucked his napkin in, then apologised he couldn't supply the wine because the butler happened to be away that day.

Captain Anthony Rhodes
253 Field Company, Royal Engineers
About an hour after the setting of the sun came the familiar drone, as the Luftwaffe came along and dropped flares, so they could see us. The sky was alight as they dropped their bombs.

Where the boats came in, there was a little nucleus at the head of the water, and then a great queue, running up from the dunes behind, perhaps a quarter of a mile long. The idea was just like a London bus queue. Nobody told us to do that – it seemed the decent thing to do. There must have been about ten or twelve of these queues running up. When we were halfway up in our queue, the bombing started, and one man ran to the head of the queue when he saw a boat coming. A naval officer turned on him and said, 'Look, go back to the place you've come from – or I'll shoot you.' He said it very loudly for everybody to hear, and the man went back with his tail between his legs.

We'd been on the fishing boat, I suppose, an hour at the most. We were trying to lie down – we hadn't had any sleep for several days – when there was a cry came up. All the men who'd been rescued and were on the fishing boat were to be transferred to a destroyer.

When we got on board, an officer came round and said, 'We shall shortly be sailing for Blighty – England, Home and Beauty.' I went right down into the hold, where I was put into a hammock, because I was dead – we all were.

At Dover when we arrived, there were a whole series of trains. All the units had been dispersed and one hadn't got any of one's own men – one was isolated, and we were simply told, 'Each of you get on the train and get up to

London. You'll find the RTO at Waterloo, and he'll tell you you'll have a couple of days to go home, and where you're to assemble to join your new units.' So we went up in the trains – they were full of civilians who got in and were going to their office in London. Sitting next to you, there might be a man who was going up to his bank. One very nice man, a civilian, pressed into my hand two half crowns – which was rather nice.

Leon Wilson
French soldier retreating from Belgium into France
We were fortunate – so fortunate. We have said thank you to England a thousand times for sending the little boats to take us to the big boats – the destroyers – to take us back to England. I was on the beach for two days, and it was so horrible. We seemed to be walking on dead bodies, not on sand. It is very hard to describe, just walking on bodies. But at ten o'clock in the evening, we reached a little boat, which should usually take about six people, but there must have been about twenty people already on it. But we were very fortunate that the boat took us. It took us to an English destroyer. I shall never forget the captain, who was one of the nicest gentlemen you could wish to meet. He said, 'Come on, Frogs, sit down and have something to eat.' It was a good joke at that moment! He told us, 'Eat whatever you want,' and we sat down to eat – and it was such that it was better than any meal at the Savoy today – bacon, cheese, everything. It was a joy for us.

Coxswain Thomas King
Aboard HMS Sharpshooter
On the way in to the beaches, our captain hailed a ship that was coming out with troops and said, 'How many are there there?' The reply that he got back was, 'There's bloody thousands!'

There was no order on the first occasion at all. It was more or less a free-for-all. Soldiers don't know the life-saving capacity of boats. We could only take ten to twelve in a whaler, and so we kept our distance from the water's edge, because it was no good us going right up on the beach, because we'd got to get seaborne again.

On the second night we went in, there was order. There was an officer at the head and he called out, 'Coxswain, how many do you want?' And I would tell him, and he would count them off. Any wounded they would pass over their heads, and you'd take the wounded first.

Al Deere was one of many New Zealanders who distinguished himself in the RAF throughout the war. One of his earliest tasks was to give air cover for the evacuation at Dunkirk.

Squadron Leader Al Deere
54 Squadron, RAF

On the 31st May, I was leading the squadron, and just as we arrived over Dunkirk, a Dornier 17 came flying up the coast. We went after it and, being the leader, I was first there. I was lining up behind to shoot it, when the rear-gunner fired. He hit my engine and the glycol header-tank, which is the cooling system. I had to break off. I crash-landed north of Dunkirk. The tide was out, and I got down on the beach, but I knocked myself out on the edge of the windscreen. When I came to, I got out and was looked after by a girl who stitched me up with an ordinary needle and put a plaster on me. Then I headed for Dunkirk, where I knew the BEF was intending to evacuate. We had been reading in the newspapers that the British Army was retreating 'according to plan'. Somewhere en route to Dunkirk, I went into a small café where I saw two Tommies. I asked, 'Am I heading for the Army at Dunkirk?' They looked at me and said something to the effect of, 'What British Army? There's no retreat, chum. There's bloody chaos.' Dunkirk was a complete shambles – burning buildings, abandoned vehicles and falling masonry.

Bernt Engelman
Luftwaffe pilot

On the beaches and in the dunes north of Dunkirk, thousands of light and heavy weapons lay in the sands, along with munitions crates, field kitchens, scattered cans of rations and innumerable wrecks of British army trucks.

'Damn!' I exclaimed to Erwin. 'The entire British Army went under here!' Erwin shook his head vigorously. 'On the contrary! A miracle took place here! If the German tanks and Stukas and navy had managed to surround the British here, shooting most of them, and taking the rest prisoner, then England wouldn't have any trained soldiers left. Instead, the British seem to have rescued them all – and a lot of Frenchmen too. Adolf can say goodbye to his Blitzkrieg against England.'

Sergeant Peter Vinicombe
Wireless Operator, 98 Squadron, RAF, aboard troopship Lancastria

Roughly four o'clock in the afternoon on the 17th June, the sirens went again from somewhere – we think the destroyers. There was an instant attack with guns going off near us. At the time, I was at the base of a funnel, and there was a terrific bang and blast which blew me off my feet – straight into the lap of an army officer. Another bomb went off and the ship lurched. He cleared off with his soldiers in rather a panic, and I got kicked in the face as they went.

The ship started heeling over. Another bomb went off. I suppose we got three because I wasn't counting any more, but I can remember these huge explosions. As the ship was going over, so loose kit and things on deck started sliding – so did the people who weren't holding on to anything. There came an announcement from someone on the bridge to transfer our weight to the other side of the ship – which we did – and she righted. But, in righting herself, of course, the extra weight made her go over towards the other side – and she went over again. Then we got the same order. Machinery like trucks, guns, stuff that was on the deck – human beings all hurtled down into the rails of the ship, into the water. One of my most vivid pictures is of the big masts of the ship running parallel to the water, and people were running along this and jumping off.

I saw a rope and I grabbed it – not realising at the time that it was attached to the ship. However, I couldn't swim, so I had to get hold of something that would keep me afloat. There were all these kitbags, so I grabbed an oar between my legs and a kitbag under each arm and just floated there.

Ordinary Seaman Frank Brogden
Crewman aboard troopship Lancastria
There seemed to be thousands and thousands of people in the water, and unfortunately, with this ship having had the attack earlier on, the fuel tanks were damaged. We had a terrific amount of oil fuel, which is almost like tar. Men were stuck in this oil fuel, clinging to various bits of wreckage. After about an hour, the attackers came over again, and they strafed us with machine-gun fire. Then various ships came in to pick troops.

I'd been in the water approximately five hours. But in the meantime, I'd come across an old broken ladder or some wood, and I was clinging to that, which I was very pleased about, because although the life-jacket keeps your head above water, it's very nice to get hold of something. I was picked up by a French tug, whose crew just threw a hook out and dragged us in. I must have been in a sorry mess, as I was black from head to toe. They gave us a mug of hot wine – very sweet red wine – and immediately I was very sick. This seemed to bring quite a lot of the oil fuel up. I found out afterwards that's why they gave it us. They must have had experience of this before.

Corporal Donald Draycott
Fitter, 98 Squadron, aboard troopship Lancastria
We were practically the last to embark on the *Lancastria*. By this time, she had round about 6,000 troops and air force on board. We were assigned to

palliasses right on the bottom of the hold. It was pretty grim and, having a strong sense of self-preservation, I thought, 'Well, on the trip home, if we get attacked by submarines or hit a mine, we wouldn't have a chance down there – particularly if the lights have all gone.' The ship was old, with no proper working gangways like an ordinary troopship, and I realised we'd have difficulty getting out if we got into trouble. So I decided to stay on the top deck.

When she was hit, I went to the bow of the ship to have a look back, and she was sinking slowly in the water. So I said to this chap, 'Well, I'm a swimmer. I'm over the side,' I just looked down about a thirty-foot drop, took my tin helmet off, my uniform, my boots, clutched my paybook and my French francs and jumped feet first over the side. When I broke the surface I was right up against the ship's plates, so I decided to strike out away from her. I swam about a hundred yards and came across a plank, which looked as if it had been blown off one of the hatches. So I sat on that, and the thing that surprised me was how calm I felt. I thought, 'Well, I'll sit on this. You'll never see anything like this again and have a grandstand view.' So I sat on this hatch-cover and turned back and looked at the ship. Fifty yards away from me, men were singing 'Roll out the Barrel'.

Private William Tilley
Clerk with Base Depot, Royal Army Service Corps

It's something that you look back on with astonishment – that from the little trawler which picked us up, we were able to watch the final lurching and sinking of the *Lancastria*. She overturned completely in the end, so you could see the propellers, and even then, you could see men standing on her upturned bows, afraid to jump into the sea – and even try to propel themselves away. That was a pretty awful sight to behold, because you realised that when she went down, they would just be sucked down with her. That was awful.

Corporal Frank Hurrell
3rd Field Army Workshop, RAOC

When we got into Dover we were put into old customs sheds. In there were these ladies from the women's services – the Red Shield Club – all the various ladies' associations. I had no tunic – I'd lost it – and one of the elderly ladies took off her fur coat and put it round me whilst I sat down, and gave me a cup of tea. Then she produced a stamped envelope – stamped and sealed – and she said, 'Right. Address it to go to your wife or whoever. Put the message on the back. Use it like a postcard – it will get there quicker.'

Tired but safe, men picked up from the beaches of Dunkirk in late May 1940 arrive
back in England aboard one of the many ships commandeered to come to their rescue.

Home, on dry land – and a smoke! Dishevelled men of the British
Expeditionary Force prepare to board trains at Dover after their return
from Dunkirk.

Lady Anne Chichester
Civilian volunteer worker in Hampshire
My husband who was in the Guards, was in the retreat, and he was picked up by a yacht with a lot of other Welsh guardsmen and brought back to England. They left every single thing they possessed except their guns – even their sleeping bags, their clothes, their equipment. They just got on board any ship that was able to take them back to England. At the time, knowing the French had given up the fight, and that the Germans were all along the coast of France, we really did think that any day they would be invading.

Reverend John Duffield
Former padre on Western Front, 1914–18, chaplain of Onchan Internment Camp
When our people had to come home from Dunkirk, it was thought that something had to be done about all the Germans who were in the country, and about whom they didn't know very much. So, in a bold step, it was decided to intern them on the Isle of Man, which was selected because of its holiday-resort atmosphere. In my parish, a great chunk of it was wired off ready for the internees. On the great day, hundreds were marched into the camp.

Senior Aircraftman James Merrett
Ground gunner, RAF
I went in the pub the first night I came back from France, and the landlord said to me, 'Oh, we thought you'd been took prisoner.' And old Bill, the postman, took one look along the bar. He said, 'I told you if there's only one bugger come back it'll be him.'

Captain Francis Barclay
2nd Battalion, Royal Norfolk Regiment
The first thing I'd pay tribute to is the men and the morale that we had in the battalion, which was absolutely wonderful. It was the most thrilling feeling to experience the spirit of the chaps who were with you.

We had tremendous respect for the courage of our men and the way they held out when the Dunkirk withdrawal was going on. They never got to Dunkirk themselves. They were stopping the Germans interfering with the withdrawal of thousands and thousands of other people – which they did successfully. The battalion was practically wiped out doing it.

THE BATTLE OF BRITAIN

By summer 1940, German invasion across the Channel was imminent. France had been conquered and Hitler's next thought was to invade Britain. The bulk of his troops and war material would have to be conveyed by sea, and in order to achieve this, he had to have air superiority. The destruction of Fighter Command was the essential pre-requisite to the invasion of Britain. For Fighter Command, all possible resources were harnessed into building more aircraft, training more fighter pilots to defend the vital radar stations and key airfields on Britain's south coast. Their task was to make sure that the air superiority Hitler needed would never be achieved. Throughout the summer, from the first mass attacks in July to the final postponement of Operation Sealion, Hurricanes and Spitfires were in action day in, day out. The pilots, many of them flying their first sorties, engaged the fighters of the Luftwaffe and the bombers they escorted, in dogfights over the south of England. The pilots and ground crews, exhausted, depleted and stretched to the limits of their endurance, knew the desperate importance of their continuing battle. Only in late September, when raids were diverted away from airfields to targets in London, was it certain that the tide had been turned and that the invasion would not take place.

Frederick Winterbotham
Secret Intelligence Service
I think the most important signal we had decrypted through ULTRA right at the beginning of the Battle of Britain, was Goering establishing his strategy with his commanders. He told them that they were to fly over Britain and bring the whole of the Royal Air Force up to battle, because only in that way could it be destroyed in the time they had.

That was the key for Dowding – to fight the battle with very small units every time they came over – gradually wearing them down and always having aeroplanes to send up. It became evident that Hitler and his generals wouldn't contemplate invasion unless they had absolute control of the air over the Channel.

Myrtle Solomon
Civilian, south of England
At the time of the fall of France there was a good deal of British joking going on – if they come here we'll do this and that – and people were making the

most comic preparations. My mother reckoned that she'd be able to keep them off with a huge log fork – a fork for sort of stirring logs, that we had at the open fire. It was a most vicious-looking instrument, it's perfectly true. There was a very patriotic woman in the village who never went about in her car without a row of pepper pots on the front. She thought she could blind the Germans when they arrived. We were told that the Germans might arrive dressed up as nuns, so every poor nun in the country went about being observed, and being looked at in a suspicious way. I remember, myself, I went on a walking holiday for a while, in Cornwall. I had a haversack on. I thought everybody was looking at me and thinking I had parachuted in. So you were a bit twitchy.

The preparations that were made by the nation – you really didn't think would keep anybody away. I mean, a bit of barbed wire on a beach – or the erection of what appeared to be sort of small concrete pyramids each side of a line – you just couldn't see how they could stop anything.

Sergeant Frederick Gash
264 Squadron, RAF

We felt we had to stop the Germans if they tried to invade. I did talk to several of my 264 friends and comrades and colleagues about that. 'What're we going to do if the Germans do get here?' And most of them said, 'We've got to stop them from getting here – so why talk about what are we going to do if they get here? We've just got to stop them.' And that was the mood of most people, and I think that was the mood of the civilian people. We would stop them.

Flying Officer Geoffrey Page
56 Squadron, RAF

I give the example of the bulldog and the greyhound – the Hurricane being the bulldog, and the greyhound being the Spitfire, one being a tough working animal, the other a sleek, fast dog. I think their characteristics were comparable to the dog world. If anything, the Hurricane was slightly easier, but wasn't as fast and didn't have the rate of climb – but during the Battle of Britain, what really evolved was that the Hurricanes would attack the German bomber formations, and the Spitfire, because of their extra climbing capability, would go up and fight the German fighter escort.

Sergeant James A. Goodson
American pilot, 43 Squadron, RAF
Once you got used to the Spitfire, you loved it. It became part of you. It was like pulling on a tight pair of jeans, and it was a delight to fly. I used to smoke a cigar sometimes – against all rules and regulations – and if I dropped my cigar lighter, instead of groping around on the floor, I would move the stick a fraction of an inch, and the Spitfire would roll over, and I would catch the lighter as it came down from the floor. That was the kind of plane it was. Everyone had a love affair with the Spitfire.

Even the Germans got to respect it. I remember Peter Townsend went to see one of the German pilots which he had shot down, close to the base. The German pilot said to him, 'I'm very glad to meet the Spitfire pilot who shot me down.' And Peter said, 'No, no – I was flying a Hurricane. I'm a Hurricane pilot.' The German kept arguing with him, and Peter kept saying, 'No – you were shot down by a Hurricane.' The German pilot said, 'Would you do me a favour? If you ever talk to any other Luftwaffe pilots, please tell them I was shot down by a Spitfire?'

Raymond Cooper
Boy, south of England, aged 14
I was excited we were going to fight the Germans. We were near two squadrons – we used to count them out and count them back in, so we used to know how many were missing. I used to do that every day during the Battle of Britain. I saw so many dogfights during that time – some planes would come quite low and be forced down, and I saw some crash into the hills near my village and saw some fall into the sea.

Once I saw some Germans get out of a plane that had crashed into the sea – they had their dinghy out and they thought they were on their way, but they were caught, and that was that.

Flying Officer Alec Ingle
605 Squadron, RAF
The first flight you made in the morning, you would get a sinking feeling in the pit of your stomach, until you saw the enemy and the minute you'd made your first interception, for the rest of that day it didn't matter what happened. The adrenalin was flowing and certainly, as far as I remembered, it flowed in reasonable quantity. Once you pressed your gun button, then for the rest of the day, you could take on the complete Luftwaffe. That's the reaction I had to it.

Pilot Officer Tony Bartley
92 *Squadron, RAF*

We did five sorties a day. We never stopped – we just went. You went to your dispersal hut half an hour before dawn, but when the tannoy said scramble, you scrambled. You went up and you fought all day long until the sun went down. Whether it be three, four, five missions a day – you just fought and fought and fought. At the end of the day we got off the airfield, because they used to bomb us at night, so we would go down to the White Hart at Brasted and drink beer.

Pilot Officer Douglas Grice
32 *Squadron, RAF*

On 4 July I was shot down for the second time. We were in the air, somewhere near Ashford in Kent, I think it was. We were told over the RT that there were Me 109s beating up Manston Aerodrome, so our leader turned and made towards Manston – and I realised that this wasn't probably a good idea.

There must have been a delay between the shooting happening on the ground, and our hearing about it in the air – and therefore the enemy would be on their way home. So, I took my section off towards Deal. It was a very cloudy day – there we were, flying along about 7,000 feet, I suppose, looking mostly downwards through the gaps in the clouds. I took one glance behind, and there were three 109s – I suppose about 400 yards away, diving on to us. For the very first time in my operational life, I froze. Most extraordinary feeling. I couldn't move, except that my hand was shaking on the stick. Of course, the inevitable happened. There was one very large bang, my engine stopped, I suddenly realised that I had no rudder control and also that I had no left-hand aileron control. So my first thought was 'I must bail out.' But by this time, I was over the sea – and the idea of bailing out over the sea didn't appeal to me.

Meanwhile, I was looking around madly – once again, there wasn't an aircraft to be seen. So I managed to get the aircraft pointing towards the land, and I was losing height. I did my second belly landing in a field not very far from Sandwich golf course. I started to get out of my aircraft, when the hedgerows erupted with brown jobs – the army, headed by an officer, who came running. Stopped two paces away – looked at me (I had taken my helmet off by then) and said, 'Hello Douglas – how are you?' And I looked at him and said, 'Hello Bill! How nice to see you.' We'd known each other as territorial soldiers three years beforehand, in the Artists Rifles – and here he was, guarding Britain with a few soldiers and a few rifles. And there was I, a

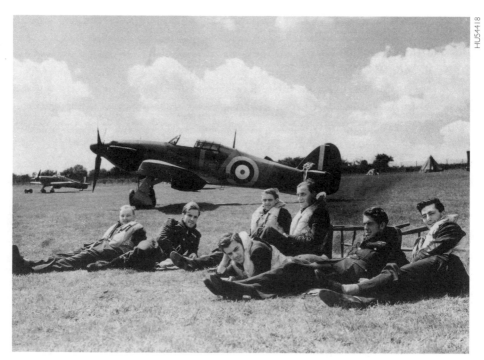

Pilots of 32 Squadron relax between combat 'scrambles' at the forward airfield at Hawkinge in Kent, summer 1940. From left to right, Plt Off Rupert Smythe, Plt Off Keith Gillman, Plt Off John Proctor, Flt Lt Peter Brothers, Plt Off Douglas Grice, with back against chair, Plt Off Melvyn Gardner and Plt Off Alan Eckford.
All survived the battle except Gillman, who was reported missing in action on 25 August 1940. Grice was shot down and suffered serious burns, but was rescued after bailing out over the Channel.

stricken fighter pilot. I was quite unhurt. His troops were very impressed to find that their officer knew the pilot.

Flight Lieutenant Al Deere
54 Squadron, RAF

We were frightened. On the way out there was an awful gut fear. When you sighted them it really was – it was quite a frightening sight. But once you got into combat there wasn't time to be frightened. But we were frightened – of course we were – the whole bloody time. But if you're in combat, you're so keen to get the other guy and, if you like, save your own skin, that your adrenalin's pumping and there's no room for fright.

I've often wondered why there weren't more collisions. There were probably more than we knew about, because if somebody collided, you didn't know about it. There was, in the initial engagement, a danger of collision. I collided with a 109 because we were both trying to come at each other head on. The closing speed was such that neither of us could get out of the way and we collided. I crashed in Kent on fire – he went into the sea.

Sergeant Rosemary Horstmann
WAAF, based at Hawkinge

It was very dramatic, because several of the girls who were working with us had boyfriends who were pilots, so they would find themselves monitoring a battle in which their brothers and fiancés were fighting, and we were writing down what the German pilots were saying – things like, 'I've got him,' or 'He's down!' and sometimes you would hear the pilots screaming.

Gunther Rall
Luftwaffe fighter pilot

I had never met the RAF before. We were not very successful – we were not very experienced at all. I had only had one experience of a dogfight with a French plane on the 12th May. We had to escort the Dornier 287, which was an obsolete aircraft, against the British Spitfires and Hurricanes. We got the order for flying direct escort – in most cases we met over Boulogne at 4,000 or 5,000 metres, and then we escorted this heavily loaded 287 across the Channel to Margate or Ramsgate – about three times a day. It was very difficult to stay with them at speed, so we had heavy losses. Right after the first missions, we lost our group commander and then my squadron commander – he was shot down. The weather was not very good, and the Spitfires just waited for us upstairs, and came out of the clouds at high speeds and dashed on us – and pulled up again. So we lost a lot of aeroplanes.

Flying Officer Roland Beamont
87 Squadron, RAF

On the 24th July, we were in the area of Purbeck, near Wombwell Airfield, and I rolled over to see this 109 going towards the sea. He was trying to get the hell out of it, but as he came out of his roll, I was back on his tail, ready for another burst. It was then that I could see that he had his undercarriage coming down, and that he was streaming coolant. He started to sideslip fairly violently, and he did another roll – this time with his wheels down, and then a diving turn towards the ground. I thought either he was going to go in, or he was aiming for a forced landing. Obviously he was a very capable pilot.

Eventually he went in rather hard, to land in a field, buckling his undercarriage. He slid on his belly across the field and ended up at the far end, near a hedge. I dived around after him and saw him lift his canopy sideways, opening the cockpit. He jumped out, off the wing and lay flat on the ground. I wondered if he thought his aeroplane was going to blow up – and then I realised he might think I was going to strafe him on the ground. Of course the thought hadn't occurred to me.

Pilot Officer George Bennions
41 Squadron, RAF

On the 29th July, the first aircraft that shot at me, I ducked out of the way, but unfortunately it had hit my port wing and damaged the flaps and the undercarriage and all the guns. Then I broke away and attempted to attack another 109. I managed to get back to Manston, but as I was coming in to land, the aircraft seemed perfectly alright as far as I was concerned. When I got near the ground, I put my flaps down, but only one flap went down, which was rather disastrous, because the aircraft slewed all over the place. Fortunately I'd left it until I was almost on the ground anyway. I'd pumped my undercarriage down, but what I didn't know was that one tyre had been blown off, and one leg damaged, and the flaps damaged – so when I hit the ground, the aircraft just spun like a top across the aerodrome, like a Catherine wheel. I came to rest completely bewildered, not having the faintest idea what had happened – but very relieved to find I was still in one piece.

Flying Officer Geoffrey Page
52 Squadron, RAF

We were all sitting around, having tea on the grass alongside a tent, which had a field telephone connected to Sector Operations. At about five o'clock, they phoned through and said there were 90 bandits approaching from the South at about 15,000 feet. There were only ten of us, but we took off. We could see the usual swarm of what looked like little insects taking shape – it was a large formation of Dornier 217s, escorted by 109 fighters. I was in the leading group of three, then I could see the tracer coming towards me from the whole formation – they had obviously singled me out as a target.

All these things which looked like lethal electric light bulbs kept flashing by, then finally there was a big bang and the aircraft exploded. The scientists reckon the temperature goes up from a cool room temperature at 15,000 feet to 3,000 degrees Centigrade in ten seconds. So, when you consider water boils at 100 degrees, that's quite a temperature change. If you don't get out immediately, you're never going to get out. The beauty of the Royal Air Force training came to my rescue and I instinctively reached for the harness and slid the hood back. I rolled the aircraft on to its back, kicked back the control column so the aircraft pointed its nose upwards, but as I was upside down, I popped out like a cork out of a toy gun.

I stupidly wasn't wearing any gloves, so my hands got a terrible burning, and face as well. My mouth and nose were saved by my gas mask. I found myself tumbling head over heels through space. I remember seeing my right arm and extending it, making myself pull the metal ring of the ripcord on my parachute – and that was agony. It was like an electric shock through my burnt hand. Again, you don't have a choice, because, if you don't, the parachute won't open.

Fortunately, my parachute wasn't on fire. One then took stock of the situation, and I noticed a funny thing had happened. My left shoe and my trousers had been blown off completely by the explosion. I was almost naked from the waist downwards – my legs were slightly burnt. Then I could hear the fight all around me, and it took me about ten minutes to float down into the water.

I had various problems to deal with. First of all, I had to get rid of my parachute, but you had to turn this metal disk on your stomach. You turn it through ninety degrees and then give it a hard thump – but it was difficult because I was badly burnt. Then the parachute was on top of me, so I was really inside a tent with the cords trapping me like an octopus's tentacles. I knew I had to get it away quickly, otherwise I would sink. Again, desperation comes into the issue, so you do turn it, and you do thump it.

The next thing was to blow up my life jacket. I got hold of the rubber tube over my left shoulder, but when I blew into it, all I got was a lot of bubbles. It had been burnt right through. My face was swelling up at this point, and my eyesight was bad because my swollen eyelids were closing up. The distant view of England, which I could see a few miles away was a bit blurred, but I started vaguely in the right direction.

Then a happy thought came to my mind, and I remembered that in my jacket pocket I had a brandy flask that my dear mother had given me – which I had filled with brandy just as an emergency measure. I thought that this probably qualified as an emergency, so I rolled on my back. This was a painful process, but I got it out and held it between my wrists and undid the screw cap with my teeth. I thought, 'Well, life is going to feel a bit better.' But as I lifted it up to take a swig, a dirty big wave came along and the whole lot went to the bottom of the Channel. I was a bit annoyed about that, but there was nothing else for it, so I continued swimming.

I heard, rather than saw the boat. There were two men in it, and they kept asking me questions. By this time I had been swimming for half an hour, and I was fed up with the whole affair, so when they asked me if I was a Jerry, I'm afraid I let loose with every rude four-letter word that I could think of, and that immediately assured them that I was an RAF officer. They picked me out of the water, and took me to the big ship, where the captain dressed my burns and gave me a cup of tea. Then the Margate lifeboat came out and took me in to transfer me to Margate hospital.

For the first time for an hour or more, I was able to laugh, because waiting on the quayside was the Mayor, dressed in his top hat and tails, saying, 'Welcome to Margate'. When you'd been in an air fight an hour before, and then there's a chap in top and tails, it is two different worlds. As it happened, it was the beginning of grouse shooting that day, August 12th. There was a certain irony in that.

Flight Lieutenant Peter Brothers
32 Squadron, RAF
Before the battle I realised that if the Luftwaffe gained air superiority then, of course, the whole country was open to them. However, one didn't have time to consider the background; you were worrying about your own chaps, your own aircraft, and your own ground crew. It was day to day, minute to minute. I realised that they were going to come in greater masses. The going then got heavier, as I think everybody realised – and one was tired, inevitably. I am a fairly equable person but occasionally used to lose my temper. Having got engaged one day I pressed the gun button and nothing happened at all, because the guns hadn't been reloaded. On landing back, I had the armourer in the office, drew my pistol, and said, 'I'll shoot you if you ever do that again.' But I was tired.

Pilot Officer Geoffrey Page
56 Squadron, RAF

I don't think at any point morale was low, because the facts of life were, we would be flying many times during the day, having taken off in the darkness, and then, as the dawn came up, we'd fly to a forward base such as Manston or Hawkinge or Rochford – and then we'd be at readiness all through the day. Then in the evening, just as the light was beginning to fail, we'd fly back to our base at North Weald. Then there 'd be a mad rush to get down to the local tavern before the pubs closed. Don't forget, we were all 19, 20, 21 years of age. We were just overgrown schoolboys.

In all squadrons, fighter or bomber, during the war, there were commissioned officers and there were non-commissioned officers of sergeant rank. But while we were lying around our aircraft or in the air, there was no differentiation between ranks at all. I always felt it was a little unfair that after a hard day's fighting and you landed, one lot of us – the commissioned officers, we would go off to the officers' mess, and the sergeants would go off to the sergeants' mess. I think men who take an equal risk, you know, should live the same way.

Flying Officer Roland Beamont
87 Squadron, RAF

On a scramble on the 15th August, the controller said, 'Bandits now twenty miles ahead of you. You should see them directly ahead.' Almost immediately the clear sky ahead started to turn into a mass of little black dots. It could only really be described as a beehive. This mass of black dots appeared, developing ahead. Our CO continued to lead us straight towards it. I just had time to think, 'I wonder what sort of tactic he's going to employ. Is he going to turn up-sun and try and dive out of the sun at them, or go round to the right and come in behind. What's he going to do?' While I thought that, it was quite apparent he wasn't going to do anything. He bored straight on into the middle of this lot until we seemed to be going into the biggest formation of aeroplanes you ever saw. Then his voice came on the radio and said, 'Target ahead. Come on, chaps, let's surround them.' Just nine of us!

I fired at a Ju 87 at point-blank range, and I hit it. I don't know what happened to it. But I could see my tracers going into it. Then I came under attack from directly ahead and below. It turned out to be a Me 110, doing a zoom climb straight up at me, firing as he came. He missed me. I rolled away from him straight behind another of his mates, a 110. I fired a long burst at him and his port engine stopped and started to stream smoke and fire, and pulled away from that.

Pilot Officer Bob Doe
234 Squadron, RAF

On the 15th August we were ordered up to Middle Wallop. We flew up there, but I was feeling very strange, in the sense that everything was distant – we hadn't been involved – it wasn't real. We landed on the grass airfield, we were put into a lorry, and halfway up to the mess, they bombed the airfield. One of the hangars was hit and a WAAF was killed in a trench. Up to that moment, we had been seeing the war from a spectator's point of view.

A bit later that day, we were scrambled over Swanage. I really had the worst inferiority complex at that time. I felt I was the worst pilot in the squadron, and I was convinced I would not survive that trip.

We took off and formed up into four 'Vics' of three in sections astern – which is the stupidest formation you could possibly fly in. There's only one person looking round, everyone else is formating. We patrolled up and down the sun, which again, is a stupid way of flying. At one point, we turned back down-sun to find we were only nine strong. We had lost three – our rear section had disappeared, one killed and the other two shot down. Then, all of a sudden, we found ourselves in the middle of a gaggle of Messerschmitt 110s and 109s. God knows how we got there – we just landed in the middle of them. I was flying number two to Pat Hughes, who turned off after a 110, gave him a quick squirt, then turned on his side and pulled away. But it didn't look quite right to me, so I formed on the 110, got quite close to it, and kept on firing until he went down into the sea. This was the second time I'd used my guns. The first was into the sea to try them out. I thought, this is something! I'm not dead, and I've done something! That feeling was really fantastic. I followed him down, pulled up from the sea, and another 110 overshot me from behind. I just closed on him and shot him down.

I shot two down without really knowing anything. I realised on the way home that I'd been so lucky, it was ridiculous. So I started to do some thinking. In fact, I went to bed early that night, and I stayed in bed just thinking. I realised that you're usually shot down from behind – so what do you do if you see bullets coming past you from behind? I worked out that, whatever I did, I must go down – straight down – because if you tried to roll or anything, you stayed in the bullet path for longer, and if you pulled up you were a sitting target. So I drilled it into my head that if I saw anything coming past me from behind, I would just hit the stick. I wouldn't think – just hit it.

The following day we met a load of 109s high up over the Isle of Wight, and I found one on his own. I settled down on him. Now, although I'd shot two down the day before, I was not certain about shooting. I couldn't trust my judgement and distance, and I couldn't trust my shooting. So I aimed above him at first, then below, and eventually I shot him down. But I had been so involved, that I hadn't seen another 109 behind me. Fortunately Pat Hughes had spotted it and shot it off my tail. I was dead lucky.

Pilot Officer Douglas Grice
32 Squadron, RAF

August 15th was my last operational flight, and we'd taken off from Biggin Hill to patrol somewhere over East Kent. I was flying what the air force called 'arse-end Charlie' – in other words, by myself, a thousand or a couple of thousand feet higher than the rest of the squadron and slightly behind. Weaving like mad, looking right, left, centre, up down – and mostly back – when suddenly, out of the corner of my eye, I saw a flash over my left wrist. The next moment, the cockpit was full of flames. The heat was enormous, and I'd done two things absolutely instinctively. My left hand had gone to the handle of the hood, my right hand had gone to the pin of my harness, and I was pulling with both hands. The next moment I was out in the open air. I'd made no attempt to jump out of that aircraft – well, I was straining back from the flames and the heat. What I think had happened was, I was doing a left-hand turn, and my aircraft had gone on turning over on its back, and I had just fallen out – unless I'd kicked the stick – which would have jerked me upwards and out.

Anyway, there I was, falling away – and I did actually remember my parachute drill, which was to wait before pulling the rip-cord for two or three seconds. I pulled it, and there was a jerk – and there I was, floating down under a marvellous canopy, about a couple of miles inland. I could look down and see the land, and I thought, 'Well, at least I won't be going into the sea.' Well, very shortly after that, I was over the coast – and a few minutes later, I was a mile out to sea – and a few minutes after that, I was two miles out to sea. Well, before that, I'd taken my helmet off and dropped it, and that gave rise to a moment of immense panic. I actually watched my helmet drop from, I suppose, twelve or thirteen thousand feet, until it disappeared from view. I suddenly realised how high I was, and how much space there was between my toes and the ground. So I hung on to my straps like mad.

Aircraftwoman Jean Mills
WAAF, plotter and tracer at Duxford

We were all pretty young – girls of only 19 or 20 – when we got assigned to Duxford, and for a lot of us it was the first time we'd been away from home, so

Summer 1940. The Battle of Britain rages in the skies of southern England – and in the Operations Room at RAF Fighter Command HQ, WAAF plotters move squadron markers on the table map.

we were laughing and joking, because it seemed like an adventure. Suddenly we reached the brow of a hill and we could see Duxford, stretching out in front of us. It was a beautiful sunny day. As we looked, we could see that something had happened. There were lots of planes – one plane seemed to hover and was nose-diving to the ground with smoke trails rising. The noise of our chatter stopped instantaneously and the mood changed. We realised it wasn't a great lark and that we were in for serious business. We were reminded of this because the pilot who was killed had an Alsatian, which kept roaming the camp looking for him. It was very sad.

Aircraftwoman Anne Duncan
WAAF *plotter*
There was a table with a map of England on it, and the whole of the map was marked out in a grid. The man on the other end of the telephone, when he was reporting things coming in, he'd give you two letters and four numbers, and from that you put down a little round disc like a tiddlywink. Then a few minutes later there would be another one – that would be a bit further on, and you could see the course gradually building of something coming in. You plotted everything. Everything came in over the radar tubes and the problem was to decide which was friendly and which was not. It was quite easy in the beginning, because anything that was friendly went from England outwards, and anything that was not, came from France or Holland and Belgium.

Pilot Officer Harold Bird-Wilson
17 *Squadron, RAF*
I was both worried and frightened at times. We were praying for bad weather – probably the only time anybody in England prayed for that! Somehow during the battle we had beautiful weather – sunshine and blue skies most of the time – and we did pray very hard. Fatigue broke into a chap's mentality in most peculiar ways. My chaps had the jitters and facial twitches. I had nightmares and used to wake up in the dispersal hut about twenty-five yards from my aircraft. I was night-flying my Hurricane.

Flight Lieutenant Frank Carey
43 *Squadron, RAF*
Altogether I did about a hundred sorties in the Battle of Britain – from early July until 18 August. The most I did was six sorties in a day – roughly about an hour to an hour and a half each one. On 18 August I was shot down. On my next sortie I nursed another plane back from out in the Channel one day. The

pilot got a glycol leak – it comes out in little white puffs that get more and more frequent. I flew alongside and said, 'You stay there as long as that thing will take you back to land. Don't worry, it's all right.' I don't know what he was suffering in the cockpit, mind you. His cockpit was open and it must have been pretty hot. When it was no longer a puff but a regular little stream, he couldn't stand it any longer and got out. I followed him down and spotted him in the sea. I circled and radioed for help until I ran out of fuel. He was never picked up. I can only suppose he got tangled up and pulled down by the parachute. When he went into the sea he was only about a mile-and-a-half off Selsey Bill. We didn't have any air sea rescue then. The Germans did. They used to fly rescue seaplanes even right along the English coast.

Air fighting is a very detached sort of warfare being fought, as it were, between machines with the human factor very much submerged in a 'tin box'. Once in a while, for a few fleeting seconds when someone bales out, one can suddenly be aware that humans are actually involved but, as the parachute descends, machines quickly regain the centre of the stage once more.

On one particular sortie from Wick, however, the human angle predominated for quite a while. The formation in which I was flying came upon a rather lonely Heinkel 111 way out in the North Sea which we naturally proceeded to deal with. After a few shots, a fire was seen to start in the fuselage and the flight commander immediately ordered us to stop attacking it. The enemy aircraft turned back towards Wick and we escorted it on its way with me in close formation on its port side where the fire was. Being only a few feet away from the Heinkel it was all too easy to become sympathetically associated with the crew's frantic efforts to control the fire and I even began to wish that I could jump across and help them. I suddenly converted from an anxious desire to destroy them to an even greater anxiety that they survive. We had got within a few miles of the coast and had really begun to hope that they would make it, when we were all outraged to see a Hurricane from another squadron sweep in from behind and without a single thought about us all around, poured a long burst of fire into the Heinkel which more or less blew up in our faces and crashed into the sea without any survivors.

It was all I could do to prevent myself from spinning round and having a crack at the Hurricane in response to the intrusion. I felt a sense of personal loss as I stared at the wreckage on the water.

Pilot Officer Bob Doe
234 Squadron, RAF

On the 18th August they sent a very formidable force over the Southampton area. We had three sorties that day. I got one on the first, one on the second, and damaged one on the third.

We were so confident at that time. There was no doubt in our minds. We knew we weren't going to lose. I suppose, in retrospect, we were bloody stupid, but it never entered our minds that we could possibly lose this war.

Then we had a new CO posted in, and he decided to come as my number two on a scramble. We found a lone Ju 88 over Winchester. Well, I had a go at it, he had a go at it – no effect. So I got behind it, got as close as I could, and filled it with bullets. He hit me through the mainspar, then stopped firing and went into the ground. When we landed back at base, the new CO, very keen, wanted to go and have a look for the Ju 88. It had crashed in a field very close to Middle Wallop. I'm now very sorry I went to see it, because someone informed me that every aircrew helmet had bullet holes in it, and that brought everything home to me.

I had to fly the Spitfire down to Hamble for repair. It was a lovely warm day, with interceptions going on overhead all the time. The foreman of the place invited me home to lunch, and his wife started talking to me. Suddenly, for the first time, I realised that ordinary people in the street knew what we were doing, and that they admired us. She was saying things that made me blush. It really was quite something. I hadn't been aware it – it hadn't entered my mind. People could see what was happening.

Aircraftwoman Jean Mills
WAAF, plotter and tracer at Duxford

From the little rooms, the little wireless and radar rooms behind the controller, we could hear the crackling voices of the pilots come back, and although we had headsets on and the work was quite intensive and required a lot of concentration, we used to manage to ease one earphone off so we could hear what was going on, and then we could listen out for 'Tally ho', which meant they'd sighted the enemy, and then you could hear them talking to each other, like, 'Look out, Blue Two, bandits to your right.' And things like that, which seemed to bring it right into the room. There was an indescribable tension about the whole thing. When there was something going on, the atmosphere was electric. We were all rooting for our boys to come back. They were very much our pigeon.

Flight Lieutenant Al Deere
54 Squadron, RAF

We were desperately short of pilots. At that stage in the Battle of Britain, August into September, the aircraft had started coming in again because Beaverbrook, the Minister of Aircraft Production, had got cracking. We were having them flown in, but we were desperately short of pilots. We were getting pilots who had not been on Spitfires because there were no conversion units at that time. They came straight to a squadron from their training establishments. Some of them did have a few hours on the Hurricanes, a monoplane experience, but not on the Spitfire.

I used to say to them, 'Look, don't do anything by yourself. Stick with your leader and just watch, and don't try and – unless you're attacked yourself, just stay out of trouble a bit until you get the feel of things.' It's pretty hard for a young chap to follow that dictum. In fact, generally what happened was they'd follow their leader and the next thing they knew they were in the parachute because a 109 got up behind them or something.

Flight Lieutenant Brian Kingcome
92 Squadron, RAF

One had to realise that there was an invasion pending – but equally, one knew there wouldn't be one. But I was quite convinced, and I think most fighter pilots were, that there was no way they could go through us. So there was no sort of nervousness in case the Germans invaded. If they did invade, we would have thought, 'What a marvellous opportunity to slaughter all these barges coming in.'

Flight Lieutenant Peter Brothers
32 Squadron, RAF

It was all fairly intense, but the waiting around at base was the hardest part. We'd either sleep, play mahjong or read. When we were 'scrambled', one of our chaps would run to his aircraft, be violently sick, and then jump into his aircraft and be off. Your adrenalin really got going once that bell went. We all swore we'd never have a telephone at home after the war – because as soon as the telephone rang you'd all automatically be at the ready. Then you'd hear, 'No, corporal so and so has just gone to get his lunch,' and you'd all relax again. It would either be that or, '32 Squadron scramble 18,000 feet over Ashford,' and off you'd go.

After we returned from an operation, the Intelligence Officer would want all the details. We weren't all that interested, it was over, finished. But he

A Flying Officer during the Battle of Britain, Brian Kingcome (in cockpit), was promoted to Wing Commander when he returned to duty after being injured in October 1940. Pictured at Manston in February 1941 his squadron's tally of kills continued to rise as the Blitz continued on British cities.

needed the information. We'd give him the information and then perhaps we'd be off again. We could be scrambled in the middle of telling him something. During one of the raids on Dover, I'd shot down a Stuka and then gone into Hawkinge to refuel and rearm. I didn't even get out of the aircraft. They were rearming the aircraft and there was a chap standing on the wing in front of me, pumping fuel into the tank. The battle was still going on up above and, as we watched, a Spitfire shot down a 109, and the pilot baled out. The airman who was refuelling me said, 'Got him!' And then, when the pilot's parachute opened, he turned to me with a look of utter disgust on his face and said, 'Oh, the jammy bastard!' As soon as they'd finished I was off again, back into the battle. But it was rather amusing. I got a 109 later on that day.

Heinz Lange
Luftwaffe fighter pilot
I flew as an escort to the bombers. I had some opportunities to shoot the opposition down – but not the luck. For us, it was more important to stop the British planes from shooting at our bombers than to have a dogfight. I came through without being hit. We mostly attacked the River Thames as far as London – targets further away were out of our range. The British flak was very good – they almost didn't have to aim, because our route was so consistent as we were always so worried about running out of fuel. But this changed later on when we could attach extra fuel.

Sergeant Ray Holmes
504 Squadron, RAF
We built up a sort of synthetic hate against them, which was a bit artificial. I wanted to shoot an aeroplane down, but I didn't want to shoot a German down. I really did not. We did hear stories of Germans shooting our fellows in parachutes, and we used to think that was pretty horrible – but we weren't sure whether it was true or not. I know I had an experience of a German aircrew getting draped over my own wing – he bailed out of a bomber and got caught on my wing with his parachute, and I was jolly careful to get him off as easily and as quickly as I could, manoeuvring the aeroplane and shaking him off. And I was very glad when I heard he'd dropped down in Kennington Oval safely. So I had no feeling of wanting to kill that fellow personally.

Flying Officer Geoffrey Page
52 Squadron, RAF

After being shot down on the 12th August, I spent a few days in Margate hospital and then I was taken up to the Royal Masonic Hospital in London, and then later on I found myself in Sir Archibald MacIndoe, the plastic surgeon's hospital in East Grinstead, where I spent two years undergoing plastic surgery.

I was there with Richard Hillary, who wrote a book called *The Last Enemy*, and there were six RAF fighter pilots. We got together and formed a little club, which we called the Guinea Pig Club. And from the six of us who started it, there've been about seven hundred have been through that hospital. We thought, well, when we were allowed to get out of bed and walk a few yards, there was a little hut, and we said, 'Why don't we form a little sort of club in there, where we can have a glass of beer and get away from the ward for half an hour or so?'

Pilot Officer George Bennions
41 Squadron, RAF

I was very concerned and very upset. I was annoyed at myself for having been shot down so decisively, and I felt terribly isolated. I couldn't see or hear very well, and so I couldn't recognise people. I felt so very sorry for myself, which is not a good situation for anybody. I felt so deflated, that half of my life had been taken, and half wasn't worth bothering with. It was, I think, the worst period of my life.

There was one person in particular who put me on a much more even footing. He had been shot down by a Hurricane. He had sent a message to go and see him. I was on crutches at the time, and I managed to get over to where he was with a hell of a lot of struggle and self-pity. As I opened the door in Ward 3, I saw what I can only describe now as the most horrifying thing I have ever seen in my life. This chap had been really badly burnt. His hair was burnt off, his eyebrows and his eyelids. You could just see his staring eyes, with only two holes in his face. His nose and lips were also badly burnt. Then I looked down, and saw that his hands and feet were burnt. I got through the door on my crutches with a struggle, and then this chap started propelling a wheelchair down the ward. Halfway down, he picked up the back of a chair with his teeth – and it was then that I noticed how badly his lips were burnt. Then he brought this chair down the ward and threw it alongside me and said, 'Have a seat, old boy.' It was then that I cried – and I thought, 'What have I got to complain about?' From then on, everything fell into place.

Flight Lieutenant Al Deere
54 Squadron, RAF

On the 31st August, I was held up taking off by a new pilot who'd got himself in the take-off lane – didn't know were to go. He delayed me. By the time I'd got him sorted out and around, I was last off, and caught the bombs – and was blown sky high – the three of us were. But I got away with it – we all got away with it. I got pretty badly concussed – my Spitfire was blown up. I finished up on the airfield in a heap. My number two finished on the airfield with his wing blown off. The number three was never seen – wasn't seen for two hours, when he reappeared at the dispersal carrying his parachute, having been blown, in his aircraft, about a mile away into what we called Shit Creek, and landed the right way out and got up and walked back to the airfield. Had to go all the way round the wire to get in.

A doctor bandaged me up and said, 'Forty-eight hours and report back.' Twenty-four hours I felt alright, so I just went back because we were under tremendous stress at the time. So I was just the night off, really. I was back the next day, all bandaged up, but I felt all right. I think I was all right.

Flight Lieutenant Brian Kingcome
92 Squadron, RAF

It was the most enjoyable part of the war. It sounds perhaps callous – I don't know – but it was enormously exciting and tremendous fun. And we had every advantage – to begin with, we were flying over our own territory, and this was a huge moral advantage. Because first of all, it gives you a reason for being there – because when you're over your own homeland, defending your own homeland, it gets the adrenalin going.

We had two extremely good controllers at Biggin Hill – Roger Franklin and Bill Igoe – and they gave you your head. Some controllers tried to tell you exactly what to do. Roger Franklin and Bill Igoe simply told you where the enemy aircraft were and left you to decide how to attack.

Flight Lieutenant Al Deere
54 Squadron, RAF

You'd go ten days, for example without actually seeing the mess in daylight. We'd go off to dispersal – if we were operating from the forward base, Manston, which we generally were, up 'til towards the end – we'd be off before first light, so we'd be landing at first light at Manston. Similarly, we'd come back in the evenings at last light. The rest of the time was spent either sitting at dispersal, which was way out the other side of the airfield with a tent or a telephone, or in the air. We used to have meals brought out to us. We never saw the public – never got off the airfield.

Flying Officer Alec Ingle
605 Squadron, RAF

We flew down to Croydon – and that was a fairly horrific sight, actually. We refuelled at Abingdon, I think it was, and then we flew right over the top of London at about, I suppose, six or seven thousand feet, just above the balloons – and the whole of the East End was ablaze. You could look right down the river, and the whole thing was sort of smoky and on fire. Your heart did go into your boots, then, when you saw that lot. It was a terrible sight.

We landed down on Croydon – 111 Squadron, I think it was, had been there. We were tucked away in the Airport Hotel in Croydon – the old airport hotel, but we only stayed there one night, because the CO decided this was not a very safe place to be – to have all his pilots concentrated in such an obvious target. So we organised and took over a complete street of houses on the opposite side – Foresters Drive. There were only about three of those houses occupied – practically everybody had gone and in some of them there were even the remains of breakfast on the table. We established ourselves there – we had a mess in number 39 Foresters Drive, and we lived in the various houses round about. One night the Germans dropped a stick of bombs right across our particular dispersal, and I slept through it, as did most people, I think. You just got accustomed to it.

Pilot Officer Anne Duncan
WAAF plotter

We didn't awfully like going into the shelters, because they were not really bomb-proof, and if a bomb landed right on one it'd leave a very nasty mess. So what we usually did was to go outside and look and see what was going on. You could see the aeroplanes overhead – you could hear them all the time. There was this special droning noise. And then one night they started dropping bombs all around us. We all lay flat. There were lots dropped on the airfield. It was very exciting. This happened night after night, so you didn't get a lot of sleep during certain periods when they were having a particular drive at London. We were right in the pathway.

Aircraftwoman Jean Mills
WAAF, plotter and tracer at Duxford

I remember coming on for a night shift and seeing a great glow in the south-east, like the biggest sunset you ever saw, and we said to the guard, 'What's that?' and he said, 'Oh, that's London burning.' That was the first time, really, that I felt it in the pit of my stomach.

Flying Officer Alec Ingle
605 Squadron, RAF

On the 8th September we met all these Heinkel 111s, and literally we took them head-on. We were spread out – we were coming straight in, with Walter Churchill leading us. Unfortunately, his eyesight wasn't very good, and he didn't see these things as soon as most people did, so he was directing us to where they were, and we all went in that direction. We met them – and it was a fairly shattering experience. You were closing very quickly, and before you knew what was happening you had a huge aircraft just in front of you, and you were coming straight at it. We advanced on those 111s and shot, and broke away underneath them. There was a fellow pilot, Jack Fleming – a New Zealander – he got a hit directly and was just a sheet of flame. I think he was hit in the header tank, and the next thing we knew of Jack, he was in a maternity hospital somewhere in Kent – he'd arrived near here, very badly burned.

It was fairly shattering to see an aircraft just go *whoof* alongside you. But it all happened so quickly, when you are closing at those speeds. You are not talking about minutes – you are talking about seconds. You are there, you fight, you break out of that particular attack and on a number of occasions, by the time you've come back again, you can't see another aircraft in the sky. The whole thing has passed you by.

This friend of mine, Passey, who was flying with me – he was rather an extrovert sort of character with a large dog called Havoc. They were a rather curious pair – but anyhow, poor old Passey – he was flying around one day, and he was shot down. He arrived on the ground in something of a hurry, and when he was found, with his aircraft, he was sitting in a seat and the aircraft – bits of the aircraft – were scattered for hundreds of yards around the place. But he was perfectly all right, sitting strapped in his seat on the ground. He had the luck of the devil, I think.

Pilot Officer George Bennions
41 Squadron, RAF

On the 11th September we were mixed up with Dornier 17s, escorted by Me 110s. I went in to attack them and splinter from an Me 110's cannon shell embedded in my left heel. It was so painful, I couldn't move my foot. I looked down and my shoe was full of blood, so I broke off the engagement and landed at Hornchurch. I went to the sick quarters, where a doctor extracted the shell splinter and put a couple of stitches in and a plaster on it. I was back in action a couple of days later, no trouble.

Pilot Officer Harold Bird-Wilson
17 Squadron, RAF

On the 24th September we were flying at about 16,000 feet and suddenly, when we were south of the Thames area, a Spitfire came down through our formations – which worried us a bit, because we hadn't realised that they were being chased by 109s. The next thing I experienced was a terrific bang in the cockpit and there were flames coming from the fuel tank. There was no Perspex left in my hood, and it was getting fairly hot, so I bailed out immediately.

One notices the quietness, having bailed out. The battle was still going on. I could hear the rat-a-tat of the guns going off in the distance, and my fellow pilots circling above me, making sure I got down safely. I was slightly wounded with shrapnel, but I was floating down peacefully. It was then that I saw a navy torpedo boat coming out to intercept me.

Forty-two years after the event, I read in a book that I was the fortieth victory for Adolph Galland – the famous German fighter ace who was made Lieutenant General of the Luftwaffe.

Flight Lieutenant Brian Kingcome
92 Squadron, RAF

It was a beautiful clear autumn day – 15 October – and I thought, now is the time to practise a forced landing – so I throttled back and glided gently down towards Biggin Hill. I was thinking about the eggs and bacon I might get for breakfast if I was lucky after landing.

Suddenly, between 15,000 and 20,000 feet, there was a rattle of bullets in the aircraft, and one went through my leg. Three Spitfires drew alongside me and took one look and rolled away. Whether they had shot me in error – which did happen – or whether they had shot something off my tail, I don't know. So I bailed out. Blood was coming out of the top of my flying boot and

I was travelling fast enough for the air to suck me out and strong enough for me to get two black eyes from the force of the slipstream. I pulled my ripcord and sailed gently down and landed on one leg in a ploughed field – which gave me a slipped disk, which I still suffer from.

A number of farmers gathered with pitchforks. I was a bit nervous, because some Polish pilots who had been shot down had been set upon because of their accents, and I was wearing a German Mae West which I had taken off some pilots who had got shot down some time earlier. As it happened they were extremely friendly, because my Spitfire had landed before me. They then asked me where would I like to go? I said, 'What hospitals do you have around here?'

Flight Lieutenant Peter Brothers
257 Squadron, RAF
The sporadic raids went on into December, then they reverted to 109s carrying bombs. Our squadron had moved from Martlesham Heath to North Weald and one day, when I'd gone over to the mess for tea, the scramble sounded. We were raided by 109s dropping bombs, and I dived under the table. They dropped a bomb right outside, where I'd parked my old open Red Label Bentley – it was filled with soil – but fortunately not damaged. The winter was coming and clearly there was not going to be an invasion. The Battle of Britain had been won.

ORAN

On 3 July, in view of the surrender by the French to the Germans on 22 June and to Italy two days later, the British government offered terms to the French naval command. They could sail to the USA, or join Britain, and when they failed to respond, Churchill and his War Cabinet saw no alternative but to destroy the French fleet at its moorings in the port of Oran. This action, to prevent the ships there from falling into German hands and augmenting their invasion fleet, was seen as a necessary evil – and was the cause of much acrimony with Britain's former French Allies.

Ordinary Seaman Vernon Coles
Stoker 1st Class, serving on HMS **Faulknor**
HMS *Faulknor* was part of 'H' Force. We met our flotilla at sea with the *Hood* and *Ark Royal*, then together sailed south. *Hood* was flying the flag of Vice

Admiral Sir James Somerville. We also had the *Valiant* in company. When we eventually arrived in Gibraltar, we thought, 'God, there's something happening here.' We were even more convinced when we saw that *Resolution* had arrived – another 15-inch battleship. There were also the cruisers *Arethusa* and *Enterprise* and ten other destroyers.

We began sailing on our own, patrolling off Mers-el-Kebir, near Oran. The French told us to shove off. Because we only had five 4.7-inch guns we withdrew and patrolled on the skyline. The following morning, 3rd July, the entire fleet arrived. Captain Holland, who spoke French, went to present terms to the French commander, Admiral Gensoul. The terms were given roughly as follows: put to sea and join forces with the British; or sail to the French West Indies and there de-militarise his ships, or sail with reduced crews to any British port; or scuttle all his ships within six hours of the offer of the British ultimatum. If there was no answer to this signal, we would open fire at 11 o'clock.

We reckoned that Somerville found this pretty distasteful. However, eleven o'clock came, and we did not hear anything from Admiral Gensoul – but we didn't fire. So the boat went in again with more terms. Admiral Gensoul refused to see the captain. He was told that we would open fire at two o'clock. It didn't happen. Then the terms went in the third time but again they were rejected. Apparently, Churchill was getting a bit hot under the collar about this. So, as there was no reply, five o'clock was given as the deadline and the battle ensigns went up. I was on number 5 gun, so I had a front-line view of the quarterdeck.

At 17.55 we opened fire. It was a sad irony – we were not attacking the Germans or Italians, but the Royal Navy's oldest enemy and our twentieth-century ally. The whole fleet was going across and ranging. What a bombardment! I had never seen anything like it. One of our destroyers out on the starboard wing had got so close inshore that she was coming under the range of their 9-inch gun, so the *Hood* just trained her guns to fire at the hill, just below a big fort which was where the firing was coming from. The fort came tumbling down because the blast had undermined its foundations. The French battleship *Dunkerque* was right under a dockyard crane and the *Hood* had to destroy it before she could get at the *Dunkerque*. Her first broadside hit the crane, it was just like a matelot dropping. The second salvo hit the *Dunkerque*. We were firing from a distance of seven or eight miles, which for a 15-inch gun is point-blank range. Our ships sank the *Bretagne*, knocked the stern off *Mogador* and badly damaged *Provence*. Admiral Gensoul then said, 'For God's sake stop firing. You're murdering us.' Over 1,100 French sailors had been killed.

The *Strasbourg* got away, along with five large destroyers. We went after her with *Hood*, *Ark Royal* and three F-class destroyers. She had a good start and we missed her. We turned back and joined our fleet. We didn't like firing on the French, but if we hadn't, they might have joined the Germans. Before we got back to Gibraltar the French Air Force came over and dive-bombed us with twin dive-bombers.

THE BLITZ

On 7 September, the Luftwaffe's attention was switched from the airfields and radar stations of the south of England to London. In a massive raid, 337 tons of bombs set much of the East End on fire, and the long-expected assault on cities and the British people had begun. Many parents in London and other cities had packed off their children to the safety of the countryside in an extensive evacuation programme during the Phoney War. Some returned quite soon, only to be sent away again. The remaining population took to their air-raid shelters or spent nights in underground stations in the capital. Others, however, braved the Blitz to serve as firemen, volunteer workers, air-raid wardens, observers and ambulance drivers. By the end of the year, nearly 14,000 civilians had been killed in bombing raids and city-dwellers lived in a strange new landscape of ruined streets, burned-out buildings and houses with their wrecked interiors open to the sky. The bombing spread from London, and on the night of 14 November a devastating raid was made on Coventry. The city centre was destroyed, along with its ancient and beautiful cathedral – but despite the relentless attacks, terrible casualties and sleepless nights, the resolve of the British people was unshaken. The army had taken a battering in France, the air force had forestalled invasion – now it was the turn of the people to prove their spirit in the face of the enemy.

Elizabeth Quayle
London ARP Unit
When you came back at night on the underground, of the entire platform, only the bit – the eighteen inches or maybe two foot – near the edge was left, and all the rest were rows of people with their belongings, cats and dogs and children. They were as good-tempered as it was possible to be. Looking back on it, everyone was much more friendly. You would have thought nothing of leaving your bags or your suitcase there – nobody would have taken anything.

For those with no gardens in which to embed their Anderson shelters, London's underground stations offered a safe, if crowded, alternative to the vulnerability of their own homes.

Frederick Delve
London-based fireman

The first daylight raid occurred on Croydon Airport. Before the war, Croydon Airport was known throughout the world. They used to run these huge Hannibal aircraft to and from Paris. The German raiders came over in the middle of the day – no sirens had been sounded at all, and they literally destroyed the whole of Croydon Airport. I was on the scene at the time and people at the airport were able to identify the pilots, because apparently these were former Lufthansa pilots who had used the airport almost daily. 'One man – we could tell him like our fingerprint – the way he always came into the airport – and he picked out every building that there was to be damaged.' Near Croydon Airport was this very large building where they were manufacturing textiles – that had a direct hit and a very large number of women were killed. The senior police officer was with me when we passed by this building, you could see arms and limbs among the debris.

When they came at dusk it was blackout conditions, and fortunately for us, the total area of the London region is 700 square miles, so it wasn't in the same streets every night that the bombs fell. They were obviously picking out area by area, which was most helpful to the fire service because we were able, generally, to extinguish most fires before the following night – otherwise they would have formed a beacon for the raiders that were coming later.

I learned after the war that the Germans chose their raid time when the water in the Thames was at its lowest. It was only possible for fire boats to be right in the centre of the river, and for firemen to take hoses ashore it would mean them standing up to their shoulders in mud to struggle ashore with lines of hose. The volume of water that could be delivered in that way was quite infinitesimal compared to what was required to deal with the fire situation that had followed, because there were more than 2,500 fires burning surrounding St Paul's. Our problem was that if you have one jet of water with just a three-quarter-inch diameter nozzle, you require 70 gallons per minute to make that jet effective.

Colin Ryder-Richardson
Welsh boy, evacuated aboard City of Benares, September 1940

I think my father could see, with a huge German army standing off the French coast, there was what you called a sense of urgency about us leaving. So it was arranged for me to go to New York. We had left Liverpool on *City of Benares* four days earlier – then we were hit by torpedoes.

There was a loud bang, a very loud bang, and almost immediately a smell of, presumably cordite – it was an unmistakable smell. There were a lot of shouts so I immediately knew what was happening and I had a slight problem because I was in my pyjamas – and I hadn't got my lifejacket, but I immediately put it on as I got out of bed. I put on my slippers – and then I had a dressing gown and now I had a problem. Did I put the dressing gown under the lifejacket or on top of the lifejacket? It wouldn't go over the top of the lifejacket and things were beginning to happen rather fast. I thought I mustn't panic, on the other hand I must think these things through rationally.

To make things worse, there was a Force 10 gale. The ship's nurse held my hand and got me on to a lifeboat. It was freezing cold and the boat was waterlogged. I clung on to the nurse, then as the night went on, lots of people were dying. This man on the boat gently suggested to me that I should release the ship's nurse, as in his view she was dead, and I was so cold that really I couldn't move my arms and legs. I was holding on for my life, holding on to her, and I didn't really want to let go of her because I felt that I would then lose whatever resource that I had in my arms. Then it became apparent to me that she was dying, and possibly was dead, and I still couldn't let go of her. I just felt that at any minute we might be rescued and there might be the possibility of life within her and it seemed to be so. There was no need to let go of her – it would be cruel to let go of her. She was a person even though she was patently dead and her mouth was open.

They said, 'Come on, Colin, let go of her, let go of her,' and I just couldn't do it. Eventually the storm solved the problem and she was swept away. We were getting fewer and fewer in numbers. There was a young man, a student, an Englishman as far as I know, who said he wanted something to eat or drink and he started drinking the seawater and everybody was telling him, 'No', in between the waves, because it was very difficult to talk. The waves were just flowing over you. He was insistent on it and the next minute he jumped from the relative safety of the lifeboat into the sea.

Ellen Harris
Reuters press reporter in Houses of Parliament
We got a bus, and we'd gone two or three hundred yards – as far as Islington Green – and the sirens went. Nobody knew what to do – this was the first ever. We'd had drill and training and what was impressed on everybody was the gas mask. And now, here was the first warning. Your mind immediately flew to the worst of everything. We were all turfed off the buses. Drivers, conductors, everybody, down into a shelter – we stopped right outside Islington Green shelter. As we all went in – mothers carrying little babies

Demonstrating the indomitable spirit that characterised Londoners during the Blitz, women organise a meal service for the bomb victims amongst the wreckage of their home.

with their gas masks on – the wardens were calling out 'Mind the live wires!' They hadn't finished the shelter. That was rather a shock.

Edward Ardizzone
Artist
Partly it's buildings – the dramatic effect of half-ruined buildings. It has a sort of dramatic quality. Partly because it was your own town – it did appeal to me enormously. Look at that – look at that strange, half-ruined street – something terribly moving about it. You know you feel almost like weeping. What was it to do with civilians – that's always hurt me about the war – to do with people who lived in the place? Poor devils – look at those poor devils going off, and the ruins behind them – that's always tragic. And again, the children dancing, because they don't mind, the children – they don't see.

Evelyn White
Nurse relocated from Birmingham to help in London
On night duty we would have to put the beds into the centre of the ward to prevent flying glass from coming in from falling bombs. The patients, who were nearly all cockneys, were wonderful. Great sense of humour. No matter how ill they were feeling, they'd always get out of bed and help us to push the beds into the middle of the ward.

There was great fellowship. The air-raid shelters in the hospital grounds filled with water, so we couldn't use them, so they converted the X-ray department into a large air-raid shelter. They sand-bagged it, they put in wooden pillars. If we were on duty at night, we would bring our mattresses over from the nurses' home, spread them out on the floor and spend the night in the X-ray room, which was well protected, we hoped, except from direct hits.

I can't ever remember laughing so much as I did in those days. I think perhaps it was a reaction, but it was great fun. There was a great sense of fellowship – 'we're all in it together – we've got to pull together'. When we used to walk back from the X-ray department, you could tell by sniffing the air where the bombs had fallen. I can remember we were crossing over to the nurses' home and we could smell burning sugar and fat, and we knew the docks had got it.

I can remember when the City got it – the infamous night of bombing – standing on the roof with others and seeing the dome of St Paul's ringed by fire. That's a memory that stays vividly in my mind.

Peter Bennett
Schoolboy in Godalming, Surrey

I remember going out with my dad. I don't know where he got the petrol, but we were taking someone home, and we thought we had seen the sunset. Then we realised that it was the London docks on fire. The sky was red.

Doris Scott
Civilian living in Canning Town, East London

Once, as I was leaving the park shelter and coming back to my house, those all around were bomb blasted, and I saw this woman cleaning the front doorstep of her demolished house as if it were business as usual.

Often when a place was bombed in the East End, the King and Queen would come and visit. It would give people a certain amount of heart and, in fact, if we knew that they had a hit, it made us feel better, because it brought them down to our level. Yes, they did inspire people in their own way.

Ellen Harris
Reuters press reporter in Houses of Parliament

We had an Anderson shelter at the bottom of the garden – and it was a fair-sized garden. On this particular evening there was a string of bombs dropped. The first in front of us seemed to be over your heads. Then all complete silence. Planes disappeared and then the next I remember the wardens coming out along the streets – because there was such complete silence – everybody seemed to be stunned. They were shouting out, 'Anybody hurt?' at the top of their voices.

Frederick Delve
London-based fireman

There was a short, sharp message sent by Winston Churchill to the fire services in London (which was not received until 11 o'clock), saying that St Paul's was to be saved at all costs. Now it was interesting because every fireman, without being told, knew that the target was St Paul's – that St Paul's was to be destroyed that night. And without telling anyone, they almost lined their backs to St Paul's and pointed their jets outwards to make sure that no fire would reach St Paul's – and generally they were successful. There was slight damage, but it was not destroyed – and yet the whole of the area around there was just devastated.

Ralph Ashill
Fireman in Coventry

A lot of appliances, both regular and Auxilliary Fire Service were sent into Coventry, particularly on the night that Coventry was, according to the Germans, 'Coventrated', when there was a tremendous amount of fire situations and bombing. I remember being told of a member of a fire crew in Coventry on the night of the big raid, who as a result of high explosive, was blown over the top of a building some fifty feet high and landed on the other side of the building behind it – and survived. These sort of stories were quite a usual occurrence.

Gunner Richard Gwillim
155th Regiment, Royal Artillery

We were stationed at a place, Kingston, near Birmingham – at an entrance to Sutton Park. The area was called Bannersgate, where there was a compound for internees. That night, the sirens went and we heard the droning – and we realised it was going to be a pretty heavy raid, but it was Coventry they were after. We were all on stand-by and went to Coventry to help. Coventry took an awful pounding. Once the cathedral had caught alight, there was nothing you could do about it. It burned very fiercely – although the firemen tried to save what they could of it. But finally it burnt right out – it was gutted. The whole roof and everything.

Margaret Couling
Civilian in Coventry

The villages surrounding Coventry were taking evacuees just for night's lodgings – just somewhere to sleep. They didn't bother about food – they just took food with them, and as long as they could get down and rest – then they drifted back next day. The men went to work, the women came home to see if the house was still standing.

Our office building was a stone building, so that was still standing – and I went up to the top floor, and we went in. We were looking around, and by this time the cathedral was in ruins and still smoking. While we were in the office, there was a little procession came from the back end of the cathedral and walked down Hay Lane. It was George VI with the Mayor and various dignitaries, and they'd just been to the cathedral. They brought their own picnic basket, so that they could have lunch before they went on elsewhere.

C.15706

While the evacuation programme saved many children from the inferno of the Blitz, those who stayed put, like these Southampton youngsters, joined the legions of the homeless as the Luftwaffe continued the attacks on Britain's cities.

Gwendoline Stewart
Teenager in Birmingham

My father built a shelter in the garden. You wouldn't know it was there. It had steps going around and around – my father said that a curved entrance stopped the blast from coming inside the shelter. He painted the walls with butterflies – there was a stove and bunk beds. It was home from home, really. That was the routine of the day – home from work, an evening meal, and sleep right through in the shelter to save on broken sleep in the house, because we had very heavy raids.

The factories were still burning, and the trams weren't running, but no matter what happened, I had to get across Birmingham, through craters, hosepipes and chaos. Even if you got into work at eleven, you received a warm welcome, because everyone else had gone through the same thing. You would find yourself walking through the city and meeting people trying to get to work – and you would become the best of friends.

Flying Officer William Gregory
29 Squadron, RAF

We were on patrol one night when a message came through to say that Liverpool was getting blitzed. When we arrived in the Liverpool area you could see the glow of the fires through the clouds, and we were at about 10–15,000 feet. I switched on the radar, and found one contact so we closed in. It was a Dornier 17, and just as we were about to shoot it down, our starboard wing was shot off by an ack-ack. I bailed out and landed on a little place next to Lime Street Liverpool, and he landed inland someplace.

I was on the roof of this house for about ten minutes when a ladder came up to the eaves and a chap came up with a gun. I said, 'Thank God you can get me off.' And I was fastened on to a chimney pot I had held on to. And he said, 'You bloody German, you can speak as good English as we.' When I got to the ground, a crowd started to put the boot in. They had every right, when you saw the fires that were going on. I was in full Irvine kit and when they ripped the coat off I was in RAF blue underneath, I was then a 'bloody spy!' Eventually a police chap came up and took me up to the police station and I put a call through to my squadron at Digby and they sent a car out.

Sergeant Frederick Gash
Gunner, 264 Squadron, RAF

I enjoyed flying at night, to be truthful. When you got above the clouds there, and the moon was shining, it was absolutely beautiful. You had to use your eyes. The pilots were flying the aircraft, and they had to keep tabs on their instruments all the time. It was left to us – the gunners at the back – to scan the skies, looking at every possibility of exhaust flames or lights of any description in the air that shouldn't be there. It was very difficult, except that I realised afterwards that even on the darkest night, if you got close enough, you could always see something else, even if it was black. If there is no moon up there, if there's something else flying or near you that was black, you could still see it.

Lilias Walker
Child evacuated from Hull to Scarborough

There was some pretty nasty bombings so we used to have to sleep in this Anderson shelter. We'd got bunk beds and were supposed to take proper shelter bedding out there – special sheets, eiderdowns and blankets. One night the sirens sounded and we went out into the shelter and I was suddenly aware of this noise above the guns and bombs – of this swishing noise. It was a landmine that was drifting over the house, and it exploded in Scarborough Street, just off Hessle Road. It was pretty close – it brought the windows in and the ceilings down, and the door, but we weren't bombed out or anything. They soon came and patched up the windows.

Eric Hill
Eight-year-old living in Southampton

We lived about four miles from the centre in a place called Bassett. The Messerschmitts and the Dornier bombers seemed to come right over the estate that I lived on, and turn round and dive-bomb Southampton. All we could see was the town ablaze – you could just see the glow. We knew that Southampton was really getting hammered.

There was an incident just before my father got called up. There was no air-raid siren blown that night, but you could tell the different sounds of the aeroplanes' engines. You knew the Dornier had a sort of gnawing, groaning effect. My father rushed in and threw my mother and me underneath the kitchen table, and we heard an almighty explosion. It was a landmine on a parachute. It landed in the next road and killed several families. I remember my father and all the neighbours went up to assist all they could. You can tell, to this day, where the landmine landed, because you have got a road full of 1930s-style houses and then you have got, in between, about three houses that are more or less 'modcon' where they rebuilt them.

One evening we were in Southampton when the air-raid sirens blew and we had to dive for cover. I remember we were in the air-raid shelter for three, four hours until we got the all-clear to come out. When we came out the high street was running with melted margarine and butter because they'd hit the cold storage. My mother and most of the women just grabbed handfuls of this butter and were ramming it into their bags.

Ellen Harris
Reuters reporter in Houses of Parliament

May 10th was the night that London was set afire. I'd been in a dugout under Liberty's in Regent Street, which my father felt safe in. I left quite early that morning to get home, wash and change and get back on duty in Fleet Street by eight o'clock. It's a good long distance from Oxford Circus to where I lived in Islington, and I was walking over hose pipes – dozens and dozens of them. No bus could have run as there were hose pipes everywhere and firemen fighting the blazes still. I got to Bloomsbury and then, walking down past Lincoln's Inn, a man who I learned had been taking cover in a shelter – a middle-aged man, almost in tears – stopped me and said, 'What are we going to do? We can't go on like this. We've got to seek peace.' He was really very panicky. I said to him, 'Do you realise that you're playing right into Hitler's hands? This is just what he's setting out to do. If he can do this to you, to get you into this state, and you start on me, and I join in – and go up the road and tell somebody and you do the same to somebody else – now, you'd get people in the state of mind and their morale goes. What you've got to do is remember you're in the front line, as if you were in the trenches in the last war. This is what I'm telling myself – this is my war effort. And this is your war effort. Buck up – you were under cover. You're all right and I know this is sad. We're going to be very upset when we see what happened last night, but take it on yourself to boost other people. We've got to keep going.' He said, 'Thank you. Thank you very much.' And he was bucked up and he went off. I hope I did him some good.

Opposite Sadler's Wells theatre was a row of little old Victorian houses with the iron railings round them. Well, what wasn't down to the ground had got all the insides out. And the houses opposite had also been badly blasted. I saw people moving children's prams which they'd filled with little things they'd rescued from their homes. There were no tears – nothing whatsoever – just firmness – 'We'll rescue what we can.' They were alright – but what got me into tears was a birdcage, still hanging in a window with a little dead canary in it.

My home and all around there was all right – except a gas main, and the

D2649

Men of the London Auxilliary Fire Service
deal with the blazes started by incendiary bombs.

PLI2041

Bombed out of their homes and left with a few treasured possessions,
Londoners pick up the pieces and carry on with a grim determination.

water mains had been hit. You couldn't have a cup of tea or anything anywhere locally. There was a local butcher man and he had some oil arrangement down in his basement. He set the stoves going and he set up a stall outside. He cooked sausages, and whatever he'd got in his shop. He cooked and put the food out there for the people to come along and help themselves. Now I saw that with my own eyes. He was the butcher – he owned the place. He seemed to me a man that you wouldn't have thought was that kind at all.

Myrtle Solomon
London civilian

We had a very big basement, and my mother said, 'We'll just open it up.' So people came in every night, for, I believe years – long after the blitz. There were people we didn't know – because you know how it is in London – how little you know your neighbours. But there were many families there, including two Italians and Austrians. Their husbands got taken away to the internment camps, which was a very grim experience for the wives, who came every night to the shelters. I remember trying desperately to help get their husbands out. The other one was a Jewish-Italian doctor, whose wife was nearly going mad without him.

It was not required at that stage, but several of us in the road went voluntarily to take a short course in what to do when incendiaries dropped. We were equipped with stirrup pumps, water and sand – nearly all of which seemed to be totally useless. Because the stirrup pump didn't work, I remember kicking incendiary bombs off the roof with my feet, or the end of a broom, just to get them into the garden away from the roof of our house. I remember throwing sand on a bomb for ages. I kept doing exactly what I'd been told to do – and throwing this sand on, and it just flared up again. The planes were still overhead, and you thought they could see you – and thought if they saw a fire going, they would drop another bomb on you. So you were absolutely petrified.

In the morning, you felt good to be alive – but with this awful sense of guilt that other people weren't – and shouldn't it really have been you?

Dorothy Hont
Teenager in Liverpool during 'May Week' bombing

It was night after night. Your life rotated around the sirens. You'd go to work and you'd close the shop early or come home a bit earlier, have a fast tea, get yourself into something warm, gather little bits of specials that you wanted to save, down to the shelter and that was it. And we used to knit in the shelter or play cards or guessing games, or just doze. Half the time you were up to your ankles in water because water used to seep in. Every day you'd have to go down and bail out. So we used to put bricks on the floor to put our feet on – cold, miserable and horrible. I wouldn't wish it on anybody.

In the very bad times, such as the week of a bright moon or early dark nights, you would have the sirens practically every night. And then if you went a few days without, that was as nerve-racking as the others, because you were waiting for them. But after we had a bit of a respite, you tended to get a little bit cheeky. You'd go to the pictures or something like that. I only went to two dances and one cinema during the whole session of the war. That was the extent of my social life.

RAID ON TARANTO

Since Italy had entered into the war, her fleet, moored at the port of Taranto, had become a threat to Allied operations in the Mediterranean. On 11 November 1940 a night-time air attack was launched by aircraft of the Fleet Air Arm off the aircraft-carrier HMS *Illustrious* to remove that threat. Twenty-one aircraft took off in two waves and met heavy anti-aircraft fire over the harbour. Two Swordfish crew were killed and one was taken prisoner – but the battleships *Cavour*, *Littorio* and *Duilio* were torpedoed and put out of action, and the blazing harbour of Taranto was left in chaos.

Lieutenant Michael Torrens-Spence, Fleet Air Arm
Aboard HMS **Illustrious**
By far the most successful and spectacular offensive action by the Swordfish was the attack on Taranto on the night of 11th November 1940. The plan was to torpedo the Italian Fleet at its moorings at a range of 200 miles from the *Illustrious*.

We would be up against 21 batteries of AA guns, barrage balloons, searchlights and underwater torpedo nets, not to mention the guns on the ships we were attacking. Clearly the outcome was going to be anything between a disaster and a famous victory. We would be using torpedoes with magnetic warheads which had just been invented. Up to this point the torpedo had an ordinary contact head which depended on hitting something. This new magnetic head was designed to go off under the ship, which would do much greater damage than hitting on the side of the ship. The RAF's Glenn Martin reconnaissance aircraft in Malta had taken some good photographs of where the ships were moored and of the location of barrage balloons and torpedo nets. It was a question of memorising these things and then playing off the cuff when you got there.

There was no precedent for judging how it would work. You had to drop the torpedo at a height of 50 feet or less at very close range because of the confined space. Half the aircraft carried torpedoes and the other half bombs and flares. Fifty per cent casualties amongst the torpedo aircraft was probably the general guesstimate. Twenty-one aircraft attacked Taranto. About three weeks earlier we had a fire in the hangar in *Illustrious*. Trying to put in extra fuel tanks, somebody short-circuited a wire and caused a fire which seriously damaged several aircraft so *Illustrious*'s two Swordfish squadrons were short of aircraft. Five were borrowed from the old *Eagle*, she not being fit for the operation.

Lieutenant-Commander Williamson led off the first wave of aircraft at about 2030. My squadron commander, Ginger Hale, led the second wave about half an hour later. During the attack 100,000 rounds were fired at us but only one aircraft was shot down in each wave. I got hit underneath by one half-inch machine-gun bullet. It was the pilot's job to aim the torpedo. Nobody was given a specific target. I dived down in between the moored ships, aimed at the nearest big one, which turned out to be the *Littorio*, and released my torpedo. While you're low down over the water and surrounded by enemy ships, the comfort is that they can't shoot at you without shooting at each other. I then made for the entrance to the harbour at zero feet and thence back to the *Illustrious*. It's difficult to know whether you have hit the target or not, because, once you have dropped the torpedo, you're away. I didn't even see any of the action around me, I was too busy looking for barrage balloons.

Once the formation had arrived over the target at about 8,000 feet, it was every man for himself. We did not know what damage had been done until the RAF took some photographs afterwards which showed three battleships sitting on the bottom. There was great jubilation aboard *Illustrious* at having had only two aircraft shot down. When we were debriefed they wanted to know if I had hit anything and I could only say that you couldn't miss a big ship at such a short range if the torpedo ran straight. The photographs of that raid appeared in all the newspapers. I was credited with a hit on the *Littorio*. But ships sunk in the harbour can always be refloated. Only one of the three was never repaired. Two were repaired but it took a long time. In March 1941 the Italians still had only one of their battleships in action – the *Vittorio Veneto* – which wasn't hit at Taranto.

Lieutenant George Going
Observer, Fleet Air Arm

We were carrying bombs and were to be the last aircraft to go in the second wave. Unfortunately, the last aircraft but one landed on top of our mainplane, but it didn't seem to do him any harm. Clifford got us repaired whilst I went to the captain and asked if we could go as soon as we were ready. He asked if we would catch the others up and I said, 'Of course,' which was nonsense, so twenty minutes later we bowled off on our own.

We had a very heavy bomb load and we arrived about twenty minutes later than everybody else – which made the navigation extremely easy because we could see what had kicked up for the others. There was nothing particularly happening when we got there. We wandered over the top of Taranto with practically no interference at all. We found our target which was a row of cruisers in the inner harbour and we managed to get into the exact position we wanted, at which point they woke up and sent up a great deal of flak. I was looking over Clifford's shoulder – he was a brilliant pilot and bomb aimer – and I'm quite certain our bombs hit but I couldn't see any nice bangs. As we were getting away, I told him I hadn't seen anything and I asked him whether we should have another go. He said 'Don't be a bloody fool.' It transpired that we did hit the target but our bombs didn't go off – they went through. It was enough to scare the Italians. Then we traipsed our way home and found the ship, where nobody had expected us to get back.

Lieutenant David Goodwin
824 Squadron, Fleet Air Arm

The major part of the Italian fleet was there – most of the bigger ships were in the outer harbour and the cruisers and smaller ships were in the inner harbour alongside the jetties. I was very apprehensive. It was the first major strike against ships in harbour and we knew that the defences were very thorough and thick on the ground. We didn't think very many aircraft would come back. It was a very dark night as we took off, so the first aircraft dropped a flame float – a float that drops on the sea and puts up a flame – and the other aircraft took formation from that and began to climb. There were a lot of clouds about and our aircraft got separated from the rest – we seemed to be flying on alone. The Swordfish was heavily laden with bombs and so we only flew at about 85 knots. It took a long time to reach Taranto and I was worried, first of all about finding the target and secondly about what was going to happen during the attack itself. Eventually, all the aircraft did arrive together over Taranto. The Italians had detected us on their sound locators and as we flew over the harbour, the amount of flak with tracers was terrific. It was quite dazzling.

The majority of aircraft had torpedoes which they were launching against the bigger ships in the outer harbour, but my aircraft was one of those dive-bombing the cruisers in the inner harbour. In order to drop our bombs, we had to go into a nearly vertical dive and pull out at a very low height. We thought we got some hits before my pilot jinked out and we got away over the seaplane base, which also put up a lot of flak at us. We set course back to *Illustrious*; there was a feeling of exhilaration. We wouldn't know how successful the raid had been until the RAF photographs were viewed the next day, but we felt that at least we'd got away with it and it seemed to go all right. These were the days before radar was fitted to help Fleet Air Arm aircraft to return home and my aircraft had no beacon so it was purely a question of navigational skill to find the *Illustrious* again. It was dark, there were no lights and the carrier was moving the whole time, unlike a shore airfield which stays stationary. One would only have to be blown ten miles off course by an adverse wind and one would never find the carrier. As it was, my pilot made a perfect landing.

1941

*I had my sea boots on and a very tight belt. I paddled around
in the water and took my knife and cut my belt so I could breathe properly.
Then I looked around and saw the* Hood *was rolling over on top of me.*

By the start of 1941, the U-boat packs were taking their toll on British merchant shipping and their escorts in the Atlantic. The British people, still suffering under the Blitz, had to contend with strict rationing imposed due to severe shortages of imported food.

In North Africa, British troops defeated the numerically superior Italian forces in February – a cause for some celebration at home, but also the trigger for German forces under command of General Erwin Rommel to be directed to the Western Desert to bolster up their failing ally. The Afrika Korps offered opposition of a very different calibre.

Having been thwarted in his ambition to invade Britain, Hitler turned his attention to the Soviet Union. It was an adversary that had defeated Napoleon in 1812, but Hitler believed he could sweep to victory before winter set in, and on 22 June launched Operation Barbarossa, an invasion to take Leningrad, Moscow and the Ukraine. The Soviet Union quickly signed a mutual-assistance agreement with Britain – at last the nation was not standing entirely alone.

The war at sea continued. In the Atlantic, the U-boat packs and German surface fleet attacked British shipping, inflicting huge losses – including the *Hood* and the *Ark Royal* – but the Royal Navy did record some significant victories against the German navy, in particular the sinking of the *Bismarck*.

In April, in the Mediterranean, British forces were ordered to evacuate Greece and make their way to Crete, where German troops were parachuted in on 20 May. Despite huge losses, the Germans managed to drive the British off the island by 1 June. A fierce battle began to keep supply lines open to the British island of Malta, and to provide sufficient defences to prevent the island from being invaded. Convoys bringing in aircraft and fuel came under heavy attacks launched from nearby Italian air bases and from U-boats that tracked the ships as they navigated the Strait of Gibraltar. The civilian population and the troops defending Malta were effectively under siege and suffered constant bombardment and severe shortages throughout the year.

As 1941 drew to a close, the final major combatants entered the arena. On 7 December, Japanese dive-bombers simultaneously attacked the US fleet at anchor in Pearl Harbor, Hawaii and British bases in Malaya and Hong Kong. Four days later, Hitler declared war on the United States. Previously reluctant to join the war, America was compelled to take action and declared war in return – her massive resources and military might were joined to the Allied war effort. Driven by the momentum of this initial attack, the Japanese turned immediately to the American military bases on the Philippines and continued their assault in Malaya. Taken by surprise by the speed of the Japanese attacks, Hong Kong surrendered and Singapore followed soon afterwards in the new year.

In the Western Desert the Allies were holding out against Rommel's Afrika Korps. And on the Eastern Front, the Russians make a successful canter-offensive on 5 December 1941 thus removing the threat to Moscow. When the curtain fell on the second full year of the war, the conflict had reached global proportions.

THE WESTERN DESERT

With the arrival of Rommel's Afrika Korps, the desert war took on a new intensity. At the start of the year the Italians were soundly beaten, but Rommel set about reclaiming the bases the Italians had lost. In June, British troops went into action to relieve the base at Tobruk which had been surrounded in April – and were driven back, sustaining over a thousand casualties and losing more than a hundred tanks. Sporadic fighting ensued and it was not until November that the Allies were able to launch a counter-offensive to retake Tobruk. After fierce fighting, Operation Crusader eventually succeeded in lifting the siege. The desert was a very different environment in which to conduct a war – a bleak landscape with little vegetation and only scattered settlements and towns – in many ways an ideal theatre in which to wage a full-on tank war.

Squadron Leader Fred Rosier
229 Squadron, RAF

Life in the Western Desert was tough and demanding. We had to put up with the extremes of heat and cold – the sandstorms which got worse and, even more depressing as time went on, the flies (particularly where the Italians had been), the shortage of water, the monotony of the daily diet of bully beef and hard biscuits – and the fear . . . that feeling in the pit of the stomach before going on operations.

Bombardier Ray Ellis
425 Battery, 107th Regiment, Royal Artillery

By the middle of the morning, as the heat of the day became more intense, you could walk about without compunction. They could see you – but only in a distorted way. They did the same thing, and we would see them walking about – but you'd see a man walking upside down fifteen foot in the air – distorted visions – you couldn't aim at it, because you didn't know where he was really. Sometimes by a trick of the light, or by fate, it would all revert back to normal again in a second and they had a complete view of the front again, maybe for quarter of an hour, and then it would go again. You'd be looking out and everything would be distorted; then it would clear and everyone dived for cover as the war started again.

A man could walk up, one shot could be fired and he would be killed. We thought about this a lot, actually. You looked for all sorts of omens – I can remember looking for omens in the sky – shapes of clouds which would suggest good things. Your mind was involved in this sort of thing. What were the omens or the chances? But I never thought of being killed – it was always the other man who was going to die. You had this feeling that, yes, you would survive – but at the back of your mind you realised you were kidding yourself.

Sergeant Stephen Dawson
339 Battery, 104th Regiment, Royal Artillery

We knew something was going on when we were ordered to travel up to Tobruk in about January 1941, because of the tension in the air – but we were just ordinary soldiers at that time, and nobody told us anything. On the way there, the convoy came to a brief halt. We'd found the body of a young British officer. He'd been shot across the chest. He had blue eyes and fair hair, with a revolver in his hand – just this one solitary object lying in the middle of the vast desert. We started to dig a grave and I made a little plywood cross – but suddenly we were told to go again, and we had to leave him there – somebody's son.

The Western Desert, 1941. Australian troops stand in fox-holes, dug in on the front line at Tobruk, where the garrison was the focus of continual fighting as the stronghold changed hands several times during the course of the year.

When we got to Tobruk there were thousands of units waiting to go into the perimeter, and while we were there in the afternoon a German bomber came along. We were all tired and grumpy, and I think a thousand men must have fired on it. I think it was already damaged, because it was flying quite low in the sky. It dipped, and then there was a flash of fire as it blew up – and we all cheered.

Sergeant John Longstaff
2nd Battalion, Rifle Brigade
I always taught the lads to keep clean – always taught them to have a shave every morning, even if it meant shaving out of a cup of tea, because it made you clean. If you feel clean, you feel your morale is good. It's when you're mucky that your morale is down. I used to make them wash their shirts in petrol, because we didn't have the water. I'd make them wash their socks, and pointed out that this wasn't just cleaning, it was preventing fleas, because there were thousands of them. They say the Italian Army brought them over.

Private Peter Salmon
2/28th Battalion, Australian Army
We moved up to Tobruk in April 1941. It was a very flat place – not a sandy desert like the Sahara – a scrubby sort of desert, and there was an incredible shortage of water. We used to get desperately thirsty. We were living in these cement dugouts with slit trenches, and doing night patrols. Night after night we set out on patrols, and we'd go so far, then we'd go to ground. Then we just lay there, a listening patrol, lying there for hours. It would get bitterly, bitterly cold, and you just hoped that you surprised the Germans and they didn't surprise you.

I was on the Derna Road at Tobruk when the Germans came. I remember it very vividly – it was a surprise to see them. They were in trucks and they came to the perimeter and I can still see them getting off those trucks. I don't know what they expected to find, but then of course we opened up on them with small arms fire and artillery – the blokes that were using the bush artillery were quite incredible, because they had no sights (the Italians had stripped the guns of their sights) but they were getting some very accurate firing, and it was amazing what they did.

An advanced dressing station offers scant shelter for the wounded as an officer from the Royal Army Medical Corps brings round water.

Sergeant George Pearson
425 Battery, 107th Regiment, Royal Artillery
I dived into the slit trench and another young chappie dived on top of me. When the bombs had finished exploding and the aircraft were going away I said, 'Come on, get up, Phil!' He didn't move and I got up and he sort of flopped over on his back. I said, 'What's the matter are you hit?' I couldn't see a mark on him, but he was obviously out – in fact, he was dead. A small piece of shrapnel as big as would cover a thumb nail had gone into the back of his neck and must have severed the spinal column and killed him, just like that.

There was one very big chap with us, and when a dive-bombing raid came, he dived into the Boyes anti-tank rifle pit. He and the 500-pounder had a race for it – and the 500-pound bomb won. He was not mutilated as such – I think it was the blast that killed him – because when we picked him up it was rather like picking up a fish – he was all floppy. It must have broken every bone in his body.

I had one gunner in my sub-section – he'd only to hear the drone of an aeroplane and he would get fidgety. If it became obvious that you were going to get bombed, he would just rush madly around. We used to knock his feet from under him and a couple of us would lie on him. It was sheer panic that it set off in him. You might say, 'Oh he's not a very good chap to have in a gun crew!' But when we were being fired on by shellfire it didn't bother him a bit!

Sergeant Harold Atkins
2nd Battalion, Queen's West Surrey Regiment
To conclude the Tobruk episode at the end of April, there was a task given to the regiment that is distasteful to any infantryman – and that was to clear up.

We had no transport and it was decided that because we were part of the Tobruk garrison, this time they sent us back to base to rest, re-equip etc. And whilst we were waiting for transport, they said, 'You will go down to the Sidi Rezegh area and you will pick up all our dead and bury them in a temporary cemetery in and around Sidi Rezegh.'

That was possibly one of the most unpleasant tasks that I, or I think anybody, has to perform. And particularly if you are an infantryman and you're still going to do some more fighting. You are aware that there for the grace of God go I.

And some of the sights that we saw and had to deal with – for instance, you have to remember that some of those bodies had been lying out there for four, five, six, seven days – and the sun had got at them, so they had deteriorated terribly – green, bloated, limbs hanging off, half off, no heads, half a body – goodness knows what.

We were asked to gather them in and bury them – and this we set about. We'd come across a chap who'd been killed, and to pick him up was impossible in one piece. One arm was half off, a leg was half off, hanging by just shreds of flesh – and one had to use a shovel and just chop it off. And then you'd try with another bloke – just to pick him up.

Gunner Ted Holmes
425 Battery, 107th Regiment, Royal Artillery

The German pilots were really good. They came so low, they nearly scraped the floor by the time they pulled out of the dive. They aimed the Stuka at the target, just let the bomb go at the last minute and machine-gunned you as well. With this fixed undercarriage, there used to be a saying that you don't know you've been 'Stukaed' till you've got tread marks on your back!

Wing Commander Fred Rosier
262 Wing, RAF

It was the time when preparations were in hand for a new offensive – Operation Crusader. The fighter force moved forward to new landing grounds at Maddalena and the operation started on 18 November. Four days later I was ordered to go to Tobruk to organise the operation of fighters from there. I set off that afternoon in a Hurricane in which I had put all my worldly goods. Two squadrons of Tomahawks escorted me. We were well on our way when we were intercepted by 109s and the fight started. When I saw a Tomahawk diving down, streaming with smoke and then landing, I decided to try to rescue him. I went down and landed close to him, he ran across and sat in my cockpit. I discarded my parachute, sat on top of him, opened the throttle and then – disaster. As we started to move, a tyre burst, the wheel dug in and we came to a full stop. For the second time in two months, I faced the prospect of a long walk. This time it would be through hostile territory, and I would be with an Australian pilot, Sergeant Burney.

My first thought was to avoid capture, for I had noticed several trucks not far away. Quickly we removed my possessions from the Hurricane and hid them under some brushwood. Then we ran to a nearby wadi, where we hid behind rocks. Soon some trucks arrived full of Italians. They spread out to search and soon found all my stuff – which included my wife's picture and a silver tankard given to me by the CO of No. 73 Squadron. It must have been the fading light that saved us. They came to within just a few yards of where we were hiding.

I decided it would be safer to walk towards the east rather than try the

The crew of a British Cruiser Mk VI tank approach a burning German Panzer Mk IV, destroyed during Operation Crusader, 27 November 1941.

shorter route to Tobruk. We started later that night, using the North Pole star for navigation. In the early hours of the third day, we began to see odd shapes around us. They were enemy tanks and trucks. There was nothing else we could do other than to continue as silently as possible. Once we thought we had been spotted, for some lights came on and we heard shouts in German. We lay motionless, and soon the lights went out and there was silence. We were making little progress. It would soon be dawn, and I was worried. But once again, the fates were with us. We saw a ring of brushwood ahead. It was around a dried-up abandoned well, and we hid there.

Later that morning – I think we had been sleeping – we heard gunfire and the sound of shells passing over us. We could see the guns and though we could hear shouting in English. Anyway, we decided to make for them. We were pretty exhausted, and Sergeant Burney's feet were in a terrible state, but we just ran and ran. At last we were safe. At first the gunners were suspicious, but then we were taken to a Guards unit who passed us on to a Brigade HQ. We were then driven back to Maddalena to find we'd been given up for lost.

Corporal Frederick Birch
No. 7 Commando, seconded to No. 11 Commando
In November 1941 we learned we would be carrying out a raid on Rommel's headquarters – the idea being to take him prisoner. The local German headquarters was at this place called Bela Littoria.

We went out in submarines – the *Torbay* and the *Talisman*. When we came to get off the submarines, we were landing in small rubber dinghies – two men in each – the first dinghy away was Colonel Keyes's, and I was in the next one. All the explosives and ammunition were sealed in four-gallon petrol tins. Ammunition and food were all in these tins, sealed around the top with solder and strapped into these dinghies.

We were put over the side off a hydroplane, and then paddled away. A couple of dinghies got washed away, and apparently, on the other submarine, only two dinghies got away. For some reason they put all the dinghies on the superstructure of the sub, and she hit a very heavy wave. They all got carried away, so there was no way that the rest of the group could get ashore.

We pulled our dinghy up the beach, and Colonel Keyes said to me and this other chap, 'Go and keep an eye for anybody approaching.'

It wasn't until it started to get light that we set off inland, and we ended up in a cave where everybody got quite warm. The next night we were due to do this raid, but during the day it started to rain – rain, and rain, and rain.

As we'd approached this cave, we were travelling in dry wadis – little gullies which were all dry. When we went outside, these things were like raging torrents, there was that much water. We were hard pushed to hold on to one another. We were walking along in single file, holding on to the back of the fellow in front.

The idea had been that we should travel to the German headquarters and leave the main party to deal with that while we blew a communications pylon a couple of miles away. We would blow our target at midnight, at the same time that the other party would be going into the headquarters. Then there would be no sort of flashback of information through the telephones.

The pylon, when we eventually got to it, was a great big, four-posted, pyramid-shaped construction with hundreds and hundreds of telephone wires on it. We'd been delayed so much that we had less than half an hour to get to this pylon before the main body went into the headquarters. We just had a small chance of making it.

We put these blast charges round the four legs and linked them all together. Then we found the one thing that was a problem – our matches were wet.

So we'd got our charges all set up and we couldn't think of a way to get them to go. Then one of the fellows said, 'What about using an incendiary bomb?' I banged one of these on a stone, and when the fire started to spout out of it, I lit the fuses. I had a big bunch of fuses, and I'd covered the lot about four times – I had far too many fuses, but to do the job, because of the wet, I had a bunch of fuses in one hand and this incendiary bomb in the other. I waited until I saw the spark coming out of the fuses, then I dropped the incendiary – and I was off.

There was so much light from this incendiary bomb, I could see my own shadow as I was running away – my shadow was running ahead of me. I eventually got behind some bushes – and then the thing went. We heard a groan, and it fell over sideways. When we come to walk away, we found that a lot of the wires hadn't broken. So I had to set the lads to cut all the wires using wirecutters.

When daylight came, we found ourselves in a cemetery. We found a tomb which had an opening which was easy to get into, and inside there were several chambers. We tried to dry ourselves, and we had our iron rations.

As soon as it got dark, we started off again towards the coast, but we were picked up by the Italians while we sheltered in a cave. We learned later that Colonel Keyes had been killed on the raid on the HQ and that in any case, Rommel wasn't there. The colonel got a posthumous VC.

Sergeant James Fraser
Royal Tank Regiment

On the 22nd November, we were doing an attack – it finished up as a tank battle on the Sidi Rezegh aerodrome. We were equipped with Valentine tanks with two-pounder guns on them. A three-man crew, of which I was the driver, a lance-corporal – an officer – his name was Pete Kitto, another lad that was unfortunately killed – and a gunner, who was a lad from Skipton.

We went into attack on the airfield – but our two-pounders were useless against the German tanks. We'd come under heavy fire, and as I swung my tank round, an armour-piercing shell went through the back of the tank, right into the engine. Obviously stopped the tank. Fortunately it contained diesel – had it been high-octane petrol, the General Grant would have been like a mobile crematorium. As soon as it was hit – *whoof* – it would just go up and explode like a bully beef can. We had to sit there because there was all hell going round us. We couldn't bale out.

When night fell, the battle subsided, and our own troops had retreated. We found ourselves practically in the middle of this aerodrome, surrounded by burning tanks. In the morning, Pete Kitto stood on top of the turret with his binoculars to have a look round to see what was happening – and was hit by a sniper, who chipped half his knee away. We carried him for a day and a half, then, much to my delight and surprise, a South African armoured car picked us up. He then took Pete Kitto immediately to the hospital, and transferred me by a lift with one of their cars, back to my own particular unit, where I picked up another tank.

THE BATTLE OF THE ATLANTIC

Throughout 1941, German U-boats inflicted severe losses on Allied convoys bringing vital arms and munitions across the Atlantic to Britain. Arctic convoys bringing essential supplies to the Soviet Union were also subjected to devastating U-boat attacks and losses were massive. However, in May, the Royal Navy scored a major psychological victory. On the 18 May, the German heavy cruiser *Prinz Eugen* and the battleship *Bismarck* sailed from the Baltic. Six days later they engaged HMS *Hood* off Greenland, and sank her with the loss of all but three of a crew of 1,400. The news was only mitigated on 27 May when, after a vengeful chase over several days by a pack of British vessels including the *Norfolk*, the *Suffolk*, *King George V*, *Rodney* and the *Prince of Wales*, HMS *Dorsetshire* delivered the *coup de grâce* to sink the *Bismarck*, after it had been disabled by a torpedo from a Swordfish from HMS *Victorious*.

Petty Officer Donald Auffret
Wireless operator, aboard RN corvette HMS *Sweetbriar, escorting Atlantic convoys*

Our life consisted of going on watch, coming off watch and crawling into the hammock for a bit of relief from the pitching and rolling. You had no real appreciation of the overall situation of what was going on. You were so miserable aboard those corvettes. You never got a regular hot meal. If you managed to grab a cup of cocoa and a few hard biscuits you were lucky. The galley was always out of action, the moment you got to sea and into the Atlantic. With the motion of the ship you couldn't possibly have put anything on the stoves – you couldn't even have lit them. They used to dance around like a cork, those Flower-class corvettes. You couldn't wash – you couldn't change. Your immediate concern was either going on watch or getting back into your hammock and praying that we'd get back to Liverpool again.

Lieutenant-Commander Colin McMullen
Gunnery Officer, HMS *Prince of Wales*

One found it hard to realise that this was it – this was going to be me versus the *Bismarck*'s gunnery officer. One had butterflies in one's tummy – but I think being astern of the *Hood* was a great morale-booster. We were with the mighty *Hood* and it was OK. Finally we were all closed up and the circuits had been tested. We'd loaded the guns. From the sighting shadowing reports of the two cruisers, we knew roughly the direction from which we could expect the enemy to appear.

Sure enough – a smudge of smoke. The captain had sent a boy up to the crow's nest as a look-out. We heard him shouting, 'Enemy in sight, bearing green 40!' which is 40 degrees on the bow. Up over the horizon came the masts and fighting tops of these two ships. This was no fault of our padre, but he'd asked permission to say over the loudspeaker the prayer before going into action. For some reason, he'd been delayed in saying this prayer, and was given permission by mistake just as we sighted the enemy. Of course, every loudspeaker through the ship suddenly started saying the prayer, just as I was giving my orders for the first procedure for engaging the enemy.

I remember being extremely angry at the time, but it was just one of those things. Our padre was finally lost when we were sunk, and was last seen tending the wounded. It was not his fault that this unusual error was made.

So we opened fire at the *Bismarck*. We never saw any of the *Hood*'s fall of shot. I'm afraid she only fired two our three salvoes. Suddenly the whole of the inside of our spotting top was like a sudden sunset. This was when our great ship which we were following blew up.

So, there we were. One moment we were full of confidence, astern of the mighty *Hood*. Next moment she was gone and we, a new untried ship, were facing the *Bismarck* and the *Prinz Eugen* – both of whom then concentrated on us. We suffered a lot of damage. The *Prinz Eugen* hit us three times – the *Bismarck* hit us five times. One of the hits went through the bridge and killed everyone there except the captain, the chief yeoman and the navigator – who was very seriously wounded. The captain, realising the state of our turrets, quite rightly went hard aport and circled round, making smoke. We were breaking off the action. I, like any gunnery officer whose shoot has been interfered with, was furious.

Petty Officer Joseph Willetts
Aboard HMS Prince of Wales

As soon as we got out of the dangerous waters – in fact we were only a few miles from Reykjavik – we buried our dead. It was quite something to see thirty or more men, lashed in canvas, sliding down a very steep structure over the side into the water. It was the first experience I'd ever had of that.

The chaplain was standing on the quarterdeck, and was reciting the burial service. The sea was very rough, and it was very cold and very windy. We couldn't hear a word, but it was very, very moving indeed.

Able Seaman Bob Tilburn
Aboard HMS Hood, *one of only three survivors*

On the 22nd May 1941, the *Hood* set sail with the *Prince of Wales* in pursuit of the *Bismarck* and the *Prinz Eugen*, which were on their way to attack Atlantic convoys supplying Britain. The *Prince of Wales* had only just come out of the maker's yard, and still had some civilian employees on board, working on her gun turrets. We went over to Iceland and refuelled there. All the time we were wondering which way the *Bismarck* was going to come. There were three possible ways she could break out – via the Denmark Strait between Iceland and Greenland, or either north or south of the Faroe Islands. The *Norfolk* and *Suffolk*, 8-inch-gunned cruisers, were keeping a look-out in the Denmark Strait. The next morning, 23rd May, *Suffolk* spotted the *Bismarck*, and *Norfolk* and *Suffolk* shadowed her from then on.

The Bismarck was approximately 300 miles away. We set off after her and at 2000 hours, went into action stations because we expected to pick her up at midnight. Then the weather deteriorated and at midnight there was a blizzard, so we couldn't see anything. But we still had reports from the *Suffolk*, saying in which direction they had last seen her. We switched off our radar in case the *Bismarck* could pick up our transmissions and know there was somebody shadowing her. We were travelling at full speed – about 29.5 knots. Then, between 5.00 and 6.00 on the morning of the 24th May, we sighted the *Bismarck* in the distance, turned in towards her and opened fire at about 25,000 yards. I was manning one of the 4-inch AA guns on the port side. The *Bismarck* answered immediately with three shells, each getting closer and closer and closer.

Then the fourth, fifth and sixth shells hit us. Everyone, even the gun crews, was ordered to go into the shelter deck. There were three of us from our gun who didn't take cover. Then a shell hit the upper deck and started a fire. The ammunition in our ready-use locker was on fire and started exploding. The gunner's mate told us to put out the fire, but we said, 'When it stops exploding, we will.' He went back inside to report to the gunnery officer, and at that moment, a shell flew into the shelter and killed the lot – 200 blokes. We three were still alive, lying flat on our faces on the deck with everything going off around us.

The next shell came aft, and the ship shook like mad. I was next to the gun-shield, so I was protected from the blast, but one of my mates was killed and the other had his side cut open by a splinter. It opened him up like a butcher, and all his innards were coming out. Bits of bodies were falling over the deck, and one hit me on the legs. I thought, 'I'm going to be sick,' so I got up and went to the ship's side to throw up. Then I looked up and saw the bows coming out of the water, and started to strip off – tin hat, gas mask, duffel coat and all the rest. By then the water had reached me and I was swimming.

I had my sea boots on and a very tight belt. I paddled around in the water and took my knife and cut my belt so I could breathe properly. Then I looked around and saw the *Hood* was rolling over on top of me. It wasn't a shadow – it was a big mast coming over on top of me. It caught me across the back of the legs and the radio aerial wrapped around the back of my legs and started pulling me down. I still had my knife in my hands, so I cut my sea-boots off and shot to the surface. I looked up to see the *Hood* with her bows stuck in the air – then she slid under.

It was 6.00 in the morning. It was dark and cloudy, but there was good visibility. A heavy swell, about fifteen or twenty foot. There wasn't anybody in sight.

Further away I could see a lot of clobber in the water, so I swam over. I thought I would get myself one of those little rafts, made of wood and about a meter square. But they were in a fuel oil slick, and I didn't want to go in. So I paddled around, and I was getting really cold by then. I spotted two other survivors on rafts – Ted Briggs and Midshipman Dundas. But there was nobody else . . . nobody else. No bodies . . . nobody else alive or dead out of 1,400 men. Just we three.

Eventually, I was getting tired and cold, so I got one of these rafts, laid my chest on it and paddled over to Briggs. You know, someone to talk to. He wasn't feeling very well, because he had swallowed some of the oil fuel, but Dundas was sitting on his raft. He'd been on the bridge, 40 feet up in the air. Tell me how he did it – he must have flown.

I tried to sit on my raft, but every time I pulled it down, the other side came up and so I packed it in, because it was falling on my face all the time. We were on three separate little rafts – Dundas, Briggs and me. Where could we go? I mean, the nearest land was one mile straight down. You can't swim, you've just got to hope for the best. An aeroplane came over once, but obviously didn't see us.

I'd read one of two of Jack London's books, where in the very cold conditions of Canada, you go to sleep and you die. So I thought I might as well go to sleep. So I actually tried to go to sleep on this thing that was tossing up and down. I thought, 'If I'm going to die, I might as well die in my sleep.' Then Dundas shouted, 'What's that?' And I woke up a bit and looked behind me – and there was this destroyer coming – the *Electra*. What a beautiful sight. Then it went straight past us – but I could see the signalman on the bridge, who was looking aft – and he suddenly sighted us and gave the flash, and told the skipper – and he turned to pick us up. It was a marvellous sight.

Leading Seaman Sam Wood
Sick-bay attendant aboard HMS **Prince of Wales**
I was watching the orange flashes coming from the *Bismarck*, so naturally I was on the starboard side. The leading seaman with me said, 'Christ, look how close the firing is getting to the *Hood*.' As I looked out, suddenly the *Hood* exploded. She was just one pall of black smoke. Then she disappeared into a big orange flash and a huge pall of smoke which blacked us out. Time seemed to stand still. I just watched in horror. The bows pointed out of this smoke, just the bows, tilted up and then this whole apparition slid out of sight, all in slow motion, just slid slowly away. I couldn't believe it. The *Hood* had gone.

The armoured wheelhouse we were in had a door which was closed by a big ratchet, nine-inch thick and made of iron. I thought, 'I'm not going to get trapped if this ship is going to blow up like the *Hood*.' So I opened the door

Pictured in 1940, members of the crew of HMS *Hood*, and mascot, enjoy themselves. On 24th May 1941, all but three of her crew perished, when the *Bismarck* sank her.

and headed for the bridge. Just as I was going up to the bridge this shell landed. It came through the front part of the bridge, passed through, and exploded on the compass platform itself. I was sucked up and seemed to float across the bridge and finally came to rest on the deck amidst a shambles of torn steel fixtures and bodies.

That was the first time I had seen casualties to that degree. First-aid parties came up to help me. They were formed of marine bandsmen, writers and suppliers. There was a multitude of injuries including Lieutenant Esmond Knight, blood pouring from his face. He was a well-known actor in the pre-war days. While we were looking after them another shell hit the radio direction room, and killed many more people.

When the bridge had been cleared of the wounded, I sat down and reflected. I was covered in dirt and blood and my head was throbbing. In my mind I could see the *Hood* sinking and felt I should have reached and grabbed the bows as they were disappearing. It was crazy thinking, but everything was crazy that morning.

We put a smokescreen up after we had been hit, but we continued to shadow the *Bismarck* all that day and part of the next. I think we lost her in the evening time. I had just one small glimpse of her afterwards, when she fired at us – that was when she was making arrangements with *Prinz Eugen* to separate, to cause distraction.

I was about three hundred yards from the *Hood*. I will never forget it. I can see it now, even see the paint on the sides of it. We didn't try to go back for survivors, as we had to keep in contact with *Bismarck*. A destroyer went to pick up survivors. There were only three.

Able Seaman Herbert Gollop
Aboard HMS Dorsetshire

Captain Martin received a signal that the *Bismarck* had been sighted off the coast of Brest, and the battleships *King George V* and *Rodney* were trying to intercept her. So Captain Martin immediately left the convoy and proceeded north. We were doing about 32 knots because she was quite a fast cruiser, and also the sea was quite rough at the time, so we were feeling that one. Everyone on board was full of excitement or fear or what. We wondered what was going to happen if we arrived first, before the battle wagons, to take on the *Bismarck* on our own, more or less.

We came up from the south and we saw the *Bismarck* ahead. She was moving very slowly then. The battleships arrived about an hour afterwards, but we kept to the south of *Bismarck* and the whole fleet sort of opened fire at nine o'clock in the morning. I was a gun-layer on the four-inch gun, and so had a grandstand view of the *Bismarck* and all the big ships firing at her. I am convinced that we put her conning tower directors out of action and disorientated her guns. We'd fired 257 eight-inch shells at the *Bismarck* altogether. She fired one salvo at us and fortunately it missed us. I think the *Prince of Wales* fired one salvo at us because she thought we were the *Prinz Eugen*. No one knew where the *Prinz Eugen* was. She eventually went into Brest, but they thought we – coming up from the south – could have been the *Prinz Eugen*, so the KGV had a go at us as well. The shells went right over the top of us like a huge express train

We were ordered to fire torpedoes, so we went as close as we could get and fired two at the starboard side. Then we went around to the port side and fired the other, and eventually she sort of rolled over to the starboard side and went down by the stern. We could see all the survivors that were left on board jumping off the bows – hundreds of them. There were bodies all over the sea and people bobbing about.

We went alongside and tried to get as many men as we could on board – but they never had much strength. They were trying to hold on to the ropes and we were trying to pull them on board. There was one midshipman called Brooks – he had the brilliant idea of jumping into the sea and helping them. He tied quite a few Germans on to the ropes and then we just pulled them in.

He was very brave, as the sea was quite rough. We did manage to get him back aboard, because there was a German submarine sighted. We couldn't take any chances of getting sunk ourselves, so unfortunately we had to leave many Germans in the sea. This was one thing that upset us more than anything else. They were just left in the sea to perish. We picked up 82 altogether. We returned and took them to Newcastle, and that was the first time we'd been back into England for four and a half years.

Petty Officer Les Sayer
Telegraphist Air Gunner, Fleet Air Arm, aboard carrier HMS **Victorious**
The Swordfish is a three-seat open-cockpit design, so the pilot is in the front, the observer is in the middle, and the TAG at the back. We could only fire backwards. The weather was terrible. We climbed in a loose formation to about 10,000 feet. We got a blip on our primitive radar and came down to have a look at what it was, thinking it might be the *Bismarck* – but unfortunately it was only an American coastguard cutter. However, the *Bismarck* was just beyond that, and we had given our position away. So, we had to do a low-level attack, and in we went. I was flying with Lieutenant Percy Gick, who was a good pilot.

As we went in, I was sitting in the back, looking down between my feet. I could see the tail of our torpedo through a hole in the fabric in the bottom of the aircraft. It was like a red fin. I'm sitting there and waiting to see that red fin disappear, then I knew that the fish is gone and we're away, taking avoiding action. We did a run in, and they were letting everything loose from the *Bismarck*. We were fortunate they didn't hit us – mainly because their range-finders couldn't get down to speeds that were less than 100 mph, and our speed was roughly 90 knots.

Gick told us over the speaking tubes that he wasn't lined up and that he was going round again. So we went out to about 25 miles and came in again on our own – all the others were on their way back. So we came in right down at sea level. I'm standing up looking forward at the *Bismarck*, and she's getting bigger and bigger – and still they didn't see us. I thought to myself, 'Well, they've only got us to aim at – they're bound to hit us. This is your lot anyway, so forget it.' But we went in and dropped the fish and turned away, and it was only then that they saw us – and they let us have everything. Gick was very good. When they started firing their heavy stuff at us, we had to count from the time they fired, and take avoiding action. Another hazard was the huge waterspouts made by their shells. You could go through the splashes and get pulled down. We did fly through one of these splashes – it came up underneath us and ripped all the underside of the aircraft out, so it was a bit draughty! We kept at about ten feet above sea level.

We felt relief when we turned around. I remember saying, 'It's bloody cold back here,' because all the fabric had been ripped away – but it was only hazardous from the point of view that we probably didn't have much petrol.

We thought we'd hit the *Bismarck*. There was only one known hit, and that was amidships – and we thought we'd got it. It jammed the *Bismarck*'s rudders and she was seen to make two big circles. I suppose it was the beginning of the end for her.

When we got back to the *Victorious* it was dark. We had been flying for about four hours and we were right at the end of our endurance. We all got back safely, even though, for some of the pilots, it was the first time they had done a deck landing at night. When we got back we were given bacon and eggs for the first time ever – and also a tot.

Petty Officer Joseph Willetts
***Aboard* HMS Prince of Wales**
Later, moored just outside Reykjavik, I heard I was required in the cipher room. When I got down there, Lieutenant-Commander McMullen took this

signal and I deciphered it. I didn't know what it was, because it was just a jumble of figures as far as I was concerned, but he knew what the transcription was. He said, 'Willetts, go on to the upper deck straight away. Lock up down here and go on the upper deck straight away, because the captain will be clearing the lower deck.' That meant that every person on board the ship who wasn't doing a job that was necessary for the safety of the ship should go on to the upper deck.

I went up – and it was crowded with all the crew – and the still was sounded. We were perfectly still, all of us, because we knew there was some imminent news. He said, 'This is the captain. I have just received a message from Admiralty, which I must read to you. The *Bismarck* is sunk.' That was the message – and there was an immediate cheer all over the ship. As things went quiet, the captain said, 'Gentlemen, I'm sure that you will agree that this is the end of a very gallant ship.'

Johannes Zimmermann
German stoker aboard Bismarck

We were in action against HMS *Hood* – she was the biggest ship in the British Navy and we were the biggest ship in the German Navy. It was the biggest against the biggest. From one end of the deck of the *Bismarck* to the other was nearly 200 yards. We received two or three hits but couldn't feel them – I was in the middle of the ship in the boiler room. The radio said there was an artillery action going on and six or seven minutes later we were told the *Hood* was sunk. Everyone was jubilant.

We had won a victory over the mighty *Hood* – but soon we were hit by a shell from the *Prince of Wales*. We were hit on the port side in Section 20 over the waterline and Section 21 underneath the waterline. So the front part of the ship filled up with water and the electric pump didn't work any more. Another shell hit the front electric turbine room which filled up with water straight away. The second boiler room on the portside was broken up and water flooded in.

At about eleven in the evening, we got attacked by an aircraft from HMS *Victorious* and its torpedo hit the armoured plate on the starboard side and exploded in the bottom of the boiler room. Then the second boiler room on the port side filled up with water. During the night we left the British Fleet behind us but the Admiral sent a message that we were heading straight to the French coast. This gave the British a chance to find us again.

On the 26th May at about 10.30, I was on the upper deck and we got the aircraft alarm. On the port side we saw a seaplane, and by now, the

Mediterranean fleet was on its way to block our escape route. At 1600 hrs I went to the boiler room and that was the beginning of the end. I didn't come out for 16 hours.

At midnight, destroyers attacked us. As we left the boiler room next morning, heavy artillery fire started up from the port side. We were told to go back the way we had come so we went on to the lower deck to where the boiler rooms are and we heard explosions on the water pumps and the sea valves. Ten minutes later I went back up and saw the *Dorsetshire* and the *Norfolk* on the starboard side. Some of us thought they were firing gas shells, as we saw what looked like green smoke coming from the shells.

The first lieutenant was standing in the doorways to Section 9 when a shell hit him. I was told to go another way. I opened the door to the upper deck and right in front of me was the turret of the first 150 mm gun. The sight of it was terrible. Blood and pieces of comrades. You couldn't tell what came from one man and what came from another. Suddenly, as the ship turned over, I slipped off the deck into the sea. It was very rough. We were all being tossed up and down by the waves. The waves were ten metres high. Nobody was powerful enough to swim in this water.

I was swallowing a cocktail of seawater and oil. I came up close to the Bismarck and it was easy enough to put your hand on the upper deck but it was harder staying there – you slipped off again each time. I was swimming alongside a friend of mine who was a neighbour from home. We had gone to the same school. He died in that water.

Finally, I was pulled on to the *Dorsetshire*. A small sailor boy gave me a big bottle of gin. I took it and started to drink. Suddenly all my insides came out – all salty water, everything. Since then I've never touched gin. I was taken down below, where they took my clothes and gave me a blanket. They put me in the library where all I did was try to read an English book I found in there – *The Last of the Mohicans*. I was treated very well. The crew made us all feel like shipmates.

Otto Peters
German stoker, aboard Bismarck

My first ship was the *Bismarck*. After ending our training in Kiel, we were sent to Hamburg. We lived on a merchant ship where I studied diesel electrics for about six months, while the ship was built. We had to study hard but at 4.30 every afternoon, we were free and we had contact with the civilian mechanics in the shipyard and we had girlfriends. In other words, we had a fine time. I arrived in Hamburg in autumn 1940 and the *Bismarck* was finished at

Soon after the destruction of the *Hood*, the tables are turned. Men of the sinking German battleship *Bismarck* are hauled to safety aboard HMS *Dorsetshire*, 27 May 1941. Of a crew of 2,200, just 115 were rescued.

Christmas. Not once during that time did the RAF try to bomb her.

I was quite proud to be posted to the ship. I was a mechanic by profession and from my point of view this ship was first class. We had four diesel engine rooms and each room had four engines and we never had any trouble at all. My superior was a petty officer named Stich who still lives near me in Hamburg. He was 'correct' – by that I mean he was kindly when necessary and hard when necessary. I was never punished. We had very little to do with the officers of the *Bismarck*. The captain was a very fine man but the first officer was strict and unpopular. I was very confident about the strength of the *Bismarck*. The first voyage was through the Kiel Canal to the Baltic Sea. We expected British aeroplanes – but they didn't come and we entered Kiel Harbour the same night. Then we had four months training in the Baltic Sea. Shortly before we left, we had a visit from Hitler. I didn't see him and he didn't speak to the crew, but we knew this meant that something was going to happen. In fact war with Russia was about to begin.

We left the harbour and soon afterwards, we were told by radio that a Swedish cruiser was following us. The British knew that we were heading for the Atlantic. We went to Norway and stayed there for one night and we saw a Spitfire, which we later discovered had photographed us. Then, we headed into the Atlantic and we knew that the British Navy were aware of us. I remember the action with the *Hood* and the *Prince of Wales*. The first officer told us by ship's radio that we were being followed by British ships – but we were not told whether they were merchant ships or warships. The captain came on the radio to tell us that we had sunk the *Hood*. Where I was in the engine room, we couldn't see anything. We just heard the news on the radio. All we could hear were the guns shooting. Nothing else. I couldn't feel the *Bismarck* had been hit by enemy shells. When we heard that the *Hood* had been sunk, there was no cheering but we did feel pride. Then our captain said that we were being followed by the British Navy. We felt a torpedo strike our rudder – but we didn't know where it had hit. The ship jumped a little bit. I was still in the engine room and I had to stay there for the rest of my shift – but afterwards while carrying out other duties, I went out on deck. It was rainy and windy. The captain came on the radio at about 2000 hours on the 26th May and told us that all the *Bismarck* could now do was sail in a circle and that there was no escape. I was frightened, but as a youngster I didn't quite believe it.

The following morning at about 0700 hours, we were informed that we would have a fight with the British Navy and we were alone, while the British had plenty of cruisers and battleships. A little later, I could hear that we got hit. I had to stay at my battle station and do my duty, but luckily my engine room was not hit. Then the order came from the first officer that we were free and could leave our battle stations. We had to try to get on to deck from the engine room. It was not easy, we had to open all the doors, and when I reached the deck below the main deck, all the lights were out and the water was up to my chest. I felt a hit while we were on this deck. There was another man there and we managed to force the last door open 10 inches. I had to take my leather clothes off to get through the narrow gap.

Finally we arrived on deck. I looked around and the devastation was awful – everything had been shot away and masses and masses of dead comrades lay around. I decided to stay on board as long as the ship stayed afloat so that I could keep my strength. It was windy and stormy. The ship was half submerged. A huge wave washed over the ship but I managed to grip something and I wasn't knocked overboard until a second wave threw me into the water. I was wearing a life jacket and I was a good swimmer and I tried to swim away. The sea was very cold but I was so excited that I didn't feel it. I was thinking about my girlfriend in Hamburg and how I had to stay alive to see her again. There was no wood or wreckage around me to cling to – which was lucky because in areas where there was a lot of wood and wreckage, there was also a lot of oil. There were shipmates nearby and we called to each other that whichever of us survived should tell the other's parents what happened. I was near one guy I knew well who wasn't saved, and afterwards I wrote a letter to his parents.

After a couple of minutes, I turned around and I saw the ship turning upside down and going right down. About fifteen minutes later, I saw a ship ahead of me through a rainy wall and I swam towards it. The ship was the *Dorsetshire* but I didn't know it at the time. I saw a Union Jack on the ship and I thought that I was going to be killed. As I got closer, I saw ropes on the side and I realised that they were going to rescue us. I grabbed a rope, but the waves kept pulling me back into the water. I tried to get the rope in between my legs and keep it tight. Finally, I came up with a wave and when the wave was high on the side of the ship, the British sailors grabbed me and pulled me on board. They rescued 78 of us.

We sailed towards Newcastle and it took us three days. On the second day, the British captain spoke to us and said, 'Well, boys, I was a prisoner of war in Germany during the First World War and I was treated well, so give us your names and I'll send them over the radio so that the Red Cross know the names of survivors.' My brother was a wireless operator in the army and he picked up my name and he told my parents that I was safe.

RUSSIA

In June, Hitler's Blitzkrieg rolled into Russia. They seemed unstoppable and by the end of the year the German Army had swept through Minsk, Smolensk, the Ukraine and Kiev; there was fierce fighting around Moscow, and Leningrad was under siege. The Russian winter began to take its toll. Unlike their comrades who had stormed their way through and now occupied Western Europe, the German troops on the Eastern Front were involved in a war of attrition against a grim and determined enemy.

Henry Metelmann
German soldier, 22nd Panzer Division
To be honest, I had a little bit of fear – of course, one never admitted it. We were in our railway compartments there, and everyone was happy. 'Now we are going to do some fighting with our division, and we do some great things.' One said these things, but I had the feeling of fear, and I am sure that others had that too, because at several places we saw the result of the fighting, and we saw the Russian tanks standing there, incapacitated of course, and buildings blown up. We saw the people in the villages – it was a very strange experience, and one sensed somehow the strength of Russia.

We got out of the train and we had summer coats and our tunics – we felt very cold – and we had just ordinary jackboots in snow. In no time you have cold feet – and you feel very miserable. I remember especially when we were unloaded at Dniepopetrovsk, the continuous cold feet, and then getting cold with it. It was miserable. That year I didn't notice it very much, because I think this escapade at Dniepopetrovsk only lasted a few weeks. But the second year we had plenty of frostbite – and the third winter we had plenty of frostbite. Yes, many lost their toes, and the casualty figures were very high.

At Christmas time the Germans get rather melancholic – we sing Christmas songs. And then Christmas Eve they attacked – came in silently in boats – and my God, they sorted us out. They beat us out of the town. I think we were in Feodosia at that time – a beachy place like Bognor Regis or something like that – but rather nicer.

They had come in very silently, very efficiently, and threw hand grenades. That was one of their main weapons. They shot at everything in sight, and threw hand grenades into buildings. We lost a large number – not only in our fighting units, but there was administration, and so many other units which were there – butcher units and baker units and a little hospital – and they blew that up. We used it in our propaganda that they had killed wounded soldiers in a hospital.

CRETE

On 20 May, German paratroopers landed on Crete and, despite suffering heavy losses on the drop and after landing, they eventually succeeded in securing the island as a base from which to protect Axis shipping and troop movements in the Mediterranean and harass Allied convoys. By 1 June 18,000 Allied troops were evacuated from the island.

Private Thomas Beel
23rd Battalions, New Zealand Expeditionary Force
We were preparing our breakfast in the early morning, when we heard the hum of planes in the distance, and it gradually increased to a crescendo of noise. Then the parachuters started coming down in the distance towards the town of Suda Bay, and the noise of firing was terrific – everything was being let loose on them. Very few came towards our position, but the ones that did we opened fire on. I don't think there was one German left alive.

We found out that after a lot of fighting, the Germans had taken Maleme airfield and that night we were being sent in to counterattack. On our approach, we were held up by German machine-gun fire by a block of stone houses, and we ended up rushing them. I felt very excited, but also frightened. I think everyone was, but we managed to capture them. Getting into the aerodrome, all hell broke loose.

The Germans opened up with everything they could possibly fire at us – mortar bombs were dropping all around us, and machine-gun fire. I'd hardly taken half a dozen steps when I felt a blow to my shoulder which sent me flying backwards, and as I fell to the ground, a mortar bomb landed quite close to me, so I was hit with a bullet in the left arm and caught with shrapnel in the right arm, which numbed my arms so much I couldn't pick my Bren up.

Marine Edmund Hill
Royal Marines
We were very much rookie soldiers. I had only actually fired five rounds on the rifle range. As we landed on the quay, a German sniper shot the tallest man in the outfit – he was about six foot four – plumb dead centre in the

forehead. This had a very demoralising effect on the men at that time.

We'd no sooner arrived, too, than we were heavily bombed by German aircraft. I realised that our potential as a fighting force was practically nil. We eventually, in our panic and hysteria – or rather our ack-ack boys – shot them down ourselves, because we'd been so used to the German aircraft coming over and bombarding us, that we just used to shoot anything that flew. My first impression of Crete was being stuck in the olive groves around Suda Bay where we were – and just being bombed to blazes all the time.

As the battle began to manifest itself, we were very lucky to have with us the Maori Regiment from New Zealand. Now, these were classic warriors of the type that would rather use knives than automatic weapons, and my first real memory of absolute fear was being in a trench, thank God with them, where when told to advance upon German positions, they would stand on top of the trenches and do their Maori tribal war dance.

We were positioned on a hill, only about a quarter of a mile from the beach, and I had a twin Lewis gun with very little ammunition – and the rest of my boys were in front of me in trenches. The Germans were laying down a creeping barrage of mortar fire, which would creep up the hill – and eventually annihilated everybody in front of me – but it took about six of these mortar shells to creep up the hill, and I can remember thinking quite clearly as I watched the creeping barrage, that the seventh one definitely had my name on it. They were coming straight up the hill, and the seventh one would obviously drop straight on my head. I was sitting at the time behind a rock, which is why I survived. We were being well raked with machine-gun fire at that stage.

Anyway, the seventh one did come, but somebody must have moved the gun – I don't know who it was – but it just went to the side and behind. I got mortar and shrapnel in the back, and although I wasn't seriously wounded, it must have hit some nerves, because my legs were paralysed. I sat there for the rest of the day while the whole hill was being raked my machine-gun fire. Then to my amazement, as it got towards evening, coming belting across this ridge calling out, 'Is there anybody there?' was an Australian.

I called out to him and he picked me up. I said to him, 'My God, you're not going to make a run for it with me on your shoulder, because they're raking the hill with machine-gun fire.' He said, 'We won't worry about that, cobber.' I thought, 'This is it – we've definitely had it.' I've always had a very high opinion of the German soldier, and in this case, they were mainly Austrian mountain troops. They must have respected this man's great bravery, because they didn't fire. He carried me down to the beach, and that's when I saw the last boat going out.

Able Seaman Arthur Stevens
Air-frame fitter with Fleet Air Arm, HMS Gloucester

On the 22nd May we had a signal round noon – I think via the tannoys – that the *Naiad,* which was the flagship, was in trouble and badly damaged in the Kithira Narrows, and would we take over her station – also that the *Greyhound* had been sunk, and that we should attempt to pick up survivors.

Well, we went in steaming to the Kithera Narrows and, lo and behold, I remember standing on the guardrail on the gun deck, and watching the *Naiad* steam by us at about 18 knots. I remember saying, 'I can't see any structural damage.' We were with the *Warspite* at the time, and suddenly we were attacked by 20, 30, 40 – I don't know how many – Stukas. I stood and watched a bomb hit the *Warspite's* after-turret and blow it to pieces. All the rage and temper and tears welled up in me – the frustration at seeing another capital ship damaged. She immediately started belching black smoke and her speed was immediately dropped. We had to carry on into the narrows to try and pick up survivors from the *Greyhound.*

Then came the holocaust, I would say, of the *Gloucester.* They came with what seemed to be hundreds of planes – wave after wave of them. There was no question of picking up survivors of the *Greyhound.* We'd have been a sitting duck.

The ship's company congregated in the sickbay flat. Like everybody else, I was worried stiff waiting for the ancillary lighting to come on. This eventually came on, and they shouted for a gangway on the starboard side of the sickbay flat to let the wounded through on stretchers.

I looked up and saw one of these 87s coming down, and saw the pilot as he pulled his stick to drop his bombs. I actually saw this 500-pounder with two incendiary bombs attached to it, whirling down. It hit somewhere forward of the forecastle. I remember then looking over the ship's side and seeing that she was laying over at a fairly sharp angle, and the cutter on the port side was being lowered into the water. I jumped and dropped between the ship's side and the cutter – then all I could feel was hands dragging me inboard.

We started to pull away, but we found the cutter was full of holes and the water was flooding in. Shrapnel had hit it, and she just sunk beneath us.

Petty Officer John Mayer shouted out, 'Grab any beams you can, lads, and I'll try and make a raft.' He lashed the three beams of wood into a letter H, and straddled the middle one. He said, 'Now, you lads, all hang on all the way round the beams of wood.' Which we did – but we were under the continual attack from the air. Slowly people slipped away.

Ginger Connolly stayed with me all night, just the two of us. Come the dawn, we started to get cold. We passed water – urinated over ourselves – to keep warm. But once you got out of the drink, you started to get cramp. So immediately you lowered yourself back into the sea to become warm again. This went on all day. The sea was becoming choppy. I said, 'Hold on, Ginge.' He said, 'No, Steve. I've had enough.' I said, 'Oh, you mustn't talk like that. Life is very sweet.' He said, 'No, I can't hang on any more.' And he just put his hands up. I grabbed hold of him, but he didn't want to know. So I thought, 'Well, probably that's the best way for him to go.' So I just let him drift, and I hung on to the beam then, on my own.

It was as if somebody'd split my brain right up the middle, and left two little men with hammers. One was saying, 'You're going to die.' The other was saying, 'You mustn't die. Your mother said you mustn't die.' Because I wasn't married, and my mum idolised me. 'You mustn't die. You mustn't die.' 'You're going to die. You're going to die. You're going to die.' Eventually, strange as it may seem, this one that was going to die got hold of me. I thought, 'Well, I'm going to die now. I'll die peacefully.' So I lay over the beam and put my head under the water. Directly I did that, the other voice said, 'You mustn't die. You mustn't die. You mustn't die.' And I struggled to the top and came to, and thought, 'Survival. Must survive. Must survive for my mother's sake. My mother must be worrying about me. I must survive.' This went on a long while. Then I looked up and saw this biplane flying around. I managed to wave to it and he circled around me. He dived, and I thought, he's going to machine-gun me any moment. But he fired a red Very light and he circled around me again. I thought, 'Any minute he's going to land.' Being stupid with exhaustion, I thought he was a seaplane. He went away, and I thought, 'You've left me here to die, even though you are the enemy, you've left me here to die.'

When I was just about all in, I saw a caique with a massive German swastika flying in the breeze, and on the bow end was a paratrooper sitting with a machine-gun trained on me – and on the gunwale side were two German matelots. They steered this caique round close to me and they lifted me out. I couldn't believe it when one of them said, 'Englander, for you the war is over.'

Leading Seaman Donald Auffret
Wireless operator, Royal Navy, aboard HMS **Warspite**
I was very frightened at Crete. We were covering the cruisers, and we were in sight of Crete. We could see the Stukas landing and taking off. We were attacked continuously from about eight o'clock in the morning. I remember

seeing *Kenya* hit, and she eventually sank. I saw the *Fiji* hit, and then there was a lull in the action and I finished the forenoon watch at twelve o'clock and went down to the communications mess desk, which was also a retire station in case of air-raids. I had a cold meal, then the bugle call for 'air attack' was sounded again, and I remember saying to this other fellow, 'I'm not staying down here.' I went to the upper deck and sat underneath B turret, and an officer poked his head out the turret and said, 'What are you doing there?' I said, 'I'm just taking some air.' He said, 'Get down to your retire station.' I was halfway down when this thousand-pound bomb penetrated the upper deck, went through two bulkheads and two decks and actually exploded on the communications mess desk. I was blown out of there like a cork out of a bottle, and I remember hitting my head on a bulkhead.

The next thing I remember they were bringing the dead and the wounded through to the temporary sick bay. I think that was the first time I was really frightened. I only had shorts on and felt so vulnerable. It seemed to me if only I had a shirt on, I would have had protection, but the idea of just having bare skin and seeing the burns and blast damage that these bodies had sustained, I felt very frightened.

Sergeant Terence Frost
Warwickshire Yeomanry
We were taken to Crete by boat from Alex, and that was quite a tough journey, because it was a very rough sea. I was so ill I wanted to die. We didn't make it to Crete – we had to turn back. Thirteen boats had been damaged. They'd done terrific damage to the *Eagle* and various destroyers and aircraft carriers, so we went back. We arrived back in Alex absolutely dying from the journey to Crete.

We were given the opportunity to get off. But although I felt like dying, I also had a sort of loyalty to my mates, so as they were sticking it out, I went back and nearly died again on the next journey. When we got to Crete, we saw nothing but Germans being loaded on to our boat who were prisoners of war.

The original intention was to take Maleme Aerodrome – which was what the Germans wanted to get, and where they were dropping their parachute corps. The boys who were there had done a marvellous job round Suda Bay – they'd knocked out seven hundred Germans – but they were just piling more and more in and dropping more supplies. Eventually, under the strain of never getting any bloody rest, and a shortage of ammunition, they had to get away because the quantity of stuff dropped on them was too much. And, because we didn't get there on time, they were let down anyway.

One morning, we were absolutely surrounded, being shot at from every angle. So our poor old CO had to walk up the road with a white flag, because there was no point in going on.

Sergeant Isaac Preddy
1st Battalion, Welch Regiment

I remember the Germans coming in – they were the first paratroopers I'd seen of the war. They were coming down from the sky and we could pick them off one by one. We took a lot of prisoners, but we also shot a lot of them. Then they brought in the gliders – about a dozen people on each one. On landing, they didn't know where they were. One came in about fifteen to twenty yards away from us. As the Germans quickly disembarked, they fired their machine guns at us. The distance was so short that we thought we had the advantage, and we could just shoot the plane as they were coming out. The last one out, was firing his machine gun, and unfortunately he killed Ernie Moss, who was by my side in the trench.

Private Thomas Beel
23rd Battalion, New Zealand Expeditionary Force

The hospital was absolutely crowded with wounded Germans and British. We found the Germans very friendly – they weren't arrogant, as a lot of them were. They were very friendly, and we were playing Ludo and all sorts of games with them. A lot of them spoke very good English. Then the hospital started to be struck by the Luftwaffe. We said to the German wounded, 'Why are they striking the hospital?' They said, 'Well, look outside – there are men out there with steel helmets on, and some of them are even carrying rifles.' We couldn't say much about that. They went out and started to wave to their own aircraft – to wave them away. They finished off by laying out a red cross on the ground outside. Eventually, the planes went away. They must have realised that there were Germans there, so they left us alone. It was then that we got the first order that the island was going to be evacuated. We couldn't believe it. We thought it was a joke.

Sergeant Frederick Birch
No. 7 Commando

A decision had been taken that they were going to have to withdraw from Crete, and to get as many men away as possible. All the fighting had been in the north-west of the island, so the commandos were sent in to fight a rearguard action while the rest of the troops were being withdrawn from the south of the island. They got us to Suda Bay, where we landed at Canea. We had full packs and plenty of ammunition and firearms – but it was not the role that we had been planned for. We hadn't got any heavy machine guns – no mortars – none of that type of weaponry at all. I think the heaviest thing we had were the Bren guns. We came off the boat, lined up in a square. They took our equipment off us and said, 'Leave your equipment there and it can be fetched up later. March straight forward.' We never saw it again. We went straight into the line around the airfield. The Germans were breaking out of the airfield, and we were trying to stop them getting into Canea.

The message came that the withdrawal had started – all non-combatant troops were to get away from the area completely. We would be fighting a rearguard action with some Australians and New Zealanders – the principle being that we would hold a line for the day to let the others get away.

As soon as it became dark, we used to send out front patrols and create a bit of a disturbance – then draw back. Then the whole line would draw back and go through a line that had been formed by the other troops who were behind us. We would withdraw through them and form another line a matter of two or three miles behind them, across the road and into the hills.

We'd have a sleep during the day, then at night this other line would then withdraw through us as soon as it became dark. We would have to hold that line while they did the same sort of thing.

The very last line that we formed, we'd almost come to the end of the queue. All troops were channelled into this very narrow road, which ran down through a fishing village in a bay. There wasn't very much room on the road, and we were still a mile and a half from the beach. We were lined up there and wondering what we should do then, because we were forming a line and during the night the other troops that had formed the line ahead of us would be passing through us – but they would have nowhere to go. So we were wondering what we were going do when it started to become dusk.

Then the word came up like a rustle to start with, and as it came nearer, we could make out that there were no more boats and that we were at the point of surrender here on the island. A few people got a bit hysterical – I remember some of the lads crying out, 'We can't surrender. British troops don't do this sort of thing.' I had my section with me, and I said, 'We're not staying here on this road. Come on, get away from this lot,' because that sort of hysteria, I felt, was catching.

When we got to the edge of the cliff we found a hole in the ground, and there was a fellow there. He said, 'There's a cave here, lads. Come on in.' So we went down through the hole into the cave – a great big water-level cave, which the tide came right into at the bottom. We thought we might be safe there for a while.

We kept watch all day, and we saw a few Germans move into the village, and we heard the sound of the Germans chivvying our chaps together in various places – then above the sounds during the day, we heard a British Tommy calling out for tombola. They were playing tombola under these circumstances!

The following day we found a landing craft, fixed the engine and got away to another island occupied by the British.

Gunner Edward Telling
113th Field Regiment, Royal Artillery
My CO called me up to his office and handed me over to an Australian officer and said, 'You are now seconded to the Australian Army, and you take your lorry.' I drove back down to a small village called Kalivis, which is just near Suda, and the Aussies started to load my lorry with tents, guns, ammunition and food. When it got dark, the officer came and said to me, 'Follow the lorry in front of you – no lights – no nothing. You just follow him and make sure you don't lose sight of him.' We went up this terrible road – it wasn't a road as one knows in England. It was gravel and pit-tar. We were winding up towards the White Mountains. The driver in front had told me, 'We are going to a place called Sphakia, but if you are taken prisoner or the Germans get to you, you forget this name and you never mention it, because this is where the evacuation is going to take place.'

Early in the morning we came to a V in the mountains – and there was the blue Mediterranean. The convoy stopped and the officer said, 'This is as far as we go. This is where the boats come in.'

The Aussies unloaded my lorry – and I fell asleep. The officer came and woke me up and said, 'Your orders are to take your lorry back and run it over the edge – and make sure it's destroyed – but if you wish to, go back and rejoin your unit.' This meant a journey of about forty miles over this winding thing, with Germans buzzing overhead.

On my return to Suda Bay, my officer stopped me at the side of the road and said, 'You have done too much – you're tired. Go up and have a rest.' Of course, when I woke up, my lorry had gone, so I had to walk 45 miles back across the White Mountains. The journey on foot was absolutely appalling. We were all absolutely dead beat. I did a lot of cross-country running at school – which enabled me to do this, but it was terror in itself, because as soon as we got on to a straight road, immediately we had Messerschmitts or dive-bombers on our tail.

Some chaps walked as if they were on parade, and others just collapsed at the side of the road and said, 'Sod it.' It was too much. You can't fight and be bombed out of your mind for ten days, and then try to walk 45 miles without food, without water. It was too much.

I made it to the boat. Throughout the journey back across the Med we were dive-bombed almost continuously. Once we got on the *Glengyle*, we were put down in the hold. A sailor sat at the top of the steps with a Tommy gun. He said, 'Anyone that tries to get out, gets the lot.' They were frightened of us being dive-bombed, and panicking and all trying to get out together.

We were bombed the next day and we all dived under a trestle table. We were all trying to get under a wooden table with a top about an inch thick – all trying to save ourselves from the dive-bombers.

Most men on Crete were so absolutely worn out, their minds had gone. There was no reason for what you did, really. When you're dive-bombed, again and again, you see men blow apart, and you bury blokes – it's so awful that you are no longer in control of all the things you do or think.

JAPAN ATTACKS

The Japanese attack on the US Pacific Fleet at Pearl Harbor on 7 December brought the Americans into the war. On 10 December, Japanese bombers attacked and sank HMS *Prince of Wales* and HMS *Repulse* off the coast of Malaya. The loss of these two great ships left the troops on the mainland vulnerable – and with few options to evacuate. There was furious activity to strengthen defences as news of the Japanese advance through Malay, reached Singapore. Hong Kong surrendered to the Japanese on Christmas Day and Singapore fell on 15 February 1942 – and 138,000 Allied servicemen were rounded up and taken prisoner.

Private Cyril Doy
6th Battalion, Royal Norfolk Regiment
In December 1941, I'd never heard of a place called Pearl Harbor. I was in a convoy on an American ship called the *Mount Vernon* heading for the Middle East. I remember the Americans on board were very upset about what had happened and I can remember one of them saying to us, 'Now we'll show you guys how to win a war.'

Karin Busch
German schoolgirl in Dresden
As America came into the war and things became harder for the German people, the more resolved the German population became. People felt that the war had to be won. German people were not politically free-thinking. In England, everyone had their newspaper, people read papers with opposing views, people discussed politics in the pub and people generally tried to form their own opinions. In Germany, it was far more important that one's house was kept tidy. All politics was left to the politicians, so the country and the mass of people followed their leader.

Able Seaman Richard Smith
Aboard HMS **Repulse**
I was so amazed – and this was the thing that's lived with me ever since – to look at the aircraft that were coming in, torpedo-bombing us. They flew in at terrific speed, quite fast – much faster than the 140 mph of the Swordfish. They were so streamlined. Their pilots pressed their attacks in so strongly, and there were so many of them. They dropped their torpedoes at a far higher height than we'd never seen anything like it at all . . . You can imagine our horror and shock when we, thought we were going to have a walk-over.

Ordinary Seaman Douglas Davies
Aboard HMS **Repulse**
These aircraft came in at various heights. It was impossible really for the best of gunners to direct as to which aircraft should be shot down – the ones at sea level, the ones at 3,000 feet, 6,000, 10,000 or even 15,000 feet.

We were below in the boiler room when there was a terrific explosion. The place went dark. There was no shouting – no nothing. The men were undoubtedly dead, and yet I was still alive and able to find my way to the ladder, which led to the top deck. I got out through the air intake on top deck, but now I could just about see with one eye – the other had been burned.

I felt all alone. I saw men being mown down by aircraft coming in at sea level, as I just lay on the deck.

But in time, I was taken down below, quite a distance down in the ship, where I was given an injection of morphia. But the morphine didn't do its work as it should have. I was still dazed. So I remained, with the countless other members of the ship's company that had been injured in the A magazine. Then there were seven or eight explosions – then I heard on the tannoy, 'Prepare to abandon ship, and may God be with you.' Why the morphia hadn't worked, I'll never know, but it actually saved my life by not working. I managed to climb towards a deck where there was a porthole.

The ship was now heeling over. Countless lads were doing what I was trying to do – escape from the ship by going through a porthole. As I hit the water, everything went black. Some time later, a lifeboat came, and the lads just heaved me aboard. I was taken to an escorting destroyer – the *Express*.

I was pulled up by rope to the quarterdeck. It seems that my clothing had been burnt off completely. On looking down I could just see the tops of my shoes. The soles had been burnt off, and I think that was about the only thing that had remained – otherwise I was completely naked – severely burnt. I had also been hit by five bullets. I was given another injection of morphia – which worked – and was sent to Singapore General Hospital. I was in a very bad condition – I was unconscious for three days with double pneumonia. I had lost all my fingernails, I'd lost all my toenails. I had my ears burnt off, my back had been burnt – my legs, my feet had been severely burnt. I still don't know how I survived.

Marine Peter Dunstan
Aboard HMS **Prince of Wales**
The Navy has a traditional saying that, if a ship is launched in blood she is a hoodoo, and there was a dockyard matey killed when the *Prince of Wales* went down the slips on her launch. She was a hoodoo from then on. A week before we went on board, the Germans had dropped a bomb between the side of the ship and the dock and it burst under the boiler room, causing some flooding. After we came aboard they decided to take her across to Liverpool for patching up. We got halfway across the dock gates and she jammed. If she had gone a bit further she would have broken her back, so we didn't go into Liverpool but went straight up into Rosyth. One or two incidents happened there. While they were putting machinery up on the bridge some silly so-and-so slipped and fell the whole length of the bridge and was killed. Another jumped in the dry dock and committed suicide.

In October 1941 we were detailed off to the Far East. Every time we stuck our nose out, something happened, so if that wasn't hoodoo, I don't know what is. I don't remember much about our last battle because I was down below transferring shells from the magazines on to a slide, which went round to the guns, which were firing like mad.

When the order came to abandon ship Sergeant Brooks, who was the turret captain, lined us all up on the fo'c'sle and counted us off. Three of the gun crew were missing so we stood there while he got the three up from the magazine. Then he gave the order to jump. From where we went over the starboard bows to the water was roughly seventy feet. But as a Royal Marine you are trained to obey an order and when Sergeant Brooks said, 'Jump!' we jumped and didn't think about it.

I swam towards a cork float raft and we pushed it towards the destroyer *Express*, one of our escorts. She was tied up to the *Prince of Wales*, getting casualties off. But the *Prince* started to turn and they had to sever the ropes with axes. I remember lying on my back and hearing them shout, 'She's going!' and watching her turn over with a number of officers in white sitting on the top of the bridge as she went over. They didn't make any attempt to get off. I was pulled aboard *Express* by a big hairy stoker who gave me a tot of rum. There was a second one a short time later and altogether I had four tots by the time we got to Singapore.

Petty Officer John Gaynor
Aboard HMS **Prince of Wales**

Give the Japanese torpedo pilots their due, they pressed home their attacks. The *Repulse* was gone – she turned upside down, and down she went. By now we had begun to take a list to the port – which meant that the starboard side was coming up out of the water. All battleships, to protect their vitals, have a nice, thick, perhaps eight- or twelve-inch armoured belt stretched along where a shell is liable to strike. But if you lift the ship up, the armour belt finishes and you expose the underbelly. The Japanese pilots knew that, so in came the torpedoes – and crunched into the ship. And now she begins to settle back again. One minute she was looking like she was going over to port – then she rocked back to starboard. Then the order came from the bridge to abandon ship – and I thought, 'Oh, I've never done this before.'

As the ship gradually turned, I hung on to a ventilator, which would be about two-thirds of the way up – uphill, in other words. Then from there, as the ship gradually turned turtle, I managed to get up on the top of the ship. I'm forever climbing upwards now. The ship is turning, and I'm climbing upwards – then I walk down the ship's side – which is now horizontal, and then find myself going over a lovely curve. Now I'm on the bottom of the ship, still floating. So I sit between the two great twin keels of the ship and I look towards the stern, where I see four enormous propellers, still idly turning, though the ship is upside down. As I looked down, I see from underneath the stern that the water now is gradually coming up towards me. What I didn't realise at the time is that the ship is going down – that's why the water is coming towards me. But it's a queer sensation, to stand on something solid, to look at the water and then the water's coming towards you, like the tide coming in.

I floated on a chunk of wood until I was picked up. A lot of the people that were brought on board, with oil fuel and shock had died. They were stacking the bodies like you would firewood in rows of five – five one way, five another. I always remember gazing into the eyes of a fellow who was a messmate of mine. He was dead, but he didn't seem to have a mark on him. I felt like saying, 'What are you doing there?'

Marine Peter Dunstan
Aboard HMS Prince of Wales

After the sinking of the *Prince of Wales* and *Repulse*, and as the fighting in Malaya came closer to Singapore, we Marines were marched to the barracks of the Argyll and Sutherland Highlanders. Colonel Stewart of the Argylls stood on a soapbox on the parade ground and welcomed us, saying, 'The Royal Marines and the Argylls had fought side by side in the annals of history, and would do so again.' So we became known as the Plymouth Argylls Battalion. But about four hours later we were at fighting stations in the NAAFI. As we had lost everything when the ships went down, we had khaki jungle uniform given to us, and that was our sum total, along with a rifle or bayonet.

We did commando work up behind the Jap lines for about a week. After that we were withdrawn back to Singapore. By this time, the Japs were advancing down the north-west side of the island and they started to mortar our barracks. There was an Indian hospital alongside our barracks, which was on fire, and I was helping to evacuate it, when I caught a mortar bomb splinter in the hand and shoulder. Out east, wounds go poisonous within the hour, and my hand blew up. I was given a Bren gun, but couldn't use it. So I had to hand it over, and was sent to Singapore General Hospital. While I was there I used by good hand to help the eye surgeon.

About a week or ten days later, we were told that we had surrendered. The Japs came in and said, 'Everybody out of the hospital within forty-eight hours.' Two of my marines died the following day. I was taken up to the prisoner-of-war camp at Changi Jail. On the way we were told to line up along the road because a Japanese general's car was going to pass by. As the car passed us, I felt completely numb. At the camp, the feeling was just numbness too. We just got on with it and kept our noses clean. We thought it would not last long.

As the stricken HMS *Prince of Wales* lists dangerously following the Japanese air attack, her crew scramble for safety.

ZZZ3130C

Sergeant Terry Brooks
Royal Marines, survivor of HMS Prince of Wales

The commanding general in Singapore ordered us to surrender. I was on the Thompson Road, manning a defensive line with my lads when I surrendered, sitting there with a rifle in my hands. The Japs gave orders to form a column and march to Changi Jail over 14 miles away, which we did. The line of men was as long as the bloody trek. As a prisoner you have got nothing. You just accept the inevitable. You have had a go and you have failed, and you expect to be treated as a normal prisoner-of-war – but of course, we weren't. They tried to make us sign an undertaking not to escape, and we refused. So they put us all on the concrete parade ground until we agreed. People were beginning to die, and the officer in charge of all prisoners-of-war said, 'We'll sign it. I don't care what you put on it.' I put BM Lever on mine – breach mechanism lever. Then five months later, we went off up into the jungle. There were no losses in Changi because we were relatively fit, but our troubles began in the jungle.

Corporal Jack Sharpe
1st Batallion, Leicestershire Regiment

Before I was captured I remember the dead and dying men we were forced to leave behind as the Japanese forced us to retreat up the Malay Peninsula. I remember the hundreds of dead I saw on the streets of Singapore. We were marched to Changi and then moved to a barracks in Singapore town and ordered to sign a paper saying we would not escape. We all refused. But the conditions were like the Black Hole of Calcutta and our senior officers agreed to sign under protest because they were worried about an epidemic.

I was then transported to Thailand to the base camp at Ban Pong. The latrines there were full of great big maggots. I'd had enough. Because the Japs thought no one would escape the guards were thin on the ground. I got out of the camp and headed north but after two days I was captured by a local Thai who had a large gun like blunderbuss.

I was handed over to a Japanese lieutenant who lined me up in front of a firing squad. They cocked their rifles. I knew for certain I was going to die. Then all of a sudden a Japanese colonel arrived and struck the lieutenant in 'luiiue. They were jabbering in Japanese and I was wondering whether they were going to shoot me or not.

In the end the colonel came across and beat the living daylights out of me with his scabbard. Every time I fell he booted me and told me to get up. My hands were then tightly strapped and I was marched back to Ban Pong and handed over to a guard. He had been a frontline soldier himself and respected me. He loosened the straps, which certainly saved my hands. He gave me a puff of a cigarette. It was the last act of compassion I was to get. I was sent to the House of Cages in Bangkok. It was a stinking place full of wooden cages, about five feet by eight feet. The Japs were forever interrogating a Chinese lad in my cell. He returned from one grilling to say he'd overheard that I was to be court-martialled for trying to escape.

At the court martial I was sentenced to two years' imprisonment. I had heard before about the place I was to be sent to, and you knew no one could survive two years there. The president of the court asked me if I had anything to say. Then I told him just what I thought of the Japs and cursed them. I was sentenced to four and a half years. The president then insulted me by saying that no Japanese soldier with a body as strong as mine would allow himself to become a prisoner.

That was it. I told him that I was going to live, not only to see him surrender, but the whole of the Japanese nation – and that I would walk out of that prison on my own two feet. His insult gave me the will to live. I was then clamped into shackles and taken down by train to Singapore where I was put in Outram Road Jail. I was put into solitary confinement for 14 months.

1942

Mountbatten gave us a lecture – said he wished he was coming with us.
Once we realised where we were going – Dieppe – I think 200 blokes thought,
'I wish he were going instead of us.' But yes, very nice talk.
We cheered him – off he went.

A t the start of the year, the Axis was making advances, except on the Eastern Front. Rommel launched a major offensive in North Africa to retake Benghazi in Libya. Japanese troops surged on through the Pacific taking Borneo, Malaya, Java, New Guinea and Burma. Most significantly, American resistance in the Philippines was quashed with the surrender of Bataan and Corregidor in April and May. At the same time, such British troops as remained in Burma completed their retreat, leaving the Japanese in control.

Rallying from the harsh winter, German troops resumed their advance to Stalingrad in August.

Montgomery took command of the Eighth Army in the Western Desert in August, and immediately inflicted heavy losses on the Afrika Korps at Alam Halfa. By the end of the year, following the second battle of El Alamein, he had retaken Tobruk, and Rommel was in retreat.

Despite Japanese advances bringing them within range to launch bombing raids on Darwin in Australia, the Australian troops finally halted their drive through New Guinea and British troops re-entered Burma to resume the fight at Arakan.

No solution had been found to the menace of the U-boat packs in the Atlantic, and in February the battle cruisers *Scharnhorst*, *Prinz Eugen* and *Gneisenau* broke out from the harbour at Brest in what became known as 'the Channel Dash'.

The other continuing feature of the war that was stepped up in 1942 was the bombing of Germany. Regular raids had been quite effective in destroying industrial targets and hampering production, but on 22

February Air Marshal 'Bomber' Harris was appointed Commander-in-Chief, Bomber Command, and in May the first contingent of the US 8th Air Force of the United States Army Air Force (USAAF) arrived in England.

MALTA

Malta was an important Mediterranean base and German and Italian aircraft launched repeated attacks on convoys bringing food, supplies, troops, fuel and, vitally, aircraft, to the besieged island. The squadrons of the RAF tasked with defending the island were desperately short of aircraft and fuel – and the people, many taking refuge in caves to escape the bombing, were driven to the point of starvation. The island was left very vulnerable following the sinking of the aircraft carrier *Ark Royal*, which had been patrolling the Mediterranean, and in December 1941 mines sank one British cruiser and one destroyer, leaving two cruisers damaged. Supply ships simply could not run the gauntlet of the Strait of Gibraltar, and Malta's situation by the end of the year was desperate, and was only relieved in spring of 1942 when, with American help, Operation Pedestal lifted the siege and Hitler postponed his invasion plans indefinitely. The fortitude of the islanders was recognised by the award of the George Cross.

Squadron Leader 'Laddie' Lucas
249 Squadron, RAF
It is only a small island, the size of the Isle of Wight, but from its strategic position, anyone could see that if we lost Malta in the spring of 1942, then the effect, not only on the Western Desert, but also on the landings in north-west Africa, was going to be serious.

It is also absolutely clear that Hitler, in February 1942, was agreeing that 'Herkules' – the invasion of Malta – should go ahead. The German and Italian General Staffs wanted it, and Field Marshal Albert Kesselring, C-in-C South, in command of the Axis air force in Sicily, got this undertaking from the Führer that the invasion order would go ahead. But Hitler got cold feet – he had lost a lot of people invading Crete, and thought he was going to lose a lot more in Malta. He was very doubtful of the ability of the Italian Navy to take on the British Navy, and he was probably quite right over that. So basically, he fluffed it. As a result, the Germans then decided that they would saturate

Malta, the three airfields, Grand Harbour and the rest – just try to starve it out and bomb it out.

The moment the Germans had to shift some elements of the air force from Sicily to the Eastern Front, on to Crete and to the Western Desert, Malta got a respite and the recuperative powers of the island were such that they could establish strike squadrons again. This was the key. If the Germans had invaded Malta, then the course of the North Africa campaign would have been radically different.

From the Allies' point of view, of course, in order to be able to hold Malta, we had to win the fighter battle. If we didn't win the fighter battle, then all the rest of it would simply go for naught.

Able Seaman Eric Beasley
Stoker aboard HMS Penelope

It seemed to us that they were bombing Malta in squares – obliterating everything. The dockyard was the prime target. In the first raids, a floating dock and an oiler tied up alongside the jetty were sunk. A destroyer that had come in with us in the convoy was sunk immediately astern of us. This was in the first raids.

Squadron Leader 'Laddie' Lucas
249 Squadron, RAF

The question was, how could we get enough Spitfires into the island? We had HMS *Eagle*, but to begin with, we could only fly fifteen or sixteen aeroplanes off that carrier, but as soon as they got into Malta, due to unserviceability or numbers lost in the air or on the ground, this simply was not enough. So in the end, Churchill, in a deal with Roosevelt, got the use of the massive American carrier, USS *Wasp*. This turned the battle, there's no doubt about it. The first fly-offs from the *Wasp* involved two squadrons, 601 and 603. They were loaded on to the carrier up in Greenock on the Clyde, with their 48 aeroplanes. One of them was cannibalised for spares, and they flew 47 off on the 20th April 1942. After going through the Strait of Gibraltar to a point roughly 300 miles out and about 700 miles west of Malta, they flew them off and 46 landed on the island. One, flown by an American, deserted. Of course, the German, under Kesselring, had monitored these aeroplanes all the way down the Med – they were ready for them when they came in and landed.

The turnaround arrangements on the island were then very poor, mainly because there had been too much secrecy and not enough detailed preparation. So within forty-eight hours, we had only seven serviceable

Spitfires left out of the 46 that had landed. This was the most terrible thing – the absolute nadir of our fortunes.

Somehow or other, Churchill persuaded Roosevelt to let the *Wasp* have another go, and she went back up to Greenock and loaded up with 48 more aeroplanes and, this time, first-class pilots. Mostly they came from No. 11 Group in Fighter Command, whereas most of the others from 601 and 603 had really not had much operational experience. Five of us, all experienced Malta pilots, were sent back to Gibraltar, to lead these aeroplanes in. USS *Wasp* and HMS *Eagle* joined up together at Gib, sailed east down the Med for about 300 miles, to a point 50 miles north of Algiers, and some 650 miles west of Malta. From there they flew off together, and got 64 aeroplanes in. *Eagle* turned round at once, came back to Gib and loaded up again with another 17 aeroplanes. So in a matter of twelve days, we flew in nearly 80 aeroplanes. After that, it was 'never glad confident morning again' for the Luftwaffe. That was the turning point of the battle for Malta. From then on, although there were some really fearsome battles right up to October 1942, the Germans never had the ascendancy that they had enjoyed before. That was really when the Battle of Malta was won.

When we shot the Germans and Italians down, we used to go and see them in hospital at Imtarfa – but one day I stopped the squadron from doing it. It was at the beginning of July, and I was nearing the end of my time with the squadron. There was a raid, and Woodall was controlling it. He'd talked this raid through, giving us a brilliant running commentary. There were three Italian bombers in a tight V formation, with a great beehive of fighter escorts – about 80 plus Me109s and Macchi 202s – and the whole ideas was that the bombers were decoys. There were ten of us – I had a four, Raoul Daddo-Langlois had a four, and the New Zealander, Jack Rae, was leading his pair of two. We were flying in line-abreast, as we always did. Woodall had got us into this marvellous position, up-sun, and at about 26,000 feet. I had pushed the thing up another 2,000 because you never lost anything by having excess height. Bader always had this piece of doggerel that he used to recite, 'He who has the sun creates surprise. He who has the height controls the battle. He who gets in close shoots them down.'

We were now about 5,000 or 6,000 feet above these fellows, so I said to my guys, 'Look we've got bags of height – we've got the sun, but there are a lot of 109s about, so we'll go straight through the lot of them, and have a go at the three bombers. After that, go straight down to the deck.' We went steaming into these bloody things. I had a go at the bomber on the left and saw it disintegrate, going down in flames. I saw Raoul's go falling away, and then

'Laddie' Lucas. During the siege of Malta, the charismatic Lucas commanded 249 Squadron, based at Takali. It was a triumph for the RAF defenders that aircraft were eventually delivered to the island, which, in turn, would protect the convoys bringing food, fuel and ammunition to the stricken island.

Jack came through and knocked out the bomber in the middle. All three of them went down in flames, then I said, 'Now roll on to your backs, fellers, and go down to the deck. There are far too many 109s about to stay and mix it.' So we went down and landed at Takali.

The next day, I took two or three of the fellows who had been flying that day, plus one of the chaps from headquarters who could speak Italian, to the hospital where all the Italians who had baled out were in bed. I walked across to the bed on the left of the ward, and there was this good-looking young Italian with his arm all bandaged up. The interpreter said to him, 'This is the CO of the squadron which shot your aeroplanes down, and these are some of the rest of the squadron.' And this young Italian, who couldn't speak English, held up his hand and said, through the interpreter, 'I have lost my hand.' It made me feel terrible. Then the interpreter asked him, 'What did you do in peacetime?' and the boy just said, 'I was a professional violinist.' I said to the chaps, 'I'm going to go out now,' and I waited for them until they had finished talking to the Italians. Then I said to them, 'Look here, we are never going to visit these wounded prisoners in hospital again when there is an emotive injury or wound. It is so terrible and bad for morale. I can't stand it.' For weeks after, long after I'd come back from Malta, I used to wake up in the middle of the night, thinking about it. It was a dreadful thing, because I had no feeling of hate for these people.

The last vital element that should be mentioned about Malta is that the island obviously depended, for its supplies, on what the convoys could bring in. And because everyone was always hungry, this spectre of starvation was always there. In my time, from February to the end of July 1942, the Navy tried to run through four seaborne convoys. The February convoy from Alexandria had to turn back as it was going through Bomb Alley, between Crete and the Libyan coast – the narrows there were the most terrible place. The Germans were bombing it from Crete and Libya. In March, the convoy with *Breconshire*, *Pampas* and *Talabot*, came from Alexandria. As it approached Malta, there was very low cloud – a mistral really – with wind and rain, and it was absolutely made for the Germans to go darting in and out as they attacked the ships. *Pampas* and *Talabot* made Grand Harbour, but as soon as they were in, they got bombed, and that was that. *Breconshire* had to be towed in and beached. Then she was bombed. They got a certain amount of stuff off the ships – probably about 5,000 or 6,000 tons – before they were sunk, but not much more. So that was the March convoy.

We were getting pretty low. Food really was beginning to get short, morale was beginning to fall, and the civilians were having their belts pulled in by the fortnight. The next attempt was in June. There were two convoys. They had this idea that if they ran two convoys together, one from Gibraltar and the other from Alexandria, it would divide the Germans' and the Italians' attacking strength. The one from the east, from Alexandria, when it was going through Bomb Alley, spotted the Italian fleet coming down from the north-east, so they were forced to turn round and go back. That was awful. The one from Gibraltar had started out with six merchant ships and in the end only two got into Grand Harbour. It was the most terrible fight. We could see a third, the US oiler *Kentucky*, which we so badly wanted, sunk as it approached the final run-in. Of the two which reached Grand Harbour, quite a lot of stuff was unloaded – enough to keep us going until August, when the '*Santa Maria*' or '*Pedestal*' convoy fought its way through.

Francesco Cavalera
Italian officer, 51st AIR Group, Italian Air Force
On the 12th or 13th of August the British were trying to get a convoy through from Gibraltar to Malta, it was a very big convoy with many ships and many planes. All of our group, 64 aircraft took off together to engage them.

During the operation we were attacked by a formation of Spitfires, my leader made a turn so hard that because of the acceleration I got as his interior wing man, I lost my vision, I saw black, and when I could see clear I realised that I was alone, all the aircraft in my formation had gone, I didn't want to leave because I didn't want people to think it was for fear, I was lucky and nobody fired on me, but eventually I looked at my fuel and it was very little so I returned to base.

Lieutenant-Commander Roger Hill
Aboard Hunt-class destroyer HMS **Ledbury**
Operation *Pedestal* was the last all-out attempt to get a convoy of merchant ships through to Malta. Their food was running out and they had no aviation fuel, no submarine diesel and nothing for the dockyard. Malta had virtually come to a halt.

If the convoy failed, Malta would have to surrender. The Governor of Malta, Lord Gort, said to me, 'You can make the garrison eat their belts, but the 300,000 civilians have to be fed or evacuated.'

The convoy of over 50 ships left Gibraltar on the 9th August 1942. Thirteen merchant ships and the 10,000-ton Texaco tanker *Ohio* steamed in four columns. They were all big, fast ships, and the speed of the convoy was 15 knots. Around them was a screen of 26 destroyers. Close round the convoy were the anti-aircraft destroyers, like my *Ledbury*, and the battleships *Nelson* and *Rodney* – each of which had nine 16-inch guns – steamed astern of the two outside columns. The anti-aircraft ship *Cairo* had a roving commission near the convoy and *Jaunty*, an ocean tug, followed along behind.

Three aircraft carriers, *Victorious*, *Indomitable* and *Eagle*, followed the convoy inside the destroyer screen. They carried a total of 72 fighters and were constantly altering course into the wind to fly off and land on the patrols. The cruisers *Sirius*, *Phoebe* and *Charybdis* careered about, keeping an anti-aircraft guard on the carriers. There was also an old aircraft-carrier, *Furious*, with her own destroyer screen, whose job it was to fly off 38 Spitfires when we were about 500 miles from Malta, as reinforcements for Malta's depleted squadrons.

As we approached down the Mediterranean, we were entering a cauldron of attack. Crete and Greece were in German hands, and would be used for air attack – then the long toe of Italy, Sardinia and Sicily was all aerodromes. About 20 submarines and 40 E-boats were also waiting for us. It was just like another Charge of the Light Brigade.

Leading Seaman Donald Auffret
Wireless operator, Royal Navy, aboard HMS **Warspite**
We passed through the Strait of Gibraltar at night, and then twenty-four hours into the Mediterranean the air attacks started, and it was almost continuous. The first ship we lost was the *Eagle*. She was torpedoed by a German U-boat. I remember seeing the planes that were on the flight decks slipping off. She went down in eight and a half minutes.

Captain Dudley Mason
Aboard Texaco oil tanker Ohio
At 0700 on the 13th August we caught up with the convoy after being led through the night by the *Ledbury*. The convoy was now in two columns, our position being at the end of the line, owing to our defective steering. At 0800 the heavy bombing attacks started again. We sustained many near-misses, but there seemed to be no damage to the ship. Then the *Waimarama* had a direct bomb hit and blew up. The *Melbourne Star*, following her, could not avoid the flames, and steamed right through them. The *Ohio* just managed to clear the edge of the flames by going hard to port.

During these attacks we were constantly receiving orders by wireless to make 45 degree emergency turns. It was quite impossible to execute these in the time given. These orders were also transmitted over the radio telephone, and the wireless orders were always several seconds behind, thus causing misunderstanding and confusion.

At about 0900, a Junkers 88 crashed into the sea close to our bow and bounced on to our foredeck, making a terrific crash and throwing masses of debris into the air. A little later, the chief officer telephoned me from aft in great excitement to say that a Stuka had landed on the poop. Apparently this plane had also fallen into the sea and bounced on to our ship. I was rather tired, having been on the bridge all night, and I'm afraid I answered him rather curtly, saying, 'Oh, that's nothing. We've had a Junkers 88 on the foredeck for nearly half an hour.'

At about the same time, a near-miss right under our fore-foot opened up the port and starboard bow tanks, buckled the plating and flooded the forepeak tank. The Ohio vibrated violently forward to aft, amidst an absolute deluge of water.

Despite these problems, we were making good headway. The weather was fine, with good visibility, smooth sea and light airs, and we were steaming at 13 knots, steering approximately east. At 1000, when we were 100 miles west of Malta, a large plane flew right over us at about 2,000 feet, banked slightly and dropped a salvo of six bombs, three falling close to the port side and three close to the starboard side. The Ohio was lifted right out of the water and shook violently from stem to stern. Then the Dorset was hit by bombs at about the same time.

At 1030, the main engines stopped as the two electric fuel pumps were out of commission. The steam pump remained intact, but it was practically impossible to keep the vacuum with this one pump. We managed to get the main engines going again, as there was only a little water in the engine-room, but we could only do about three to four knots. Then one of the boilers blew out and extinguished the fires. Enemy planes continued to bomb, but our gunners and crew kept up a deadly and accurate barrage, and no further damage was done.

Ledbury offered to take us in tow, and we reckoned that with our own power we would be able to make 12 knots. But at 1045, the second boiler blew out, extinguishing the remaining fires, and the vessel stopped. The Ledbury then signalled that she had to leave us to go to the assistance of the cruiser Manchester. Bombing was still going on.

At 1130 the Penn came alongside and we gave her a 10-inch manilla tow rope from forward, but the attempt to tow from ahead was hopeless, as the ship just turned in circles, finally parting the tow-rope. I signalled to the Penn that the only hope of towing the Ohio was from alongside, or with one ahead and one astern to steady the ship. We were still being bombed while stopped, so I asked the *Penn* to take off my crew until more assistance was available.

At 1800 two motor launches and a minesweeper, *Rye*, came out from Malta to assist us. I called for a small number of volunteers to return to the *Ohio* to make the tow ropes fast, but the whole crew voluntarily returned. The tow ropes were made fast to *Penn* and *Rye*, both towing ahead. The bombing attacks were still going on, and at approximately 1830 a plane dropped a bomb directly on the fore part of the boat deck, which passed right through the accommodation into the engine-room, exploding on the boiler taps. It made a shambles of the after-accommodation and the boiler-room, and the crew were blinded and choked by the powder from the asbestos lagging.

Captain Eddie Baines
Aboard Hunt-class destroyer HMS Bramham

On the 12th August the bombing started in a big way and at around 1300 the *Deucalion*, one of the merchant ships, got hit by one bomb and had a near-miss with two others. She was not vitally damaged but she came to a halt because she was making water and they wanted to see what was wrong with her. *Bramham* was a 'rescue' ship so we came up alongside her.

We were greeted by the sight of the *Deucalion*'s boats being lowered in great panic and people tumbling into them and rowing over to us. The officers and particularly the captain standing on her bridge were absolutely apoplectic with rage and he was shouting, 'Send the boats back!' which I would have done, anyway.

So when the boats came alongside our scrambling nets, we jumped on the men's knuckles as they came up over the edge. They called us a few choice names but we invited them to choose: either they could get back into their boats and stay there or go back to the *Deucalion*. So they thought better of it, recovered their nerve and returned on board.

Deucalion now could only make 13.5 knots, so we were ordered to escort her to Malta by what was known as the inshore route, along the coast of North Africa. It was just as unpleasant on the inshore route as anywhere else and we got bombed on the way. Then at dusk a couple of torpedo-bombers came out of the murk and popped a torpedo into *Deucalion* and blew a bloody great hole in her stern. She was burning down below and there was obviously no hope for her, so the captain gave the order to abandon ship.

Then we had to sink her by going up close and dropping depth-charges. We didn't want her to get picked up by the enemy as a propaganda prize. The scare was that she would blow up as we went alongside, as all the merchant

After the attrition of the Pedestal convoy, the *Ohio*, severely damaged and sitting very low in the water, limps into Malta's Grand Harbour.

ships were carrying high-octane aero spirit and huge amounts of ammunition. She seemed to be settling by the stem so I left her, and when we'd been steaming at 23 knots for about an hour, I saw an explosion astern and it was the *Deucalion* blowing up.

I was standing by the damaged *Dorset* when, about three or four miles away, I saw the problems that people were having with the poor old *Ohio*. The *Penn* and the *Rye*, a minesweeper that had come out from Malta, were trying to get the *Ohio* moving and I could see without even using my binoculars that they had got it all arse about face and really were not achieving much.

Then the *Dorset* was sunk and after picking up the survivors I made my way over to the *Ohio*.

I went up to the *Penn* and said to him over the loud hailer, 'Wouldn't it be a much better idea to tow with one destroyer on either side rather than one ahead and one on the stern?' He agreed and decided that, come dusk, we would do that.

At about one o'clock in the morning I went to the starboard side of the tanker and *Penn* went on the port side. Unfortunately, on the port side of the ship there were some big flanges sticking out which had been blown out by a torpedo. The *Penn* was bigger than my *Bramham* and his stern overlapped this flange. He was very frightened that he would damage his own ship by bashing it against this flange, so he said he was going to cast off. I said, 'Look, can't we stay put and get on with it? The sooner we get to Malta the better.' But he said he didn't want to get to Malta with a ship with just one screw. I saw his point, so we both cast off.

At first light *Ledbury* arrived back from her search for *Manchester* and offered her assistance. I went alongside the port side and positioned myself so the flange was clear of my stern. *Penn* went to the starboard side and so we secured and made tracks for Malta.

Through trial and error we discovered that if the *Ohio* took a swing to starboard the *Penn* should increase speed by a third of a knot which would very slowly check that swing and would bring her back again. And the swing would go past the right course and come towards my way so then I would increase speed slightly. So in fact, the actual course was a zig-zag, but it worked extraordinarily well.

At 0900 a bomb holed the tanker aft and she started sinking. By this time the remaining merchant ships in the convoy, the *Port Chalmers*, *Rochester Castle* and *Melbourne Star*, had safely reached Malta with their escorts, leaving us poor sods with this old crock, tied together with cobwebs, sinking slowly in the middle of the sea.

Lieutenant-Commander Roger Hill
Aboard Hunt-class destroyer HMS Ledbury

On the morning of the 14th August we headed towards where we thought the *Ohio* would be, but she was much further behind the rest of the convoy than I had expected. We found her in the company of *Rye*, a minesweeper which had come out from Malta, *Penn* and *Bramham*. *Ohio*'s boilers had blown up and there was no hope of getting her engines going. So we had three destroyers and a minesweeper circling around the damaged tanker, whose cargo was intact and Malta less than a hundred miles away.

It was absolutely vital to get the tanker to Malta but the difficulties were immense. She was slowly sinking and she had this great big plate sticking out and, as you tried to tow her, she turned to port all the time. I put a wire on to her quarter and when they tried to tow her I pulled on this wire to try and keep her straight, but I put too much power on and the wire broke. So then I went and took her in tow with a big manilla rope. *Rye* took a line from my fo'c'sle to keep my bows up. *Penn* lashed herself to the *Ohio*'s side to keep her straight. This was fine and we were off, making about two knots.

Then a crowd of nine dive-bombers came screaming down at us. It was horrible to be held by tow ropes at each end, moving at two knots and quite unable to dodge. We all lay down on the bridge as a 500 lb bomb whistled over the top of the bridge and splashed alongside the fo'c'sle. Luckily for us, it did not explode; it was an oil bomb, designed to set the tanker on fire. *Ohio* had a near-hit in the raid and started to settle by the stern.

When the attack was over, we were in confusion. The *Ohio* and *Penn* were pointing towards Malta and *Ledbury* and *Rye* were pointing in the opposite direction. The chaos of wires, ropes and cables hanging down into the sea had to be seen to be believed.

We finally got ourselves disentangled and then *Bramham* lashed herself on the port side of *Ohio* and, by shouting to each other, she and the *Penn* got the *Ohio* moving and kept her on the right course. The destroyers alongside were about half the length of the tanker and she was very unwieldy. When she swung badly I put my bows against her and pushed her round.

The afternoon dragged by slowly and we longed for darkness when there would be no more threat of attack from the air. I felt if we had any more bombs around I would lie down on the deck and burst into tears. That evening at dusk we spotted the cliffs on the south side of Malta. All the sailors and survivors on deck cheered at the sight. Now we only had our own minefields to get through and perhaps an E-boat attack to face in the night. We stayed at action stations all night with permission for everyone to sleep except the man on the phone.

In the night there was quite a circus act. A tug came out from Malta with masses of people on her bridge all shouting at once. Then she rammed *Penn*, made a hole in her wardroom and disappeared into the night.

During the night *Ohio* made several attempts to blow herself up on our minefields as she swung off course, but each time the destroyers alongside pulled her up and I gave her a push in the right direction. As we were pushing her round the last point for the run to Valletta, the coastal defence opened fire. They thought they had spotted E-boats. We made signals to try and stop them firing but they kept on. So eventually I got a big light flashing and I said, 'For Christ's sake, stop firing at us!' and they stopped.

In the early morning, as we approached Malta, I walked round the ship and looked at the sleeping members of my crew. They were lying in duffle coats, one head on another chap's tummy, faces all sunburnt and lined with the strain of the last few days. I felt proud of them, and grateful we had got through it all without a single casualty. The pom-pom's crew were closed up and ready, training their guns. I climbed up and said, 'Good morning, aren't you going to get any sleep?' and they said, 'Oh no, please sir, just one more attack, can't we have one more attack?' I said, 'Christ almighty, haven't you had enough attacks?' They were great people.

At daylight we came round the corner to the entrance to the Grand Harbour. I pushed the *Ohio* round with my bows and followed her in. It was the most wonderful moment of my life. The battlements of Malta were black with thousands of people, all cheering and shouting and there were bands playing everywhere. It was the most amazing sight to see all these people who had suffered so much, cheering us.

The *Ohio* was pushed by tugs to the wharf to discharge her oil. Her stern was so low now that water was washing over her after deck. Within five minutes they were pumping her out in case she was sunk by enemy bombing.

We berthed the *Ledbury* in the French creek. I went quickly around the ship, looked in on the wounded, then got some dope from Doc, took off my clothes and then, oh boy, did I sleep.

THE CHANNEL DASH

No solution had been found to the menace of the U-boat packs in the Atlantic, and in February the *Scharnhorst*, *Prinz Eugen* and *Gneisenau* broke out from the harbour at Brest in what became known as 'the Channel Dash', with the intention of making for Germany to Allied shipping. Both

Scharnhorst and *Gneisenau* were damaged in the 'Dash' and put out of action for months. Despite the best efforts of the Royal Navy and RAF, bad weather conditions favoured the German battle cruisers, and the aircraft which had been called to give chase suffered severe damage.

Sergeant Robin Murray
214 Squadron, RAF

It was a cold day on the 12th February – overcast, 10/10ths cloud – and from 9,000 feet down to about 900 feet was solid cloud, snow cloud. We took off in our Wellington, and flew out on course – but we didn't see a thing because of the cloud. Then we iced up very badly. The port engine packed up, and after about twenty minutes, part of the propeller broke away – came through the side of the aircraft and damaged the hydraulics. We eventually came down in the sea at about a quarter to five in the evening.

When we hit, the Perspex area behind the front turret broke and the wave took me right back up against the main spar. I came to underwater, pulled myself along on the geodetics and came up by the pilot's controls. There were four of them already in the dinghy, which was still attached to the wing. I was the last one in. We'd lost Flight Lieutenant Hughes and George Taylor. We paddled around with our hands looking for them, and Andy Everett swam round to the turret which was under water, because the plane had broken its back just behind the main spar – but it was no good. I had swallowed a lot of salt water and was very sick. We were all sopping wet. We made ourselves as comfortable as we could. There were five of us in the dinghy – McFadden, Stephens, Wood, Everett and myself.

For the first few hours there was nothing around – just the sea. It was quite choppy, and that was uncomfortable. Unfortunately, whoever had put the rations in the dinghy had forgotten the tin opener, so we couldn't open the tins. Then the knife fell overboard, so we didn't have that either. So all we had was Horlicks Malted Milk tablets. It was cold – the coldest winter for nearly a century.

We were hoping that someone would come out and pick us up, because the wireless operator had sent out a Mayday signal – but what none of us realised was that the navigator must have got his co-ordinates wrong. We had done a 180 degree turn, and we were heading out to sea again, so we landed off the Frisian Islands instead of, as we thought, 20 miles off Orford Ness.

I had read about how you mustn't go into a deep sleep when you're cold, because you get hypothermia and that's it – you die. So I suggested that we

Robin Murray was one of five crew members left in a dinghy after ditching their Wellington bomber in the Atlantic. Three days later, when he finally reached shore, he was the sole survivor.

always had two people awake so that we didn't all go right off into a deep sleep – and that's what we tried to do.

Everyone survived the first night. We thought that any moment somebody was going to pick us up. We saw quite a few aircraft flying very high – unrecognisable, of course. There were flares on the dinghy, but we didn't see any aircraft that was low enough to have seen us. Once we thought we saw a ship – that was on the second day. We set off a flare, but nothing happened, and we tried to send off another. But it wouldn't work – it was damp. None of the flares worked at all after that. We saw quite a few aircraft that evening, just before dusk, flying very high. We came to the conclusion they were probably German.

We hadn't got a paddle on board – we were just sitting there. It was very strange, because people just went into a coma. They just sort of lost themselves. Stephens went first, on the second day at four o'clock.

That second night was very cold. We just talked about various things. There was no despondency – we never thought we weren't going to be picked up.

At dawn of that morning, Wing Commander McFadden died. There were no visible signs of injury. McFadden was firmly under the impression in his last hours that he was in his car, driving from the hangars back to the mess. He was the only one who got delirious in that way. People sort of went into a coma. They would be talking quite normally – and they would gradually drowse off. You'd shake them to try to keep them awake, but they'd gone. You could feel that they were going. But it was peaceful – there was no suffering at all. They weren't in pain – they just quietly died.

Pilot Officer Woods died about three hours after Wing Commander McFadden. He was very quiet. Finally, Sergeant Everett died at dawn. I was disappointed that he had gone so quickly. He went while he was talking – just drifted off. I kept them all on the dinghy, and was able to keep my legs out of the water by resting them on them. It sounds terrible, but by this time they were beyond help.

The final morning was the worst time, because we drifted in towards land. The water was as calm as a millpond, and the cliffs were about 150 yards away, with a gun emplacement on the top. It was about eleven o'clock, I suppose, by the time I drifted into the shore. I got a tin lid and caught the sun, and somebody came out of the gun emplacement.

Then the tide started to go out. I was starting to drift out to sea. That was a bad moment. Then a German Marine Police boat with a Red Cross came out and they hauled me aboard. I was able to stand up, and they got me on to the deck. They tied the dinghy on the back with the bodies of my crew and came slowly back.

They took me into Flushing dock. I'll never forget that moment – the deck was above the quay, and they put a ramp down, and as I walked down the ramp to the ambulance, there were five or six German sailors there, and they all came to attention and saluted me.

RAIDS ON OCCUPIED FRANCE

Hitler's 'Nacht und Nebel' (Night and Fog) decree cleared the way for his troops and the SS to eliminate without trial anyone 'endangering German security' – but despite the dangers of expressing any opposition, there was resistance. The British Special Operations Executive (SOE) assisted the French in setting up a network of circuits that would help prepare the ground when the time came for the liberation of France and the rest of occupied Europe.

In Scotland, selected soldiers underwent rigorous commando training to prepare them for special missions – the first of which was a raid on the northern French coast to capture the Würzburg radar set from Bruneval. This raid on 28 February was a great success for the paras, and a month later a combined naval and commando raid succeeded in destroying the dry dock at St Nazaire. This was the only dock on the French coast capable of accommodating the mighty Tirpitz, and disabling it would severely curtail the battleship's operations. On 28 March, 18 small coastal assault craft accompanied the veteran US destroyer HMS Campbeltown on a ram-raiding mission. The Campbeltown, packed with explosives, rammed the dock gates at dawn and the commandos on board rushed to destroy the gate-opening gear for the submarine pens. Despite the element of surprise, German resistance was savage and of the 611 commandos who took part, 185 British troops were killed and over 200 taken prisoner. Senior German officers arrived to inspect the damage to the dock and were accompanied by two commando officers who had been taken prisoner. Aware of the explosives about to detonate, they remained silent and died as the massive explosion shattered the dock gates and sent the remains of the Campbeltown halfway down the dock.

The raid had been a success – but a costly one. The next, more ambitious raid cost more than a thousand lives. Five thousand Canadians and a thousand British and American Rangers took part in an amphibious raid on Dieppe – the largest such raid of the war – on 19 August.

Supported by 237 warships and landing craft, and 69 squadrons of aircraft, two battalions were to land to either side of the main port, and then tanks would land in the main, central assault, covered by fire from eight destroyers offshore. The plan was for army commandos to take out the coastal batteries and marine commandos to attack the harbour, destroying military installations and gathering vital intelligence and taking prisoners for questioning.

One of the initial side landings was delayed, and the Canadians remained pinned down under fire on the beach. The other side landing was made at the wrong place, and only one battalion advanced inland. The main assault was a disaster. The destroyers failed to silence the guns and as the tanks struggled over the shingle, they came under heavy fire. The infantry on the beach also suffered heavy casualties and the Royal Marine Commandos, prevented from even attempting their role, went instead to the aid of one of the infantry battalions. All the marines who landed on the beach were either killed or taken prisoner. Official reports recorded that a radio beacon station and a flak battery had been destroyed, along with a six-gun battery and an ammunition dump, and that it had been a valuable exercise in the deployment of substantial numbers of troops in an assault, and in the transport and use of heavy equipment during combined operations. The raid gave a clear sign that the Allies were far from ready to land in occupied France.

SAINT NAZAIRE

Sergeant Robert Barron
No. 2 Commando
After we left Falmouth, the sea journey was calm and pleasant. I was with Captain Hodson's assault party on Motor Launch 341. We were third in line on the port side column but we broke down some time before our rendezvous with the submarine *Sturgeon* so we had to transfer to Motor Launch 446. We fell behind but the captain put on full speed and we tore through the night with sparks coming from the funnel and we caught up the convoy at the entrance to the River Loire. From then on, the atmosphere was tense. It wasn't too dark as we sailed up the river. I no could see the outlines of the shores. Everyone was ready for action. There was no opposition from the defences except for the odd searchlight and some sporadic gunfire until suddenly everything opened up when they realised we were an enemy force. The searchlights along the banks lit us up like a stage show and gunfire was

coming from all sides. It was fantastic the amount of fire and noise, the coloured tracer, it was like a firework display. I was using an anti-tank gun to fire at the searchlights. I may have put one out of action. Then we had a direct hit on our funnel area behind me. I was wounded in the foot and leg. During all the activity, I was unaware that the captain of the motor launch had missed the mole entrance where we were due to land and assault the two flak positions on the east jetty. Subsequently, the captain decided to withdraw down river. This again was a hazardous time as were running the gauntlet of fire from the riverbanks.

We were lucky to get out of the river and find the destroyer *Tynedale* in the entrance on which we were transferred and came back to Plymouth

Captain Robert Montgomery
Royal Engineers, attached to No. 2 Commando

All the officers were called together by Lieutenant-Colonel Charles Newman. We all went down and Charles was there with a model and a blackboard and he told us that a raid was on. He didn't say where the raid was going but as soon as I saw the model, I knew exactly where. A day or two later, all the soldiers were briefed as well. Newman had been told that if anyone had any reason for not going, they would be given the chance of opting out and no-one would think any the worse of them, as the chances were that we weren't going to come back. Newman asked if anyone wanted to fall out and there was not single voice raised. I went over to HMS *Campbeltown* and I was called in by Newman to have a look at some air photos, which showed the five German destroyers in the Loire. That was a slight worry. He also said that the *Tirpitz* had started moving up the Norwegian fjords, which made the dry dock the priority target, and if we hadn't finished the job when the re-embarkation took place, we were to remain behind and make certain it was done.

My party on the *Campbeltown* were the ones who were going to do the dry dock demolitions. One team was responsible for the demolitions in the pumping station, another for the winding station at the seaward end of the dry dock, another for blowing the gate at the seaward end of the dry dock in the event that the *Campbeltown* did not hit it fair and square. Those were the three parties at the seaward end of the dry dock. There were two parties who were going to operate at the other end of the dry dock, one which was to attack the winding station and the other was to blow the caisson gate. There were a number of other demolition parties with the job of destroying all the other dock machinery and installations. Each block of demolition parties had a protection party supplied by 2 Commando. These normally consisted of an officer and four Tommy gunners. There were also assault parties whose job it was to hold the perimeter of the area in which we were carrying out the demolitions. All of these parties were to be carried on HMS *Campbeltown*.

Just before we set off on the *Campbeltown*, I went down to the petty officers mess to see that the sergeants were all right and I was met by the chief bosun who gave me a large glass of Navy rum, saying 'Have this, sir, it'll give you your sea legs.' It was pretty powerful stuff. People had begun to realise fairly early on that the *Campbeltown* wasn't intended to come back but that it had been victualled for a trip to Gibraltar as part of its cover plan. So there were lots of goodies on board that we hadn't seen very much of, like butter and bacon and chocolate. When the chaps went to the canteen to ask for a Mars bar and the man running the canteen gave them a crateful, they thought they were in heaven.

One of the big parts of the raid was for the *Campbeltown* to hit the harbour gate. She would then be blown up hours later with delay-action fuses. So in her front end was a chamber which was filled with depth charges – about 450 lbs of explosive – and they had been put in a steel tank and concreted round. The captain actually held a sherry party at lunchtime as we were on our way into action. In the afternoon, we tried to get a bit of sleep, went through the dress rehearsal and then after dark we met up with HMS *Sturgeon*.

We then went to action stations. My job was liaison officer between commandos and the captain, so I was with the captain on the top bridge. We suddenly began to slow down and we heard a lot of churning and we realised we'd hit the top of a sandbank. We looked at each other but luckily she cleared. If we'd got stuck we'd have been a sitting duck. As we came up the Loire, we saw searchlights and heard British bombers overhead, but there was no sign of any bombs. A bombing raid was supposed to coincide with our ground-level raid in order to keep the German guns firing into the air and paying less attention to the river. In fact, the RAF pilots had not been told about our raid. Their orders were not to drop their bombs unless they could see their target – which they couldn't, so all they did was to wake up the gun crews and then disappear.

Petty Officer James Laurie
Wireless telegraphist aboard Motor Launch 192

On the way across to St Nazaire we had masqueraded as a German anti-submarine striking force, just out on patrol. In fact, we were flying a swastika. The *Campbeltown* destroyer had been altered to look like one of the German Moewe-class destroyers, and we got away with it. We bluffed our way up the estuary. Signals were exchanged with the German shore batteries by the signalmen on the bridge of the *Campbeltown*, coming with casualties, requesting ambulance assistance and so on. It worked for a minute or two. We were almost in the mouth of the river Loire when the Germans saw through the disguise. We hauled down our swastikas, hauled up our white ensigns and from there on it was into battle.

Captain Robert Montgomery
Royal Engineers, attached to No. 2 Commando

The shooting started rather slowly, but pretty soon all hell broke loose. There was banging and crashing and lights and tracer. The bridge was hit and the coxswain was killed, so another naval rating took the wheel and then he too fell away. I seemed to be the next in line, so I grabbed the wheel but I wasn't very certain what to do with it. I desperately tried to remember which way to turn it for port and starboard, but luckily at that moment someone else took it away from me.

The searchlights came in handy because they showed us we were fast approaching the lighthouse on the old mole and we were able to change course right away. If we hadn't seen that, we might well have rammed the mole rather than the gate. Soon, we hit the gate with an almighty crunch which threw me back against the bridge. The assault parties immediately began clambering off the front end. It was quite a game climbing down the ladder as there was a fire blazing in the fo'c'sle. Corporal Calloway's trousers caught fire as he climbed down and he had to take them off. He carried out the whole operation in his underpants.

I followed Chant, who'd been hit in the hand, and when he got to the door of the pumping station he found it locked. I had a six-inch-long limpet mine, which I slapped on to the lock. I lit it and we blew it in. In order to control the demolitions, Sergeant Jameson and I tried to get on board one of the two tankers in the dry dock, but there was a machine-gunner on board. We threw a couple of incendiary devices at him but I don't think they did any good. Then Chris Smalley came up and asked permission to fire the winding house. When he tried, nothing happened because his igniters failed and he had to go back in to sort that out. Then Chant showed up, having laid his charges in the pumping house, which went up almost immediately. That was wonderful. Chunks of concrete the size of a bench came off the roof. We went inside and saw that two of the motors which pumped the shaft had fallen through the floor. The other two were leaning drunkenly. Two of the men destroyed the switchboards and dials, cut the transformer pipes and threw in a couple of incendiaries. They had a fine time. I then sent Chant and his boys back and went up the dry dock.

While I was on my way up there, there was a splendid explosion came from the winding house, and that was obviously a write-off. Coming back, I met the party on the caisson gate who had had a bit of trouble. Gerald had been wounded early on and Burtenshaw had been killed while trying to lay the demolitions. They hadn't been able to get into the caisson because the Germans had covered the hatches and built a road on top. Eventually, they put underwater charges on the dry side and it was reported that water had been heard going into the dock at either end of the caisson, so we reckoned it was off its seating and wasn't going to be much good. That completed the operation very nicely and successfully.

On the way back, I found a railway truck and lit an explosive and hurled it in. The truck disintegrated in flames. It was lovely. I then came to a bridge, held by Donald Roy, who told us not to cross but to go over on the seaward side, using the girders underneath, because it was under heavy fire from the basin. I reported back to Newman, thinking everything was marvellous. Our operation had gone 95 per cent according to plan. I asked Newman whether I should to go to the embarkation point or go off to see how Pritchard was getting on. Then, the adjutant, Stan Day told me to look out in the river, and that was when I realised we were unlikely to get home because all the little motor launches were burning all over the river. We fired the signals for rallying but none of the other demolition people came in. It was very depressing.

Newman decided that we would have to fight our way into the open country. He put us into parties of about fifteen or twenty and off we set. I was in the front, quite by accident. I promptly came up against a brick wall which forced us to turn round. After that I was at the back – a much happier situation. We moved along the edge of the submarine basin, when suddenly a grenade burst just beside me and I got a tiny bit of metal in my bottom, and it was just as if you'd shot a rabbit. I went head over heels, thought 'O Lord, I'm dead,' and then got up and realised I wasn't. By that time, we'd got into the old town square and we had to get across a bridge if we were going to get out of the town. So Newman assembled us again and we decided to charge. George Hands, the troop Sergeant-Major, gave covering fire with a Bren gun as we ran across the bridge. From the amount of fire that was coming at us, we should have been absolutely massacred, but Newman had a theory that they'd been firing at us from long range and they forgot to drop their sights. Everything was going over the tops of our heads. There was clanging against the girders on the bridge but we got through.

We found a truck which Bill Copeland tried to get going, but all he managed to do was turn on the headlights and that caused a lot of screaming and shouting from us about blackouts. As we went on, an armoured car came down the street firing at everything, so we had to clear off the street. We split up into parties and so began the St Nazaire obstacle race. We were over walls, into people's gardens, through houses, and when another armoured car came along, we decided to stay where we were. We were in a house with an air-raid cellar so we went to ground and gave some of our wounded chaps morphia and tried to bandage them up and make them comfortable. Someone operated on me with a fighting knife and cut a small chunk of metal out of my bottom.

Then the Germans began searching the house. They searched upstairs and found nothing and were just about to leave when there was a cry in German from upstairs – whether it was from a Frenchman or not I don't know – 'Have you looked in the cellar?' At that stage, Newman surrendered. I don't know why the Germans didn't just chuck a hand-grenade into the cellar – I'm sure that's what I would have done – but they pulled us out and took off our tin hats and moved us about a bit and there was a lot of shouting and screaming. One of us pulled out a fighting knife and another chap pulled out a hand-grenade and they lined us up against a wall and trained a machine gun on us and I thought that was it. But Newman explained to them that we were just trying to get rid of our weapons.

An officer came and took us into the house opposite which was the German headquarters – we hadn't really chosen our hiding place very well. We were there for quite a long time. More and more chaps were brought in. We were a bit worried because the *Campbeltown* hadn't yet gone up. It was supposed to have gone off at 4.30 in the morning and it was now half-past ten. Then suddenly, it did. There have been all sorts of stories about why it was so late. I believe that it got so hot that some of the acid in the acid pencil fuses distilled away and it took rather longer for the acid to eat through the copper and set off the fuse. Just before the *Campbeltown* exploded, Sam Beattie was being interrogated by a German naval officer who was saying that it wouldn't take very long to repair the damage the *Campbeltown* had caused. Just at that moment, she went up. Beattie smiled at the officer and said, 'We're not quite as foolish as you think!'

Able Seaman Herbert Dyer
Aboard Motor Launch 457

When I came back, they were still dropping these hand-grenades, and one dropped right into the bridge and cleared them right out. It took the captain's leg off and took my Scots boy's insides out – he was still alive, but it killed another one. The lieutenant had got killed on the fo'c'sle, and the gun crew fo'c'sle were both dead, so the skipper gave orders to push off, and we pushed off midstream. Then we got set on fire, so he said abandon ship. We threw a Carley raft over the side – four got on it. The skipper came on, the young man with his stomach wound, the signalman and myself – we were unhurt. The tide was taking us out. It was similar to the Thames Estuary – it was a wicked tide. We went by a boat that was sunk, with its mast sticking up, and we caught hold of this to hang on there, and tied a rope to it. The skipper wasn't very good – he must have been dying – you could see him change colour. He just let go and went under. The signalman wasn't hurt, but he just said 'cheerio' – he said he couldn't hang on and he went under. In the meantime, the tide was going out, and the rope went too high and was tipping the boy into the water, so we cut it and let it go. We were stuck there until the morning when the Germans picked us up.

DIEPPE

Sergeant George Cook
No. 4 Commando

Mountbatten gave us a lecture – said he wished he was coming with us. Once we realised where we were going, I think 200 blokes thought, 'I wish he were going instead of us.' But yes, very nice talk. We cheered him – off he went. Then we started priming grenades, drawing ammunition. Our troop were doing the demolitions, so we drew explosives and we'd a fair amount of stuff which we packed up – ammunition, spare Bren pouches, spare mortar shells, grenades – which we'd all primed. Then we had a meal and we sailed – a beautiful evening, as we went down the Solent and past the Isle of Wight.

Suddenly an officer said, 'Oh – they've got all the harbour lights lit.' I looked over the prow of the boat and you could see lights on the shore. The lighthouse at Varengeville was flashing, so I thought, Cor blimey – everybody awake. We're going to have a pretty bad welcome here.

When we landed, there was some barbed wire. We'd a roll of wire netting which we threw over the barbed wire so we could run over it. The Germans were firing tracers from their pill-boxes, and Lord Lovat said, quite casually, 'They're firing too high.' He was about six foot – I'm five foot four – so I thought, 'If they're firing over his head, there's no danger they're going to hit me' – but they did fire their mortars, and four or five blokes were killed on the beach.

We kept firing as we moved, but we were getting a lot back. Somebody shot a bloke out of the ack-ack tower. He did a lovely swallow-dive off the top. We arrived in an orchard, and Sergeant Horne and I had to cut some barbed wire. He started cutting, and then I heard an 'Ugh' – and when I looked, there was Sergeant Horne, blood spurting out of his chest. He looked as though he was dead – which was a bit of a shock to me, because he was about the toughest fellow I ever knew, was Geordie Horne. Then I got hit in the face and the shoulder. That was me out of it.

Albert Quesnée
French seaman aboard the Bayonne

On the 18th August I was aboard the *Bayonne* and we went to Dieppe on a raid. We were taking some Canadians to drop them on a quay at Dieppe, but of course the Germans were there. That was a bad day, a bad day. I've never seen so many planes come down in the water.

The captain – he was a good captain. We couldn't land at first because the Germans were firing, so the captain turned and we went in backwards, because at the back we had all the big guns and the smoke screen, we dropped them and then went back.

Major Pat Porteous
Temporary Major, Royal Artillery

We hit the shore, a steep shingle beach which had three or four yards of wire at the top. We were prepared for this and had rolls of chicken wire to lay over the barbed wire, which made a sort of bridge which we could stagger over. While we were getting that on, the Germans opened up with mortars, which they had obviously ranged very closely on to the beach, and caused about a dozen casualties.

After we got over the wire, we had to wade alongside this river, because the Germans had flooded the valley. It was fairly heavy going for about a mile directly inland. Then we swung left across open ground behind the German defences. This brought us round to a little wood at the back of the battery we were to assault. The battery had barbed-wire entanglements around it, but there was a spot where the German soldiers coming home late from leave or something, had trampled a path through the barbed wire. We managed to get in without any problem at all. As we got into this area of the battery, we bumped into a truck of German soldiers who were just disembarking. We managed to kill them before they got out of the truck. We then started working our way through this very dense bit of country – all these little cottages and hedges and so on. Roger Pettiward, the troop commander, was killed by a sniper, and John Macdonald, the other section commander, was

Pnt Portecus, VC. Decorated for his courage in what was the only successful element of the costly Dieppe raid in August 1942, he recovered from his injuries and returned to France on D-Day.

J E 'Johnny' Johnson. He flew to give fighter cover to the ill-fated Dieppe raid, 19 August 1942, and went on to notch up a Fighter Command record of 38 kills, being awarded the DSO and bar and DFC and bar before transferring in 1944 to the Second Tactical Air Force.

killed by a stick grenade. This left me in command of the troop.

I was going along a little lane towards the battery when I suddenly saw a German pop up. I threw a grenade at him and he threw a stick-grenade at me. As soon as they went off, I popped up – but unfortunately he popped up a little bit quicker, and he shot me through my left hand. I put on a field dressing, and we pressed on. We got close to the battery and lined ourselves along a low bank about four feet high. I made contact with commando headquarters, who were approaching the battery area, and he said, 'Come on, it's time we went in.' We made a bayonet charge into the gunpits.

The German guns were fully occupied dealing with the other party of commandos who had landed, and so we got very little opposition, but I got a bullet through my thigh, which slowed me up. The first gunpit I came to was the one which had been hit by the mortar bomb, and was just full of corpses. I staggered on to the next gunpit and then I rather gave up the ghost. I'm glad to say I didn't actually bayonet anybody. I couldn't have done, because my rifle had been smashed and my pistol had run out of ammunition, and I couldn't load it with one hand. Two chaps came along and hauled me out while the demolition team went into the gunpit.

All the guns were loaded with a 100 lb shell and then with a bit of plastic 808 behind it. The shell exploded as well as the plastic, and opened up the guns like a banana skin. Having blown the guns, that was our job completed. We then made a quick withdrawal. I was loaded on to a door somebody had pulled off a shed, and carried by two German prisoners, down a gully. They didn't like that, because they had laid the mines there, and weren't quite sure where they were – so they were very nervous.

When we got down to the beach, there was a bit of shooting, so the assault craft laid a smoke screen. We had to wade out almost shoulder deep. I was loaded by these two poor Germans, who were scared stiff. They thought they were going to have their throats cut. However, they were all loaded in and taken home safely. I was then transferred first to Peter Scott's steam gunboat, where there was a medical orderly who tied up my leg and hand as well as he could, and then transferred to a destroyer.

I never discovered why I was awarded the VC, but I think the main thing was ours was a very successful raid – the only bit of the Dieppe operation that was successful. I was very lucky, I think – very lucky to get the award of the VC. The citation said that I'd been wounded in my hand, and had then led this bayonet charge against the guns, got wounded again and carried on. But I felt it was rather like being in a rugger scrum – you got kicked about a bit and the object was to get over the line. Which was all that we did do, in fact. I was

After the Dieppe landings, dead bodies and burning Churchill tanks lie abandoned on the beach, and in the shallows, a landing craft is in flames.

Canadian troops who managed to escape the carnage on the Dieppe beaches on the fateful raid, in which 907 Canadians were killed and 1,874 taken prisoner out of a landing force of 5,000, return to England aboard a Royal Navy vessel.

scared from the moment we started getting shot at – or before that – as soon as we realised we were going on an operation which was all rather frightening – it has to be. I don't think there's any man on earth who is not frightened if he's going into an operation.

My feeling is that it was an absolute disaster. It should never have taken place. A great deal has been made about the lessons learned from the raid which were put into good use for the main landings in Italy and later on in Normandy. But my feeling was that 90 per cent of those lessons could have been learned training in Britain on the beach at Weymouth or anywhere else. But as it was, they had something like 1,000 killed and 2,000 taken prisoner – and what did they achieve? Absolutely nothing.

The whole plan depended entirely on success on the two flanks, or the three flank parties, the two Canadian and the two commando parties. Without that, the beach itself is an absolute killing ground. The headlands on either side were firing straight down, enfilading down the beach – no one had a hope. The people at Puys – the Royal Regiment of Canada – I think only about one man actually got over the sea wall – and they had the most appalling casualties, the whole regiment. I think twelve men got back to England out of a battalion of 700 or 800. All the rest were either killed or taken prisoner. It's an impossible piece of coast. It's cliff all along, except for these few little gaps where odd rivers came down or gullies came down. It was quite impossible to get up. I'm very, very bitter about it, and I think most Canadians are too, who were thrown into it.

The only French civilian we came across was a little lady who emerged from a cottage just near by the spot where we landed at Ste Marguerite – who appeared from her cottage in her nightdress, waving a bottle of wine, which she offered to the troops, saying 'Vive les Anglais!'

Squadron Leader 'Johnny' Johnson
616 Squadron, RAF

There was supposed to be a headquarters ship, HMS *Calypso*, that was supposed to be the radar-equipped controlling ship. But I could never establish communications with it on the four times we flew that day. The ship wasn't sunk, it was just impossible to communicate with it. This was supposed to be the controlling ship with RAF controllers on board, who would give us instructions, but we never heard a thing from them all day.

We could see very little except a bloody great pall of smoke over the town, and lots of shelling going on down below. But we could do nothing about it because the attackers and defenders were all within a hundred yards of each other. We couldn't help the army. When we got home after the first patrol, we knew that the whole thing had been a disaster – but there was nothing we could do to help them.

THE WESTERN DESERT AND EL ALAMEIN

Rommel had the upper hand in the desert in the early months of 1942. The tide began to turn, however, when Montgomery took command of the Eighth Army on 7 August, following the inconclusive battle at El Alamein ending in late July. The British now inflicted heavy losses on Rommel's troops at Alam Halfa on 31 August and, with the greatest artillery barrage ever delivered, the Second Battle of El Alamein began on 23 October. By 4 November, Rommel's troops were in retreat and on 13 November the Allies retook Tobruk.

Corporal Peter Taylor
2nd Battalion, Rifle Brigade
Rommel attacked and pushed us back through Tobruk. He pushed us right the way back into the Alamein position which had been prepared for months. They'd prepared properly constituted minefields and defences in some depth. It was bounded on one side by the Qattara Depression, which was impassable to the normal wheeled or tracked vehicle. So Rommel couldn't do any flanking movements and come up behind the defensive forces. Everybody pulled back into the Alamein position. We were the last British units over the Egyptian border, which was called The Wire, because the Italians had laid a huge border of barbed wire in peacetime, separating Egypt from Cyrenaica. I was bringing a truck back which was in a pretty bad state and being towed. We got to a place called Fuqa, where there was a huge NAAFI, which had been abandoned that morning. Such was the rapid advance of the German forces, that they'd had to just down tools and take off. But there was a terrific cauldron of hard-boiled eggs still bubbling merrily on the fire. There were cases and cases of stuff all over the place. We got into the NAAFI, picked up one or two nice bottles of drink and a few of these boiled eggs and took off down the road.

Sergeant James Fraser
Royal Tank Regiment

I was driving a General Grant tank – which was the same tank that I would eventually take over and drive Montgomery in. It was a place called the Knightsbridge Box, and we came under heavy fire. The tracks were blown off the tank. The tank commander gave the order to bale out. We baled out and we got underneath the tank – which normally one wouldn't do, because the tank is a main target – but we had no option. There was machine-gun fire and heavy shellfire, so we got underneath the tank.

One would say it was a thousand-to-one chance, but a heavy explosive came underneath the tank, lifted it. I blacked out and when I came to, dazed, I looked round to find three of the tank crew had been killed. That left myself and another lad. In making our way away from the tank, we were fired on by a machine gun, and I was hit on the leg. I was picked up by one of our own squadron's tanks, taken back to the line, and then to the advanced field ambulance for treatment.

Corporal Vernon Scannell
Argyll and Sutherland Highlanders

One of the most memorable and still chilling and nightmarish things is hearing the voices of those who'd been badly wounded, their voices raised in terror and pain. I can remember one particular sergeant who'd always seemed to me almost a kind of father figure. He wasn't that much older, but at that time I was twenty and he'd probably be pushing thirty, which seemed to me a lot older. He was rather a tough, leathery kind of man. He was badly wounded and hearing his voice sort of sobbing and calling for his mother seemed to be so demeaning and humiliating and dreadful. I felt a kind of shock that I can't fully understand even now, because he'd been reduced to a baby.

One of the things that struck me about being in the battle, on reflection was, when you consider the amount of stuff coming over in terms of the actual shells and mortars, bombs and small arms and the rest of it, when you consider the expenditure of weaponry – how few people were hit. That's what always amazes me. I've been under heavy bombardments of one kind or another and really very, very few people were hit. You're in a slit trench, you get your head down – but it always surprises me really that there weren't much heavier casualties.

Sergeant John Longstaff
2nd Battalion, Rifle Brigade

This was July 1942, and we are driving through the desert road until we come to the Ruweisat Ridge. Nobody had told our lads that there were British minefields. Nobody had told our lads about the sand storms – the dust storms. Nobody had told our lads even how to brew up a cup of tea. Nobody had told our lads what compass bearings we were working on. In any case, it didn't matter – we had no compasses. If the company commander got lost, you all got lost.

All of a sudden, there's a hell of an explosion. I could hear shouts. Lieutenant Peter Coryton with his driver on a scout car had run into a British minefield and been killed, and his driver badly hurt. I went along to see Sergeant Turnbull and asked him what was happening. 'I haven't a clue, Johnny.' So I said, 'I'm going to make a cup of tea.' Three of us got down, trying to pump a bloody petrol burner to brew up. We couldn't – it was thick with sand and we didn't have any nozzle cleaners. Somebody said, 'Open a tin of petrol, put some sand in and light it, then put your dixie on the top, and brew up that way.'

I was told that we were going to attack at first light, and follow the tanks. That night we could hear the rumbles of the guns where the Australians were attacking. We could see the desert flashes. So, about six o'clock the next morning, we didn't even have time to brew up. I think we had a biscuit and a piece of bully beef. The lads were nervous – I could see that. I could even feel myself nervous. I knew I had a responsibility. The lads looked to me as an old soldier – I'd gained their confidence in England.

I hadn't forgotten what had happened only about six hours before – of the running on to a minefield. I didn't believe it would happen again – but it did, that morning. We weren't far behind in our truck when I spotted more mines – the wind had been blowing and exposed them.

Then we started receiving all this shit. Our sand was making the storm – so all the enemy had to do was fire into the dust storm that we were creating. 'Major Francis,' I said, 'you can't go any further. We're only soft skins. I don't know where the tanks are.' Nobody knew. So Francis did the right thing – he stopped the attack and put us in this wadi.

At midnight that night they took us out of the line. We got Stukaed. Again, it was a brilliant night and this time I had a Tommy gun. I fired that and the lads started firing. 'Hit the bastards! Hit the bastards!' Nobody got hurt but in twenty-four hours, the 23rd Armoured Brigade no longer existed as an armoured brigade. It became an infantry support tank brigade. Some

El Alamein, the Western Desert, 1942. With visibility ahead obscured by the dust and smoke of battle, British infantry advance through the barren landscape.

officer of senior rank should have been shot for the debacle he brought the 23rd Armoured Brigade into. There wasn't a cat in hell's chance of breaking through Rommel's line.

We marched up through the dust to relieve a company of the East Yorkshires. There were seven men left out of that company. They'd been in the attack, and seven men were now going to be replaced by about eighty of us. There were tears coming down all our faces when we realised what these lads had been through. It was a foul position. There were dead Senussi – the tribe from Libya, who were fighting with the Italian Army. There were dead bodies all over the place and never buried for days and days – they stank.

The only good thing about it was there was an Italian truck nearby. I went over and found a bottle of brandy and a couple of big carafes holding probably about eight or nine litres of vino and a load of French letters (which we used, funnily enough, to carry water in later on, and I used to keep my guns clean). We also found hundreds of packets of Italian cigarettes. Since we'd landed in Egypt, three weeks before, we'd not had a single issue of cigarettes – or of anything you would call the niceties of the NAAFI. We went into battle without a fag between us. I can tell you, fags for a soldier were very important in those days. Two things won the psychological war in my view – a cup of char and a fag. Whatever morale a Tommy was in beforehand, it's right high up after he's had his fag and a cup of char. So long as he can sit quiet for a minute or two.

It was a quiet position – probably it was just as well, because the worst enemy we had was the flies – millions, billions, living on the dead around us. Yet we didn't even feel that we wanted to bury those dead that were all now burnt up.

Evelyn Cottrel
British nurse, with Hatfield Spears unit in North Africa
When we got to Tobruk in 1942, Mrs Spears couldn't see anyone about, but there was a large tent, so she said to us, 'I'll just go and have a look in there.' We found out later on that it was full of officers debating on what the next move would be. The officers later told us that she barged in and said, 'I am Lady Spears, and I am here with my gals to set up a hospital in Tobruk.' They tried to tell her she couldn't, but she just said, 'We are staying – we have orders from the French, and we are staying.'

We were there for quite a long time and saw a lot of the battles, which meant we had to deal with some terrible cases, and of course we were bombed all the time and there were no windows. It was terribly hot and sometimes when the bombing was bad, we'd have to get patients under the bed.

I remember one of the girls writing a letter for this one man to send back home after he'd been shot in the eyes. He was saying, Don't worry. You know, I may have lost my eyes, but I'm alright.

Sergeant John Longstaff
2nd Battalion, Rifle Brigade

We were now going out on patrol, night after night after night. There was five miles distance between us and the enemy, so we'd go out on strict compass bearings. We'd go out making sure that there were no lights on the vehicles, making sure the milometer was working, that we had proper watches that we could rely on for distances. We would leave the driver in charge of the truck. He would be armed with one thing – a form of incendiary grenade that he would push into his petrol tank if he or his vehicle was going to be captured. So he stayed there while the rest of us went forward to try and hear who the enemy was in front. At that particular position it was the Ariete Division and the Folgore Division of the Italian Army, backed up by heavy machine-gunners of Rommel's Afrika Korps.

We had a nice little way of capturing people. In the desert, if you wanted a tom tit, you would squat somewhere on your own. When you get up, if you've got some paper to wipe your bum with, you're bloody lucky. You can't use any bushes out there, because they're all prickly, so you wiped your arse on your trousers. As simple as that – this is war. So, I used to squat down as near as we could to the enemy lines – or we'd see somebody else squatting down – and we'd just go over, pretend to pull our pants down – never wear our steel helmets. We'd squat down and bring our Tommy guns to bear on the soldier who was opposite us. They never came away shouting – they were only too pleased to have their tom tit and be captured.

Captain David Smiley
Royal Armoured Car Regiment

Until Monty launched his big attack at Alamein, there was nothing really more than what I call patrol activity in the no man's land. You advance, and they shot at you. You withdrew and you were able to go back and say, 'They're there still.' That was how it worked. That's what the role of an armoured car was – reconnaissance and keeping in touch with the enemy. If they had withdrawn, we'd not been shot at. It's a very nice way of fighting. Of all the units to be in, I think an armoured car unit, certainly in the Western Desert, was the most fascinating and most pleasant. You had casualties – we had our fair share. I remember being attacked by our own fighters, mortared by our own infantry – shot at by German artillery, all on the same day. We had no casualties at all, but being in the no man's land, there was the question of identification. Certainly from the point of view of a pilot flying an aeroplane at high speed, we were probably nearer to the German lines than we were to our own, so he probably took us for the enemy.

Montgomery was what I call a bit of a bullshitter, but I think that was part of his act, and very effective, I think. He had to publicise himself and build up a reputation against Rommel, whose reputation was extremely high. We all thought the world of Rommel. If you were opposite Rommel, you expected something to happen. He did have a very demoralising effect on British troops. He was a bloody good general.

Sergeant John Longstaff
2nd Battalion, Rifle Brigade
Montgomery came to the southern sector of the Alamein front at Alam Halfa, and one of the first things he asked was, when did we leave England and had we had any post? Not a single soldier had had a letter. Had we any NAAFI? We hadn't even seen the NAAFI. We were scrounging as much as we could from other units – cigarettes – and understandably, other units weren't prepared to give them away or even sell them. He wanted to know why our shirts were stained – because we only had one shirt, and there was sweat – and they were hard, like bloody cardboard. He wanted to know if we'd had any leave. Nobody had had any leave at that stage. He made sure his adjutants took note of everything. He wasn't talking to the officers – he was talking to the riflemen – he was sitting inside little dugouts with the lads.

Before Montgomery, we never knew what our role was – where we were going, what was going to happen, who was on our left flank, right flank – who were our reserves. We didn't even know who the enemy was prior to Montgomery. He gave the order that every soldier will be told who is on his left and who is on his right – who is behind him and who is in front of him, and he will be told what he's going to do. When a man is told those things, he starts getting confidence. He doesn't feel that he's fighting by himself.

Sergeant James Fraser
Royal Tank Regiment
My earliest memory which is very clear, is when Montgomery came with his first journey up in a tank. He came and spoke to the crew. Straight away he was communicative. He wanted to know who we were, what we did, what our family was all about, and all the other bits and pieces.

He was wearing this Australian hat, with all the badges that were around the brim, and a pair of 'Bombay bloomers' – KD shorts, which were a lot wider than the normal. Now, dressed in that hat and shorts, and with his thin legs, he looked like matchsticks in a pair of boots. Very high-pitched voice – and he didn't look like a general at all.

Reverend Douglas Thompson
Chaplain with Essex Regiment

We got stuck. We were ordered to stay just five miles westwards of the Alamein line, to hold the Germans back while the Alamein line was completed and Montgomery's plans came into effect for the push forward that he made later. The South Africans were in entrenchments, deep fortifications on our right. The New Zealanders were out on the desert on our left, and we were in the middle of this line. It had to hold for perhaps forty-eight hours while things happened behind us.

I was up with the Regimental Aid Post, just behind the front line of troops – the first dugouts – and between there and the second line. That's the station for a chaplain in an infantry division, and I was there with the doctor. We made for the hole which was to be the Regimental Aid Post. I was there, going from there up to the front line, back and forwards, and fetching chaps out who were wounded, with a couple of drivers. I was in that position when the line fell. We kept out the German motorised infantry, but then they pushed down the tanks on us. Then Rommel's own corps came down in its tanks, and it was a case of the sand and the rifle against the tank – which was no bargain at all, so they mopped us up. As they came through, there was one tank commander standing in the top of his tank in the turret with a heavy rifle, potting off British chaps in holes. He came as far as the Regimental Aid Post. I was outside it with a couple of drivers who'd been hurt. He just took one pot at me and I got it in the liver. Then a young German sergeant, who was a very decent lad, came up, and he talked to my driver, who asked him for a stretcher for me. The young German gave him one and got four of our chaps to pick me up. I was taken in and they laid the stretcher down just beside Rommel's command car.

I was moved by ambulance. My driver put a young artilleryman who'd been shot through both legs, in beside me, so the two of us were humped off across the desert. This German driver had made friends with my driver, and he took us from one hospital to another. He couldn't get us in. On one occasion we got to an Italian hospital and the chaplain came out and gave him a drink. He wouldn't give me a drink because this German doctor had said I had three

November 1942. General Montgomery meets the commander of the Afrika Korps, General von Thoma, now a prisoner of war. Monty's arrival boosted morale among the 'Desert Rats'.

days to live, but if I didn't eat and drink, I'd stay alive for at least three more days. He just gave me a kiss and a sweet to suck. We got back and we landed up at a place just a mile or two out of Sidi Barani, in an Italian hospital which was full of German troops which our RAF had caught coming ashore. They were in a shocking mess. I was laid with them in the hospital.

The chap next door to me had got third-degree burns. When the Italian orderlies removed his clothes, they took most of his skin off with them. He was in a shocking state. Sometimes he was calling for a maid, or a servant, in a Channel Islands café, for beer, and then he would change his tune. He would begin to cry for his mum. He was just raving. I put out one hand and took hold of his hand and held it. I think he must have thought it was his mother's hand, because it quietened him down, and he died in peace before the morning came.

Sergeant John Longstaff
2nd Battalion, Rifle Brigade

We were told that the last battle of the Alamein line – of Rommel's attack – would take place right in the sector that we were in front of – at Alam Halfa. We had something unique. We had magicians in charge of our camouflage. Large tins that had held potatoes were made to look as if they were anti-tank guns, vehicles were made with hessian to look like tanks – tanks were made to look like vehicles. Petrol supplies were made out of any old rubbish. Water points were made where there were no water points.

Our 2nd Battalion lads had the responsibility of going up on the 22nd October to take a position and to start making a gap through a British minefield. They went out without any mine-detectors, digging their bayonets into the ground to discover mines, then putting a bandage on a steel post. As soon as they found a mine, they'd tie a wire to it, then somebody would yank the mine out. They were generally Teller mines, and one Teller mine could put a British tank out of action.

It was eerie seeing the flashes of our guns on the 23rd October at ten o'clock. The gunners seemed to be firing rapid fire with 25-pounders. The sky had to be seen to be believed. Round about seven o'clock that night, we received orders to march. B Company under John Francis was to lead the battalion. We were now through the second of the British minefields, which meant a journey of about two or three miles through a narrow gap, no wider than say two tanks could get through. These gaps had been made by the Rifle Brigade and the Royal Engineers – and they did damn good work.

We got into our positions while it was still dark. We were in front of the

Australians and the 51st Highland Division. We started to dig in, but it was rock. I found some old German army mortar bomb boxes, which I filled with rocks to build a sangar in front of my men. Then we put some boxes over the top of us, so that the overhead shrapnel bursts wouldn't come down like rain and chop us up. A shell doesn't have to explode underground – if it explodes above, it creates more casualties, because it's coming down like an umbrella. My lads were well trained on this.

Our position was called 'Woodcock' and the next one to us was called 'Snipe'. It was in that position, two days after our first attack, that my battalion knocked out 14 tanks in the major attacks – it was the most tanks knocked out by any battalion of the British Army ever – a record. But that record was only to last two days, because the 2nd Battalion, the Rifle Brigade, under Colonel Vic Turner, who received the VC, became immortal over the battle of Snipe. They knocked out 90 odd vehicles and tanks.

Through a dust storm, Bill Stanbridge the quartermaster, brought up his 30 hundredweights with rations for the whole of B Company – all in sacks full of bully beef and biscuits and the luxury of a few tins of sardines. He had gallons of petrol and boxes of ammunition, including sticky bombs and extra mines. I was horrified the next morning to see that I had about 200–300 gallons of petrol about ten feet away from me, bags of bloody mines. We had to crawl out and disperse this stuff, knowing very well that if one shell had hit the petrol or the mines, bits of us would be floating around the desert.

As it was, we'd suffered a hell of a lot of casualties – our machine-gunners had suffered in particular. I had one vehicle for the whole of the company and we put the wounded on it. They got back all right.

As we were marching or walking through, tired, lacking in sleep, and hungry but proud, with our rifles slung over our shoulders, we were stopped by a redcap at one of the points. 'Who are you, Sergeant?' 'My name is Longstaff, Sergeant. Rifle Brigade.' He looked, and he was smart, this redcap. He shouted out to the gunners, 'It's the RBs.' The gunners cheered and even now I cry. The redcap saluted every one of my lads – every one. I don't like bloody coppers, but that one redcap to me personified the best that the military police had ever had in the desert.

Sergeant Harry Simpson
7th Battalion, Black Watch
In the main battle of El Alamein in October 1942 it was our job to bring out the carriers with food and ammunition behind the main attacking lines. When the forward infantry had secured their positions, we had to provide

them with our supplies. The further advanced we got, the more horrifying the experiences were. There were our mates, lying prostrate on the ground in a terrible state. We gave the wounded what help we could, and then we advanced further up. We also helped the enemy if we could, because you felt sorry for them.

One chap I do remember, in the odd silence you got when the guns stopped, he was swearing at us in Italian, so we gave him a drink of water and a cigarette. But he threw them on the floor, so I said to Captain Miller, 'Let's put a bullet through the bugger,' and we laughed like Albert – so we left him there and we carried on. What happened to him I don't know – and frankly, I wasn't even bothered.

Martin Ranft
German gunner, 220th Artillery Regiment, Afrika Korps
El Alamein was my home for quite a while, because we were stopped. On the 23rd October, nine o'clock in the evening, that's when we heard that terrible artillery fire from the British line. I was facing the front line and suddenly the whole sky was red with the gunfire. The shells were howling over you and exploding all around you – it was just horrible. We thought then that the world was coming to an end.

Captain David Smiley
Royal Armoured Car Regiment
I was pretty impressed the night of Alamein, when the guns opened up. It was tremendous. All our searchlights were facing upwards in the sky to make a false daylight, to make things easier. When we went through the minefields and got to the first positions, there were dead Italians everywhere. I can remember seeing a man in his trench with his mess tin in front of him. He was dead. The barrage had opened up so suddenly, it had caught them well and truly unprepared.

As we pushed ahead, the Italians were surrendering in their thousands. We just said, 'March east – march back to Cairo.' We left the mopping up to be done by those behind us. Eventually, when the thing came to a grinding halt in our area, we spent about a week going out in patrols finding pockets of wretched Italians. Their officers or the Germans had pinched all their transport. Some were starving and had no water. I remember getting sixteen Italians on my armoured car, hanging on like grim death. They were absolutely delighted the war was over. They weren't very enthusiastic, to put it bluntly. They were conscripts – Mussolini had called them up. I think half those poor devils didn't want to fight at all. It was the Germans who put up most of the tough resistance.

Sergeant John Longstaff
2nd Battalion, Rifle Brigade

Then there was the second part of the battle of Alamein. I got my reinforcements – although the battalion was not ever again to be up to strength. We were to take up the positions held by two battalions – the Norfolks and the Durham Light Infantry. Those lads had been through hell far more than we'd been through, no mistake about that. They'd tried to break through, but they'd suffered badly.

I told Harry that I thought we'd had our chips that night. I think it was the only time I really felt that I was going to be killed. If I'd been in A company, I would have been, because of the way the enemy was dug in in depth. When A Company advanced, the enemy allowed them to get so far forward, and then just devastated them. We in B Company could do nothing except drop on the ground where we were and try and give covering fire. In the meanwhile, our Bren-gun carriers were supposed to bring up our pickaxes and shovels and blankets and water and ammunitions and all the other items used by soldiers in the front. The signal was so many flares – but we couldn't send any flares up – we hadn't got to the position. I think there was a real balls-up. They had decided that the Royal Artillery and supporting guns would give an artillery barrage to our left flank and to our right flank where the KRRs and the 2RBs were attacking – but we would go in silently.

So, when we went in again, another bastard accident took place. An order was given for one of our platoons to attack a machine gun. They attacked it – but it was our own machine-gunners. Half of my bloody platoon was killed in that one bloody battle by my own mates. Then we had to withdraw. I followed the moon for direction, with Johnny Judd badly wounded and another lad called Latchmere, who was supposed to have played football for Spurs, also badly wounded with four or five machine-gun bullets through his guts. Johnny was never to fight again. We deposited them at the first-aid station and we goes back.

Corporal Peter Taylor
2nd Battalion, Rifle Brigade

It was about the 12th day of Alamein when the enemy really started to go. The desert was littered with Alpine boots and rucksacks with a cover which was made with the hide of a deer or elk or something – hair-covered rucksacks. We found out afterwards that this Alpine regiment had been hurriedly sent from Italy across to Tripoli and whistled down to the battlefield almost before they could pause for breath. All their Alpine boots had been hung on the outside of their packs. They'd been put straight into the front line to hold positions. This stuff was all over the place – the dross of an army, if you like – tins and cans and bullets and guns and rifles, boots, packs, hats – a hundred and one things everywhere. Burnt-out vehicles and tanks – and a few graves, though not many. The dead on our side had all been taken away. They were taken away and buried. I should imagine the engineers had burial details – had graves prepared ready for the possible number of casualties. The casualty evacuation and withdrawal of people of ours who were killed was incredible. The wounded were got away extremely quickly in jeeps and little armoured cars with stretchers built on to the back of them – strap him down and whoosh – off. They'd have an orderly sitting on the back to see the chap didn't get bounced out. The medical evacuation was heartening because people had been told, 'If you get wounded, you'll be whipped away straight away.' We'd never had this sort of thing before.

Everything had been thought of – that was why the spirit was so good. After years of being pushed about by the Axis forces, at last we were holding our own and doing a bit better than holding our own. We were actually beating them. Everybody could see we were beating them. It wasn't because they were short of weapons – they had almost as much as we had – but we had a little bit of the edge with the Sherman and the anti-tank guns. We had a bit of the edge.

North Africa after El Alamein

Colonel Charles Dunphie
Assistant Chief of Staff to General Patton with US II Corps
Patton had this sort of blood-and-guts reputation, but he was also extremely kind-hearted and sentimental. To show his blood-and-guts thing – he issued an order that the corps at least were to look like soldiers, and everyone must wear a steel helmet and none of these knitted caps any longer. I was driving him in a jeep when we passed an officer by the side of the road in a knitted cap, and Patton shouted 'STOP!' He got out, took him by the neck and shook him like a rabbit – took his cap off, threw it on the ground. Fined him 10 cents for the Red Cross and then stumped off and got into the jeep again. I said, 'Steady, General. Wasn't that a bit rough?' And he said, 'It'll be all round the

corps by tonight and you'll never see one of them Goddamn caps again.' And I must say I never did.

But, equally, when later at El Qatr, after a successful operation, we were moving forward and got stuck, he sent General Bradley, who was second-in-command of the corps, and myself forward, with his ADC, a boy called Janssen, whom he was very fond of. We were to see the divisional commander and find out what was holding him up. Rather stupidly, I think, our jeeps were parked together, and three Junkers came over, opened their bomb doors and let out these anti-personnel bombs, which landed right amongst us. It killed Janssen and wounded me, and General Bradley was luckily not hit. When I was in hospital, Patton came round to talk to me about Janssen, so I told him. He sat down on the bed and burst into tears. He was also very good to me, and I remained – on two sticks – with him for the rest of the campaign.

THE FAR EAST

The British Army in Burma was driven into retreat. In March, Rangoon fell to the advancing Japanese, who by May had entered China. The Japanese offensive continued, with bombing attacks on Calcutta in December, but by the end of the year, the Allies were fighting back.

Second Lieutenant John Randle
7/10th Baluch Regiment
We arrived in the middle of an air raid at Rangoon, and moved by train to lower Burma in the general area east of the Sittang and west of the Salween. The part we went to was rubber not jungle, and we were used to the vast open plains of our training area in India. I like trees, but in rubber plantations, with no horizon, it is a bit depressing and confining. The Japs had barely started their offensive, we guarded bridges, then deployed on the West Bank of the Salween, before pulling back to Kuzeik on the River Salween opposite Pa-an. A Company were in a patrol base at Myainggale seven miles south of the battalion position. I was told to take over from A Company, and my Subedar Mehr Khan went off with one platoon as advance party. During the night the Japanese attacked and wiped out my platoon, and a platoon of A Company. As I was moving to Myainggale with my remaining two platoons, I ran into the middle of a Japanese regiment just getting across and taking up positions on the west bank of the Salween. I had a hairy old night, lost a few chaps, but

managed to get my two platoons out and back to the main position.

We were in single file when a man charged into our column. I thought it was one of my soldiers running away, and shouted at him. It was a Jap who ran off into the bush. A couple of Japs were then shot by my men, the first dead Jap I had seen. There was quite a lot of firing, and I realised there were quite a lot of Japs about. I tried to get through on my radio, which didn't work. So I sent my runner, the company bugler, back with a message to my CO. The Japs cut in behind us and we could hear the runner screaming as they killed him with swords and bayonets. This was followed by an enormous lot of firing a couple of miles away from the base we were going to relieve. The Japs were running about, in a fair state of confusion too, having just come across the river. We had no idea what tactics we should adopt. I just formed a circle, which looking back was the best thing to do: river on one side, Japs on two sides. It was pure luck not cleverness. It was clear to me there were a considerable number of Japs to the south of me, so I decided to return to the battalion position.

The next day they dive-bombed our positions near the airfield at Chiang Mai across the Thai border. That night the CO decided to send out one of my platoons on patrol. God knows what for. So I was down to one platoon, and a section of MMGs. At about twelve o'clock the Japs came in and we had hand-to-hand fighting. They overran us and C Company. They came in with no artillery support in what started as a silent night attack. When they got close, they screamed *banzai* and came charging in, shoulder-to-shoulder. The Vickers fired across my front and caused heavy casualties to the Japs, but they surged into Company HQ, where I killed the chap coming for me, while my CSM was grappling with another, but my batman was killed by a grenade. Just before dawn, realising if we stayed we would get taken prisoner, we charged out and then lay up about 150 yards away, and after first light heard a second assault going in, on Battalion HQ. We then had a pause, but at seven o'clock the next morning they finished us off. We lost 289 killed, and had 229 taken prisoner in our first engagement. It took me two days to get back to our lines. We were staked out there like a goat for the Jap tiger and sacrificed for no reason. The CO was killed and we lost over 60 per cent of our officers. Only about fifty of the Battalion got away. With the exception of one officer, the Japs butchered all our wounded. News of this got back to us and this conditioned mine and the whole Battalion's attitude towards the Japs. We were not merciful to them for the rest of the war. We didn't take any prisoners.

The Japs fought with great ferocity and courage. We were arrogant about the Japs: we regarded them as coolies. We thought of them as third-rate. My goodness me, we soon changed our tune. We had no idea about jungle fighting, no pamphlets, doctrine etc. Not only were we raw troops, we were doing something entirely new.

Lieutenant Donald Day
1st Battalion, 4th Gurkha Rifles
The Gurkhas were a bit bewildered. We keep lambasting the Jap and then had to retire. They did not understand this constant retreat. Every time they met the Jap they beat them, and then had to retire.

Gurkhas prefer the kukri to the bayonet, they can cut a man in half with it. A standard blow is cross-cut to the shoulder. They cut off heads. It is a terrifying weapon and, used in the hand of the Gurkha, is lethal. I have used the kukri in anger only once. I was using it to sharpen a pencil by a haystack, when a Jap suddenly appeared round the corner, and I had to hit him with my kukri as I had nothing else to attack him with. My orderly was so convulsed with laughter at my ineptness, he failed to dispatch the chap quickly. The Gurkhas have a strange sense of humour. I made a mess of him and my orderly finished him off.

Pilot Officer James Thirlwell
3 Photo Reconnaissance Unit, flying Hurricanes, based at Magwe
I was sent to Lashio to investigate the possibility of flying out the squadron personnel by China Airways to India. I went to the orderly room Flight Sergeant for transport, and he said, 'You can have this Wolseley Fourteen, but I want something in return.' So I swapped a typewriter I found in the house in which I was billeted for this car, and drove to Lashio. Having confirmed the availability of China Airways, I was flown to Calcutta, only to be sent back to Burma, where I spent most of my time rescuing the special cameras from crashed photo-recce aircraft.

After getting out of Burma for a second time, I had an extraordinary period based at the Great Eastern in Calcutta, the most expensive hotel in town. I would get into my Hurricane at Dum-Dum, fly to Chittagong where I refuelled from petrol drums using a hand pump. Having spent the night with the British Consul, I would fly to photograph Rangoon, where the Japs seemed to want to shoot at me, before returning for more fuel at Chittagong, and on to Dum-Dum to get the film processed as quickly as possible. After a shower in the Great Eastern, I would sit down to dinner being served by bearers in white coats and gloves.

As the Japanese advance reached the British base of Singapore, on 15 February 1942, running out of water and with little ammunition left, General Percival had no alternative but to surrender.

1943

There were excited yells over the R/T, 'It's gone! It's gone!'
The whole dam had collapsed and the water had started spewing
out down the valley.

This was a year of pushing back the tide of Axis advances. On 3 January the Germans began to withdraw from the Caucasus and in February the last German resistance was crushed in Stalingrad. In the same month the first of the 'Chindit' campaigns set out to drive back the Japanese in Burma in a war of jungle attrition. The round-the-clock bombing of Germany continued, in greater numbers and with greater accuracy, despite heavy losses. Some queried the morality of raids where civilians came under the attack, but raids continued to destroy industrial targets and demoralise the people

The major move in Europe was the Allied invasion of Italy. Following landings on Sicily, the troops moved on to Salerno on the mainland. Despite the speedy capitulation of the Italians, the troops met heavy German opposition as they fought northwards to Rome.

In the Atlantic, at last the tide was turning. The U-boat packs had been concentrating their attacks to the south of Greenland, where neither British nor US aircraft could escort the convoys. The result was 120 Allied ships sunk in March. In retaliation, the Allies deployed support groups of warships centred around aircraft carriers to protect the convoys, and added the air assistance of long-range Liberator bombers. Soon, despite losses to shipping, U-boats were sunk in significant numbers and Dönitz was forced to withdraw them to safer waters. The sinking of the Scharnhorst on Boxing Day was the icing on the cake for Britain's sea-war success.

BOMBING GERMANY

Based in East Anglia, the USAAF started daylight raids over Germany on 27 January, but the main force of bombing raids was against German cities by night and, on 16 May, the famous 'Dam-busters Raid' was carried out against the Möhne and Eder Dams, by 617 Squadron, using the newly developed bouncing bomb. Further raids brought devastation on the ground, but there were still heavy casualties among Allied aircrew and planes.

Doris Scott
British civilian in Henley, Oxfordshire
The Americans were a jolly and friendly crowd. It was like Hollywood come to life – the way they spoke in different voices like Kentucky or New York Bronx. Many girls were bowled over by them, and I think the British soldiers didn't like it very much. The reserve of the English was in sharp contrast to their friendly 'got any gum, chum?' way of talking. They certainly made an impact.

Marion Bryon
British civilian, evacuee organiser, Rushden, Northamptonshire
There was a local prostitute known as Cora in a local pub. Someone tried to make an appointment with her, and she said she had found a nice GI, and she was going to America. There was a piece in the paper about her as a GI bride.

Sergeant Ronald Buckingham
RAF prisoner of war in German camp
At Sagan we had in the camp one of the most celebrated RAF escapers who never got back to this country, and whose final end had never been established completely. That was a chap named Grimson. I saw a bit of the escape – but obviously, we just carried on walking. One didn't stand and stare, but it was the most fantastic daylight escape, in that he was dressed as a German civilian, carrying a ladder, which had been taken from the theatre block. He worked his way across from the centre of the camp, up against each electricity pylon, with a box, purporting to test the connections – and so he came until he got to the warning wire. Whereupon, he shouted to the postern in the box – he spoke perfect German, and had false papers, of course – and took his ladder over the wire. He put it up near the postern box, twiddled around with his box of tricks and dropped them down between the two main wires, into the coils of wire.

In the absence of signposts, removed in case of a German invasion, a British policeman gives directions to US GI Elco Bolton from Florida.

The all-American boys of the United States Army Air Force. In Britain at the outbreak of war, James Goodson (immediately left of the map-holder) was spurred by the sinking of SS *Athenia* on the night of 3 September 1939 to join the RAF, where he flew with the Eagle Squadron. In 1942 he rejoined the USAAF and flew with them until shot down on an impromptu attack on rocket-powered aircraft at Peenemünde.

I am told that he swore for a good three minutes in German, and then said to the postern, 'Well, you know, I'll be in the dirt for that. I'd better go and get another one and continue the job. I don't want to go all the way round there and out through the Kommandatura, and so on. I'll just nip over . . . all right?' He showed his papers to the postern, who said, 'Ja, ja, ja,' then Grimson just went over the wire, I'm told, and away. Then, of course, there was a ladder up against the wire. The guards changed, so there was a different guard in the box, and a ladder against the wire, and our blokes got hold of a Jerry officer in the camp and said, 'Hey, one of your blokes pinched our blooming ladder out of the theatre block, and left it against the flaming wire. We want it back, please.' So the officer went with a group of our blokes – called to the postern – got the ladder back and put it in the theatre block. There was no evidence at all that he'd gone. That's the coolest escape I know.

Sergeant Leonard Sumpter
617 Squadron, RAF

When we first saw the experiments with bouncing bombs – well, we thought it was marvellous. It's hard to think, when you first see it, that when about five tons of metal hits the water, whether its spinning in a backwards direction at about 450 revs a minute will make any difference to it. You'd think, 'Well, it'll just go straight in – straight down.' But it didn't. It just hit the water – and up she came, and did about three bounces to the beach.

It was an impressive sight – mine did four bounces to the beach. That's why I got chewed off. I dropped it too soon, and it would have hardly reached the dam wall. The idea was to bounce it up to the dam wall, and it was spinning against the wall and sticking to the wall by its spinning, until it got to the depth where the hydrostatic fuse exploded it.

Flight Lieutenant Harold Hobday
617 Squadron, RAF

We were going to try and hit the aqueduct which carried the Dortmund–Ems Canal over a valley, to release all the water. We had a different bomb – we didn't have a bouncing bomb – we had a very large bomb on board.

We took off, but fog in the area meant we couldn't see the target, so we had to return and land with a bomb on board. I think it bent the hook it was on when we landed, because we weren't supposed to land with this bomb on board – but we had to because there were no other supplies of the bomb.

The following night they decided to send us again. Mosquitos were sent in advance to reconnoitre and beat up the defences. But we couldn't find the

The United States Army Air Force was based largely in the eastern counties of England and are seen here at a dance at a Women's Land Army camp in Suffolk.

The pilot and co-pilot in the cockpit of an RAF Wellington bomber. The constant night raids over industrial targets in Germany exposed the bombers to heavy anti-aircraft fire, and by the end of the war over 50,000 aircrew had lost their lives.

aqueduct because the weather wasn't good enough. The moon wasn't bright enough either, and so we were stooging around, trying to locate it. We did a wide circle a couple of times, with our pilot trying to see if he could see the target, when suddenly the bomb aimer in front of our aircraft, said, 'Pull up, Les!' and Les and I pulled up, because we were aiming straight for some trees on a hill. We brushed the trees and two of the engines were damaged – and the tail.

We managed to ditch our bomb and climb up, but because of the damaged tail, the aircraft kept wanting to go around in circles. Eventually it got worse and worse, and the pilot couldn't hold it, so he told us to bail out.

The crew in the front bailed out, but the people in the back, who were shovelling ammunition out to lighten the load, didn't hear the 'bail out' order. They sensed Les was coming down, and called over the blower, 'Are you ditching, Les?' and Les said, 'Jump out quickly.'

He tried to land the aircraft in a field, but it hit a tree and he was killed – but the other two got out. Naturally we didn't find each other. I landed in a tree, clambered down and started walking.

I found someone who could speak English. I was given some clothes and told to shave off my moustache, as Dutchmen don't have them. The underground movement looked after me in a wood for a month, then eventually they fixed up that I should go up to Rotterdam, stay with somebody there, and get used to mixing with Germans.

Then I was met by a fellow who took me down to Paris on the train, which was very overcrowded. This was done on purpose, of course. We had to go through the customs where the Germans were on the Holland/Belgium border, and also on the Franco/Belgian border, which was a little hair-raising, because there were two Gestapo people at each place. I had to hand my papers in. I'd got forged papers in which I was supposed to be a deaf and dumb Dutchman working on an airfield in the South of France. Sounds a little bit of a tall story. They were just about to ask me a question, the Germans, and then said, 'Well, go through, ' and I didn't have any trouble.

Squadron Leader John Shannon
617 Squadron, RAF

Hopgood's run-in attracted tremendous flak, and he was hit – hit in one of the petrol tanks, because his wing on the starboard side caught fire. I think his bomb-aimer must have been hit, because the bomb was released late and bounced over the wall. There was a tremendous explosion. Hopgood did his best to gain height, and he gained some four to five hundred feet when the entire aircraft exploded in mid-air beyond the dam wall in a steep climb. Goodness alone knows how it happened, but one survivor from that terrible smash was his rear gunner, Burcher, who was taken prisoner of war. He was obviously blown out, and must have had sufficient sense to pull his parachute cord. He was the only survivor. That was the second bomb against the Möhne Dam – the wall was still standing.

The next chap to go in was Mickey Martin – and the same thing happened again. He was hit several times going in, but to try and draw off some of the flak, Gibson was flying down one side of the lake, just out of range of the flak, but with his navigation lights on under the aircraft to try and fool the gunners. It was a bit of a spoof, but it did work. It drew some of the fire off. Martin's bomb was released, as far as we could tell, exactly on site. Again, there was this tremendous, vast explosion of water up into the air, and then when the whole thing had subsided again, the wall was still there.

So the next Vic was called in. The leader of that was Squadron Leader Young – Dinghy Young, as he was known. This time, Martin was also flying down one side and Gibson on the other, trying to draw the fire to get some of the flak away – to give the flak gunners three aircraft to shoot at instead of one. This worked to a certain extent. Young dropped his mine – again, as far as could be assessed, in the right place. Again there was a tremendous explosion of water. Young called up and said that he thought the wall would go – as far as he could tell it had been a perfect run – but when it subsided, the wall was still standing.

The next one to go was Maltby, who was flying his number two. The same procedure was carried out again, and Maltby, as far as he could tell, had dropped his bomb in exactly the right place. Again, we had this tremendous explosion of water. It settled down – and still the dam wall was there.

I was then called in by Gibson to start my run, and I was just starting the run and Gibson was flying down one side and Martin was flying down the other side, when there was a tremendous explosion. There were excited yells over the R/T, 'It's gone! It's gone!' The whole wall had collapsed and the water had started spewing out down the valley. It poured out of the lake, taking everything in front of it. After a few minutes, it was just an avalanche of mud and water rushing down the hill, so we moved on to the Eder Dam.

Gibson rapidly said to me, 'L-Love' – which was my aircraft – 'Steer off the run. Stand by. I think it's gone!' Then he came back and said, 'Yes, it has gone!' and they circled and saw that the whole thing had gone. So we then moved across to the Eder Dam, the aircraft that were left.

I tried, I think, four times to get down, dropping down – and each time I was not satisfied with the run that I'd made, and told the bomb-aimer not to release. To get out of this predicament, we had to immediately pull on full throttle and do a steep climbing turn to the right to avoid a vast rock face that was up in front. The approach on the Eder Dam was pretty hairy.

Gibson said, 'Well, have a rest from that and call in Maudsley,' who was the leader of the next flight, to come along. He had one dummy run at it – unsuccessful – and did the same thing that I'd done. Then he did another dummy run and dropped his bomb, but the bomb overshot and bounced over the wall, and again exploded below – and there was a tremendous flash. We don't know what happened to Maudsley – his aircraft was never found and he never returned.

Then Gibson told me to have another go, so I had another dummy run. Then I got what I thought was an excellent run-down, and we released the mine – as far as we could tell, there was a small breach made on the port side . . . but there was no significant sign there – and so there was only one aircraft left. That was Les Knight, and he was called up. He had three or four runs before he could release his bomb and when he released it together with mine – his was in the same place – the wall gave.

After that, Gibson told us to get the hell out of it, because there was no more that we could do. We had no bombs and we didn't have enough fuel to go on to the Sorpe. The second wave had gone to the Sorpe – but the Sorpe Dam was never broken. It was an earth-wall dam, and the bouncing bomb wasn't the right weapon for it.

We went back individually – not in formation. I just got down on the deck and opened the throttles and went. We landed back at 4 a.m. on the 17th May. I had been away about six and a half hours.

The costs had been high. Out of the 19 aircraft that had set out, only nine returned – we had lost 52 lives.

We had a tremendous reception from the top brass in Bomber Command when we touched down. There was Bomber Harris, Sir Ralph Cochrane, and of course, Barnes Wallis. We had proved his bombs would work, but he never for a moment thought the cost would be so high. He was in tears, and a more distressed figure it would have been hard to imagine by the time the last aircraft landed.

I suppose we had become hardened to loss – we could shrug it off. We had to, otherwise we could never have flown again. We were debriefed, then we all went back to the Mess and opened the bar and started drinking. The beer started flowing till late in the morning when we struggled off to bed, and slept for a few hours. Then there was a stand-down for survivors for a week. The

HU62923

The pilots and crew of 617 Squadron at Buckingham Palace to receive decorations for the Dam-Busters Raid. From left to right, Flg Off Taerum, Flg Off Spafford, Flt Lt Trevor-Roper, Flt Lt Maltby, Wing Commander Guy Gibson, Flg Off Johnson, Flt Lt Martin, Flt Lt Shannon, Flg Off Hobday and Flt Lt McCarthy.

Bill Reid was awarded the VC for his courage in continuing on a bombing raid to Düsseldorf, in spite of his aircraft being badly damaged and being seriously injured in the head, face and shoulder. Such was his modesty, he never mentioned his award to his fiancée before their marriage in 1952.

whole thing really took off because it got so much publicity. The press were allowed to write about it, and some brilliant journalist coined the name, 'The Dam-Busters'.

Flight Lieutenant Bill Reid
61 Squadron, RAF

On the night of my tenth raid, we'd set off as usual – we were heading for Düsseldorf. As pilot, I got the full briefing, whereas the rest of the crew only had a specific briefing for their particular section – navigation, wireless operator etc. All pilots made sure they knew the courses roughly anyway, for safety's sake, because it sometimes happened in training that the navigator would put Red on Blue – meaning an error of 180 degrees, and give you the wrong heading. That's how I knew the rough headings after the navigator in my aircraft was killed.

We had just crossed the Dutch coast, when, suddenly, there was a great bang in my face. I thought it was predicted flak. We lost about 2,000 feet, and I felt blood running down my face. I pulled the plane up and then I felt this pain . . . something had hit my shoulder too, it was just like a hammer blow. The crew were all right, except for the engineer – I think he'd been hit in the forearm. I didn't see any point in saying I'd been hit, in case they panicked. So I checked that everyone was OK. I trimmed the plane and we flew on. I still thought we'd been hit by predicted flak, but Cyril the mid-upper said, 'No, it was a Focke-Wulf 190.' But the first instruction I received was, 'Dive starboard.' I think his guns had jammed, but we flew on. We were at about 19,000 feet when – *wham* – again. We were really hit this time, and we started to spin down.

At about another 2,000 feet below, everything went dead in my ears. There was no intercom, nothing. My hands were a bit bloody, skinned, really, when the windscreen had shattered. So I pulled on my silk gloves, then my leather ones, and put on my goggles because the windscreen was out. Then Jim Norris was hit in the arm, and the port elevator damaged, so there was only half an elevator holding the aircraft straight and level. Together, we held the stick back and I trimmed off as much as I could. I asked Jim to get me another heading from the navigator and he came back and signalled that Jeff was unconscious, but I felt that it was not a permanent situation.

I looked out and got the pole star and knew we were heading about 120, south-east. And I thought, 'Well, we'll just carry on like this.' That night we were actually aiming towards Cologne, dropping spoof flares there, and then turning at the last minute for Düsseldorf. I thought we were all right for timing, and I could see other planes beside me, so I knew we were still fairly well in the stream. Then on time I saw these flares come down ahead of us, obviously Cologne, and I turned up on to 060, the bombing run. As for Les, the bomb-aimer, he didn't really know what had happened yet, because we had been keeping things going, but let him know that we were now heading for the target and he set up the bombsight and switches. I opened the bomb doors and looked for the three target indicators which I aimed at and kept her straight and level, and held it until I felt the bombs go off. Held it for the photograph, then turned and headed back to base. I just kept going. The oxygen supply had been hit, so Jim fed me little bottles of oxygen. I occasionally slumped forward on the way back and he would change the oxygen bottle. We came down to about 12,000 feet by then.

When I saw water I went down to 7,000 feet and that was below our oxygen height. Then all four engines cut. The engineer usually kept the tanks fairly level, in case they got hit, so you didn't lose your petrol, but he'd forgotten about it in all the hubbub. He just turned them on and they started up again. My biggest problem actually, was how to hit England. Then I saw some beacons flashing, and it was a wee station, EEH or something, and we couldn't get down. We headed off, and I spotted a big canopy of searchlights further north, and headed for that. But on the way there I saw this big aerodrome with a Drem system of lighting, and it was big enough for us to land on. So I circled there, reduced my height, and said, 'Stand by for a crash landing.' And, of course, we'd no hydraulic pressure, because the bomb doors had stayed open. But we used the emergency air-bottle and let down the undercarriage, then I flashed my landing lamp on and off, and kept circling. They put some big sodium flares out because it was a bit foggy, and we took a low approach coming in. As we touched down, the undercarriage legs collapsed – they'd been shot through. We went along on our belly for about fifty yards, and it was only then that I realised Jefferies was dead, because he slid forward down beside me.

We'd landed at an American aerodrome, Shipdham in Norfolk. They took us into their hospital – the only thing I remember is that I was as dry as a bone, dying of thirst, and they gave me a drink of water. They stitched me up, and I went off to bed. The next morning they took us to Norwich Cottage Hospital, and two days later we were shipped down to the RAF hospital at Ely. Jim Mann, the wireless operator, died the next day.

Air Vice-Marshal Cochrane, the Base Commander, came to see me that first week. He said he'd heard my story from the rest of the crew, but he wanted to hear it from me. He asked me why I didn't turn back, and I said that

I'd thought it was safer to go on, rather than turning back among all the other planes; I mean eight or ten miles of aircraft all flying in the same direction. I said if one of the engines had packed up I'd have turned round right away, but the plane was still flying. It wasn't that I was determined to drop the bombs or anything, but I just thought it was the safest thing to do at that time. Then he said, 'You know, Reid, the returns from ops have been practically nil since your raid. It's as if they all said, "That bugger Jock, he went on even though he was wounded, so we can't turn back just because of a faulty altimeter, or something like that."'

THE ITALIAN CAMPAIGN

With Malta's safety secured by August 1942 and American troops under Patton fighting in French North Africa and driving east to meet up with the Eighth Army moving west, North Africa offered good bases from which to launch an Allied invasion of Italy. This began with landings on Sicily, on 10 July, followed by mainland assaults at Salerno on 9 September. In the wake of the Sicily landings, Mussolini was deposed, and on 25 July, Marshal Badoglio replaced him.

The Allied advance in Italy met with heavy German opposition as British, American, New Zealand, Indian and Polish and Free French troops pressed north through the Apennines in worsening winter weather. Only in June 1944 could the Allies liberate Rome following fierce battles around the ancient monastery of Monte Cassino.

Lieutenant Bill Jewell
Commanding submarine HMS **Seraph**
After the North African landings, the next obvious target was Sicily, indeed it was so obvious that, as Churchill said, 'Anybody but a damn fool would know it is Sicily.' Operation 'Mincemeat' was devised to hoodwink the German High Command that Sicily was only a cover target, the real objectives being Sardinia in the west and Greece in the east. Lieutenant-Commander Ewan Montagu of Naval Intelligence dreamed up the idea of putting a body into the water so it would be picked up. 'Major Martin' was supposed to be a Royal Marine officer on Mountbatten's staff. The corpse could carry what purported to be vital secret documents to ensure that the other side was misled in predicting where we were going. Among them was a personal letter to

General Alexander from General Archhibald Nye, which was actually written by him.

In spring 1943 Montagu and an air force officer came up to the depot ship at Holy Loch to deliver 'Major Martin'. They came alongside with a refrigerated canister about six foot long and about the width of a man's shoulders. It looked like a small torpedo. We lowered it into the fore-ends and hung it on the torpedo rails . Nobody except myself knew what was going on, and there was quite a lot of speculation about what this thing could be. There were rumours that it was a secret weapon. We sailed within an hour of taking delivery and set off for the Mediterranean. We had no real problems, apart from being bombed twice – which was par for the course, anyway.

On the 30th April we arrived south of Huelva where Spain and Portugal meet. Intelligence hoped that the canister would drift inshore from this position, where it would surely come to the attention of the Spanish authorities. By this time the crew had decided that the canister was some form of meteorological device for predicting the weather. I explained that they were on no account to talk to anyone about this, either then or in the future.

When it was really dark, we got as near as we could to the estuary. The first problem we encountered was an enormous fishing fleet, which came out, passed over us and beyond. We closed into the coast and lifted the canister on deck on to the fore-casing. We shut everyone else down below and put the hatch down. All the other officers and I went down on to the casing, unscrewed the lid of the canister and took the body out. Both my father and brother were doctors, so I didn't have a problem handling the corpse. The poor devil had died in a lunatic asylum in London and was about thirty-eight. That was the macabre aspect of the whole scenario. I was supposed to check that he had all his private impedimenta about him. He was dressed in a Royal Marine uniform and all his letters and documents were in a case attached to a chain which led to the pocket of his greatcoat. They'd been able to find someone who looked very like him in the Admiralty, so they were able to take a photograph to produce his official pass.

Intelligence had taken every precaution to ensure the authenticity of their decoy. As well as the false plans, he was provided with passes, theatre ticket stubs, keys, money and personal letters, including two from his fiancée, Pam. These rather imaginative love letters had been written by some of the girls at the Admiralty who probably had plenty of experience in writing to absent loved ones.

Previously I'd had a look through the prayer book and got some idea of how the burial service should be. You never do burials from a submarine, and I'd never done a burial at sea before. So we read this out over him and pushed him quietly over the side. We ran the propellers full out astern to move his body towards the shore and sent him on his way, having no idea whether he would get there or not. We then set off to Gibraltar. Absolutely everything had gone according to plan. The greatest difficulty we had was getting rid of the canister, because it was designed to be refrigerated and had tiny compartments all around it. We started off by putting a charge inside the thing – but nothing happened. The charge went off – but the canister didn't sink. Then we tried firing machine-guns through it – but it took about 400 rounds and still didn't sink. So we had to blow it to small pieces with another charge, and eventually it went down.

As we tied up in Gibraltar, somebody came on board and handed me a folded piece of paper. I opened it and read it. It said that the body had arrived successfully. Really that was the last I had to do with it. The enemy must have swallowed 'Mincemeat' whole, because they mobilised a lot of troops to Sardinia and to Greece.

Lieutenant-Commander Roger Lewis
Magnetic mine expert

During the early part of planning for the Sicily landing, we chose which beaches we were going to land on, and it turned out that one of the best beaches on the south coast was not going to be used. We also had some intelligence that the Germans and the Italians were pretty certain that we would use that beach, so, in the course of the planning stages, we decided to set up a hoax on that beach – and Douglas Fairbanks Jr was detailed off to run the hoax. He and I got together to fix this.

The plan that we produced was to equip four American PT boats with towed balloons – the balloons to be painted with suitable radar-reflecting paint, and a certain amount of 'window' attached to the tethering hawser of the balloons to make the MTB and balloon look, radarwise, at night, like a large transport.

We then fitted out the PT boats with huge loudspeakers and a gigantic amplifying set, with a selection of gramophone records. These gramophone records were made to represent the noises made by four transports creeping up the anchorage, anchoring, hoisting out their landing craft, the landing craft starting up engines, the embarkation of troops, and eventually the landing craft setting forth from the four transports, fanning out and approaching the beach.

So on the night of the landing, at the right time, these four PT boats proceed to anchor at the right distance off the beach, at the right distance apart, to represent an assault convoy. The Italians and Germans on the beach noticed this and signalled for reinforcements. Hundreds of troops who would have been at the real landing bases were rushed down to this beachhead, only for dawn to break, and for them to see four PT boats and four balloons, at anchor in the bay! And that was Douglas Fairbanks Jnr's contribution to the Sicily landing.

Lieutenant-Colonel Alastair Pearson
1st Parachute Battalion

The outline plan for Sicily was that the Airlanding Brigade would capture the Ponte Grande Bridge outside Syracuse on D-Day. Then 2nd Para Brigade would secure a bridge north of Augusta on D+1 and 1st Para Brigade would seize and hold the Ponte di Primasole some ten miles south of Catania on D+3, or any subsequent date. My task as CO of 1 Para was to capture and hold the bridge. The codeword was 'Manston Tonight'.

The 2nd Para Brigade operation was cancelled due to the speed of the advancing Eighth Army. On D+3 our operation was postponed for 24 hours. The next day we went to an airstrip outside Kairouan. They told us the operation was on but they didn't tell us the time of it – that depended on how well the army was doing.

The airfield was a sandy strip in the desert. We got there at midday and the only shade was under the wings of the Dakotas. We lay underneath and waited and slowly baked. By the time we got the code word, the problems of the Airlanding Brigade had filtered back. The fact that a large number of our aircraft had been shot down by friendly naval vessels did not help our morale. We were assured, however, that this would not happen again. At dusk we set off. Inside the Dakota I was reading my book and the rest of the soldiers were chattering away. Then all of a sudden there was the clatter of machine-gun fire. I could see all these ships below belching fire at us. They thought we were Italian torpedo bombers.

Eventually we settled down, then one of my signallers told me we were over Mount Etna, which was nowhere near where we should have been. I struggled out of my parachute in order to get to the cockpit to see what was happening. As I passed one of our soldiers who'd been an RAF officer I said jocularly, 'Can you fly one of these things?' and he said he could. I got up to the cabin and realised that we were heading back again.

I said to the pilot, 'The DZ's down there, what are we doing?'

His co-pilot was sitting with his hands over his face crying, 'We can't, we can't.'

'Can't do what?' I said.

'We can't go in there.'

I could see quite clearly blobs of fire. I knew what was going through his mind, it was going through mine as well, because on the ground were what I thought were burning Dakotas. I said to the pilot, 'There's nothing for it boy, we've got to do it. If your co-pilot's no good I've no hesitation in shooting him.'

I pulled out my revolver. The pilot continued with his protests. So I said, 'I could shoot you as well.'

'You can't do that, who'd fly the aeroplane?'

I said, 'Don't worry about that, I've got a bloke in the back who can fly this.'

'Yeah, but he won't know how to land it!'

'No one has asked him to land the bloody thing – you don't think he's going to hang about to land it do you? He'll be stepping out very sharp!'

He decided very reluctantly to go in. I got back into my parachute, the bell rang and we all stood up. I thought we were going in too fast. We seemed to be going downhill as well. Out I went over the DZ and I didn't think my chute had opened, because I was down on the deck as soon as I'd jumped. I'd gone out number ten, my knees hurt, but I was all right. My batman at number eleven was all right but the remainder of the stick all suffered serious injuries or were killed. I was very angry. We all got to our RV and soon discovered the burning Dakotas were no more than haystacks alight.

With only about 200 men including a couple of platoons of 3 Para, I formed a defensive position around the approaches to the bridge. The Germans put in a series of attacks in the afternoon. We weren't in any danger of being overrun but we were suffering casualties and were running short of ammunition. But I considered we could hold out until dark.

However, at 1830 hours I was ordered to withdraw by Brigadier Lathbury, with which I disagreed. But in the end I had to do as I was told and withdrew my battalion up to the hills. Before I withdrew I took my provost sergeant 'Panzer' Manser and my batman, Jock Clements and made a recce of the river bank because I had a gut feeling I was coming back again. It was stinking and the mosquitoes were there in their millions. About 500 yards along I found a ford, where we crossed and made our way back to battalion lines. The following morning I had a grandstand view as the 9th Battalion of the Durham Light Infantry, who were the leading element of the Eighth Army, put in a full-scale infantry attack on the bridge. It was unsuccessful and they suffered very heavy casualties.

I was called up to Durham's Brigade HQ to see what the next move was. I listened in amazement as the brigade commander put forward the idea of another attack that afternoon. I said, in a voice louder than I should have done, 'If you want to lose another battalion, you're going the right way about it.' There was deathly silence as the two brigadiers gave me a long look. But Brigadier Lathbury, who was also at the meeting, saved my bacon and persuaded them to listen to what I had to say. I told them that I would take the 8th DLIs across the river that evening by the route I'd recce'd.

The brigadier just looked at me and said, 'All right, Pearson, what do you want?' In other words, how many tanks, what artillery; so I said, '2,000 yards of white tape!' 'What's that for?' he said. 'If we're going to get lost we'll all get lost together,' I said. He agreed. I then said that it was to be a silent attack with two companies and I wanted the remainder of the Durham Light Infantry with its armoured support to be in a position on the road, ready to move as soon as they saw the success signal, a green Very light.

At midnight I asked the CO of the DLI and his two company commanders to come with me while the remainder moved down the tape. The CO was a bit anxious and said to me, 'What's out in front?' I said, 'My bloody batman, I hope!' Panzer Manser was leading with the tape. One of my soldiers who was two behind me had one up the spout. For some reason he pulled the trigger and the bloke in front of him dropped dead, shot straight through the back of his head. The noise was unreal – a single shot at night. I really thought we'd passed the line of no return. But the Germans made no response.

Jock Clements, my batman, was standing there. So I said, 'Away across the river Jock.' 'What me, sir?' 'Aye, you, yes. Here's my torch. If you see anything, give it a wee wave. If there's anyone on the other side you'll soon know about it.' The Durhams' CO was with me, and he couldn't believe that batmen talked to their COs like that. I told Clements to make it towards the bridge with the tape.

We crossed over the river and got on to the bridge. It was about 0400 hours. I told the Durhams' CO that the Germans would probably attack at first light and he was to get his two companies out to the edge of the orchard, because if the Germans got in he was in trouble. He did not agree. By this time it was beginning to get light and the remainder of his battalion should have been joining him as the success signal had been fired. I had done my job and the three of us left and made our way up the road. I expected to see the Durhams go into action – streams of jeeps and tanks – the only person I met was a War Office observer on his bike. I told him the form and he pedalled off – but it was dawn before they crossed the bridge. By then it was too late.

Later that day the remains of Para Brigade were moved by transport to Syracuse. I was fast asleep in the front of the truck when I was awakened by

Clements to be told that the Commander-in-Chief, Monty, was behind. Just at that moment, the familiar khaki Humber passed with its pennant flying and signalled for us to stop. I thought a rocket was impending for being asleep, but not so. He greeted me by name like a long-lost friend and congratulated us on our efforts and then said he'd like to talk to the men.

My RSM who was right behind me was pretty quick-witted and moved off to wake them. But he was a clever bugger, old Monty. He got his ADC to throw some packets of cigarettes into the trucks where the men were. Then he said, 'Walk with me, Pearson.' So we went about 200 yards down the road while he told me that although our casualties had been high, the cost was well worth it. He then walked slowly back again. When we got to the trucks he was greeted by cheering men all smoking Monty's fags and saying, 'How's Alamein, sir?' There he was, lapping this all up – all the cheers. It was very, very clever how he knew where I was, and a great morale-raiser.

Sergeant Norman Travett
2nd Battalion, Devonshire Regiment

In the early part of the attack on Sicily the opposition was nearly all Italian. It wasn't really until we got to the area of Regalbuto Ridge that we really encountered the German forces. They were a completely different kettle of fish. The Italians would surrender without much problem at all, but the Germans, especially the Hitler Youth – the young fanatical Nazis would continue fighting when it was absolutely hopeless to carry on. When we captured them, they were very arrogant.

Major Martin Hastings
2nd Battalion, Devonshire Regiment

We were struggling up a ploughed field which had vines in it, and I met two Americans – paratroopers – sitting under a vine. I said, 'What on earth are you doing here?' 'I don't know,' they said, 'we dropped.' And I said, 'I see you have, but I think you must be something like fifty miles out of your proper place.' I said, 'You'd better go down to the beach.' I think it gives some idea of the chaos that the paratroopers had, of being dropped in various different places, because I think the same chaos happened to our own paratroopers.

I went on with my two platoons and company headquarters, and eventually we came to where an Italian battery was supposed to be. I couldn't see any Italians at all – but I could see one or two of the guns. We went charging into these guns – and there wasn't a soul. So I thought, 'Well, that's extraordinary,' and then I heard some noise coming from a dug-out, so I had a flash grenade, which made a lot of noise, didn't do much harm – so I chucked one of these down it, and all hell was let loose. After a lot of shouting, out came about fifty Italians with their hands up. So I thought, 'Gawd, what do I do with this lot?' So we sat them down and I went on a little bit, until I saw a hat sticking up on the end of a stick on the other side of a long wall. I fired my Tommy gun along the top of that, and up jumped another fifty Italians, all wanting to surrender. So I had to get rid of them, and I sent them off with a section down to the beach, and I didn't see that section for twenty-four hours – so by this time I was getting a bit thin of men.

Having captured this battery, my other platoon at last arrived – exhausted, having tried to catch up. At that moment, the Italians had some little two-seater tanks – R35s which had a little machine gun in them. I said to my chap in Company Headquarters, 'Where's the Piat?' the Projector Infantry Anti-Tank, which we had in those days, and he said, 'The platoon's got it.' So I said, 'Well, go and fetch it.' But while he was fetching it, we lay down at the side of the road, underneath this wall. Then down the road came a small boy and girl, walking together. So I grabbed them and put them in the ditch beside me. Then down the road came two Italian civilians, so I grabbed them too and put them in the ditch. The Italian noticed these two children in there, so he got up and gave me a kiss on both cheeks, which rather startled me, to say the least. However, at that moment, one of our tanks at last had arrived and put an end to the R35s, so we had made quite sure of our final brigade objective.

William 'Bill' Jordan
British cameraman Army Film and Photographic Unit

Near Taormina, I did a bit of filming of a sapper. It was repetition after the first initial coverage. He swept on and then he found a piece of metal, which gave him some detection. He stooped, picked it up, and then took one step forward to sweep on – unfortunately, by the side of the metal he'd picked up was an anti-personnel mine – he trod on it. It was the type with the three prongs that stick up with a container underneath full of ball-bearings. The initial charge sends the canister up in the air about five or six feet, and then the whole canister explodes and sends out a shower of ball-bearings. Unfortunately, the sapper got some through his head, and the sergeant behind him got some in the head as well – they were both killed outright. I got four – two in my left leg and two in my left shoulder – and it was that that sent me back to North Africa to base hospital.

Salerno, Italy, 9 September 1943. A landing craft lays down its own smoke screen to provide cover for the arrival of British troops. Although the Italians had already surrendered, their German ex-allies continued to put up strong resistance.

SALERNO

Major Armin 'Sheriff' Puck
Marshal Provost, HQ Commandant, 36th Division, United States Army

I wondered how I would react when the ramp of that landing craft dropped down, and I started to get across the beach to the old temple ruins. I prayed on it for about five minutes – and I said, 'I'm just going to get my head down and my tail up, and I'm going to go.' And I did.

Sergeant Ike Franklin
111th Medical Battalion with 3rd Battalion Aid Station, 143rd Infantry, United States Army

It was one long nightmare, really. I remember one time, a buddy of mine and I got pinned down there at Altavilla between artillery crossfire. The Americans were over-shooting and the Germans were undershooting, and we were pinned down between the two. My pal said, 'Ike, what are we going to do?' and I said, 'We're going to stay right here.' And he said, 'What about the shells?' And I said, 'Well, they're going to kill me the same if I'm asleep as I'm awake. I'm going to have some sleep. I haven't had any sleep since we landed.' And that was the only damn sleep I got from the time we landed until after I got captured.

Private (First Class) Arnold Murdoch
Company K, 143rd Infantry, United States Army

When I got hit, I pushed myself up and yelled real loud. The man immediately in front of me looked back and he saw me and gave a scared, nightmarish cry and he tore out of there. The other guys didn't want to leave me, but I knew they couldn't help me, and Jack couldn't do anything for me. I said, 'Jack, you can go back and send a pill-roller over here.' He went off and left his rifle – and I'll tell you, I started praying. I thought, 'This is for real,' so I said, 'Well, listen God, if you'll help me to get back, I'll try and be a better boy.' When the medics came, they turned me over and cut my pants leg off, and the sleeve off my arm. My arm was real bloody, and my leg was too. My leg was hanging there, so they put some sulphur in the wound, then they took Jack's rifle and took it in half and put it for a splint. They left again to look for a stretcher. I was there for about two hours after I was hit.

Major Armin 'Sheriff' Puck
Marshal Provost, HQ Commandant, 36th Division, United States Army

The tanks were between us and Paestum, and they were hitting our left flank. OK, so what happens, Finney somehow after this initial tank battle was over, went down to the beach and got a 105 Howitzer. He jumped into a hole and sets up this 105. He lays down direct fire and gets four of these big monsters coming towards us. Then the group in 636 Tank Destroyer Battalion got some tanks, and that was kaput for the German armour that morning.

Sergeant Ike Franklin
11th Medical Battalion, with 3rd Battalion Aid Station, 143rd Infantry, United States Army

We were up at a place called Albanella, where they had knocked out some tanks. There was a German soldier laying beside one of them. He was pretty badly burnt, and he cried out, 'Water!' and no one gave him any water. An American lieutenant said he would have anybody court-martialled for giving aid and comfort to the enemy. I told him, 'Lieutenant, I'm a medic, and I have been trained to give aid to anybody that's wounded, whether they're friend or enemy,' I said. 'He was enemy maybe five minutes ago, when he was shooting at us, but right now he's in pain and he needs water.' He said, 'We don't want to do anything for him until after we've had a chance to question him.' So this fella wouldn't let me give him any water.

Lieutenant Payne Rucker
Squad/Section Leader, 2nd Battalion, Cannon Company, 143rd Infantry, United States Army

We didn't have radios, and so we were going to stay right in our position until somebody come to fix the track on our tank. So we were sitting there in this area with the gun during the night, and I had to put out guards. Finally I put Red Cantrell and another guy down at the end road. Anyway, I heard a bunch of girls laugh in a house, and I could hear that laugh and I knew it was Cantrell. I said 'Fojtosec, get up there and see what the hell is going on.' Cantrell was up there with these girls, in a battle zone – drinking wine and having a big time. Fojtosec came back and said, 'It's Cantrell. If you shoot him, I'll swear to God it was the Germans.' He wanted me to shoot him – I should have killed the son-of-a-gun up there – but you don't go killing American soldiers.

Private Ralph Jetton
HQ Company and B Company, 504th Parachute Regiment, US 82nd Airborne Division

It was daylight on the 13th September, and we parked our jeep outside town, where we saw this big old barn. We got out and walked down through the streets, me and Major Wellans on one side, and Captain Gorham and his bodyguard on the other. We probably got 400 yards down into the town of Albanella when we heard, 'Psssst,' and looked over and there was this old Italian man at the door. Major Wellans hollered for Captain Gorham and his interpreter. The interpreter talked to the old man, who told us we had just missed a patrol of 60 Germans, but they were still in town. And we thanked him and sprinted back to the jeep. Before we got to the jeep this barn disintegrated – exploded. The Germans had zeroed in on us with mortars and 88s. We got in this jeep, and me and this interpreter was holding on the back, while Captain Gorham was driving, and we were zig-zagging and missing the shells bursting. If you've ever seen a wild picture show with jeeps going here and there, and if you can imagine the wildest you've ever seen, that was us. We finally got some high ground between us and the artillery and we slowed down, but it was a hair-raising thing.

Corporal John Hummer
Technician Grade 5, C Company, 1st Ranger Battalion, with rocket-launchers in 2nd Platoon, United States Army

The 4.2s had clobbered the knoll with white phosphorus shells – it just tore up the trees and shrubs and tore a platoon of Germans to pieces. That was a mess and one of the ugliest scenes I ever saw up there.

Private Ralph Jetton
HQ Company and B Company, 504th Parachute Regiment, US 82nd Airborne Division

On the fourth night on Hill 414, I was sitting there in the hole, dark as pitch. Things had been quiet all evening. The Germans had pulled back, and I was sitting there thinking of home, and wondering about my brother. A lieutenant out of the 141st came by and he asked me where the Command Post was, and I told him. But first I said, 'What outfit are you out of?' and he said 141st – so I said, 'What battalion?' and he said 'Third,' so I said, 'Do you know a fella the name of Jetton?' and he said, 'Yes. He was, a few minutes ago, sitting down on the side of the hill, waiting to come up here and relieve you.' I jumped out of my hole and run down that hill – it was pitch dark, you

After the Anglo-American landings at Salerno on 9 September 1943, British soldiers man a machine-gun post in an exposed position near the beach.

couldn't see anything – and I got down to the little hacked-out road and started calling his name quietly.

I was walking down the road with the guys laying down on each side of the road. I couldn't really see them, but I knew they were there in the dark. He didn't say a word until I got up close, and he said, 'Yeah, what the hell do you want?' He didn't know who I was – he thought he was going to get detailed out on a patrol or something – and I said, 'This is Dub,' and he said, 'You little sonofabitch!'

Everyone was delighted, and they gathered around and we were beating on each other and hugging. Best moment of the war for me.

Major Roy Murray
Company Commander, 4th Battalion, US Rangers

There were a lot of booby traps around, and mines that had to be taken off the road – we made our advance to Sele very slowly.

Wherever they thought you might stop and get off the road, my God, they had artillery shells wired up, grenades wired up, just have them so that we walked into them, not seeing them. There would be a trip-wire, and they had all sorts of things booby-trapped. They would have a nice artefact off some place, and a guy would say, 'Oh, a souvenir,' and *boom!* You can't convince the American soldier that he shouldn't look for souvenirs and loot. He's very curious – has to lose his arm before he realises this is not the way to go.

Private Ike Franklin
Company C, 111th Medical Battalion – liaison agent with 3rd Battalion Aid Station, 143rd Infantry, United States Army

After I was taken prisoner, I worked with German doctors to treat the wounded of both sides. There was one American doctor, Captain Munro, but the Jerries wouldn't let him work. They had captured some American medical supplies and the German doctors used the plasma to treat the American wounded. But there were some Germans that could have used it – but they wouldn't give it to the Germans. This was because Hitler said it might have some Jewish or Negro blood in it, and they didn't want to contaminate the bloodstream. I told them, 'You are scientists – you know better than that.' And their doctor said, 'Well, Hitler says that, so I've got to go along with it.'

TA2142

A truck carrying American troops arrives in the rubble-filled streets of Naples, October 1943.

NA9367

As the Italian winter takes a grip, British stretcher-bearers work in the driving rain during the battle for Monte Camino, early December 1943.

Fusilier Gus Platts
6th Parachute Battalion

We left from Bizerta in Tunisia. The whole of the 6th Battalion, less A Company, went aboard HMS *Abdiel*, a fast mine-laying cruiser. The mine decks were piled with 1st Airborne Divisional stores and about 400 troops in all. We were in the illustrious company of HMS *King George V*, HMS *Howe*, the USS *Boise* with the 12th Cruiser Squadron and the 14th Destroyer Flotilla. Seemingly nothing could go wrong as we arrived at Taranto late in the evening of the 9th September. We were due to land some time after midnight and were already inside the harbour wall, at anchor, in a balmy evening breeze. I was on deck with the mortar platoon, and we had our mortar bombs and equipment on our backs, waiting to go ashore, just lying down to take the weight off our feet, with our belts unfastened. Then, all of a sudden, there was this unholy bang, immediately followed by what I thought were tracer bullets, but were actually sparks shooting out of the funnel. It looked like we had been attacked – been bombed. After the explosion the ship trimmed by the stern and listed to port. About 30 seconds later she righted herself partially for a few seconds and then went rapidly over to port, sinking by the stern. In actual fact she had broken in two and burst in many places from stern to stern.

I was thrown upwards and hit the bottom of the lifeboat I was under. As I got to my feet, the ship was already listing badly. A naval officer appeared in front of me in his whites saying, 'Get over the side.' I didn't need telling. I had to climb up the deck to get to the rail, and could actually sit on the ship's side as she was turning over. At that moment Bill Dillerstone, one of my mates, was having trouble blowing up his inflatable life-jacket. I blew it up for him – he couldn't swim. Into the water we went, and then we became separated. I struck out away from the vessel as fast as I could – I was dressed in denim trousers, shirt, one boot and one gaiter. I must have swum about 100 yards in the dark, in water full of thick fuel oil and shoals and shoals of jellyfish. I came across another mate of mine, from the machine-gun platoon, struggling in the water. We ended up with a barrel between us, holding ourselves up. You could see in the distance only the bow of the *Abdiel*, still sticking up out of the water, and there were men sitting on it, smoking cigarettes. It was only for a second, and then she went completely.

A large rowing boat picked us up. There was a rat clinging to my shoulders – I threw it off, but it came back again. The damned rat stayed with us until I was pulled out into this boat, and I slung it away in the water. There were eight or nine guys in the boat, one of them was very seriously wounded, with a leg coming off. It took us only a short distance and we got picked up by a little Italian tug flying a Red Cross flag. We got aboard – we were a bit shell-shocked, wet and smelly, and covered in black oil – and we were taken ashore. There were probably about 20 of us and we were put in a cinema near the docks. It was there that I came across Bill, as black as I was, and with a big grin on his face. I thought he'd gone under because he couldn't swim, but he had swum all the way in – a hell of a way. He pulled a tin of cigarettes out of his pocket, a 50-tin of Players; he opened them up and they were perfect. He gave me a fag and we handed them around – they went very quickly. The only thing I had that wasn't contaminated with oil was my beret, which I had rolled up and put inside my shirt.

We thought we were going to be in the cinema for a long time, but when it got light, a navy launch took us aboard the *Howe*. The first thing we did was go into the showers, scrub down and get all the oil out of our hair. Then someone gave me a packet of fags and a pair of blue naval overalls, and we got our heads down on the floor and on the tables. We were given big mugs full of what the Navy called 'kia' – like cocoa. It was very tasty. The next thing we knew the bugle was blowing for reveille. We gathered on deck trying to sort out who was who.

Brigadier Pritchard from our old battalion – 'Charlie Orange' to us – came aboard from a launch. He told us we were going ashore and carrying on the fight. There were three big cheers, but none of us had anything to fight with. Things got going on the *Howe* somehow, and we were supplied with gear. We were given the Marines' equipment – all prewar stuff – and for many many years afterwards you used to find ex-6th Battalion men still walking about with distinctive white waistbelts, which immediately identified them as coming from the *Abdiel* sinking.

There were less than 100 of us on the *Howe*. The CO, Lieutenant-Colonel Goodwin, and the RSM, Langford, were lost; the senior man was the PTI Sergeant-Major, John Reid, who called the roll that morning. We were shipped out with all our strange gear. I got a pair of white Navy plimsolls, blue Navy overalls – no shirts or anything else – and white webbing equipment with a pack and some pouches. I was given a Lanchester sub-machine gun, a typical Navy weapon, like a Browning. It fired 9 mm and they believed we would find plenty of ammo in Italy – we had none ourselves.

The next day, after a night ashore, we sorted ourselves out into something like a fighting unit, though we looked more like a band of guerrillas. I discarded my Lanchester at this stage for an Italian Breda. For a while I found myself a machine-gunner in an infantry section because at first we had no mortars with us.

Part of the brigade went up to Foggia, then Bari along the Adriatic coast to Manfredonia. All our kit had come into Bari docks from Africa, and the whole lot went up in the big bang when the Germans raided Bari and hit an ammunition ship. So going into Italy I hadn't got a single piece of equipment except my beret – I lost everything else.

Along the eastern side of Italy, every few miles there was a river, and in winter they were raging torrents. Jerry had dug himself in on the Sangro River. When we got there it was in flood – it was very, very strong. The REs built a bridge that was swept away in a night. The Indian sappers eventually rebuilt it and we got across and some tanks followed. It was a fairly rotten time – the weather was bleak and it was one big mud hole. We were in the same gear we'd got from the *Howe* – I was still wearing my Navy overalls. It was cold. You could find yourself a coat or the odd thing, but for a few weeks it was grim. We didn't wait for stuff to come through to us – we just got on with it.

After the Sangro we joined up with the 2nd New Zealand Division – we had been everybody's poor relations until then. We went on to Lanciano, a little up the coast. By December 1943 the 1st Airborne Division had gone home. We stayed on as the 2nd Independent Brigade Group – it was a fairly big unit, spanning the three infantry battalions, the 4th, 5th (Scottish) and 6th (Royal Welch), with a squadron of engineers, a battery of gunners and even a glider-pilot section.

Just before Christmas we had taken a place called Casoli, a village on top of a hill, seemingly a favourite place for villages in that part of Italy. We set up our position on a day when it was snowing. We dug our mortar pits four or five feet down, did one or two shoots during the day, and then at night the snow really came down. We were just below a ridge about ten feet high. I went into my slit trench, put my groundsheet on top of me and in next to no time I was asleep, sitting on my steel helmet to keep out of the wet trench. I was found absolutely snowed under and had to be dug out. If they hadn't found me I would still have been there now, frozen solid. My sergeant gave me a tot of rum to thaw me out.

Throughout this time our casualties were coming from shell and mortar fire. At Arielle, in front of Chieti, the route coming up to our position from rear echelon was under such constant shell fire that it became known as the 'mad mile'. You were more likely to get killed going back to base there than staying in the line. We used to go down it like a bat out of hell – yet every day a supply truck would get blown up.

Every time the Germans stopped they got into a prepared position which they defended. Our brigade never ever went back – always forward – but the

Germans had mountains, rivers or prepared defences to pull back to. While they were holding one defensive line, they were getting another ready. We were constantly having to find our way in – they could call the tune. The only time they couldn't was when things like Anzio happened, when we got behind them and interfered with their plans.

WAR AT SEA

The German battleship *Tirpitz* was ready for service in 1941 – but spent an inactive war in harbour in Norway – where she tied down Allied shipping by the threat of her presence. On 22 September 1943 she was attacked by midget submarines and disabled, but following the Channel Dash in February 1942, the *Scharnhorst* was at large and, according to decrypted German naval signals, was en route in late December to sink two Allied Arctic convoys. British warships were sent to attack the *Scharnhorst*, and the *Duke of York* sank her on Boxing Day, delivering a major blow to German naval power.

Wing Commander Donald Bennett
10 Squadron, RAF
They believed that although a torpedo or a bomb couldn't touch the Tirpitz because the armour-plating was too thick on her sides and deck, the construction of the bottom was such that mines, rolled down the surface, could have burst the hull from below.

The ship was moored very close to the shore, and all we had to do was drop these mines between ship and shore and they would go down and do their stuff. When they got down to a certain depth, they would go off. Each one of us, on our aircraft, carried five of these things weighing about 1,500 lb each. We went down over an island to get a pinpoint, and an exact run-in. I was a flamer, so I was picked on all the way. The theory was that we went to a point on the coast, about ten miles short of the ship, and did a stop-watch run from there – exact speed, height and timing – and we would drop. Had I done so, it would have been perfect, but in fact there was man-made fog filling the whole of the fjord. You couldn't see a thing, so the drop was not very accurate, and I had to make a second run – which I did. It was pretty hopeless because of this fog – a very clever chemical thing. They sprayed chemical on the water and it produced a fog about two hundred feet thick. They had it going for hours because somehow they knew we were coming. Anyway, the result was that the ship was undamaged.

We lost about half of the aircraft that were on the raid, and I was lucky to get away with it myself. In those days the pilot of a Halifax aircraft didn't wear his parachute – it was not a seat parachute as fighter boys wore. It was a pack that you clipped on your chest. When I ordered 'Abandon aircraft', all the boys got out as fast as they could, and there I was, sitting in my seat with a flaming aircraft – and a very hot one – ready to do what? Bale out without a parachute? I'm pleased to say that the flight engineer, a man called Coughlan, realising my predicament, came back into that aircraft, knowing it was about to collapse, and handed me my parachute, which I clipped on.

As I started to get out of the seat, the starboard wing folded up. I got out in a hurry and pulled the plug, and hit the deck just as it opened. If I'd counted three seconds – or if there had been any other reason for a slight delay, I wouldn't have made it.

Lieutenant Godfrey Place
X-craft submariner, RN

At 6.40 a.m. we sighted the *Tirpitz* at a range of about a mile. My plan for the attack was to dive down deep about 500 yards from the target, pass under the torpedo nets at 70 feet and lay the charges, then escape under the nets. At 0705 I took X7 down to 70 feet for the attack but we hit a net and had to disentangle ourselves. We tried again at 90 feet, but got even more firmly stuck this time. When we finally came clear and rose up to the surface I saw that, somehow, we had got under the net and were now about 30 yards from the *Tirpitz*'s port beam. We actually broke surface at that point but no one spotted us, even when we gave the target's side a glancing blow. So we slid underneath and dropped one charge forward and one aft. As we dropped the second charge at 0720 we heard the first sounds of counter-attack from the enemy. It was not directed at us, as it turned out, but at X6 which had been spotted after dropping its charges.

Our charges had a time delay of about an hour, but the timers had proved unreliable so it was imperative we escape through the nets as quickly as possible. The charges dropped by the other X-craft might go up at any time after 0800. For the next three-quarters of an hour we nosed around just feet from the sea floor, looking for a gap in the nets and rapidly losing all sense of our exact position. We tried most places along the bottom of the nets, and even broke water sometimes, but couldn't find a way out anywhere. The HP air was getting dangerously low and eventually the situation was so desperate that I decided to try going over the top of a curtain net between two buoys. We surfaced, gave a strong thrust and flopped over the net. Then we dived down to the bottom and tried to get as far away from the *Tirpitz* as we could before the charges went up. But at sixty feet we hit yet another net and while we were struggling to get free, the explosion went up, a continuous roar that seemed to last whole minutes.

The explosion shook us free of the net but also damaged X7, so I took her down to the bottom to assess the damage. The situation was not promising. Water was coming in through the hull glands, but none of the pumps worked and our HP bottles were empty. When we surfaced to check our position our night periscope was hit by enemy fire, and at this point I decided to abandon ship. As the Germans were dropping depth charges, we decided to try a surface surrender. With some trepidation I opened the fore hatch just enough to allow me to wave a white sweater.

The firing stopped immediately so I climbed out on to the casing, still waving the sweater. We had surfaced close to a battle practice target so I thought, 'That's fine. I'll hold on to the practice target and bring the crew out.' Just then, the X7 bumped into the target and the curved side of the target forced our bows down, letting water into the hatch before I had time to close it.

Unfortunately the boat hadn't got enough buoyancy to stay on the surface and she went down, leaving me standing on the practice target. I felt fairly confident that the others would get out all right but, as it turned out, the only one to escape alive was Aitken, who was a trained diver, and he was picked up in a comatose condition. Whitham and Whitley had run out of oxygen before they could escape.

So there I was, standing on the battle target, wearing just my underclothes, sea boot stockings and army boots. I felt ridiculous as I was taken on to the quarter-deck. The *Tirpitz* was in chaos. One chap kept running up to me and saying, 'How many boats?' and 'You will be shot.' I had a sudden vision of Gabby, the town crier in a cartoon film of *Gulliver's Travels*, saying, 'You can't do this to me, you can't do this to me – I've a wife and kids, millions of kids.' What I actually said was, 'I'm an English naval officer and I expect to be treated with due courtesy.' But I wish I had known at the time that the likelihood of my being shot on a crowded deck was very small.

Also aboard the *Tirpitz* were Cameron and the crew of X6, who had scuttled their craft and surrendered after laying their charges.

Petty Officer George Burridge
Radar operator, aboard HMS **Belfast**

On the 25th December 1943 we were called to action stations, and we were eventually told that we were likely to be going into action fairly soon. The

Boxing Day 1943. HMS *Duke of York* and the cruiser HMS *Jamaica* sank the German battleship *Scharnhorst*, and all but thirty-six of the crew of over two thousand perished in the icy Atlantic. Picked up by HMS *Dorsetshire*, the grateful survivors were brought ashore blindfolded for security reasons.

ships were reported to be close enough to cause us problems. On the 26th we were told that it was the *Scharnhorst*, and that it had taken the *Norfolk* out of action. We fired star shells to get its position, and then we had a report from the *Sheffield* saying that they had engine problems. So we were told to engage the *Scharnhorst* alone – and that frightened the life out of us, because we knew we were completely outgunned and outclassed.

We couldn't see it, but we were plotting its position and shadowing it. Everyone was as tense as could be. The battle started later that day. We were going in, firing, then coming out again, in the hope of staying out of range. We got a message that the *Duke of York* was coming to support us, because without that we wouldn't have lasted long.

We continued firing along with the *Duke of York*, and I can see it now – the entire *Scharnhorst* on fire from bow to stern – literally just a mass of flames. We went in with torpedo attacks two or three times, then we pulled away and the destroyers went in to finish it off.

THE FAR EAST

Following the sudden and hurried withdrawal by the British during 1942, the Allies were ready to drive back the Japanese and win back Burma. Jungle warfare proved deadly in many ways other than fighting – malaria, illness, heat – and the Japanese proved an unpredictable and ruthless enemy, willing to sacrifice themselves rather than suffer the ignominy of capture. Early in 1943, British losses in the Arakan were heavy, and it was not until General Slim took command of the 14th Army that the tide began to turn.

Wing Commander Arthur Gill
84 Squadron, RAF

At the time we did hate the Japanese – they were regarded as not fighting fairly. I think it was considered that we had always played cricket when we fought a war up to those times, and some of the atrocities carried out by the Japanese were resented by the British forces, particularly for the torture and the ill-treatment of prisoners. On one occasion, our airplane was filled with fumes and the gunner, thinking it was on fire, baled out without instructions from the pilot. He landed in Burma, safely enough, but was captured by the Japanese. They assumed he was a spy. They tortured him and eventually he was killed. All the chap had done was to fall out of an airplane inadvertently.

But the Japanese were known to be pretty ruthless little men. And it didn't go down well with the British forces.

Ursula Betts
British anthropologist working with refugees from Burma, known as 'the White Queen of the Nagas'
I and four Nagas went down and ran a canteen – supposedly for Europeans – and we did keep European food for the Europeans coming down on the refugee trains. But of course we got swamped every day by the two thousand-odd Indian refugees who were streaming out. And the temperature was in the nineties – up in the hundreds during the day. It was very hot, and we got through sixty gallons of tea in the day.

We went down to the railway station, and the water for the tea had to be carried in four-gallon kerosene tins with a wooden bar across. You carried one in each hand, and the five us carried sixty gallons that way. We stacked the cans – at first we just had open fireplaces on the platform with iron bars across to sit the tins on, but as we got a bit more organised, the railway built us a little shed with proper brick compartments. We went down to the railway coal bunkers and came staggering back with loads and loads of coal – it was very sooty coal. I used to go down a blonde and come back a Carmen brunette – hair absolutely black with smoke and soot. About five, the train would pull in, and we'd be swamped by these mobs and mobs and mobs of clamouring Indian refugees. And poor devils, it was very hot. They were packed into the trains. Half of them were sick with dysentery and cholera. If anybody died on the train they used to try and get the body out for proper burial or cremation.

Then, of course, the trains were being shunted into sidings for hours at a time. They were supposed to go right through. There was a complete breakdown of communication in all possible directions. You fended for yourself, but they were supposed to get through in eight hours. It was believed in Shillong the trains were getting through in eight hours. If they got through in twenty-four, everybody was lucky. And of course the body would start to go off, and they just chucked the corpses out on the line.

It got towards the end – we used to have a patrol down the train, looking into the carriages to find out if they were trying to conceal a body – and then try and get it removed.

The wounded were marvellous. They'd be leaning out of the windows and see me doubling down the platform with my cans. Having had their tea, the train would pull out with everybody hanging out of the windows and waving and shouting, 'See you on the road to Mandalay!' Quite often they were badly wounded men who had smelly wounds, whose clothes were in a mess. One of my tasks was to do a patrol down the train – look in every carriage to see if there was anybody who wasn't getting anything.

I found one chap who'd obviously been next to a friend who'd been hit, because there was blood all over his uniform, and I said, 'Look here, go up and get some tea. Can you walk?' 'Oh yes, I can walk – but there's ladies there, and I didn't like to go.' I said, 'All right, here you are.' And passed him in his tea and bun. He was very grateful.

The Japs were coming up Burma like a piston up a car cylinder – and quite a lot of the refugees had come out by the side exits, through Manipur. But once the Japs got past those exits, there was only one way for the refugees to go, and that was right over the most appalling mountains, where no arrangements for food or anything else had been made. I heard some accounts of conditions on that road – they were quite appalling. The place was littered with corpses – you were walking over them.

Wing Commander Lucian Ercolani
159 Squadron, RAF

On one occasion, I dropped into the mess to have lunch. We had only just had our first glass, when a distraught villager burst in. Would we help? A leopard had just mauled a child in their village and it was still there.

Armed with rifles we set off in a jeep with Frank Carey – a distinguished Battle of Britain pilot – with the villager to show the way, and us not quite knowing what we were going to find.

We saw this poor child with a great lump torn out of her side, which they had filled with a cow pat. Apparently they had healing properties! The womenfolk were in a terrible state and the men were going in all directions, armed with spears, bows and arrows, and an assortment of quite fearsome weapons!

There, in the branches of a great mango tree, in this tiny collection of huts, was this lovely creature, draped out along a branch. The two valiant gentlemen took careful aim and fired, obviously wounding the animal but, unfortunately, not killing it. It came bounding down the tree, scattering us all as it went, and disappeared. We realised that honour was at stake and we were duty bound to track it down, but didn't quite know where to go.

The Headman then took charge and pointed to the eaves of one of the huts where it had taken refuge. We were pushed forward by all the villagers, they were all around us, until we were only about ten yards away. There was a great roar and out leapt the leopard. We couldn't even lift our rifles properly with everyone crowding around us and by great good fortune, the leopard didn't touch any of us, but bounded right through between us all. Unwisely for him, he again took refuge up this tree and this time we didn't make a mistake.

When the leopard skin was returned from the curers in Calcutta, the skull, which had been sent with the skin in order to give the appropriate savage appearance to the ultimate fireside rug, had not been properly cleaned. The head of the rug had rotted, to become a hairless, flat and wrinkled grey mass. This prompted the story that Frank hadn't actually shot the leopard at all, but had paid some local lads to club it to death.

THE ARAKAN

Sergeant Reuben Kitson
Royal Corps of Signals
Everybody that went into the Arakan to start with would be pretty certain they'd have malaria three times in the first twelve to fifteen months. Malaria was sometimes followed by jaundice.

The diet was alright – I wouldn't think our intake of calories was anything like we should have had, because my normal diet before going abroad would be something like 3,500 calories a day, and I think that for long stretches of time, our intake would be down below 1,000 calories. We didn't get any bread. We didn't get any potatoes. We didn't get any green vegetables. We took ascorbic tablets in lieu of vegetables. We had tinned stew, soya sausages, bully beef, and the diet wasn't much varied from that.

Sergeant-Major Martin McLane
2nd Battalion, Durham Light Infantry
Before the attack on Donbaik, we formed up in a dry nullah bed. There was a series of them every few yards. We were carrying an average of 60 pounds of kit. The artillery fire was going over, and everything was dusty in the early morning light. The company commander gave the order bayonets on, smoke if you want to. The men dragged on their cigarettes, and were hanging on to them for grim death, because let's not be heroic, a man is only going to do a job if he's ordered to. He's going into an attack and the chance of him being killed is tremendous. The order came, right, get ready, over the top. I had the signallers and company clerk with me. As we went over the top, I saw a Jap. I up with the Tommy gun and the bloody thing wouldn't fire. I was disgusted – here I was a professional soldier and I couldn't hit him. He had been throwing

grenades, but scarpered. I never heard our Brens firing, only desultory shots from rifles. I had been in attacks in France and knew what it should sound like. All there was was Japanese firing – nothing of ours at all.

The CO spoke to me on the set. He asked what was happening. I said this is the funniest attack I've been in, I can't hear a Bren, I can't hear a rifle. There's nothing moving, all I can see is bodies. He said, 'Do something about it then.' 'What can I do?' 'Get the men in.' Well, I only had Company HQ with me, the other two platoons were off on their own. I found the company commander wounded. He'd been wounded in France in the knee, and his same leg had been hit again. He was bleeding badly. I dragged him back through the nullah, found A Company commander and put my company commander on a stretcher.

I went to find the two rifle platoons, I passed a stretcher with Lieutenant Greenwall on it. He was full of shrapnel from a Japanese plastic grenade, lying smoking a cigarette. He said, 'Well, Sergeant-Major,' stroking his old man, 'they didn't hit that.' He was newly married. I found seven of his platoon lying down. I shouted 'Come on lads, bayonets!' A corporal said, 'Wait, wait, Sergeant-Major, these Brens and rifles won't fire.' I didn't believe him and got down behind a Bren. One round fired and then the gun jammed solid. I went through all the drills, but nothing would work. I slung it aside in disgust. 'Give us your rifle.' I fired it, but the bolt stuck solid and I could not eject the round, except by putting the butt on the ground and booting the bolt with my foot.

Sergeant Clifford Jones
1st Battalion, Royal Welch Fusiliers
At 0500 hours the attack on Donbaik began. All hell was let loose. Three-quarters of A Company got on to the bunker, but couldn't hold it. They got into some of the trenches on the outside which were empty. I came in from the right and lost half my men trying to attack similar bunkers. I was told over the radio to move up to A Company, and take over. I wriggled and grabbed hold of the first man I could see and asked what was going on. He pointed to my officer doubled up down in a foxhole. He said 'Are you taking over?' 'Yes,' I said. 'Leave me here and get on with it.'

I then got a message to go back to the CO, who said 'D Company are cut off. The Royal Scots are going to reinforce us and attack to get D Company out. I'm coming back with you to A Company,' which he did. The Japs were very astute, and shouted out in English, things like, 'British soldier, why are you here? Your wives are waiting for you.' The CO shouted in Welsh through a loudspeaker to D Company, to hold on. That flummoxed the Japs. A

Company and the Royal Scots' attempts to reach D Company went well for the first fifteen minutes, but then came under Jap bombardment. After two hours of fighting, we did get out about 40 men of D Company. There were no officers alive.

Lieutenant Michael Marshall
4/5th Royal Gurkha Rifles

I was posted to the 4th/5th Gurkha Rifles in the Arakan in September 1943. To get there, we went by train to Madras, by steamer to Chittagong; from there to Dohazari by train. From there we marched on a mule track over the Goppe Pass to Goppe Bazaar – it poured with rain all the time. I met the quartermaster of the 4th/5th before starting the march. I was wearing the trench coat I had brought with me from London and he said abruptly, 'We don't wear raincoats in the Arakan, we get wet.' I took the point and never wore one again.

As the battalion had suffered some casualties the previous week, and the numbers of sick had increased, they were delighted to see how many reinforcements we had brought. The monsoon had only recently finished, and this part of Arakan consisted of a series of hillocks surrounded by water. The paddy fields were about a foot deep in water. The four companies were spaced out on hillocks wherever there was dry ground. All the rivers were flooded. We were permanently damp.

Our positions were about six to seven miles from the Jap forward posts. Colonel Mac, as he was known, posted me to B Company, whose commander had been drowned four days earlier. He had been demonstrating to his men how to swim the Kalapanzin River in full battle order. He was a strong swimmer, and it was thought his legs had become entangled with weeds. There were no other British officers in B Company. I became a full lieutenant at the age of 19 years and four months. The battalion's task was active patrolling. As I was totally inexperienced I was sent out to learn what I ought to be doing. This was not easy as I had a limited knowledge of Urdu and my knowledge of Gurkhali was not much better. On one patrol I had ten men, plus a very experienced Subedar. He always spoke to me in Gurkhali, and if I didn't understand that, in Urdu. It was only back at base when I heard him talking on the inter company telephone system to the CO in perfectly good English that I realised that he had no intention of making my life easy; I would only learn Gurkhali by speaking nothing else.

One night, I led a standing patrol with a Jemadar from my own company and about six men, through paddy the whole way. At about two o'clock in the morning we were shot at. We all got down into the water and stayed for about half an hour. We had probably been heard by a small Jap patrol who had fired – but did not stay to investigate. When we moved on, most of us had forty to fifty leeches hanging off us, and we spent a good half hour removing them when we got to a bund. Some leeches are so penetrative that they can go through lace holes in boots.

Captain Alexander Wilson
2nd British Infantry Division's jungle battle school

Most British people, many brought up in towns, have never really been in the dark, because there are always street lamps, or some sort of light. Few of our soldiers had ever been alone at night. We have lost our sense of hearing and smell. These are basic animal-like instincts which are vital in the jungle. The Japs smelt different to us, and you could smell them in a defensive position, or if they had recently passed down a track. The Japs smelt rather like scented powder. Indians smelt differently to us too – it depends on what you eat.

At night you feel very much on your own and are susceptible to noises deliberately made by the enemy, and you shoot at these, and at shadows, which you mustn't do. Slim's adage was, 'the answer to noise is silence'. It was almost a crime to shoot without having a corpse to show for it in the morning. The antidote is endless training at night. We practised movement by night, the use of pole charges to attack bunkers, and bringing down supporting fire from mortars and guns very close to us. There was a very great deal to learn. Radio communications were a problem in jungle and hills. You found an enormous number of blank areas for communications, specially at night. You had to find the right spot for siting wireless sets by moving around.

Lieutenant Michael Marshall
4/5th Royal Gurkha Rifles

It was the first time I had heard Gurkhas actually shouting 'Ayo Gurkhali!' (The Gurkhas are coming!), a fearsome noise at close quarters, which undoubtedly scared the Japs. It was also the first time I had seen them using their kukris at close quarters. They mostly went for the throat. The Japs ran.

The next morning I was told to take two platoons back to this position to bury the dead. I instructed the Jemadar to carry on, and went off. I returned to find that instead of digging graves, the Gurkhas were using the foxholes dug by the Japs. The bodies had rigor mortis, and would not fit, so the Gurkhas were cutting them up and stuffing them into the holes. I stopped this, but they thought I was being pernickety. The Gurkha has all the nicest characteristics of the British soldier – he likes sport, drinking, women and gambling. However, he has little feeling for the dead, either the enemy or his comrades. Once gone they'd gone, and there were no feelings of sadness nor remorse. When killing the enemy he is elated, and Gurkhas' eyes become bloodshot when going into action at close quarters. The Jap was a very courageous opponent and suffered enormously – but the Gurkhas were better. I was glad I was with them not against them. My battalion took no prisoners until well into 1945 and none of our men were taken prisoner – neither side took prisoners. At this time in the war, the Japs were thought to be invincible by some people, including many British troops. This was not the attitude of my Gurkhas.

Captain Peter Gadsdon
A Company, 4/14th Battalion, Punjab Regiment, Indian Army
We mounted standing patrols in the paddy fields in the valley. In a mist so thick you couldn't see anything, the patrols heard troops coming and said, 'Halt, who goes there?' Some Indians replied, '*Tikka bai* . . . it's all right . . . don't bother . . . no problem,' and they walked straight past. The sentries came and reported this to us. This column, which had gone straight through our position, hadn't been some of our own ration parties as the sentries had thought. In fact it had been the Japs with Indian troops fighting with the Japanese.

Major Henry Cree
2nd Battalion, West Yorkshire Regiment
Nobody thought that a dressing station would be attacked – but it was. The Japs got into it and did the most appalling execution there amongst the wounded and sick in this hospital. We could hear it going on – shouts and screams and shooting. I was asked by the CO of the Indian hospital to counterattack the hospital and take it, but I said I couldn't. It was pitch dark by that time, and I said it was impossible for us to attack. You couldn't tell friend from foe, and we should only end up by shooting all our own men if we tried to attack it by night. We didn't know the ground, anyway. It was impossible to put down any sort of covering fire with mortars or guns, or anything – we'd only have made matters worse. So I said, with great reluctance, 'I don't think I can do anything about it tonight.'

Early the next morning, A Company went in and counterattacked the main dressing station. The Japs were still there in full force and had to be just winkled out, inch by inch. We lost 15 men ourselves in that attack – but we eventually got them all out of it – booted them out.

It was horrid – they'd shot men lying in their beds. They just shot them. They shot several doctors too – they just lined them up and shot them. It made everybody very furious and determined to get the better of them – which we did. What happened was that the whole of the 9th Brigade, B Echelon was in the position, just a little way from us on both sides of a deep chaung. This chaung ran up into the main dressing station area, getting much narrower as it went up, but it was a well-defined channel. That night, Japs started passing down this chaung on the way from the main dressing station. Both sides of the chaung were held by our B Echelon personnel, muleteers, orderly room staff, sanitary men, quartermaster's storemen, chaps like that – nearly all old soldiers, including the regimental Sergeant-Major. They twigged what was happening. They just let the Japs have it. They killed an enormous number of them in that place, which became known as Blood Nullah afterwards. These were the chaps who had raided the main dressing station, so we felt we avenged that one.

I was quite scared of the Japs, myself. I thought they were very nasty people. They would die, but they wouldn't lie down. They literally did hold their positions absolutely to the last man and the last round. They were immensely determined. On our advance down the Tidim Road, we used to come upon pockets of these Japs, all lying dead under a tree or something. They had either died of complete starvation, or in some cases they had committed suicide by holding a grenade to their bosom and pulling the pin out, rather than be taken prisoner. We found that their food consisted only of an old sock full of rice and some bits of raw fish – terribly smelly and nasty. They'd been living on this for ages – extremely hardy.

Group Captain Frank Carey
267 Wing, RAF, based at Magwe

The Japanese aircraft were considerably more manoeuvrable than ours were. If we got down and mixed it with them at low altitude we were in trouble, because we couldn't accelerate away from them unless we had a bit of height to dive away and they could run rings around us. The Japs at that stage were flying fixed-undercarriage monoplanes called Army 97s. They were extremely light and, for their weight, had very powerful engines, but not much in the way of gunfire. They also didn't have any armour plating behind them. If you got a good squirt at them they used to fold up.

They really worked, those Japs. One Jap that I shot down had deliberately crash-landed, trying to dive into a revetment with a Blenheim there. He missed it. We got the whole aircraft and body and everything else – he'd got

27 bullets in him and he was still flying that thing round the airfield looking for a target. They always used to try to dive into something. That was what we were up against. We also had to deal with an appalling lack of facilities – no spares, no tools, no equipment. Sometimes, to get an engine out, we wheeled a plane under a palm tree, pulled the tree down, tied it to the engine and slowly released it. Often we cannibalised one aircraft to keep others going.

When we made our first advance against the Japanese down the Arakan border with Burma, I flew to a recently repaired airfield at Cox's Bazaar to test its suitability for operations. On the return journey I had to refuel at Chittagong, which had only emergency fuel supplies on it. The refuelling party were in the process of finishing their job, and I was sitting in the cockpit waiting to start up, when I noticed a number of fighter aircraft appear from behind a cloud – about 27 in all. I knew they must be Japanese, because we didn't have that many aircraft in the place.

Being without radar cover or any other warning was always a hazard, and here it was in large lumps! I started my engine, yelled to the ground crew to get under cover, and then had to taxi a long way to get to the end of the runway. I opened up, but long before I was airborne the bullets were flying and kicking up the dust around me. I got up in the air and immediately began to jink and skid to make myself an awkward target. I was helped by my own fury with myself for having been stupid enough to take off into such a suicidal position! However, luck was with me again and I led the Japs on my tail up the river at absolutely nought feet between the river boats, finally working my way up into the hills and leading them away from their own base at Akyab. Eventually they had to break off – I suppose their fuel was getting low. I thought I saw one of them crash behind me, but that was never confirmed. I really lost a lot of weight on that sortie.

Wing Commander Lucian Ercolani
159 Squadron, RAF

There was an entirely different atmosphere flying in the Far East compared to the European show. The risk from enemy action was considerably less in the Far East, but, really, the anxiety and fear was probably worse. However badly one thought of the Germans, at least there was an element of European civilisation, as against our real fear of the Japanese and of coming down amongst them.

Our bases were always in the Eastern part of India, in Bengal, 56 miles from Calcutta. This meant that there was a lot of flying before we actually got to the business end, across the Bay of Bengal and, more often than not, flying over the Burmese mountains. To start with, this was mostly at night.

Returning back in the mornings, though, could be a joy – the sun rising behind you a glorious gold, lighting up the tops of the mountains, the valleys shrouded in mist, still in the dark. Although you had the worry of getting over them, they were very beautiful. The aircraft with less fuel and no bomb-load now, light to the touch, quite free and relaxed. It was quite an emotional feeling. I often thought I could hear the 'Ave Maria' being sung.

Pilot Officer Roger Cobley
20 Squadron, RAF

The Mark IIC Hurricane was fitted with two 40 mm cannon for anti-tank work and they made the aircraft a bit unwieldy. You couldn't do aerobatics safely. We carried high explosive or armour-piercing shells. Each gun was loaded with only 16 rounds, which you had to fire singly, not in bursts like 20 mm cannons or machine guns. You had to line up very accurately on the target, and attack one at a time. We were supposed to have Spitfires as top cover, but didn't get it to start with. But operating very low as we did, with jungle trees below, it was difficult for Jap aircraft to see us, and in any case there weren't many about.

I commanded a section – a pair of aircraft. In the Arakan in late 1943 we started by operating from a jungle strip called Brighton, near the coast just behind our front line. After which we moved even nearer the front and flew from a strip on the beach, called Hove. This was an agreeable place, living in bamboo huts. We swam, but had to look out for stingrays. We had a ration of drink dropped to us by parachute – four bottles of beer per month for the airmen, and one bottle of gin or whisky for the officers. We had a good mix of over half Commonwealth chaps. Our targets were bunkers, river boats, and occasionally trucks. We lost quite a few people, shot down by flak. I was shot down during an attack on Akyab, where a Japanese general was supposed to be visiting. I was leading, and was hit by flak. There was no target so the others peeled off. My engine kept stopping then picking up, and glycol smoke was coming out. I had 80 miles to go, and wasn't going to make it. I told the others to go home. I headed for the Kaladan Valley where I knew there were some relatively bare hillsides, and the West Africans were still about. I landed wheels-up on a barer patch, and it was right by a West African forward patrol. The West Africans arranged for an L-5 to come into a strip they had prepared and fly me out. I was back in the squadron before nightfall that day. I was very lucky.

Group Captain Frank Carey
267 Wing, RAF, based at Magwe

A group of us – all pilots temporarily off ops in Eastern India – formed a club called the Screechers' Club. There was a tendency for the young to hit the bottle when the pressure let up, myself included, I must admit. The idea was, you were allowed drink only as long as you remained amusing. The club also had ranks. At the bottom was Hiccough, then Roar, Scream, and Screech at the top. Everybody but me had to start as a Hiccough. I permitted myself one grade up at the beginning, since I was running the thing. Everybody else started at the bottom. You had to behave yourself because, if you went over the top, you were downgraded. The only way to move a grade up was to hang around at the bar and buy drinks for one of the higher grades. When we had graduation night – about once a week – if a chap had bought me four drinks, he was certainly worth a grade higher. Chaps would hang inverted from the ceiling punkahs and things like that, which would gain them a higher ranking as long as they weren't stupid and injured themselves.

Somebody gave us a grand piano there. We used to have singsongs and I started to compose two pieces of music. One was called the 'Prang Concerto' and the other was the 'Symphonie Alcoholique'. I could play the symphony all ways – you didn't necessarily have to use your hands! The 'Prang Concerto' had three movements, and the last movement demanded the complete demolition of the piano. I had to go through and play the third movement on my last day there, before being posted to the Middle East. It cost me quite a lot to replace that darned piano. Actually, I never did really complete the third movement, because it's almost impossible to break the heavier wires of a piano, even using a broken-off piano leg! Humour relieved everybody's feelings.

Squadron Leader George Butler
11 Squadron, RAF

We carried napalm in the Hurricane's long-range tanks instead of fuel. It was very effective against the Japs, especially close to our own troops. Napalm strikes were controlled by our own troops, firing coloured smoke on to the enemy position. The colour was changed each day, to keep the Japs guessing. I as leader went in first, followed by the other eleven. We would make three runs each, until we had expended our bombs and ammunition.

Pilot Officer Harry Morrell
211 Squadron, RAF

When I arrived at 211 Squadron, the adjutant came out to greet me and fell flat on his back – he was drunk. We had a brilliant CO, Wing Commander Marr, DSO and bar, DFC and bar, who had shot down six Japs. We had 16 aircraft in our squadron, and in the year before I joined had lost 35 crews. I didn't know this at the time.

I did my first op sortie on New Year's Eve, as one of a pair attacking river craft. We lost touch with the other aircraft in cloud, but got there OK. Pagodas were especially useful for navigation – you could see the Shwe Dagon's gold dome 40 miles off in daytime. We were highwaymen and we hit anything that moved. The big prize was a train. If there were no trains about, we attacked the stations, or the engine sheds. The Beaufighter was a formidable aircraft and had four 20 mm cannon, six machine guns, eight 60-pounder high explosive rockets or eight 25-pounder PA rounds. We always used HE on river craft.

We normally flew alone, but on one occasion, we flew as part of an eight-aircraft sortie to look for Jap Motor Torpedo Boats up a chaung. We were to attack a position given over the radio by an Anglo-Burmese chap on the ground. He would guide our rockets, saying 'fifty yards right' or whatever. We formed up in a taxi-rank, but none of us could see what damage was being done. We later found out that we'd killed the Burmese chap with one of our rockets.

Pilot Officer Basil Hewes
82 Squadron, RAF

Once a water buffalo strolled across a forward strip at Kalewa as a Mosquito was taking off. The pilot didn't see it, the aircraft caught fire, and as we had no fire or crash equipment we had to watch them burn to death. The operating conditions were more dangerous than the Japs. If you landed in the jungle, the chances of getting out were remote. You were briefed on what to do, but few made it.

Flight Lieutenant Ernest Bambridge
60 Squadron, RAF

Bombing and strafing fast and low was occasionally frightening, but as I was not very old, the fright did not last long. We went in pairs. The bombs had an 11-second delay to give you time to get clear. I lost my number two on one strafe. He was hit and baled out OK, but he came across a Gurkha patrol who mistook him for a Jap and shot him dead. I flew with a survival kit consisting of a .38-inch revolver, a field dressing, a kukri and some K rations.

Pilot Officer Harry Morrell
211 Squadron, RAF

We had to take off in the rain – sheets of spray flew up. You wouldn't do it nowadays. As you flew across the paddy fields, flocks of birds would fly up and hit the aircraft, hitting the windscreen and engines. The blood and feathers would soon blow off.

Wing Commander Lucian Ercolani
159 Squadron, RAF

We got involved with the infamous railway line linking Singapore right up through to Burma, built over the bodies of thousands and thousands of prisoners-of-war. It was a real 'hate' operation.

Bridges and the trains themselves were the bomb targets. The Liberators were designed for medium- and high-level bombing, but as they were the only aircraft available which could do the considerable distances involved, we had to evolve new low-level techniques. We could hardly claim ever converting a Liberator into a fighter-bomber, but we must have come fairly close!

Having flown 1,000 miles plus to find our objective on the railway line, we would have to come right down on to the deck to try and knock out the engines. The terrible worry in our minds was that these trains, and the lines, were crowded with our own people. It was a very deep emotional experience to see your own people on the ground, right down there in those terrible places, waving to us and encouraging us on. I cannot believe that some accidents did not happen, as many were very close to the engines, but their welcome was always the same. We felt awful when we had finished and pulled up to go home again, leaving them all behind.

We also evolved a new method for low-level bombing to knock bridges down. Bridges are, in fact, quite difficult to hit. Amongst many other successes, our squadron led the flight that knocked down the famous bridge over the River Kwai. Great annoyance was caused later amongst the crews by the film when it was said that the bridge was too far away for the air force to reach!

The technique we worked out was to go as low as possible and fly slightly diagonally across the bridge, and on each run to only use three bombs. Flying diagonally gave one just a little latitude fore and aft and also sideways. We used delayed-action bombs, certainly to avoid blowing ourselves up, but particularly so that they could really settle down before exploding, trying to get them as close as we could to the bridge.

1944

I found myself banging the bridge with my clenched fist,
'By God, we're ashore in France, we've done it, we're back in France again.'

There were bodies – dead bodies, living bodies. All the blood in the
water made it look as though men were drowning in their own blood.
That's how it looked.

Overstretched on two fronts – in Russia and Italy, where Rome finally fell on 4 June – Germany was struggling to survive. All the same, they still had the ability to spring surprises, such as the last-ditch attack in the Ardennes in December.

Allied bombers continued to pound industrial – and civilian – targets in Germany, yet production actually increased.

In the Pacific, American planning came to fruition with land, air and sea forces committed in an island-hopping campaign to lever the deeply entrenched Japanese troops from their island fortifications. Turning the tide with the effective destruction of the Japanese fleet at Leyte Gulf in October, the Americans had the Japanese on the back foot, while in Burma the British Fourteenth Army laid on the pressure and halted the Japanese at Imphal and made a counterattack towards Mandalay.

The stage was set by June for the Allies to launch the invasion of Europe to liberate France. The troops had trained and prepared, planners had put the final touches to the invasion scheme, and the resistance cells in France and the Special Operations Executive had prepared a programme of sabotage to support the landings – whenever they should take place. D-Day began the fight-back in North-Western Europe, and with the Allied troops landed in the South of France pressing north, the German Army was in an untenable strategic position.

ITALY

After the first attack on Cassino had ended in failure, the Allies launched an amphibious assault at Anzio, 70 miles behind the Gustav Line and 30 miles south of Rome. They met little opposition, but instead of exploiting this and pressing inland, the Allies consolidated their forces. The Germans reinforced the area and four months of bitter fighting ensued with heavy casualties. In some of the toughest fighting of the entire war, four major battles were fought before Cassino fell to the Allies, the road to Rome was opened, and the city was liberated on 4 June – two days before D-Day in Normandy.

Corporal James Orr
Irish Guards
When we landed at the Anzio beachhead, we didn't go in for three or four days; then, when we made the push, Jerry had brought up reinforcements and we didn't get very far. If we'd gone straight for Rome, we could have captured it in the first two days.

Captain Russell Collins
16th Battalion, Durham Light Infantry
In Naples I went into a little bistro place and had some spaghetti, and sitting at the next table were a couple of American troops – American Negroes, who had come straight over from the United States – from their speech they must have been from the Deep South. Presently, one of these chaps, who was sitting only a few feet from me, turned and sort of beamed, sort of jovially, and said, 'How do?' And I said, 'How do you do?' and he said, 'Nice day,' and I said, 'Yes, lovely weather here, isn't it?' 'Gee,' he said, 'you sure do speak American very well – you speak it almost as well as I do.' And I thought that was lovely – and he'd never been outside the States before – and I'd never met an American Negro before – but a nice little illustration of how people are thrown together, you know, from different parts of the world.

We found ourselves in this little village, and it was apparent that we were concentrating there, and there was some big battle afoot, and we could see this mountain range ahead – Monte Camino – which was just a bare escarpment. Hence the name, Bare Arse . . . we assembled there and we were in little platoon groups, just basically waiting for our turn to go into the attack, and there was all sorts of reconnaissance going on.

I remember a particular thing – there was a wind-up gramophone, with a 78 record or two there, and that's the first time I heard the intermezzo from the *Cavalleria Rusticana*. Then it was another song, 'When It's Moonlight on the Colorado'. We played these for days, over and over again.

Captain John MacAuslan
5th Reconnaissance Regiment
We arrived in the dugout and it was just like pictures of the First World War. It was a biggish dugout underground, with a timber roof and paraffin lamps, and people poring over maps.

We were given our orders, and I remember when we went out of the dugout, an American officer said, 'Don't go that way – there's usually a stonk on that area.' The colonel said to me, 'John, what's a stonk?' I said, 'I don't know, sir.' He said, 'You don't know?' I said, 'No – what is it, sir?' He said, 'I don't know either.' Actually, a stonk is a concentration of artillery.

The battle had finished. The Germans attacked and attacked and attacked – and then they stopped, because they couldn't get anywhere. And the reason they couldn't get anywhere was that we had such a weight of artillery. It was shellfire that stopped them. My division was on the coastal side of the Anzio perimeter, and opposite us were the German 4th Parachute Division, who were extremely fine troops.

I was at regimental headquarters, and I slept in a dugout, which was about six feet by three feet, underground with lots of sandbags on top. It was fine, except for when it rained I got soaking wet. We seldom operated at all during the daytime. There were only limited places in which one could move, but everything came awake at night. The days were all more or less the same, really. You spent most of your time forward, then we had a few days' leave in the base areas.

There were notices everywhere 'Dust means Death' – which meant that if you raised any dust, the Germans could see it and they would fire at it straight away. You moved very carefully, especially in a jeep, so as not to raise dust. Our great treat was the pin-up, Jane, in the *Daily Mirror*. Seldom fully clothed, she was used to keep morale up and even encouraged us to take our mepacrine for malaria. The marshes nearby were full of mosquitoes. Actually, we thought the mosquitoes ate the mepacrine – but it was a court martial offence to go down with malaria.

We were told when we were going to Ostia that we were going into the killing ground – which didn't please me very much. We started off with hordes of photographers and journalists – I'd never seen a photographer or journalist in the war before, but we had about eight. I went in the colonel's car, and on the first day we ran into a little ambush. I was really totally exhilarated. I'd never been like that in my life before, and never have been since. We went round a corner and we were fired on by a machine gun. The driver backed very skilfully round this little hillock. If you were fired on and you backed up, you normally ended up in a ditch upside-down and you were dead. But he was very good. I remember the colonel stuck his head out of the car with his steel helmet on and called up one of the squadrons. You could feel bullets whistling all around you. I hadn't got my steel helmet – I'd lost it – and he said, 'John, put your steel helmet on and get down.' I just grinned at him. I'd never felt like that before. I got out of the car and I walked along the road – and the squadron came up. My exhilaration had evaporated by that time, but for a couple of minutes it was really wonderful.

Sapper Stanley Fennell
23rd Field Company, Royal Engineers

The Americans were astonished at the Grenadier Guards. They were used in all the bad places where the enemy were probing. We went with them and gave them support, in that we laid minefields for them, or did demolitions for them. These brave Guardsmen whom I watched go into action – I cringed at the sight, because I was sitting in an enormous armoured car, and they were completely soft-skinned, as it were. The shells burst amongst them, and they marched steadily forward in the attack.

The Irish Guards, the Scots Guards – to see them go forward in attacks was awe-inspiring. I suppose it's esprit de corps, and that's a kind of morale-booster. We thought we were better off than the infantry, but the infantry said they wouldn't like to do our job.

The Yankees went rolling past in their Shermans, which brewed up very easily. They used to wave to us, and throw us tins of food. If they were going into action, they wanted to get rid of it anyway. We used to look at them and say 'You poor devils!' – and they used to look down at us, clearing mines, and say, 'Wouldn't do that for a fortune.'

When I was captured, the Germans treated us very reasonably – they kept saying, 'We are the front swine. You are the front swine.' And we laughed. They seemed to have a very simple kind of humour – very straightforward. As the daylight came and the shellfire slackened, they marched us back along the road that we had been attacking. It was strewn with the debris of our original advance. Our vehicles and tanks, still smouldering, and the bodies of our people were strewn everywhere.

It sobered us to see the shambles of it all. We'd been pushed back miles.

Italy, May 1944. Polish troops hurl grenades during the tough fighting at the battle for Monte Cassino.

There were units of the Reconnaissance Corps, from the really early days. They hadn't buried the bodies – their own bodies even. They just laid covers over their faces.

We prisoners were decimated by the British shellfire on Aprilia, which we called 'the Factory'. There must have been thirty or forty dead, piled up. I had to climb over them to get out of the room. Some of their soldiers that had been guarding us were killed and I remember holding people's hands as they died. The Germans were most attentive and they made every effort to treat our wounded and look after them the same as their own.

We were marching and it so happened that this chap near me was limping. Suddenly we heard, 'Halt, halt!' and a German officer got out of the armoured car, came round and seized hold of this chap. 'You're wounded', he said, in German. 'You mustn't march.' These things shook me at the time, because it was so contrary to everything I'd ever been told about the enemy.

While we were marching, we were still under heavy shellfire from our own aircraft. The Allies had said they must stop the German attack with aircraft – and they were flying directly towards us. We just stood in a group in the road – and the German guards stood there, petrified.

We stood and watched as this huge armada of aircraft came at us. Everybody ran, and the salvoes of bombs – whole formations of bombs – dropped on the road where we'd all been standing. It was a most awe-inspiring thing to see these bombs getting larger and larger in flight. And the noise – the thunder of these bombs! When the dust cleared and we got up, I couldn't hear. I could hardly speak. We were deafened – some of the bombs were only yards away.

Some of our men fell down a hole. They were standing there when the ground gave way – it must have been some subterranean passage or workings. They were wedged in the shaft. With the Germans' help we actually rescued them. We lowered ropes that the Germans fetched, and that helped us get over the shock.

The Germans then said, 'Right. On the road.' The German officer said, 'Unload all those vehicles.' The vehicles had been blown to the side of the road – they were damaged, but were full of provisions. Some officer said, 'That's not right under the Geneva Convention.' The Germans threw back their heads and laughed. That was the first time I ever heard the Geneva Convention mentioned. The English-speaking German interpreted for us. He said, 'You are now in our hands. We may do with you what we wish. We carry the principles of the Geneva Convention only where conditions allow – and the conditions don't allow it at this time, and we are not asking you to load those rifles or anything. They are just stores. We must move them. If you don't move them, we shall shoot you.' Of course we all started to unload the provisions immediately.

Herbert Holewa
German soldier

The fighting on the Volturno was very tough. We had paratroops, some remnants from the Afrika Korps and units from the infantry. We were opposed by very good British forces, including some from the Eighth Army, who we had fought against in North Africa. The terrain was hard and the Allied fighter-bombers were very effective. You couldn't walk on the road. Even if you were on a bicycle, they would come down and shoot at you. The firepower of the Allied forces was enormous. Even to this day, I can't understand why they didn't achieve more at that time. They were far superior to the German forces. We were positioned forward on the bend of the river and during the night, the Allies bombed and strafed the roads. We needed it to defend ourselves, but we needed every bullet. We still had a very good fighting force. A lot of the old ones were still around and the young ones looked up to them. We had very little contact with the Italian civilians and they were actually very hostile to us. I remember we were stationed at a vineyard where they never used to look at us and doors were always being shut in our faces. I remember just one occasion when an Italian man went down into the wine cellar and fetched up a dusty bottle of wine, covered in cobwebs. He opened it and poured it out for us. That was nice.

William 'Bill' Jordan
Cameraman, Army Film and Photographic Unit

I always feel that sound could have captured far more than the visual medium. You'd hear a shell burst, but by the time you'd swung your camera round, all you got was just a cloud of dust drifting away. You were incapable of capturing the physical situation you found yourself in.

We got to the outskirts of Cassino – crawled, literally on our tummies into a couple of shell-holes, I suppose just half a mile short of the foot of castle hill. There were one or two Indian soldiers passing through and there was sniper fire everywhere. Literally just to put your head up above ground was fatal. They'd got it so pinpointed that one couldn't move during daylight. We did a bit of filming – general stuff of Cassino itself – and then decided that we still weren't getting enough, so we came back and found a first-aid post. I spoke to the sergeant there and he said, 'Well, there might be a bit of material for you here. We go out every now and again with a stretcher party and pick up the wounded. We go between the lines and pick up our own and sometimes German wounded.' I said, 'Well, that's excellent. I'll come along with you.' He offered me a Red Cross armband, but I said, 'I don't think I need that,' and off we went.

I tagged along with the stretcher party and we got within five or six hundred yards from the foot of castle hill again. Walking along, suddenly I thought to myself, 'Terrific shot – first-aid party going along with the ruins of the monastery in the background and castle hill, as they're picking up the wounded.' I went down on one knee – I think I'd got a 25-mm lens on, which is a fairly wide angle – I wanted to catch the whole situation with the whole section of medics. Let them get no more than fifty yards in front of me to get the shot . . . and boom. I knew no more. I got a mortar bomb right by the side of me. I woke up four days later in hospital with so many holes in me they thought I was a pincushion.

Sergeant Bill McConville, who came to see me in hospital about four days later, told me that at one time, when they put me on a stretcher, they said I was dead, because I was bleeding from the mouth and nose, had blood in my eyes – and I don't remember a single thing. They cut me from the base of the stomach, right up to the chest. This was all done under canvas, just outside Cassino. I don't know whether they used a penknife or a boy scout's knife, or what, but it's the most amazing scar you could ever see. The surgeon got half way up the stomach and decided he'd gone the wrong way, so he came back again and made another cut. Some stitches are something like six inches long, some are a couple of inches long – but thank God I'm still here.

Captain Russell Collins
16th Battalion, Durham Light Infantry
We had been a long period between Volturno and Camino, and even though I was dog-tired, and I knew my men were, I always made them wash and shave, and they thought it were ridiculous sometimes when we had no hot water. But when we'd been in the trenches overnight and we were going to move the next morning, or go on an advance or an attack, I always insisted that everybody got his mess tin, got down behind a hedge somewhere, put a drop of his water in it from the water bottle and washed and shaved. It had a tremendous morale-boosting effect.

I remember going on quite a deep patrol, and we got into this gully and realised were in a position that I was going to have difficulties extricating ourselves from. We were spread out to some extent, and Private Morson was in a leftmost position, and lower down the gully than I was.

There were maybe as many as twenty of us – but I saw that we'd gone too far, and we came under fire. We just had to get out of the gully as soon as we could. But poor Morson was hit and he couldn't move. It was a question then whether anybody could go down and recover him or not.

He was some thirty or forty yards from me to my left. I agonised as to whether or not I should go or send anybody to try and get him out. You couldn't rely on the Germans – it wouldn't be any use taking a Red Cross flag. If anybody else went down there they would have been fired on as well.

We came to Hill 320 – these are metres above sea level – where we dug in and had airmail from mum, and sea mail from dad. Even then the post would come up to those positions with the rations when they came.

My platoon occupied a farmhouse on the near bank of this Cassina River. The enemy were across this river, in a large group of farm buildings. We were there awaiting orders and generally keeping observation.

We tried to sally forth to make an exploratory patrol across the river, and they opened fire and drove us back. Then I went upstairs in the farmhouse to an observation point to look through a window to try and locate their machine-gun posts.

I remember standing with my binoculars searching the ground, when suddenly there was a long burst of machine-gun fire which splattered all around this window and broke through the wood and plaster on the walls either side and through the window – yet nothing hit me. You get to a point where you think, 'I'm leading a charmed life.' I felt by then that I must have been being preserved to do something when I got back from the war.

When the first stage of the attack went in on those farm buildings, I was keeping observation from that same window. I saw the Germans get up out of this same trench, and put a white flag on the end of a stick and walk, not towards us, but back towards the farm buildings. I was very puzzled by this. I thought, 'Now, is this is a ruse to get us to come out again?' I'm afraid I was very suspicious about the whole thing. I thought, 'Is it a decoy – are they trying to get us to come out?' Because there was no obvious sound of a battle – but in retrospect, they must have thought their base had been taken and occupied. I shot them. I couldn't afford to risk my men. There are very few people I've shot in cold blood like that, particularly in the back when they're waving a white flag, but you know there was nothing else for it.

In the battle for Cassino, in Italy, May 1944, British crews manning 4.2-inch mortars brace themselves against the deafening noise of their own bombardment.

On the fourth attempt, Allied troops finally took the German stronghold of Monte Cassino – the focal point of the heavily defended Gustav Line. On 18 May Sherman tanks and jeeps roll through the ruins of Cassino.

Captain Anthony Harvey
1/5th Battalion, Royal Gurkha Rifles

We were overlooked by a thing called the Platform, and the Germans were dug in there. We couldn't move out without them firing on us. We had been supported throughout the campaign by the Canadian Tank Brigade, and somewhere down in the water meadows I saw one tank, struggling to get up to our village. I can't remember if I went to him or we did it on the wireless, but I got in touch. It was one solitary tank which had managed to get over this impossible bridge, and had not bogged down in the water. There was a Canadian sergeant in charge, and I asked him if he could come up – crunch through the rubble which had once been the village of Saint Angelo, and use his tank gun to blow the Germans out of the Platform.

This he duly did, and I sent in a platoon and we mopped up the Germans, who were very happy to surrender, because they were being blown out of their dugouts. We were able to consolidate and we later moved forward, took up a defensive position and eventually the 78th British Division passed through us.

The Germans fought from the rubble of Cassino and had to be winkled out – particularly the parachute regiments. They had a reputation for being tenacious, and they deserved it. On that particular occasion maybe they were shell-shocked – a tank gun's round bursting in the dugout next to you is a very persuasive argument for giving up – but I wouldn't want anyone to think that they weren't good. They were absolutely marvellous adversaries. The whole retreat up into Italy, which was based all the time on riverbanks and rivers, was conducted in a most masterly way by, of all people, an air force general – Kesselring.

The abiding thought from Cassino about the Gurkhas was that they didn't rush around shouting and bawling in a vainglorious way to win VCs – though they did it when it was necessary. The great peace in one's mind was that if you discussed a battle and then gave your orders, there was no question – they did what the orders said. You didn't have to worry about them being carried out. You would know that when the report came back, 'Position taken', it was taken. Then you could plan for the next move. It removed all the doubt. That is what I loved about my service with the Gurkhas. Their motto is that it's better to die than to be a coward – and they believed that.

Sergeant Gus Platts
6th Parachute Battalion

Eventually we moved over from the Eighth Army front to the Fifth Army front, for the fourth battle of Cassino. To us, Cassino was just another place, another name. We came out of the line, loaded our mortar platoon windscreen-less jeeps and trailers, and just went straight across the country in one night. It was early May, but pretty nasty. We got there late at night, off the trucks and a long carry. We took all our equipment through, but not the mortars because we were going to take over the Welsh Guards' mortars in their positions. We got to our positions and we made ourselves familiar with the fire plan. Then the Welsh Guards left and all of a sudden there was a lot of noise behind us – they were going off in their Bren carriers or whatever – and Jerry didn't want to lose a moment, he had been alerted and started stonking us. We were also under sniper fire, and one we called 'Schmeisser Joe' paid us a visit almost every night across the Rapido.

We were in on the final attack on Cassino, on the 11th May. For this we moved over into the mountains, a steady climb of two or three hours, into a new position for the attack. We brought the ammunition up over two or three nights using mules. We had Italian animals – very good beasts really. They were very sure-footed and you never had to help them the way you did the little Indian mules.

About eleven o'clock at night the balloon went up. Something like 1,600 guns went off at the same moment. That's forgetting all the mortars – we were just small fry, firing on targets already selected. It was like the earth opening – a tremendous noise – and the whole mountain lit up. And we had a hell of a shoot ourselves. We ranged on a target – a crossroads or an area where there were German positions – and fired continuously until the barrels were red-hot. We had to urinate on them to get them cool. All night we were firing. We pulled out at dawn the following morning, when the attack had gone through, and the Germans were moving back to their next defensive line. Cassino had been broken at last!

Captain John MacAuslan
5th Reconnaissance Regiment

General Mark Clark has said no one was allowed into Rome except Americans – the British troops would be shot if they went near Rome. A patrol from my division of the Green Howards got in at half-past six – illegally – and I reckon I got in at half-past four. I wasn't quite in the centre, but we got quite a long way in. Then I turned round and came back again, because I had second thoughts. Common sense actually crept in, and I went back to Ostia. I found one of the troops putting up the statues there and starting to shoot at them with machine guns, with a very agitated curator trying to stop them. They took no notice of him at all, so I stopped them doing that. I think that's quite the most useful thing I did during the whole war.

Captain Anthony Harvey
1/5th Battalion, Royal Gurkha Rifles
It was in November of 1944 – we had been in a rest situation as a division, and we'd come forward. We turned due east from Florence and had gone up through a little village called Marudi. We had to go over the spine of the country – which wasn't terribly high. It was a lovely sunny day, and I had gone forward with the patrol.

The leading scout, Thaman, came upon two Germans in a sentry post. Luckily for him, they were both asleep. He charged with his kukri and they both surrendered. The German position somehow was alerted to the fact that their sentries had been captured. Within a very short time, mortar fire of some intensity was coming down on our position.

We couldn't move forward, and a message came from the leading section commander that we were to retire. There was a sudden lull in the firing and I, with my runner, ran for it. What we didn't know until afterwards was that Rifleman Thaman had gone to the top of the hill and had seen the rear positions of the Germans and engaged them with grenades. He had then fired his Tommy gun until his ammunition ran out. He then grabbed a Bren gun from one of his chums and said to them, 'Run for it. I'll keep the Germans' heads down.' He continued firing, in an exposed position, until he was shot through the throat. He died, but the rest of us got away. There is no doubt that he saved our lives, and long after this courageous action, a court of inquiry was set up and all the witnesses were called and told what they knew about his enormous bravery. As a result, he was awarded the Victoria Cross.

BOMBING RAIDS OVER GERMANY

Massive bombing raids – sometimes carried out by as many as a thousand bomber aircraft – by the RAF and USAAF from bases in England continued to pound German cities.

Flight Lieutenant Arnold Easton
Australian, 167 Squadron, RAF
I remember one of the navigator's jobs was to log down the position of any aircraft that were shot down. During the Nuremberg raid on the 30th March 1944, they were just going down like flies, particularly from the German frontier to the target. That was my dominant memory of that raid. It was a

very hectic, disastrous raid. There were dozens of planes going down and blowing up on the ground. It was dreadful.

Flight Sergeant Norman Jackson
106 Squadron, RAF

I was shot down on the 26th April 1944. Our target was the ball-bearing factory at Schweinfurt. We'd had a lot of goes at that already. Anyway, we'd got our bombs down, but the flak was coming up and there were fighters all around. We all thought we were going to make it. I was sitting in the cockpit when we were hit, and I saw flames coming from the starboard inner engine, so I grabbed the fire extinguisher and put it inside my Mae West – it was smallish. We'd decided that either the bomb-aimer or myself would have to get out if there was a fire, since we were the only ones who'd been trained to deal with that sort of thing. I released my parachute inside so that the bomb-aimer and navigator could hold on to it in case I slipped. It was my duty to get out. There was a hatch behind me. I got out and slid down on to the wing. We were doing about 140–160 knots and we were at 22,000 feet. I hung on to the air intakes on the leading edge of the wing with one hand, and tried to put out the fire with the other. I'd got it under control, but the German pilot had seen me and was aiming at the engines, so the aircraft was shaking all over the place. I couldn't even jump, because they were holding on to my chute. Then I was shot off the bloody wing, and they threw the parachute out of the plane.

I was going down and watching it burn about me. It was in flames, and the holes in it were getting bigger all the time. I hit the deck fairly hard – bushes and I don't know what else broke my fall. I could hardly walk, my hands and my eyes were badly burnt, and I got a couple of bullets and bits of shrapnel in my legs.

Anyway, I crawled to this village, picked a house and knocked on the door. The bloke opened the door and was bawling and shouting in German. Then two young girls came and pushed him aside. They took me inside and gave me schnapps and bathed my wounds. They were nurses from the hospital, and I thought, well, 'Maybe this won't be too bad, after all.' The rest of the crew had been rounded up. The pilot and rear-gunner had been killed but the others were all right, so we were taken to a police station. The others were knocked about a bit, but I was in the worst shape. I could only just see.

After the police station I went to a German hospital where they patched me up. I was in there for about eight or ten months. As a matter of fact, the pilot that shot us down later came into the hospital to say hello, which I thought was nice of him, the bastard.

Norman Jackson, VC. On 26 April 1944 Jackson climbed out on to the wing of his Lancaster at a height of 22,000 feet in an attempt to put out an engine fire. For this act of courage he was awarded the Victoria Cross.

CH12871

The ground crew of Lancaster 'N for Nuts' and mascot, Pat, while away the hours as their aircrew and bomber carry out a mission to destroy railway yards in Paris. From take-off to return, the crew could only wait – and hope.

CL276

Geoffrey Page was shot down over the Channel on 12 August 1940, was badly burned and spent two years in hospital. He returned to active flying duties in 1942, to pilot the new fighter-bomber Spitfire Mk IX.

D-Day

Planning for D-Day

Massive secrecy surrounded all elements of preparation for D-Day, from troop training and movement to the administrative planning and setting up of deliberately misleading feints to lure the German command into deploying troops far away from the intended landing points. Tragedy marred the preparations at Slapton Sands near Dartmouth in Devon when a training exercise was spotted by nine German motor torpedo boats on a routine patrol, and three US tank landing ships were torpedoed, killing 749 American soldiers and sailors. Many of these men were specialised engineers, whose role would be hard to fill.

The invasion was time-critical – the tides had to be right and the weather calm enough for safe landings – but eventually, after one day's postponement, the massive armada set sail for Normandy on the night of 5 June.

Eighteen thousand paratroops landed at dawn to capture essential bridges and disrupt German lines of communication, and the first US troops landed with tanks at Utah Beach at 6.30 a.m. These were followed by British landings at Gold and Sword Beaches, and Canadians at Juno Beach. At Omaha Beach the Americans were tied down to a small perimeter, but by midnight 155,000 Allied troops were ashore. The misinformation programme had worked, and German defenders had to be hurriedly recalled to Normandy to bolster up the defence. Sheer weight of Allied numbers began to tell as the fighting pressed towards Paris and north and east towards Belgium and Holland, and the marshy islands of Walcheren to the north of Antwerp.

Lord Louis Mountbatten
Head of Combined Operations until October 1943
In October 1941, I was recalled from Pearl Harbor to take up the job in charge of combined operations by Mr Winston Churchill. The very first day I reported to him, he said, 'You are to prepare the invasion of Europe for unless we can land and fight Hitler and beat his forces on land, we shall never win this war. You must devise and design the appliances, the landing craft and the technique to enable us to effect the landing against opposition and to maintain ourselves there. You must take the most brilliant officers to plan this great operation. You must take bases to use as training establishments where you can train the Navy, Army and Air Force to work as a single entity. The

whole of the south coast of England is a bastion of defence against the invasion of Hitler. We've got to turn it into the springboard for our attack. There are three conditions necessary for a successful invasion. First, obviously, to get ashore against no matter what opposition. Secondly, having got ashore to stay ashore no matter what the weather conditions. Thirdly, to stop the enemy from building up his forces against you quicker than you can, otherwise he'll throw you back into the sea.'

Brigadier Arthur Walter
Director of Ports and Inland Water Transport
In 1942, when the planners were planning the invasion, they came to the conclusion that it wouldn't be feasible to have an invasion in which the stores came over the beaches. That was for two reasons: one, there's a 25-ft rise and fall of tide on the Normandy beaches and you can only discharge at certain times either side of high tide, so that the amount of time you had for discharge was limited and the amount of stores you could get over would be limited. The other was that if there was a storm or bad weather on the beaches, nothing could come ashore and the prospect of capturing a fortified port was negligible. It was only then that the bright boys – British boys – thought up the idea of an artificial harbour which would be built in pieces in England, towed a hundred miles to the beaches and there put down, piece by piece by piece. And so came about the building of the Mulberry Harbours. The combined Chiefs of Staff, British and American, said that this project was so vital that it might be described as the crux of the whole operation and it must not fail because it was the only way we could safeguard the getting of stores to support the operation.

Ordinary Seaman Kenneth Bungard
Aboard craft towing Mulberry Harbour caisson
We arrived at what seemed like a huge office block without windows, sixty foot high. We were told to clamber up on top, not knowing at the time that this lump of concrete was actually floating and when we got to the top we found that it was just a huge hollow concrete box. Next to it was a tug. We thought the tug was tied to it but, in fact, it was tied to the tug and the tug towed us away. There we were on top of this thing. There was nothing we could do. We just had to sit there while we were towed along at four knots, which isn't very fast, and as the dawn began to break we found ourselves in a bay by Dungeness where we promptly went down inside this concrete box, opened the sluices and sunk it on the sand and wondered what the hell we

Preparing for D-Day, June 1944. Men of No. 4 Commando learn their role in the forthcoming landings at a briefing from Lieutenant-Colonel Dawson. They would only know their actual destination when embarked on the night of 5 June.

were doing – 'cos nobody tells you anything. We soon realised why they asked for volunteers, because these things had never been taken across an ocean. I mean, it was like trying to drag a brick across the Thames.

Brigadier Arthur Walter
Director of Ports and Inland Water Transport

I'd been to a meeting in the morning and I was taken to lunch at the In and Out Club in Piccadilly. I had my usual black civil service case in which I had locked the papers for the meeting and I placed it under the table during lunch. Afterwards I went back to Norfolk House in St James Square but when I arrived, I realised I hadn't got the case. I'll never forget that moment. I'd left it in the In and Out Club and it contained not merely the plans of Mulberry but also information as to where we were going to invade. At that moment, I wanted to die. I wanted to be instantly shot – not that that would have helped much, but I really have never forgotten to this day my feelings of utter horror. I rang up the club and the hall porter answered and said, 'Yes sir, a case was left here and I've got it in my cubby hole,' and I galloped the whole way from Norfolk House to the club and he handed it over to me. It was still locked.

Lord Louis Mountbatten
Head of Combined Operations until December 1943

The absolutely crucial thing for an invasion is to get the troops across the water and for that you want landing ships and landing craft – and we just didn't have them. They had to be designed, they had to be built in large quantities at a time when all shipbuilding facilities were required to fight the battle of the Atlantic. With the support of Mr Churchill, I managed to get a great many built in England. When the American, came in, I got them to build, to our plans, in a really big way. So the date of the invasion depended on the date on which we had enough landing ships and landing craft to take the troops over.

Ordinary Seaman Jack 'Buster' Brown
Aboard fleet minesweeper HMS Kellett

On the 28th April 1944, our captain received the signal to proceed to Slapton Sands where German E-boats had attacked a fleet of US landing craft who had been rehearsing for D-Day landings. I remember the dozens of corpses covered in fuel oil floating in the sea, and our ship's boats being lowered to recover them. We had about 70 brought aboard, but only one was still alive, and he died shortly afterwards. The flotilla returned to our base at Portland, where the dockland abounded with ambulances, but there was not much that could be done for the poor blokes. There were 749 killed.

Ordinary Seaman Geoffrey Cassidy
Aboard HMS **Riou**

On the night of the 28th April, my landing craft berthed in Weymouth harbour and I was told to keep all sightseers away. Ships started to unload dead American soldiers on the quayside. The story was that there were three E-boats hiding under the cliffs when the US convoy went past. All they had to do was full steam into the convoy, fire their torpedoes and then head for home. That night, US ambulances were taking the dead away, six to a van, and it went on until four in the morning. All the ambulances left on the Weymouth to Dorchester road, so they went away from Slapton Sands. I read about Slapton Sands in the papers after the war – but the papers got it wrong. The stories said that the dead had been dragged up Slapton Sands and buried in nearby fields. That was all wrong. It was lies. There were no dead in them fields – the dead were treated with respect and they were all taken away in the correct manner.

Lieutenant Albert Morrow
Canadian officer commanding MTB 726 in British coastal waters

An American torpedo boat under the command of Commander Buckley had arrived at Dartmouth amidst talk of an operation to try out landing craft in advance of D-Day. Lots of officers had tried to give Buckley advice about how the German E-boat tactics worked but his attitude had been, 'Oh, we don't need that advice.' His skippers had wanted it – but he didn't. And then one night in April 1944, they carried out an operation called Operation Tiger. They were to do a landing at Slapton Sands – and Jerry sat out there and torpedoed these ships. It was exactly what we'd warned Buckley about. So this is one of those things – no matter who you are or where you are, it's foolish not to take any advice when it comes to enemy tactics. It was a tragedy that could have been averted if he'd only listened.

Lieutenant William Jalland
Platoon commander, 8th Battalion, Durham Light Infantry

As the preparations for D-Day gathered pace, I remember being open mouthed at some of the equipment that was being assembled. Part of PLUTO that looked like an enormous bobbin floated about in Southampton Water. We didn't know what that was. We saw pieces of Mulberry, some with cranes, some without. Again, we'd no idea what they were. We saw the crabs, the scorpions, and the flails. We didn't know what any of it was, but we knew we'd be on our way very soon.

Lieutenant-Colonel Allan Younger
26th Assault Squadron, Royal Engineers

We were given Armoured Vehicle Royal Engineers (AVREs) equipped with improvisations for getting over or through any obstacle we might meet on D-Day. These included fascines, which were huge bundles of chestnut paling about 12 feet across which were held on a little ramp which could be released to fill up a ditch. There was an assault bridge, which could be dropped. The tank didn't have the ordinary gun. It had a thing called a 'Petard', which was a codename for a Spigot Mortar that fired a charge of about 25 pounds of explosive a limited distance, I think about 50 yards was the maximum range. The object of this was to break up concrete so that if, for instance, you met a wall and you couldn't get over it any other way, you could smash it down. We also had a lot of shaped charges called 'General Wades'. They each weighed about 25 or 30 pounds and they could be placed on concrete to smash it up – but you had to get out of the tank, clamp them on to the concrete, get back in, pull the string and there'd be a terrific bang and with a bit of luck, the concrete would fall to pieces and you could climb over it.

Sergeant Anthony Bashford
44th Royal Tank Regiment

I remember seeing all these enormous tins, enormous piles of Compound 219. This was simply grease with lots of fibre in it – a bit like putty – which you applied around any particular crack or crevice in the Sherman tank to make it waterproof for the beach landings. Sherman tanks had an escape hatch in the floor of the tank through which the driver and co-driver could escape. Obviously it wasn't water-proofed so that was where the Compound 219 was placed. The engine inspection doors were also sealed with it. As you went up the hull, the turret ring was sealed with a type of plastic covering and tape. The gun mantlet was sealed and of course the gun barrel was sealed and these seals had little explosive charges attached to them which ran back inside the tank, the theory being that as the tank came off the landing craft and rolled up the beach, the gunner or the crew inside could activate these charges and blow away the waterproofing membranes so that the turret would be able to rotate freely.

Major Peter Martin
2nd Battalion, Cheshire Regiment

On exercise at Hayling Island, we were landed in water up to our waists, and by the time the soldiers had marched 12 miles inland with wet trousers, they had become very raw in the crotch. It was decided therefore to issue oilskin trousers, which were part of the anti-gas equipment, which sat over the boots, and high up the waist so that everybody would land with dry trousers and would not become all raw and red by the time they reached the objective.

Major Ian Hammerton
2nd County of London Yeomanry, Royal Armoured Corps

We had a visit from Major General Percy Hobart, who thought up the canvas flotation collar, which displaced enough water to keep the tank from sinking after it left the landing craft. He gathered everybody round him and said, 'I have some news for you. You've heard of the Lord Mayor's Show?' and everyone's heart stopped beating. 'You know that people come round afterwards to clear up the mess? Well, your job is going to be the very opposite. You're going round first to clear up the mess. You are going to be mine clearers. Flails.' None of us had ever heard of them.

Brigadier Arthur Walter
Director of Ports and Inland Water Transport

We were summoned to a cinema in Portsmouth. There were about 400 officers there and redcap police all round the place, it was all very secret and we sat down in this cinema and Monty came in. He told us something about the plans for the invasion. He said this is what we're going to do, this is what we expect the Germans to do – and this is what I'll do to the Germans. It was terribly inspiring, because I'd been planning my own little corner of the invasion, getting more and more puzzled, not knowing quite where it fitted in, and he suddenly put everything into perspective and I can only say that he raised my morale just like that. He was a leader and I would have followed him to hell.

Sergeant-Major William Brown
D Company, 8th Battalion, Durham Light Infantry

Eisenhower came to have a chat with everybody. He was great. The finest general there's ever been. We formed a whole square right round this great big field. And he walked into the middle of the field and he said, 'Righto, gentlemen. When I give the signal, all come in and sit down. Never mind the officers, they'll walk in with the men. I want everyone to hear what I have to say.' That pleased everybody. There was no bullshit about him. He was immaculate. He could have been cut out of chocolate. He said he'd heard all about us down in Southampton, how we'd been living it up and now the time had come to get aboard ships and fight alongside each other. He did more to lift the morale – certainly my morale – than anything else.

Sergeant George Self
8th Battalion, Durham Light Infantry
When we moved to a camp near Romsey, we had battles with the Yanks nearly every night in Southampton. The cause of the friction was money and their arrogant behaviour. Eisenhower came to see us and gave us a lecture about the American soldier. He agreed they were overpaid, oversexed and over here – but when they got over the other side, they would show us the road home – how to fight. That was the worst thing he could have said. That night the blood flowed in Southampton.

Major Cromwell Lloyd-Davies
Aboard HMS Glasgow
We foregathered at Belfast, and immediately were put under complete security. No one was allowed ashore – no one was allowed on board. Then, for the first time, the operation orders were opened. These were very extensive and consisted of several sacks of orders. They also included a sort of rubber model of the whole of the Omaha Beach, which we were going to attack. It had been made in sections about a foot square. I understand that each section was made in a different part of the United States, so that they were never put together until they finally arrived in this country for D-Day. We assembled all of this in our hangar, and we were able then to sit down and look at the beach from a suitable distance. You saw the exact beach, including the background – as we would see it on the day. The security was intense, and even if a man went sick, he was sent to one special hospital in Belfast – which was under guard – and was not allowed to be removed.

Brigadier James Hill
3rd Parachute Brigade
As the great day was arriving, all my battalions were penned in their camps – which they weren't allowed to leave. This period was very interesting to me. All day long the Canadians, with whom I'd pitched my tent, were playing games – baseball, throwing balls about – and I thought what tremendous

vitality these Canadians had got. Then in the afternoon I would visit my English battalions, and find half a dozen chaps desultorily kicking a football, and the rest asleep. I thought to myself, here is the difference between the Old World and the New – the élan and joie de vivre of the New World of the Canadian – and the maturity and the not worrying, not bothering, and having a good nap while you can, of the British.

Captain J.H.B. Hughes
Aboard HMS Danae
When HMS *Danae* was nominated as a member of the In-Shore Bombardment Squadron for Operation Overlord, the commander addressed the ship's company on a freezing quarterdeck in Greenock. His comment that we had the honour to be expendable was smartly countered by, 'Fuck that for a lark,' from the ranks of the stokers' division.

DELAYS AND DECEPTIONS

Lord Louis Mountbatten
Head of Combined Operations until December 1943
To prevent the enemy from building up reinforcements so quickly that he can push you back into the sea, you have to do two things. First, you have to have a deception plan to make him think you're going to land quite somewhere else and make him build up all his reinforcements and his defences there. That was easy in our case because obviously it was the Pas de Calais – the Straits of Dover, the shortest way across. It was not only that the German generals thought we were going to go there but all the British generals actually wanted to go there. Secondly, having got them all concentrated in the wrong place, you had then to prevent them from being moved to the right place when they discovered their mistake. For that purpose you wanted weeks of interdiction, bombing, destroying roads, bridges, railway junctions, tunnels and everything. And for that purpose, Bomber Command had to be turned on to the job way ahead of D-Day.

Squadron Leader John Shannon
617 Squadron, RAF
The operation was called Operation Taxable and it was one of the biggest spoofs ever played on the Germans. The raid was carried out on the night of the 5th and 6th June and the object of the exercise was to simulate a landing of troop

Preparing for time off in France, men of the Royal Electrical and Mechanical Engineers
swot up on what to expect.

carriers and troop ships across the channel in the Calais area to try and put the Germans off the scent of where the real D-Day landings were going to take place down in Normandy. The object was for eight aircraft to fly in rectangular orbits at a steady speed of 200 mph at 3,000 feet, dropping out bundles of 'window' – strips of metal foil – which once released into the air, gave a blip on German radar. Intelligence sources had calculated that the radar blips appeared every 12 seconds, so we had to drop our bundles of 'window' every 12 seconds. We would fly for 32 seconds ahead, turn onto a reciprocal course and fly for 30 seconds and turn again and fly ahead on a forward course for another 32 seconds and then turn again and fly 30 seconds back. The effect was that we were slowly, very slowly, moving forward. We had to fly-line abreast eight aircraft with something like a mile distance between them. It was all pinpointed over the radar navigation. All the timing was absolutely synchronised so that we all got on our positions and started at the same time. In each aircraft there were two pilots and two navigators, because the work was so concentrated that we had to have a break every so often. We had three additional people in the aircraft with stop, watches, dropping window out at 12-second intervals – they'd drop a bundle out and as soon as it hit the airstream it would scatter and the blips would start coming through on the German screens. The operation tied up a tremendous amount of German reserves in that area. We could tell that they thought something was happening because we watched their guns on the French coast firing into the Channel, in the belief that they were lobbing shells into the middle of a landing force.

Sergeant Jack Nissen
RAF radar expert involved in use of radar-jamming techniques
Two hundred ships were each equipped with two to three kilowatts of Mandrel jammers, which were used on that 'one-night-only' basis. When Eisenhower said 'Go', everybody on board their ships, wherever they were, threw this big master switch. Nobody had been told what the switch was but when it was thrown, the German radar operators saw some hash on that bearing. Hash can be caused by a faulty valve and I can imagine the German radar people on that night – they'd be sitting in their tiny ops rooms, cut off with just a telephone, dawn approaching, when all of a sudden the front end of their receiver goes on the blink. When that happens, you'd normally just give it a tap. If that didn't work and you were tired out and fed up and waiting to go off duty, you might say forget it for tonight, wait till the mechanic comes on duty, he'll replace the valve and everything'll be fine. If that's what the German radar people did say, they made a fatal mistake. Because at first light

on the next morning, all the capital ships were in position, laying four or five miles offshore with their big guns. And by then it was too late.

Private Peter Fussell
No. 1 *Commando*

At about four o'clock in the afternoon we were told to stand down – the invasion was off. We were given the reasons, we were told the weather had broken and it was unlikely that we would be landing for the next twenty-four hours. We were told that a decision would be made by midday on Sunday. After that, every man Jack – whatever your religion – went to church. It didn't matter what denomination you were – agnostic, atheist, Church of England, Roman Catholic, Presbyterian or Jewish – you stood in some church and someone blessed you.

Lieutenant-Colonel David Warren
1st Battalion, Hampshire Regiment

What we all felt – and this was the most astonishing thing about the Normandy landings – was that everyone was 100 per cent confident that whatever happened to you or to anyone else, the operation would be successful. There was no question that it might not be. And everyone was glad to get on with it because it felt like the green light for the end of the war.

Yvonne Cormeau
Agent, F Section, SOE. Working with the French Resistance

We listened to the radio for messages all the time. The men could not, of course. It fell to the people who were in the home – whether it was grandma or children – everyone contributed to try and listen in. The main times were the six and nine o'clock broadcasts from the BBC. One day we had a message, which said 'Listen in to the broadcasts twenty-four hours a day,' so the boss and I installed a little set in the hay up in a loft outside the farm, and we listened. We were told it might happen any time, 'You must listen in, you might hear your message. Get yourselves ready, put on the clothes you will wear for work when you go away and make all arrangements for those who stay at home looking after the animals, that they have food.' Then finally the message came through that the armada had sailed, and there was terrific rejoicing, and a little crowd came up to our village during the night. We had been up all the time, cleaning what weapons we had. They had been hidden in the beehives. Then by morning, the others had turned up, and we allocated them to various people in the village we knew we could trust. They went out,

The Paras prepare for D-Day and black up their faces to make a pre-dawn drop.

despite the fact that they'd only had about five hours' sleep – they went out as soon as possible to blow up the railways and bridges – get trees knocked down so as to block the roads – the bigger the tree the better.

The airborne invasion

Major John Howard
Commander, D Company, 2nd Battalion, Oxfordshire and Buckinghamshire Light Infantry

It was a *coup de main* operation – glider-borne to capture two bridges in Normandy and to land soon after midnight the day before the seaborne landings on the 6th June 1944. For this operation I was given two extra platoons and 30 Royal Engineers, so that was 150 infantry, 30 Royal Engineers – a force of 180. We landed in six gliders, each glider containing one platoon of around 25 infantry and five Royal Engineers. Three gliders went for a bridge over the River Orne and three gliders for a bridge over the Caen Canal, now known as Pegasus Bridge. This bridge was much more important, it was more heavily defended – it was a waterway used for commercial purposes up to the port of Caen. Most of the defences of the two bridges were around this bridge. That is one reason why I went in No. 1 glider. We were so thrilled to have this special job – the spearhead of the invasion as it's often described – that we wanted to get the job done and done successfully, and that seemed to overcome all fear.

Staff Sergeant Roy Howard
Glider Pilot Regiment

As a glider pilot, my objective was a small corner of a particularly tiny field of rough pasture close to the Orne Bridge. If I overshot, I would crush us all against a 14-foot high embankment – if I undershot I would destroy my seven tons of powerless aircraft and its human cargo on a belt of 50-foot-high trees. There was simply no room for error. The significance of the two bridges to be attacked by a *coup de main* force was emphasised to us. With the 6th Airborne Division landing to the east of the river, and the whole invasion coming ashore to the west of the canal, it was vital that these troops should be able to cross the two bridges over the Orne and the canal. These two bridges were the only ones where you could do this between Caen and the sea. So it was absolutely vital that we had the maximum surprise element, and the only way to do this was for us to carry out our operation before the rest of the invasion started. So we were going to sneak in just after midnight, and some six-and-a-half hours before the seaborne invasion came ashore.

Someone had made a most marvellous sand-table, a perfect model of what was on the ground in Normandy – even down to the last tree and ditch. The chap who'd made it had put some wires above the area, and slid a cine camera down these wires, filming all the way, and therefore had simulated what a glider pilot would see on his approach. It was incredibly clever, and impressed us all very much. So we were very confident. Each Horsa glider with its 88-foot wingspan was going to carry 28 troops, a mixture of Ox and Bucks Light Infantry, plus two or three Engineers – we were also going to carry an assault boat, and numerous other bits of equipment, because it was thought that the bridges might be blown before we got there. We got out on to the airfield about 9.30 p.m. on the 5th June. I think everyone knew on the airfield what was happening except one of the ground staff from the Air Force, who came up to me and said, 'Are you bringing this one back tonight, Staff?' I said, 'No. I don't think so.' He walked away looking dazed.

We'd met the Ox and Bucks lads a few days before and they were a very good bunch. However, on the night they arrived all blacked up, loaded with arms and ammunition, they looked a right bunch of cut-throats – I think I was more afraid of them than I was of the Germans. We loaded up, drank a cup of tea, chatted and at about twenty to eleven, when it was nearly dark – we had double summertime in those days – we mounted up and when somebody fired the green flare, the engines started and one by one we got under way.

Private William Gray
2nd Battalion Oxfordshire and Buckinghamshire Light Infantry
We were literally staggering under the weight of the stuff we were carrying. I personally carried four fully loaded Bren-gun mags plus two bandoliers of .303 ammunition. I had six Mills 36 grenades, two 77 phosphorus smoke grenades, two Norwegian-type egg-shaped stun-grenades that just made a bang when you threw them. We carried a twenty-four-hour ration pack that consisted of cubes of tea, soup, oatmeal, toilet paper, sweets, matches and some fuel for our little Tommy cookers.

Lieutenant 'Tod' Sweeney
2nd Battalion, Oxfordshire and Buckinghamshire Light Infantry
At eleven o'clock, we took off from Tarrant Rushton to spearhead the invasion into Europe. It was rather like being picked to play for your country at Lords. The exhilaration buoyed us up and kept us going. We were all scared

stiff, of course, but we'd been waiting and waiting for this stage from 1940 onwards, and none of us had even been in action before.

Sergeant Henry Clark
D Company, 2nd Battalion, Oxfordshire and Buckinghamshire Light Infantry

Suddenly we became airborne. We could barely see, it was quite dark, there were a few cigarettes going and there was obviously a tenseness and nervousness because there wasn't the usual idle chatter – nobody was singing and there was almost silence in the glider, but within about ten minutes, the usual round of conversation started, people began to sing, the tenseness evaporated and it became just another glider flight.

Major John Howard
Major, 2nd Battalion, Oxfordshire and Buckinghamshire Light Infantry

The flight at about 6,000 feet over the Channel was very, very quiet – so much so that for the first time in a glider, I wasn't sick. It was a sort of company joke that I was going to be sick and some bright lad at the back of the glider would always shout through 'Has the company commander laid his kit yet?' which of course caused a lot of mirth amongst the rest of the men, but that night nobody used their brown-paper bag.

Sergeant Henry Clark
D Company, 2nd Battalion, Oxfordshire and Buckinghamshire Light Infantry

We heard the glider pilot shout, 'Casting Off!' and suddenly the roar of the aeroplane engine receded and we were in a silent world. It was like being trapped in a floating coffin in mid-space. Immediately the glider cast off, the singing, the talk, the conversation stopped. People realised what we were heading for. There was no going back now. We'd reached the point where we could only go forward. We were dropping rapidly and the pilot was a bit concerned that we were coming in too fast, but there was nothing he could do about it. David Wood, the No. 2 Platoon commander shouted out, 'Brace for impact!' We all linked arms and lifted our feet off the floor and prayed that our number wasn't up. We went in at a steep angle. I felt the jerk of the parachute opening and we hit the ground with an almighty thump and lost the wheels, then we came down again on the metal skids and were airborne again, and then there was another bump, with sparks shooting up from the skids hitting flints in the field. Then we came to a halt.

Private William Gray
D Company, 2nd Battalion, Oxfordshire and Buckinghamshire Light Infantry

The glider was twisting and turning a bit and, looking over the pilot's shoulder, you could see the bridge. It was exactly like the model we'd been shown but it suddenly vanished as the glider veered to make its approach to landing and the next thing – *crash!* – as it hit the deck. Sparks were flying left right and centre, and all of a sudden it just came to a halt and there was silence again – just the creaking of timber in the glider. The undercarriage had gone and the front of the glider had caved in. Den Brotheridge, our platoon commander, quickly slid the door open and said, 'Gun Out!' which was me, so out I jumped and stumbled on the grass because of the weight I had on me. I set the Bren up facing the bridge and the rest of the lads jumped out. Den looked round to make sure that everyone was out and he said, 'Come on, lads!' We were about thirty yards from the bridge and we dashed towards it. I saw a German on the right-hand side and I let rip at him and down he went. I still kept firing as I went over the bridge. On the other side was another German and he went down too.

Captain Richard 'Sandy' Smith
D Company, 2nd Battalion, Oxfordshire and Buckinghamshire Light Infantry

In the flurry, I remember a German throwing a stick-grenade at me, and I saw the explosion – felt the explosion. I was extremely lucky, because the grenade exploded very close to me, and hit various parts of my clothing – but not my body, although it made holes in my flying smock. He was the first German I actually shot. Having thrown his grenade, he tried to scramble over a wall, and I shot him with my Sten gun as he went over.

Major John Howard
2nd Battalion, Oxfordshire and Buckinghamshire Light Infantry

As I came out I had the most exhilarating moment of my life, for three reasons. First of all, less than 50 yards away I saw the tower of the canal bridge that I had been studying for so long. Second, the nose of the glider was right through the wire of the enemy defences and, third, there was no firing, so we had been a complete surprise. Everybody realised this and took full advantage and ran to the bridge. I moved up the track to my command post. I heard two more gliders crash on the landing zone behind me – I could hardly believe my ears because they were so near. By now the leading section of No. 1 Platoon had hurled grenades into the pillbox, while the rest of the platoon, led by Den Brotheridge, doubled over the bridge. David Wood's platoon arrived and I gave them the number-two task of clearing the inner defences. The enemy had been woken now, but they were low-grade troops of mixed nationality and we didn't have much trouble with them, except the NCOs who were all German. No. 3 Platoon had a heavy landing, and when their commander, Sandy Smith, came up he was limping very badly. At the same time I got the message that Den Brotheridge had been shot in the neck and was apparently dead. I told Sandy to coordinate the two platoons on the far side and I would send somebody over to help him.

I then got a message from David Wood, the No. 2 Platoon commander, that he, the sergeant and his radio operator had all been hit by enemy machine-gun fire the other side of the pillbox and were out of action. After that I started to worry about the Orne Bridge about a quarter of a mile to the east, because I could hear no firing from there, nor had I received any radio messages or had a runner from those three platoons. I was considering whether I should send at least a patrol over there to help to capture the bridge. But then, as often happens in battle, luck changed for a while in that Captain 'Jock' Nielson, commanding the Royal Engineers, came up and told me that there were no explosives under the bridge. Almost simultaneously I got a message by radio to say that No. 6 Platoon had captured the River Orne Bridge. So about 15 minutes after the first platoon had landed we started sending out our success signal 'Ham and jam' over the radio! I got the operator, Corporal Tuppenderry, to keep repeating it, 'Hello Four Dog, Hello Four Dog, Ham and Jam, Ham and Jam, Ham and bloody Jam,' he shouted in all his excitement. While we were giving out this message I hoped that Brigadier Poett would pick it up as well because he had dropped at about the same time we landed with the 21st Independent Para Company – the Pathfinders.

At 0050 hours we heard the sound of our bombers flying low and coming in from the coast. As they got over the dropping zone east of the River Orne we saw 7 Para parachuting down – a great sight. As prearranged, I blew a Victory V signal on my whistle. Some had landed in haystacks or in floods, but they heard this whistle. It must have meant a lot to them, because not only did it signify the bridges had been taken intact, but it also helped them to orientate themselves.

In all the excitement, down the road from Ranville came an open German Mercedes-Benz staff car. No. 5 Platoon waited for it to come over the river bridge, then opened fire. When we got to it there were four badly wounded occupants. Inside there was ladies' lingerie, and it smelt of perfume. There were also plates of half-eaten meals so it must have been one hell of a party. It turned out that the German officer in the car commanded the bridge's garrison. He insisted, in perfect English, that, as he'd lost the bridge, and his honour, we kill him. The doctor came up and gave him a dose of morphine and put him to sleep, but he didn't survive.

Shortly after this, two enemy tanks came very slowly towards the canal bridge from the west. However, Sergeant Thornton of No. 6 Platoon blew up the leading one with a PIAT (Projector, Infantry, Anti-Tank) bomb, and the other retired quickly. The bomb had hit the ammunition inside and it went up like a fireworks display. When 7 Para heard this they thought we were really in trouble because some of them arrived soon afterwards. As soon as 7 Para got across the bridge and into Bénouville, more fighting started straight away. Soon after first light wounded were taken into the Gondrée's Cafe, which had become a medical aid post. To celebrate us being the first Allied soldiers into occupied France, the patron, Georges Gondrée, went into his garden and dug up ninety bottles of champagne to give to the wounded. The whole of my company decided they wanted to report sick!

The first aircraft we saw were three Spitfires at 6,000 feet. We put up a ground-to-air signal about our success and they came in low, circled the bridges, did a 'victory roll' and dropped a container full of the early morning papers from Fleet Street. The troops were fighting over the *Daily Mirror*, because it had a strip cartoon called 'Jane'. Jane was always in her undies, or nothing at all, and she had a superb figure, so everyone wanted to see what she was up to. There was no mention of the invasion of course, and that gave rise to a few quips.

Staff Sergeant Roy Howard
Glider Pilot Regiment
Once the chaps had gone, this was a dodgy time for a glider pilot. I leapt out of the glider and crawled to the nearest ditch. There I threw off my flying helmet and equipment and proceeded to kit myself out as a soldier. It was a strange transition. We were trained soldiers, be we were also trained pilots, so our objective was a quick return to the UK for further flying, not to be involved with the fighting for longer than necessary. By the 8th June I was back at Tarrant Rushton, having been released by the operation commander at 2100 hours on D-Day.

PARACHUTE LANDINGS

Captain John Sim
12th Parachute Battalion, 6th Airborne Division
Finally the evening came – the evening of the 5th June, when we got into our lorries and we were transported to the airfield. We collected our chutes and the lorries took us around the perimeter, miles away into the countryside where our aircraft had been dispersed. The aircraft we were going to jump out of was the Stirling. It was a peaceful June evening – lovely and calm.

We just sat and talked for a while amongst ourselves, and then the padre came whipping up in his jeep and we had a little prayer. He wished us well before he dashed off again to another aircraft. Then came the jeep of the RAF crew roaring up, and they got out and said, 'All right, you chaps. Don't worry! Piece of cake! We'll get you there!' It was a tremendous, exciting, light-hearted atmosphere.

Corporal Dan Hartigan
1st Canadian Parachute Battalion
Here we were, C Company, just over 100 of us, taking off in little bombers to drop behind Hitler's 'impregnable Atlantic Wall' and take on Rommel's soldiers. We were perfectly aware that attacking infantry should have a three-to-one ratio in its favour, but according to intelligence reports we were going in to do our job at close on one-to-one. We were loaded to the hilt with grenades, Gammon bombs, flexible Bangalore torpedoes around our necks, two-inch mortar bombs, ammunition, weapons and water bottles. Our exposed skin was blackened with charcoal, the camouflage netting on our helmets was all tied up with burlap rags, and the space above the harnesses in our helmets was crammed with cigarettes or with plastic explosive.

Captain Dennis Kelland
8th Parachute Battalion, Regiment, landing east of River Orne
I was dressed in what was jocularly called 'Christmas Tree order' because one's parachute harness had to be sufficiently tight to stop it being jerked off one's shoulders when the chute opened. As a consequence, I could barely walk in an upright position. Strapped up in this way, I had a .45 Colt automatic, a Sten gun through my harness and a cartridge-pistol. On the run in to Normandy, the flak started to come up and when the pilot started to jink, I fell flat on my back in the doorway of the Dakota plane and it took two men to lift me to my feet again. This was despite the fact that we'd been briefed

that we would go into Normandy on a flak-less route. In actual fact, the Germans were on an anti-invasion exercise in the very area in which we were to land. The man who said that he wasn't scared when he did a parachute jump was a liar, because every jump one did had its attendant nervous tension – but on this occasion we had the strain of going into battle for the first time.

Flight Lieutenant Alec Blythe
48 Squadron, RAF

I had met the Royal Engineers, whom I was to drop on D-Day, and they seemed jolly nice chaps. However, when they came up to the Dakota on the night of the operation with blackened faces they looked a fearsome lot. One pulled out his dagger and said that it was going to find a German that night. I was rather glad they were on our side.

Pathfinders were supposed to set up a radar beacon, called Eureka, which would guide us to the dropping zones. Unfortunately very few Pathfinders were dropped accurately, so most of us found there was no Eureka beacon to track to and we had to fall back on our own navigational equipment. My DZ was one and a half minutes flying from crossing the French coast to dropping. The briefing therefore had to be tremendously detailed. Accurate models of the Normandy coast and hinterland were constructed. From these models cine films were made of the tracks to each of the dropping zones. So we were prepared with a mental picture of what we could expect to see as we flew in. The films, however, were made in daylight, whereas we would be dropping at night.

As we crossed the coast, my navigator reported two large houses which we expected to see before a line of trees came out of the murk. I was getting ready to drop my troops south of the road to Caen. There was a fair amount of moonlight and I could see that the Germans had flooded the area south of the road where we were supposed to drop. I didn't have much time to think, but decided I had better drop to the north of the road rather than in the water. The red light was on and the engineers were standing ready. There was some flak but I hadn't had to take evasive action. I was intent on making as steady a run as possible when suddenly the aircraft banked almost 45 degrees. In a flash of light from the ground I saw a Stirling bomber passing in front of us. Clearly we had been caught in his slip-stream which threw us off course. I had therefore to bring the wings level and regain heading as quickly as possible. The paratroops in the back no doubt were hurled about and were probably cursing me for taking violent evasive action. I never saw them again to explain the reason for their discomfort. Unfortunately the accuracy of the drops on D-Day wasn't as high as one would have hoped. I would like to think that my engineers were accurately dropped, especially as the two bridges assigned to them were blown up. When I got back to Down Ampney and had been de-briefed, I quietly cycled home.

Corporal Dan Hartigan
1st Canadian Parachute Battalion

A few minutes before the drop, we passed over a town where the streets, a few hundred feet below, were full of promenading people. That was the toughest moment of all, for each of us knew that we might never have the chance to do something like that, ever again. Somebody said, 'For Chrissakes gimme a cigarette,' to which the sergeant growled, 'You know better'n that – stow the cigarettes 'til after Varaville.'

Captain John Sim
12th Parachute Battalion

With about five minutes to go, we all moved up closer. I was astride the door, looking down at the sea, and I hoped to see some of the task force – some of the Armada – but I didn't see any ships at all, just the speckly wave tops of the sea below me. Suddenly I saw the parallel lines of waves coming ashore on the dark yellow beach, then a cliff, woods, copses, hedgerows – this was all about 800 feet below me.

It was a moonlit night so I could see the ground quite easily. Then – red light on, green light and I jumped. The roar of the engine, the whish of the wind around one's body and then quietness. Just like an exercise in England, I found myself floating down to a field just to the side of a grazing horse. I landed without any harm and I heard others landing around me.

Brigadier James Hill
3rd Parachute Brigade

On D-Day I was jumping No. 1, which gave me a problem. In camp, to keep the Canadians amused, I'd given them a football with Hitler's face on it in luminous paint. Everyone knew I was proposing to drop this, along with three bricks, which they gave me with some rather vulgar wording painted on them, on to the beach to astonish the enemy. So there I was, as brigade commander, standing in the door of the aeroplane with a football and three bricks! As we got over the beaches, out went the football and the bricks and myself. As I orientated myself, it appeared that I had been dropped with my stick bang in the middle of the River Dives. However, what the Germans had done in anticipation was to flood the valley of the Dives. On either side of the river were water meadows with very deep irrigation ditches. The Germans had wired this area before they flooded it so they had really created a very impenetrable barrier.

Lieutenant Nick Archdale
7th Parachute Battalion

Just before I jumped, I threw out a stuffed moose head which we'd purloined from a pub in Exeter, and was planned to put the fear of God into any German it hit. Then out we went.

Lieutenant-Colonel Terence Otway
9th Parachute Battalion

We arrived on time over the coast and quite suddenly, anti-aircraft fire – large and small – opened up on us. I was waiting to jump and there were some explosions near the tail and I was thrown out of the aircraft, closely followed by my batman. I saw tracer coming up and one or two tracer bullets actually went through my parachute. I realised the danger when a Stirling bomber passed under me and I wondered if it was going to hit it. It was completely chaotic. Aircraft going in all directions and levels – except the right ones. Anyway, it was clear that I was not going to drop on the dropping zone. It looked odds-on that I was going to hit a building, which I recognised as the headquarters of a German battalion. I hit it at first-floor level – my shoulder was about the level of the windowsill, and then I dropped down to the ground. Somebody threw open the window and looked out, and I was fumbling around for a grenade to throw at him, when one of my corporals suddenly appeared from nowhere and picked up a brick and hurled it up at this man who vanished from the window. We had to get away from the building, but we didn't make our way straight to the dropping zone, because if there were German troops following, we didn't want to lead them straight to the dropping zone. As we went along, we met two rather stout German soldiers on bicycles. We stopped and told them we were British troops. They replied that they were sick and tired of the SS dressing up in British uniforms and doing exercises, and could they please get back to barracks. We eventually convinced them that we really were British troops, and we took their rifles and threw them into marshy water, and told them to get on their bikes and get the hell out of it – which they rather thankfully did. I've often wondered what happened to them.

Company Sergeant-Major Sid Knight
9th Parachute Battalion

We were to attack the Merville battery, a group of four massive concrete gun emplacements with full overhead cover, surrounded by a lot of barbed wire, an anti-tank ditch and a minefield. These guns were all facing the coast and covered Sword Beach where 3rd Division were due to land, so they had to be destroyed. My orders were to take a diversionary party of six men around the perimeter and make a noisy break-in at the main gate while the rest carried out a main assault through the breaches in the perimeter. I actually dropped quite a way off target because when I'd gone to jump, my harness had somehow hooked on to a handle on the door leading to the pilot's cabin. I'd hammered on the door, which opened and set me loose, but this delay of a few seconds meant that I landed in a field full of cows.

Suddenly these Lancasters started dropping their 400-pounders around me, so I was bouncing up and down in a ditch. As these bombs were coming down and the cows were being blown to bits, I suddenly thought of this old Cadbury's advert, which said, 'Where is your chocolate?' I thought, 'It's with a soldier alone in an unfriendly country!'

Anyway, things became a bit quieter after the bombs dropped, so I made my way round to the rendezvous. The planning was so good that when I dropped I knew where I was immediately. The first bloke I saw was Sergeant Salter, so we ran together to the rendezvous. When I arrived, there was hardly anyone there at all. Then one of my old mates turned up plus a few more. My diversionary party was attached to Headquarters Company so we were given orders to do what we could, but we had no weapons. I had just one pistol, one Bren gunner and one Sten in my party. Anyway, Colonel Otway then decided that we'd go off to the battery, and do our job there.

It was night-time, very dark and we all went through the lanes from the rendezvous at Varaville to the Merville battery. When we got near to the battery, everybody had his job to do. We numbered about 150, that's all. At the battery we found Major Alan Parry with the battery reconnaissance party. I was close to the Colonel and Hal Hudson the adjutant all the time.

There was hardly any noise whatsoever, and the battery loomed out of the darkness. You could see the outlines of the four big guns facing the sea. We'd come over the barbed wire and there was an old perimeter track leading up to the battery so I started to make a movement around this road when machine-guns opened up from both sides. Someone shouted out, 'Get those bloody machine guns!' I had only one man with me and I took his Sten gun from him. We found there were three guns, one outside and two inside the perimeter, in front of No. 1 battery. I got the bloke on the outside corner by the forming-up point, then we went into the battery. It was very dark, but I could see that one of the gunners was by a whacking great lump of concrete that had been blown up. His tracer gave him away, so I got right round behind him and put my gun on him, which soon quietened him.

I had a go at the third one, whether I got him or not I don't know, but it all went quiet. I went back to report to the Colonel and was just going towards the actual objective when I saw Major Parry on the right-hand side of the track wounded in the leg. On the left side was Captain Hudson and he had a terrible wound in his stomach – I think a shell must have hit him. I carried on with my diversionary party inside the perimeter and as we reached the main gate, we saw some Germans walking in, waving white flags. A couple of our blokes were shouting out, 'Shoot them.' Of course, I shouted, 'You can't shoot them – they've got the white flag up,' and so we rounded them up. I went and had a look in the batteries myself. Some chaps put two shells in the gun – one at the breech and one in the barrel! When the gun fired, the shells blew one another and the gun to pieces, I did not see the actual firing but I heard the explosions.

THE SEABORNE INVASION

Able Seaman Ken Oakley
Royal Naval Commando
On the evening prior to the D-Day landings, the senior arms officer gave us a briefing and I will always remember his final words. 'Don't worry if all the first wave of you are killed,' he said. 'We shall simply pass over your bodies with more and more men.' What a confident thought to go to bed on.

Lieutenant George Honour
Midget Submarine X23
For D-Day we were to leave on Friday night, the 2nd June to cross the 90 miles from Gosport to France and land at a fixed position. We marked our position and sat on the bottom until nightfall. On the Sunday night, we surfaced and dropped our anchor so we would stay right on our marking position. We could see a lorry load of Germans playing volleyball and swimming. Little did they know that we were there, and what was waiting for them. We hoisted our radio mast and got a signal that the invasion had been postponed, so then we had to retreat to the bottom again and wait until

Monday night. That night we resurfaced and received a message that the invasion was on. So we went back to sit on the bottom and at about 4.30 a.m. on Tuesday, 6th June, we surfaced again, put up all our navigational aids – 18-foot telescopic mast with a light shining seaward, a radio beacon and an echo-sounder tapping out a message below the surface. This was for the navigational ML's to pick up as they brought the invasion in.

Our particular operation for D-Day was called Gambit. When we looked it up in the dictionary, much to our horror it said the pawn you throw away before a big move in chess – which didn't encourage us too much.

Captain J.H.B. Hughes
Royal Marines, aboard HMS *Danae*
Just before dawn, those of us on the bridge of HMS *Danae* had a tot of the most superb 1812 brandy from a bottle laid down by my great-grandfather in 1821 – sent to me by my father with the comment, 'You may find this of some use in the near future.' We then commenced the operations for which we had been trained, namely engaging and knocking out three enemy batteries. At about 10 a.m. we closed the beaches to knock out the opposition to the landing forces in the Ouistreham area. Our open 6-inch and twin 4-inch guns went into independent fire – the guns being laid, trained and fired by the crews stripped to the waist. This was real 'Nelson Stuff'. We knocked up a fantastic rate of fire. X and Y guns were firing at least 19 rounds per minute on occasion. We all joined in, jumping in to relieve the exhausted crew members where we could. It was exhilarating beyond description and even my thirteen-year-old boy bugler fired Y Gun with the lanyard while the captain of the gun, a corporal, leapt to get more charges into the breech.

Then it all came to a halt and we sailed to Portsmouth for re-ammunition.

Lieutenant-Commander Hugh Irwin
Commanding 591 LCA (HR) Flotilla
Rommel had placed beach obstacles all along the Western defences. These were in the form of tetrahedrals, steel posts, which had shells and mines attached to them. Our landing craft were fitted with twenty-four 60-pound spigot bombs and the object was to blow up the beach obstacles at half-tide, clearing a passage for the LCTs that were carrying tanks with flails. The flails would clear any mines that were left and then the troops could go in. As we arrived thirty yards off the beach to do our job, destroyers were bombarding inland, but at precisely H minus one minute, the bombardment lifted. We let go our spigot-bombs and there were tremendous explosions.

As landing craft arrive on Normandy beaches on D-Day, troops equipped with bicycles dash through the shallows to begin the liberation of France.

Sergeant-Major William Brown
D Company, 8th Battalion, Durham Light Infantry
I watched these tramp steamers firing bloody great big rockets. They were absolutely blasting the hell out of the beaches. The beaches were cleared really when we got there, the way these things had been going in. It was the first time I'd seen rocket-launchers used.

Squadron Leader Geoffrey Page
132 Squadron, RAF
It was fascinating to see our troops and the Americans and the Canadians going into France again. I was sitting over the beaches at about 1,000 feet and I had a dress-circle view of the whole of the Normandy landing. We felt sorry for the troops who were coming across in the landing craft. There were thousands of vessels from big battleships down to landing craft, and the little landing craft were taking a tremendous pounding from the bad weather conditions. The Channel was rough. I should think a tremendous number of them were being ill from sea-sickness – and of course, to get out of a landing barge on a beach – to be fired at and to be a brave man and attack the enemy is not the easiest thing in the world. And of course, after I'd been there for about an hour, I'd fly back to England, and I'd tuck into a breakfast and I'd be comfortable, while those poor chaps were still out there on the beaches. That was our several-times-a-day routine, going back out over the beaches – and it became a little boring, in fact, after a while, because the Germans, I think, thought that the Normandy invasion was a dummy attack – they put up no air resistance at all. I believe two German fighters, which I never saw, came over once during the first fortnight.

Lieutenant-Commander Cromwell Lloyd-Davies
Aboard HMS Glasgow
The scene in the Channel was quite amazing. It was almost like Piccadilly Circus – there were so many ships there, and it was incredible to us that all this could be going on without the Germans knowing anything about it. But we never saw a German aircraft the whole time. Our air force had kept them completely out of the air. We arrived off the approaches to Normandy, and *Glasgow* was then told to take the head of the line of the force going into the Omaha Beach. As we steamed down the line, the padre said to me, 'Shouldn't we say a prayer?' And so I said, 'Why not say Nelson's Prayer?' because it was exactly right for this day. So he started to read Nelson's Prayer, and as we passed the *Texas*, all their ships company took off their helmets as they heard us reading the prayer going in.

Major Ian Hammerton
2nd County of London Yeomanry, Royal Armoured Corps

As we crossed the bar, I said, 'I suppose I better open my bag' – my sandbag with the maps in it. And while I was going down to the cabin to get it, I passed the exhaust from the motors of the engines of the ship – and I began to feel queasy. Up to that point, I'd enjoyed the smell of diesel smoke – but from that point onwards in my life, I didn't. I got them opened – I got the relevant maps to the other tank crews on the ship, and that was it – I was sick. As the landing craft headed into the rollers, there was a thud, and it slipped sideways and upwards and downwards and all ways. Water splashed on to the deck and began sloshing from one end of the ship to the other, carrying with it sandwiches, oil and vomit. This went on all night as we were going pretty slowly.

When I opened the sandbag, I found a map, which showed where we were landing and showed all the defence information – the height of the seawall, the kind of beach, the kind of guns in the DUKW houses – the minefields, the telephone lines, the wire – everything. But in addition to that, there were several photographs. There were photographs of families sitting on the beach, building sandcastles – with the seawall in the background. These had been collected during the previous two years, and it must have been a tremendous job, sorting out thousands of holiday snapshots, because the government had asked for snapshots of beaches from Spain to Norway. In addition to these photos, there were aerial photographs taken a couple of weeks before from a low-flying Mosquito, showing the Germans working on the sea defences on the beach – and running as the plane approached. The only thing all these photos didn't tell us was how the enemy were going to react.

Lieutenant-Colonel David Warren
1st Battalion, Hampshire Regiment

We had the advantage of having marvellous models of the part of the coast where we were going to land, and so before we ever got on board the ship, we were able to brief everybody from the model. They were very good indeed. They had all the intelligence about the enemy – their positions and anything else that would be relevant. We knew a great deal about the beach on which we were going to land, but going in, I suddenly realised that with the bombardment, there was such a lot of dust and smoke from fires that it was difficult to see exactly where we were supposed to land. We knew where we wanted to land, but we couldn't tell where it was.

Sergeant-Major William Brown
D Company, 8th Battalion, Durham Light Infantry

Morale was getting pretty low then. People were getting sick and spewing. The smell when you went downstairs, where the men were trying to lie in the bunks with their equipment on – the smell was vile. Chewing gum was supposed to stop you from being seasick – but in fact it made you worse. The handiest things were the spew bags, because you could take them and throw them over the side.

Able Seaman Ken Oakley
Royal Navy Commando

All around the sea was one mass of craft, landing craft of all kinds, shapes and sizes. A lot in our immediate area were LCAs because we were going for the initial assault. There was a good feeling as we went forward – except that most of the army was seasick. I wasn't very happy myself. However when we got within sight of the shore we were getting spattered with light gunfire, nothing very heavy at this moment. Finally we got within sight of the stakes, the dreaded stakes, with the shells and mines on, which protected the beaches. Our coxswain did a marvellous job. We were headed straight for this stake and I could see the 56-pound shell lashed to it. In just the last second, he missed it. He got it just right. He steered us in between the stakes and got us ashore without touching one of those shells. At the order 'Down ramp,' we were all surging ashore. We were in a few inches of water. All around were craft beaching and chaos and more gunfire was pouring down on us. We ran, under fire, up to the top of the beach where we went to ground, about a hundred yards from high water. People were going down and screaming and crying all around us. As we hit the sand at the top of the beach we took stock of our bearings and realised we had landed almost exactly in our correct positions. We landed on Queen Red One, Sword Sector, Colleville sur Orne.

Lieutenant-Commander Roger Hill
Aboard HMS Jarvis

We watched them going ashore. From the bridge of my ship, they looked like little models – moving forward, stopping, firing, and moving forward again. Coming in from the big ships were the flotillas of the landing craft, and as we watched, the guns still blazing away, they formed in line abreast and were rushing for the surf line of the beach. I found myself banging the bridge with my clenched fist, 'By God, we're ashore in France, we've done it, we're back in France again.'

Corporal Bernard Slack
Royal Marines

Where we landed we found 'Rommel's Asparagus', as we called it. It was four triple bars and triple wooden stakes, and on the end of every one was an 88 mm percussion cap shell, strapped to blow the bottom out of you. But the Royal Navy Beach Commandos had gone in first and cleared pathways.

Corporal Thomas Finigan
Mine Clearance, 85th Field Company, Royal Engineers

We carried metal-detectors ashore but we found them quite useless for the simple reason that there was so much shrapnel around, that as soon as you switched on your detector, you picked up noise. So we had to do it the old-fashioned way – we prodded for the mines with a bayonet. Once you got the pattern of a minefield, it was quite easy. The Germans were very methodical and laid them in very regular patterns. You just went forward in lines, carrying white tapes, and cleared and marked an area about three or four foot wide. We had Pioneer Corps people with us and after we'd disarmed the mines, they would take them back along the beach and blew them up twenty at a time. These explosions were going on all the time, which was reassuring.

Lieutenant William Jalland
Platoon Commander, 8th Battalion, Durham Light Infantry

The LCIs started going round in tight circles towards the beach and when they were within striking distance, they peeled off one at a time, rammed their prows into the beach and then the next LCI would come alongside it and ram in there and so on – and it worked like a charm. The prow of our boat went into the shingle and the American sailor lowered the ramp and I knew exactly what I had to do. I was to walk off the gangway and on to the shingle and get off the beach quickly because a lot of shelling was expected. I went down, manfully I hope. I stepped off the ramp into the water. The water rushed over my head and I went straight to the bottom on my hands and knees. The prow was smashing into the shingle next to me and I watched it smashing against my legs and arms whenever it came near me. My waders were full of water and I couldn't get to the surface. I threw away the folding bicycle that I was carrying. Then I started to tear at the waders and I managed to get them off. I unfastened my webbing and slipped that off and eventually I landed on Hitler's Fortress Europe on my hands and knees, wet through, very frightened and completely unarmed.

Signal Sergeant James Bellows
1st Battalion Hampshire Regiment

All along the beach, there were men lying dead and not just in the waves. Some of them still had their tin hats on. A lot of them had been overridden by their landing craft as they came off. The landing craft became lighter as men came off and as it surged up the beach, any man that was in front went straight underneath.

Petty Officer Alan Higgins
Telegraphist, Royal Navy

As we began unloading the first men, casualties were sustained. Orders were for all wounded to be landed on the beach. There was one soldier being helped by two others, his left foot and boot as one, in a mangle of flesh and leather. I shall never forget the almost apologetic look he gave me as he passed by. A landing craft shot alongside us and on to the beach with its cargo of tanks ablaze and ammunition exploding. The air was alive with bullets and shrapnel. As I ducked back into the wireless offices, we sustained a direct hit. The smell of cordite and the cries of wounded men came from the packed No. 3 troop space, where the shell had exploded, leaving wounded and dying men. As we disembarked the rest of the men, our skipper shouted down the voicepipe for me to see what was happening in No. 3 troop space, as it had to be cleared. As I was halfway down the ladder, a soldier said, 'Come and help my mate, Jack.' I replied, 'You better get off quick, all the rest have landed.' He replied, 'I can't – my leg has had it – help my mate.' The water was pouring in so the wounded were in danger of drowning. I went to his mate and I saw that his leg was hanging off below the knee, so I opened the tin of morphia ampoules and jabbed one into his thigh with the attached needle. Turning back to the other man who was semi-conscious, I undid his webbing and tried to set him on the seat next to his wounded mate. He was a big chap, and his gas mask kept catching under the seat. I said, 'Try and help yourself, mate,' but all I got was a vague, incoherent mumbling. I finally got him seated and saw that both his legs were shattered below the knees, so I jabbed a needle of morphine into each of his thighs.

By now, some other crew members had arrived in the troop space, and the task of getting the dead and wounded up to the deck above began. One soldier looked all right at first, but a closer look revealed a hole of about one inch in diameter behind his ear. He just sat dribbling in a semi-haze. We got him and the rest of the casualties put aboard a destroyer, which carried a medical officer. We had only one wire stretcher, so most of the wounded were carried up the ladder, one man supporting the shoulders with his hands under the arms and one man supporting the legs. Not the most satisfactory way of handling wounded men, as the one supporting the shoulders would be kicking the wounded man in the back as he struggled up the ladder. One of the men I was helping must have had internal injuries, for his face was a leaden colour and he just sighed and gave up the ghost as we reached the top of the ladder. The dead and wounded were placed along a narrow passage on the port side, and the wounded were kept as comfortable as was humanly possible.

Sergeant James Kelly
No. 41 Commando, Royal Marines
It had just broken daylight when we arrived – and the shambles! I was the third man out, and when I saw the things going on in the beach I thought, 'How the hell are we going to get through that?' We waded ashore, and all I remember next is a blinding flash and a smell of cordite, and my mate Charlie Orrell lying down on the deck, the blood was pumping out of his neck. I lay down next to him, then in a matter of seconds a voice said, 'Get going. You're not supposed to stop. Get going.' So I went, and just before I got to the wire, a captain shouted at me, 'Give me a hand here!' and he was trying to get the waterproofing off the Bren-gun carrier. When we got it open, it had had a direct hit inside it, and it was all just a mess. But that's the shambles that an organised beach landing becomes, I suppose.

Signal Sergeant James Bellows
1st Battalion, Hampshire Regiment
We grounded and dropped the ramp. We were a hell of a way off the shore and the waves were coming by the side and I thought they were pretty bloody high for shallow water. I said, 'We're not in shallow water, here. We're in deep water, you know!' and this sub-lieutenant said, 'We've grounded!' All sorts were going on all around us but we were in our own little world. We started arguing about the depth of the water and so he called for a stick that he put in the water and said 'Four foot six'. I said 'You must be bloody joking! We're in deep water! We're on an obstacle!' 'No we're not!' he said. 'I'm in charge of this ship! I'm the captain!' Stupid sod. So I went to my chaps and I said, 'This is going to be a bloody wet landing.'

Sergeant William Spearman
No. 4 Commando

There were bodies – dead bodies, living bodies. All the blood in the water made it look as though men were drowning in their own blood. That's how it looked.

Captain Eric Hooper
Motor Transport Officer, 9th Battalion Durham Light Infantry

As I was standing on the top of the ramp, we hit an underground mine that exploded and blew the ramp up and made a hole in the sand. They'd issued us with oilskin trousers, which came right up to your chest, which you tied up with a string. When I got in the water, I couldn't touch the bottom and I started to float. The air was trapped in the trousers and the bubble rose up to my chest and I became buoyant and I started turning over. Just then the trousers burst and I sank back into the water.

Sergeant-Major William Brown
D Company, 8th Battalion, Durham Light Infantry

The water filled the gas trousers. We could feel it sloshing around inside and we stood on the beach, like idiots, in trousers full of water.

Sergeant Norman Travett
2nd Battalion, Devonshire Regiment

We beached – I can't remember how far out, but we had to jump into the water, which came up roughly to our waist. As we were wading ashore I became aware that the bombing had left craters in the water, which you couldn't see. Some of my mates walked into these craters and, because of the weight of their packs, were drowned.

Sub Lieutenant Frank Thomasson
RNVR, aboard LCT 1192

The Marines, who had been awoken from their slumbers very early, so they could put the final polish to their buttons and check over their equipment, seemed in no hurry to leave us. It soon became clear why. As soon as the way off was clear, the NCO fell them in, dressed them by the right, turned them into line – but instead of then marching them off at the double, as one might have expected, they were stood at ease. At this point, they all took their steel helmets off and replaced them, from their kit, with their normal peaked caps, ignoring our suggestion to, 'Chop, chop!' The right-hand marker then changed his helmet for a top hat and a raised umbrella. Called to attention, they marched off and up the beach to start their job. The inspiring result of this transformation was that large numbers of others, dashing about, paused as they saw the marching Marines. They seemed to be saying to themselves, 'Why am I rushing?' and slowed down. This action by the Marines had a calming effect on all.

Able Seaman Peter Thompson
Aboard LST 304
In our tank landing craft, we went about a mile in, opened the bow doors and eight DWKS went off towards the shore. Then 12 tanks, which had flotation buoys on the side and a propeller on the stern, went off. There was still a little swell and one or two of the tanks went straight to the bottom. Poor sods. Later we unloaded the rest of the tanks and equipment and waited for the ambulances. They brought three or four hundred wounded men straight on board for us to take back to England. It was busy but for me, being a youngster, it was exciting. There was more excitement than fear. You just felt that this scene was amazing. It took your breath away.

Corporal William Dunn
26th Assault Squadron, Royal Engineers
The atmosphere in the tank as we hit the beach was a little bit tense because we were battened down and I was the only man that could see. Shells and bullets were coming across the top of us. My co-driver was sitting behind me asking me what was going on and could he have a look. My main concern was the infantry that were lying on the beach. I only had this little visor to look through and I didn't know if they were dead or not, so I had to pick my way through.

Able Seaman Ken Oakley
Royal Navy Commando
We were now left with the business of organising the beach, getting everything moved off the beach and getting the signs laid. The beachmaster's responsibility was to get that beach cleared – get it organised – and he was the senior officer on the beach, irrespective of rank, whether the army guy was a general or whatever. He was the man in charge of the beach. He sent his various teams to do the clearing, get the stakes out, get the roads laid down for the heavy vehicles.

After some time, one of our chaps came up to me and said, 'Oh, Ken, can you help me? Sid is down there, very badly wounded.' Sid was an old friend. I went and found that he was severely wounded. The assistant beachmaster said, 'He caught it across the back. His kidneys were hanging out. I've pushed them back in and shoved on this dressing. Can you get him to the first-aid-post?' We had to half carry, half drag him but we got him to the first-aid-post and left him there under a bit of canvas. I had to go back to my duties on the shoreline. More and more craft were coming in continuously, and I was directing them. The trouble was, when the soldiers came ashore, their first reaction was, 'Let's group up and have a little check, and then we'll have a cup of tea.' We had learned on exercises that you must not allow this to happen. You must keep the beaches clear and the momentum going. If the beach is clogged up, the whole impetus is lost. You have to keep it moving. There is no other way. This is what we were doing – chasing them, telling them to get off the beach. That is your exit. That is *your* exit, over there, over *there*.

Private Peter Fussell
No. 1 Commando

We cleared the beaches straight after we hit them. Unfortunately, some of the infantry, who'd landed along with us, started to dig in. It seems that was what they'd been taught to do, as part of their training. Well, that wasn't what *we*'d been taught to do. Our idea was to get the hell out of it as quickly as we could. One of our officers shouted at these chaps, 'For God's sake, don't dig in here. You're going to get shelled and mortared. You're going to be counter-attacked. For God's sake, get clear of the beach.' The infantry chaps didn't know what to do but they followed us – which was probably just as well, because it cleared the beaches for other people to land and bring in supplies. No-one wanted the beaches cluttered up with holes and infantrymen.

Sergeant William Spearman
No. 4 Commando

The planners might have gone through a lot of campaigns at a very high level but nobody can know what it's like to be on a beach where you can do nothing. Where you're under severe fire and you've got to get off. And it's only a person who's been through it a number of times who can know – you stay and die or you get off and live. People doing it for the first time – no matter how many times you tell them – they don't realise it. And people didn't get off the beach. They were so transfixed with fright, they couldn't get off. I was transfixed with fright but I had the certain knowledge that you either stopped and died or you got up and got away. So I took the coward's view and got out of the bloody place.

Able Seaman Ken Oakley
Royal Navy Commando

To our left the patterning of mortar fire seemed very intense, but we seemed to be just under the arch of fire so that we were relatively safe. The main part of the mortar fire seemed to be to our left, further down, which suited us fine, but for the people that were under that, it must have been awful. A commando was screaming, 'Help me, help me,' and I looked at the beachmaster as if to say, 'Should we go to help him?' but we couldn't. My duty was to stay with the beachmaster – he was my prime responsibility. The commando had a huge pack on his back anyway which would protect him from various splinters and shrapnel. It didn't look good at all, but he wasn't the only person who was in dire straits all around us. The mortar- fire was very intense. Some people were filtering through, only some, not many. Then behind us came the roar of a tank. A duplex-drive tank had managed to get ashore. He pulled up behind us, opened his hatch and fired, and that was the end of the mortar-fire. One shot, honest, no more than that one shot screamed over our heads, whoosh, and it must have gone straight down into the bunkers. Fantastic, I thought – a great job.

Corporal Bernard Slack
Royal Marines, on mechanised landing craft

We could see men getting shot down. Not everyone got hit – some of them made it right up the beach. As callous as it seems, we didn't bother, although we saw some terrible sights, because it was nothing to do with us. I saw some of my mates die. We saw the hospital ships lifting them up on the stretchers, on to the decks to tend them – but you don't bother. You just get on with your job. This is what you're trained for.

Able Seaman Ken Oakley
Royal Navy Commando

Suddenly the air was split by a piercing sound of bagpipes. Along the beach, some hundred yards away, a piper was marching up and down. There was Piper Bill Millin filling his bag up and getting his wind. Lord Lovat had asked him to play a few tunes. Lord Lovat came up behind Bill, formed up his troops and they marched off in parade-ground style, straight up into the village of Colleville. It was amazing. How could he have the pipes on the beach amidst all this hurly-burly? Shells screaming and fire all around. And silently, as the sound of the pipes died away into the hinterland of the beach, we got back to work bringing the landing craft in. That was a real high point in the whole landing.

Sword Beach, 8.40 am, D-Day. Commandos of the 1st Special Service Brigade land at the La Brèche area, accompanied by Brigadier the Lord Lovat to the right of the column and, nearest the camera, still aboard, the brigade bagpiper, Bill Millin.

Sergeant Bill Millin
Piper, 1st Commando Brigade

'Give us a tune, piper!' 'What tune would you like, sir?' I asked. 'Play "The Road to the Isles",' he said. 'Would you like me to march up and down?' 'Yes, yes! March up and down! That would be lovely!' So there I was, going backwards and forwards, piping away when I felt a hand on my shoulder and it was this sergeant I recognised and he said, 'What are you playing at, you mad bastard? Every German in France knows we're here now!'

Staff Sergeant Geoffrey Barkway
Glider pilot, 2nd Battalion, Glider Pilot Regiment

I felt this bang in my wrist, and that was it. The next thing I remember was being in this house on the floor with my arm in a sling across my chest. My right arm was pretty mucky. Because I had lost a lot of blood, I was terribly thirsty all the time. The next thing I remember is lying on the beach, under this tarpaulin cover. Then we were put on a DUKW and taken out to a tank landing ship. The doctor had got a sort of emergency theatre. He redressed my arm, which by this time had begun to smell a bit because gangrene had set in. After a while, I felt wet and uncomfortable, so I called a nurse and she turned the bedclothes back and there was all blood everywhere. I had haemorrhaged, she left the clothes turned back and rushed off to get the sister. I looked down, and instead of my arm across my chest as I thought, there was nothing there. My arm had gone. Which was a bit shattering.

Francis O'Neill
Photographer, Army Film and Photographic Unit

As we came off the beach we started coming across bodies – British bodies. I remember the first one I saw was an infantryman, and what fascinated me was that he had no head. He was just lying there, with no head. There was no sign of his head, but I don't think I was particularly shocked. It sounds a cruel thing to say, but I was quite surprised at not seeing much more carnage. Then, as we started to get to the little sand hills, which were just below a concrete promenade – we did start seeing bodies and some wounded fellows. I was out of the half-track by this time, and I started taking pictures of the troops coming ashore. Then I suddenly spotted two very tiny infantrymen marching along with a very tall German soldier who was absolutely terrified. He had a bandage round his face and there were these two rather cheerful – I think they were cockneys – on either side of him. I said, 'Just a minute!' and they posed as though they might be posing in Piccadilly Circus for their picture, with this German in between them.

Corporal William Dunn
26th Assault Squadron, Royal Engineers
I was driving a Churchill tank and when I got to where we had to drop the fascine, I said to our tank commander, 'Jim, I can't see the culvert.' He radioed back to Captain Ewart who was on the beach, but our orders were to carry on so I put the tank in first gear. As soon as I started to move we went straight down, because the Germans had flooded the area. Water started pouring into the turret. Everybody had to get out a bit sharpish but with me being the last, I started to swallow water. As my co-driver got out he put his knees round both sides of my head and dragged me with him. There was quite a bit of water in my stomach by then. When I got outside, Bill Hawkins hit me once in the stomach. We hadn't time for any niceties, he just brought the water up and that was it.

Sergeant Norman Travett
2nd Battalion, Devonshire Regiment
We got whatever cover we could underneath a wall, because there was still considerable enemy fire-power coming from land. In no way could you possibly advance until these troublesome pillboxes had been destroyed. We lay there in our wet trousers with water oozing out of our boots for what seemed ages. Eventually the pillbox on our right was silenced. That was where I saw my first dead Germans. It was gruesome. I thought really those chaps had probably been called up for service like myself, and had no wish to be where they were. They didn't stand a chance, really, not there. What could they do? Nothing, really.

Corporal William Dunn
26th Assault Squadron, Royal Engineers
We just lay down behind the sand dunes and Jim Ashton started to sing 'Kiss me Again'. He was a father figure, he was a good man and he always did this to settle us all down. I was the youngest one in the tank crew and he'd just started to sing when a mortar-bomb came and dropped between us, which killed three, outright. I was wounded, the co-driver had a hole in his back I could have put my fist in. But he was so brave and said 'I'll crawl for help.' I saw him roll over when he got a hundred yards from us and that's where he died.

I rolled down into a minefield. There was a big board – 'Achtung Minen' – straight above my head. I thought 'Cor blimey'. I managed to get up on to my feet and I ran about fifty yards, then my legs gave way and I collapsed. Two lads came and dragged me back and gave me a cigarette and a drink. I was left there for quite a while and the first one to come on the scene after that was a Canadian medical officer who gave me an injection of morphine. He told me that I couldn't possibly have run because I had five compound fractures in one of my legs. I said to him, 'Well, when you're fighting and there's bullets flying around, that makes you do queer things.'

Sergeant-Major William Brown
D Company, 8th Battalion, Durham Light Infantry
When we were finally off the beach, we met up in a 'hide' where we had a self-inflicted wound in D Company. I heard a rifle shot. An old fellow of forty, a bundle of nerves, had shot himself in the hand. I said, 'You've shot yourself, you bastard!' He said, 'I'm sorry, Sergeant-Major. I can't go on.' 'It's all right, ' I said. 'Leave your rifle there. Get yourself back. You've been hit in the hand.' I wasn't going to court-martial him.

From the hide we moved off on our bicycles, trying to keep at the pace of the battalion. We'd used the bikes to get to the hide and they'd been useful, but cycling at a marching pace was pretty hard work. So when we stopped, I attracted the attention of a passing tank commander. I asked him to do me a favour. 'What do you want?' he asked. 'Run over them bloody bikes. With your track,' I said. 'Run them over?' he said. 'Aye,' I said, so he just ran them over. And then I said to my officer 'The bikes have gone, sir!' 'The bikes have gone?' 'Aye, the bloody tanks have run them over,' and he said, 'Oh well, if you haven't got a bike, you haven't got a bike.'

Sergeant William Spearman
No. 4 Commando
All the way along, you'd have snipers firing at you, and by the time you heard the crack, it was too late. You couldn't really take evasive action from snipers other than to zig-zag or to go behind a car or lamppost. And you couldn't stop. There was no point in stopping. You had to go on. The mortar-bombs were very frightening. You'd hear one whistle as it approached and then just before the loudest pitch as it reached you, you'd have to throw yourself on the ground. If you didn't get down quick enough, the shrapnel could hit you.

Sergeant Henry Cosgrove
Royal Marine Commando
Once we left the shore and we were on our way, four of us played cards for hours in our LCT. We nearly wore the cards out. Our job was to get to the Orne bridges as quickly as we could, to relieve the paratroopers who were holding the bridge.

When we got to the bridges, there were a lot of dead Germans around, and some of our paratrooper fellows. Then I suppose the brigadier had a meeting with somebody, and we set off over the bridge. There were snipers about and they were firing at us now and again, and a fellow got hit – but the brigadier – Lord Lovat – he must have thought he was on his estate. He marched along with a bloody bagpiper playing alongside him. We went over the bridge and then the problems really started. We started to lose a lot of men, so we moved to a higher piece of ground and dug in. I didn't know what the hell was going on, other than I was digging a hole as fast as I could, because we were being mortared from a battery that had actually been taken, but our troops had moved on and the Germans had come back.

Captain John Sim
12th Parachute Battalion

My company commander, asked me to see if there were any Germans in four houses nearby, where we were going to establish our Battalion Headquarters. I took a sergeant and two soldiers and when we got to the first house I noticed there was a light on inside. I knocked, and after probably about a minute, a middle-aged lady in her day clothes opened the door. At two o'clock in the morning this was a bit unusual. Behind her, her husband and two kids were also dressed in their day clothes. I said, 'Bonjour Madame, nous sommes soldats d'Angleterre; nous arrivons ici par avion, parachutistes. L'heure de libération est arrivée. Ou sont les soldats allemands? Les soldats allemands restent ici?' She looked blankly at me. I was a dunce at French at school, but I thought I'd done quite well. I had another go but now she looked dazed and terrified – we were all camouflaged up with blackened faces. I then asked my sergeant, a right raw Yorkshireman, if he could speak French – he couldn't and neither could the other two, so I tried again. I'd barely started when she burst into tears, embraced me and said, 'You're British soldiers, aren't you?' So I said, 'Yes, I've been trying to tell you this for the last three or four minutes. You can speak English well, can't you?' 'Yes,' she said, 'I am English, born in Manchester, and I married a French farmer before the war and settled here.' I asked her why it took her so long to come out with it. She explained that there had been Germans masquerading as British commandos or parachutists in the area to test them out. Then she said, 'It wasn't until I heard your frightful schoolboy French and your backchat to your sergeant that I realised that no German could possibly have acted the part!' She told us there were no Germans in the area.

D-Day, 6 June 1944. British troops of the South Lancashire Regiment land on Sword Beach, backed up by amphibious tanks of the 13th/18th Hussars.

Chief Petty Officer Albert Barnes
Quartermaster, aboard a Royal Naval tug, towing Mulberry Harbour caisson
A Force 9 gale was blowing and I think it was one of the worst tows that we ever had. I mean, you think of towing, you think of the tug being ahead but there were times when the block was abeam – it was really close. When we got over there, we shortened the tow and went to this long row of ships that had been sunk as a marker for us. Small tugs tied up alongside and guided her in and then they opened the seacocks and sunk them and that was more or less the start of the Mulberry Harbour. There was a Royal Navy commander with a ginger beard who called us all sorts of names, but we did it in the end.

NORMANDY

Brigadier James Hill
3rd Parachute Brigade
In the days following D-Day, I experienced some of the hardest fighting I had seen in the war. Involved were the 9th Parachute Battalion, 1st Canadian Parachute Battalion and 5th Battalion Black Watch. Imagine what it was like for a 9th Battalion soldier. These men had never seen a shot fired in anger until forty-eight hours before. Their average age was twenty. They had suffered an appalling night drop on D-Day. They had stormed the Merville battery and attacked Le Plein. They arrived on the ridge on the 7th June, 90 strong, having set off from England with over 600 officers and soldiers. They were minus their equipment and not exactly fresh. In the first eight days of the Battle of Normandy, my brigade, which started around 2,000 strong, lost about 50 officers and 1,000 other men.

A narrow road ran along the ridge. We had to hold this ridge at all costs. If the Germans had secured it, the bridgehead at Ranville would have been untenable. Alistair Pearson and his 8th Battalion were denying the enemy the approaches to the ridge from the south. The 9th Battalion, whose numbers fluctuated during the battle, held the wooded area and the road adjoining Château St Côme. Brigade HQ and their defence platoon were in the middle. The Canadians held the Mesnil crossroads area immediately to the south. My Brigade HQ with their strong defence platoon, numbering some 150, and the Canadians with some 300 men were concentrated over a front of about one mile, astride the Bréville–Troarn Road, running north to south on top of the ridge.

Enemy attacks concentrated first on the Canadian battalion at Le Mesnil then swung against the 9th Battalion after the Germans had occupied Bréville on D+2. It was then that I realised we were up against a first-class German infantry division – 346 Grenadier Division – supported by tanks and self-propelled guns. During this period, some six attacks were launched against the 9th Battalion from Bréville and the east – three of which were coordinated with attacks on the Canadian positions at Le Mesnil. There was constant patrolling activity and on one occasion, my defence platoon accounted for 19 Germans.

My room was on the top floor of a barn with access only from the outside staircase. I sat on the top step with my left backside overhanging the steps which was good as I smelt of gangrene poisoning – I had lost most of my left backside during a mortar attack on D-Day. From my position, I had a bird's-eye view of the German break-out from Bréville on D+4 and their attack on Peter Luard's 13th Battalion holding the north-east perimeter of Ranville. The 13th held their fire until the last moment and then mowed them down. For the next two days the Germans filtered back through the rear of our positions. I knew it was irregular to see Germans creeping about, but we had neither time nor resources to chase them.

It was about this time that we were strafed by our own Typhoons. Unfortunately the lady of the château, walking in the garden with her husband, was hit and killed. Our doctors tried to save the baby, to no avail, and we buried her in a shroud in her garden with what dignity we could muster under such circumstances. Soon after that, the husband and housekeeper left and my Brigade HQ occupied the château.

Sitting on my steps, looking down on the bank below, I saw the adjutant of the 9th Battalion, Hal Hudson, lying on the bank looking like a shrivelled parchment, waiting to be operated on by my Field Ambulance unit in the adjoining building. His story was unusual. He received some 18 shrapnel wounds in his stomach during the capture of the Merville battery. He thought, 'I must kill one German before I die.' He imagined he saw a figure looming up and he shot it with his Sten gun. It was in fact his foot. The pain was such that it took his mind off his much more severe wounds and thanks to that and the treatment he received from the Field Ambulance, he lived to tell the tale.

On D+5, the 5th Battalion of the Black Watch were put under my command to capture Bréville. The attack went on in the early hours of the morning and was repulsed by the Germans with heavy losses. I then told them to hold the Château St Côme itself and coordinate their defence with the 9th Battalion. At this juncture, the German Divisional Commander decided that our positions at St Côme and Le Mesnil must be liquidated for once and for all and a major attack was launched on D+6 on both the 9th Battalion and Black Watch positions and the Canadians. This attack was in strength, preceded by a heavy bombardment lasting some three hours, and it went on supported by tanks and self-propelled guns. The Black Watch were driven back and came back through the 9th Battalion and my defence platoon positions.

At 1600 hours, I received a message from Terence Otway commanding the 9th Battalion to say that he was doubtful whether he could hold out much longer. I knew that he would not send me this signal unless things were urgent and that something must be done about it. I had no bodies to spare so I went to Colonel Bradbrook, whose HQ was 200 yards away at the end of our drive, and asked him to help. At that moment, German tanks had overrun the road to his right and were shooting up his company HQ at close range. To his eternal credit, he decided that he could deal with this problem and he gave me what was left of his reserve company under Major Hanson, a very tough commander, together with cooks and any spare men, and we set off to the 9th Battalion area.

Company Sergeant-Major Sid Knight
9th Parachute Battalion

The 12th Battalion were ordered to attack Bréville to relieve us. You could look down on them and actually see the battle taking place with our boys attacking. They relieved us tremendously by doing that, and then they took Bréville. The ridge was held and the Germans didn't contest it again. Marvellous job. I don't think I'd be here today if they hadn't done that. They lost an awful lot of men, though, some killed by our own gunfire.

We then moved up to the crossroads at Le Mesnil and my little party dug in at the brickworks. Of course, the Jerries had a fixed line on it, so as soon as we got into the brickworks, boom, boom, down came the shells and RSM Cunningham was hit. We picked him up and called the medics and put him in the ambulance. He looked at me and said, 'I'll tell you this, when we get back to barracks, I'll remember who the real soldiers were.' I said, 'All right, Bill, you get yourself better.' Later the medics came back and I asked, 'How is the RSM?' They said, 'He's gone.' Terrible waste, because Le Mesnil was our last place to go before being relieved.

Normandy, June 1944. Following the landings and the drive inland, the 13th/18th Hussars encountered the German 21st Panzer Division. Following the engagement, men of the Hussars remember a fallen comrade after the Reverend Victor Leach had read the burial service.

Captain John Sim
12th Parachute Battalion

I decided that I would take the dead from one action to Ranville church. Among them was a German soldier. While we were being mortared, this lone soldier had come down towards us, from the castle fence carrying a rifle. I quietly said to my batman, 'Harris, you see that soldier coming down? Shoot him.' And he did. Much later I thought, 'How could I have given such an order?'

Lieutenant-Colonel Alistair Pearson
8th Parachute Battalion

Practically everyone was out on patrol every night to give the enemy the impression that we were very strong – which we were not – and to keep the enemy off balance. It is easy to knock the German off his stride. If you disorganise him, he finds it hard to reorganise. You have to keep on hitting him, not necessarily cause many casualties – just keep at him.

Captain John Graham
Argyll and Sutherland Highlanders

The Germans were unquestionably the best army in the world. They fought with great skill. Their use of ground was remarkable. Their ability to plug gaps by junior commanders taking the initiative, without waiting for orders from on high, was superior to ours. Much later, when the German army had been defeated in France, pulled back over the Seine and chased into Holland and Belgium, they were able to produce a cohesive defence against us by bringing in remnants of batteries, regiments and battalions. They formed battle groups on an *ad hoc* basis to produce a swift and resolute defence. If the German army had not been bled white in the East and continued to be engaged by the Russians, I do not know how we would have defeated them.

Flying Officer Ken Adam
609 Squadron, RAF, Second Tactical Air Force

I had a gold ring made up of the wedding rings of my mother and father. Before I went on an op I would turn this ring three times. On one particular occasion we had to attack a Gestapo headquarters in the middle of Dunkirk. As I started my engine I went to turn my ring, but it wasn't there. I must have dislodged it when I went to grab my parachute. So I said to myself, 'Well, this is it.' I started to look for any reason to abort the mission. But the plane was behaving perfectly. I took off, and it was a particularly nasty attack in which we lost the squadron commander and three other pilots. I was hit several times, but managed to get back. As I climbed out the fitters were walking towards me, great grins on their faces, holding my ring, which they had been turning for me.

Major Peter Martin
2nd Battalion, Cheshire Regiment

At 2330 hours on the 7th June, orders arrived to assemble the armoured column at first light the following morning, and to advance to Villers-Bocage. I was quite certain that if an armoured column had set off on the afternoon of D-Day, there would have been absolutely nothing to stop it, but having wasted 36 hours, it was too much to expect an easy drive to Villers-Bocage. We assembled, but no move was made until 1000 hours.

As we advanced, we found that the whole complex of hamlets that make up the village of Audrieu was held and the 1st Dorsets were fighting hard. All that night, the Dorsets battled away in Audrieu and as there was nothing for my company to do, I went to sleep. Shortly after midnight, I was ordered to report to the Brigadier. He told me that a squadron of Sherwood Foresters, by following a circuitous route, had reached Point 103 – a dominant feature south of Le Haut d'Audrieu, the southernmost hamlet. My company was to move across country to join them. We had a nightmare journey through enemy territory. By 0230 hours, we were up on Point 103.

At first light, German tanks approached from the south and engaged the forward tanks of the Sherwood Foresters, knocking some of them out. The remainder withdrew to the reverse slope of Point 103, leaving my two platoons totally isolated.

The enemy tanks stood off about 120 yards away, hull down, and began shelling our bank with high explosive, causing casualties. On several occasions, when the Tigers cruised too far forward, with turrets open, our machine-gunners fired at them to make them close down. The situation was precarious, because if the enemy put in a determined attack from the south, he would be right on top of us before encountering our tanks or anti-tank guns. So we were very cheered when soon after midday, recce parties from the 1st Dorsets arrived to say that Audrieu was being cleared and the Battalion would soon come to join us. At about that time, one of my platoons came up on the wireless and asked for help with evacuating a seriously wounded corporal. The only way was by jeep over an open field being shelled like fury. I thought I'd better drive the jeep myself so I told my driver to get out. To my disappointment, instead of saying, 'No sir! I will go with you!' he said, 'Right,

Normandy, 18 June, 1944. An echo of home – on Derby Day, British troops pause for a flutter on the big race. Sergeant Dalziel of the Royal Signals takes the bets, while Lance Corporal Day holds the cash.

sir,' and hopped out. I drove the jeep to a gap in the hedge of a field where the shells were bursting. I remember saying, 'Oh God, please stop the shells. If you stop them, I'll be good for always.' The shells promptly stopped and I got the corporal to safety. Many times during the war, I promised I would be a better person if I was allowed to survive. The promises never lasted very long.

For two days, the battle for Point 103 raged on. Eventually, the enemy began closing in. Shermans were blazing everywhere. I was hailed by the CO of 24th Lancers, sitting on the ground, with his arm in a sling. He handed me a rifle, saying, 'Put a round in the breech, at least I'll take one of them with me.' I thought, 'Good God, it's as bad as that.' Shortly afterwards, all firing ceased. It was the final attempt by the enemy before pulling out and leaving St Pierre.

Sergeant Doug Woodcraft
9th Parachute Battalion
On about the 14th June, I was told to go into Escoville and see if it was still held by the Germans, So off we went, followed a track to the edge of the wood and there, six or seven hundred yards away, was the village. At the edge of the wood was a slit trench occupied by Jocks from the 51st Highland Division. I asked them if the Germans were in Escoville. The answer I got was in broad Scots and had more fucks than a Sergeant-Major's blessing. They didn't know – they didn't want to know. They were up to here with Normandy – give them the Western Desert any day.

It took the best part of an hour to make our way along a hedge through the thick undergrowth until we were almost to the village. I saw two Frenchmen digging a hole beside a very dead cow. After a bit, I managed to attract their attention. They dropped their shovels and to my horror, came running over, shouting 'Tommy! Tommy!' at the tops of their voices, with me shushing away like mad.

We followed them to the village centre, where there was a small café with eight or nine Frenchmen seated around, each with a glass in front of him and there was a war going on outside! I shook hands with everyone, then the owner of the café came from behind the bar, moved a small carpet and pulled up a loose floorboard, and came up with a bottle of clear liquid. I didn't know it at the time but I was about to be introduced to Calvados – the real stuff – you could run buses on it.

We all toasted De Gaulle, Roosevelt, Churchill and Stalin, each swallow causing a minor explosion at the back of my throat. All the time, I was pointing in all directions and saying, 'Boche? Boche?' whilst everyone replied in a torrent of French. I was getting nowhere when I suddenly remembered that we had been issued with a leaflet that contained a number of English-French phrases and it was in my wallet. Also in my wallet, which I had forgotten about, were five contraceptives, loose, no packaging. As I opened the wallet, they fell on to the floor. One Frenchman with a yell of delight that could be heard in Caen, grabbed them, held them above his head and punched the air with fist, screaming, 'British Tommy jig-a-jig!' At this the small crowd started cheering and clapping. It was obvious there were no Germans in the vicinity with all this noise going on and I decided to get away as soon as possible.

Before we could leave, the Frenchman went into a house opposite and returned with a dozen big brown eggs. My pouches were full with Sten magazines and my pockets had grenades in them, so I placed the eggs carefully inside my smock, said, 'Au revoir,' and left.

On the way back, we heard the now familiar sound of German mortars firing. As one man, the three of us dived headlong into a ditch and as the bombs burst around us, I became aware of a wetness spreading over my chest and stomach. I thought, 'God! I've been hit!' Then it dawned on me. I'd landed on the eggs.

Corporal Norman Habetin
Wireless Operator, 8th Battalion, Rifle Brigade

Operation Epsom, which began on the 26th June, wasn't very pleasant. It was our first do and we had some very, very rude awakenings. It made all of us feel a lot sadder and a lot wiser, because we found out the enemy was a very real one and there was no question of a walkover or anything like that. We drove through Cheux, which was a bit of a mess. People all over the place had been killed. It was quiet, there were no guns firing. There was nothing in front of us except the Germans, but that didn't sink in because everything looked so normal – farmhouses, the sort of country we were used to. It was hard to believe that this was a front line.

We parked in an orchard, then without warning we were mortared. As we sat in the carrier, clods of earth came flying in and we couldn't do anything about it. We just kept our heads down. The Bren-gun carrier was lightly armoured but it didn't have a roof. When it stopped and we looked around, a number of people were lying dead. After a while, I walked over to one of the other chaps who was pouring brown-coloured stuff into a tin from a jug. 'Water's a bit rusty, isn't it, Bart?' I said. 'It's not water, you chump. It's Calvados,' he replied. He had found barrels of it down in a cellar. I told him he was a fool. The cellar might have been booby-trapped. 'I'm still here, aren't I?' he said. We tried it. It was horrible but we drank plenty. The next morning was grey and overcast and we moved up to Hill 112 – one of the most notorious hills of the whole campaign. Four of us got together and dug in and then we started being mortared. It went on for the rest of the day. It just never stopped.

The night turned into a kind of nightmare of tanks milling about in the dark, exploding mortars and shells and the expectation of a sudden bayonet attack because we'd been warned that the Germans would counter-attack. At three o'clock in the morning we were told that we were going to withdraw from the hill as it had become untenable. I could see that we had become surrounded. The only way out was across the Odon Bridge, which was the same way we'd come in – but there were shells going off continuously. I thought 'Christ, how the hell are we going to get a whole armoured brigade across that?' As we approached it, the shelling stopped. I couldn't believe it – it seemed unreal. We passed a scout car with a dead crew sitting inside it, but we got through without a scratch.

Everything was quiet. By then, we were exhausted, we'd lost a lot of men – in fact most of the platoon had gone west. What shook us most of all is that we hardly ever saw any Germans and yet we were losing men left right and centre. I'd had this idea that I was going to see a mass of men in grey uniforms but it wasn't like that. They were always nearby but they were hidden, popping off at you from a concealed spot.

Captain John Graham
Argyll and Sutherland Highlanders

The aim on the 26th June was to capture bridges across the River Odon to the west of Caen. We in 227 Highland Brigade were to follow behind the other two brigades in the Division and subsequently push through to capture the bridges. The plan for the leading brigades did not go as predicted. We spent a dreary day moving forward behind them. Our inexperience showed. We couldn't tell the difference between incoming and outgoing fire. The cry would go up, 'Sniper!' The soldiers would go to ground and fire at the trees. I don't believe there were any snipers at all. But if you get a large body of soldiers firing skywards, other people a mile or so away will receive these bullets and will fire back. My memory of the first two days is of almost continuous fusillades between our people, who thought the Germans were firing at them, and some other British unit perhaps a mile away.

Corporal Gordon Fidler
Tank Driver, A Squadron, 2nd Fife and Forfar Yeomanry
Our company's first encounter in France was Operation Epsom, the attack on Cheux. We didn't come across the Germans until late in the afternoon. One of the tanks on my left got to within about fifty yards of this anti-tank gun and then erupted. It was literally engulfed in flames and I remember two lads coming out and their clothes were alight, in flame – and they lay on the grass burning. We had to leave them, though, because were still going forward. I won't forget that sight.

Corporal Robert Nurse
Tank driver, 2nd Fife and Forfar Yeomanry
We got into a sparsely wooded area at dusk and suddenly all hell broke loose. Tanks were blazing and our commander was even more frightened than I was. He was absolutely rigid with fear. The next morning, we could not understand how we had survived. We got out of the tank because by now obviously the German vehicles had withdrawn, and there was a metal casing on the turret about 18 inches from my head and a 75-mm hole straight through it. It had gone in one side and out the other. The German gunner must have seen the flash when his shell hit and presumed he'd knocked us out, and left us alone. Two close friends of mine were burned alive in that attack.

And then Hill 112 – oh God, I didn't like that place. We were on a forward slope overlooking a valley and suddenly four German Tiger tanks started crossing my bows so I fired and I hit one of the bloody things and it went 'BOOM!' Up into the air. But I'm talking about the shell, not the tank. It just bounced off and then I saw these four barrels turning round towards us but we reversed pretty bloody quickly and we were back on the other side of the hill before you could say 'knife'.

Private James Bramwell
224 Parachute Field Ambulance, RAMC
A chap was brought in with the top of his head blown off, brains spilling out into the stretcher. The MO took one look at him. I said, 'Is there anything we can do?' He shrugged. So I gave him a lethal shot of morphine. When the MO came back, I told him what I'd done. He said, 'It's OK, you did quite right. There was nothing we could do.' I'm sure there were many others like these, but we did not talk about them.

Normandy, 26 June 1944. Armed with a Sten gun and rifles with fixed bayonets, British infantrymen advance tentatively in Operation Epsom – a drive to outflank the city of Caen from the west.

Major Peter Martin
2nd Battalion, Cheshire Regiment
All these battles had a purpose, although we did not know it at the time and we became rather disillusioned. It's about the only time during the whole war when I was ever less than happy with the high command. Little did we know the great Monty plan to keep constant pressure in our area to open the way for the Americans. Because I was part of the Brigadier's Tactical HQ and went with him wherever he visited, I saw more of the Brigade than many more senior officers. I could see the effect of casualties on battalions.

By the end of June, 50 Div had lost, killed, wounded and missing, over 300 officers and 3,000 soldiers. Reinforcements came up every day to plug the holes before the next day's attack. The individual soldiers were as super as they had always been, the courage was still there, but the skills were going and it showed. If our own artillery or mortar-fire failed to dislodge the enemy, our infantry seemed to become at a loss about what to do. Instead of using fire and movement to get forward, they stopped. Untrained or semi-skilled 3-inch mortarmen would fire their mortars from underneath trees, killing themselves with their own bombs exploding in the branches above.

I began to see worrying signs in my own company. Because there were four brigades in the Division, and only three machine-gun companies, we never got a rest. My soldiers had been with me right through the Western Desert, the invasion of Sicily and now Normandy. Battle fatigue was beginning to show. A superb corporal suddenly burst into tears and had to be sent back. We had this problem with the new people, too. One new officer who'd never seen a shot fired in the whole war, broke down completely under enemy artillery fire. In the First World War, I suppose he would have been taken out and shot but we felt sorry for him, not angry. He probably went and did a good, if less demanding, job elsewhere for the rest of the war.

Sergeant Charles Elsey
6th Airborne Armoured Reconnaissance Regiment
The most unusual recce job we had was on the 8th July on the day of the 1,000-bomber raid on Caen. The colonel asked me to take out two tanks to protect the war correspondent Chester Wilmot and his BBC wagon. The colonel told us to find a place where Wilmot could see what was happening. So we prowled about and found a nice little hillock, which gave us a good view towards Caen, about two miles away. It was an awesome sight – the bombers came over and the sky was black with them. Chester Wilmot was doing his recording and I sat next to him. He described the planes coming in,

'Oh another plane's been hit. It's all right, it's all right, everybody's getting out!' He had to say everybody got out or else people listening at home would panic. 'Could it be dad? Could it be my husband?'

Flying Officer Ken Adam
609 Squadron, RAF, Second Tactical Air Force
There was a Canadian pilot called Piwi Williams who went to his death, fully aware that he was going to die. It was unbelievably touching.

We were flying an operation over France and I could see his aircraft gradually losing height and I called on my radio, 'Piwi, what are you doing?' He called back and said that he was hit and paralysed, and he went slowly down for several minutes. I'll never forget his last words, just before he hit the ground. 'Order me a late tea.'

Corporal Norman Habetin
Wireless Operator, 8th Battalion, Rifle Brigade
We were briefed for Operation Goodwood, which was going to be the attack to end all attacks. It was going to start from where the airborne troops had landed, near Caen. The objective was Falaise, about 15 miles away. It was going to take three days. It would open with a bombing attack, bigger than the one on D-Day, then an artillery barrage – then ourselves. We drove all night to this place where the gliders were – the start point. We got there in the early hours – started digging slit trenches. I remember, it was a warm day and we were bitten by mosquitoes. Bitten to bits. We were digging these trenches, then about five o'clock in the morning, we saw the first Lancasters overhead – masses and masses of them, bombing the enemy front line.

Then the barrage started. It was being fired from behind us to somewhere in front of us. The noise was just as bad as the aeroplanes. I don't know how high these shells were, but I remember thinking to myself, 'God, fancy being on the end of this lot. No one could survive.' At seven o'clock we started. We drove through a lane taped through a minefield – got into a large field, then fanned out with the tanks, the 2nd Fife and Forfar Yeomanry, with a carrier tank – spread out. We rolled forward as our artillery put down a creeping barrage. But in amongst us, enemy shells were bursting. We were all going along together in some kind of horrible devil's dance. It's a very nasty and frightening experience. No question about that. I thought 'Christ, this is dreadful.'

Then to my surprise, I began seeing Germans all over the place – very much alive, running about. I thought to myself, 'This is ridiculous. How the hell can people be alive after all this lot?' They mostly had their hands up, trying to get to hell out of it, because their lines had been overrun. There was nothing they could do against a gigantic Armoured Brigade driving all over them. There were tanks on fire – our Shermans – in large numbers. We just went on through all this until we came to our first objective – the Paris–Caen railway line – so we stayed there. Made some tea.

Time drew on and we were told to move back two or three hundred yards to give the tanks room to manoeuvre, because we were on top of a hill, overlooking a village called Bourgúebus. Apparently, the Germans were in there – hidden. The tanks were going to move forward to clear this village. I watched as they accelerated down the hill, but within minutes about three-quarters of them were on fire. The whole hillside was a horrible graveyard of burning tanks.

Corporal Bill Scott
2nd Fife and Forfar Yeomanry

On the 17th July 1944, Operation Goodwood happened. By the time we got through the minefield on to this open ground, we didn't have flank protection because there were a limited number of lanes through these minefields. The Germans knew the exact yardages and they could knock you out quite easily, and they did – from both flanks.

We moved through but there was black smoke and tanks going up all around us. It was a very selfish feeling, but I was just glad it wasn't us – but then we still had to move forward. We couldn't stop. I think we lost about a hundred plus tanks that day.

I remember – this comes clearly to me – at one point some infantry came up to me and said, 'There are two of your men in that tank over there.' And I went across to the tank and there was the driver and the co-driver, strapped in. They were black red, but they weren't dead. I could still see their lips and things moving, but there was nothing that could be done for them. We had to move forward otherwise we would have been sitting ducks.

Norman Clark
British civilian correspondent for News Chronicle with US Third Army

After a few days we were told we were breaking out to Le Pas de Calais in a scheme called Goodwood. We were ferried over the bridge that the 6th Airborne had captured, and then went into the north of France. It was clearly going to be a big job, because there were thousands of troops waiting to start – but Goodwood was a calamity. The bombers went in and then we followed.

We took quite a number of prisoners, but some of the Germans had got the high ground, and started mortaring and shelling us. I remember a shower of mortars landing among my company and I got blown up myself. I did my ears in there, and couldn't see a thing, because there was so much dust around. Anyway, we still advanced, and we got to within about two or three hundred yards of the objective itself, and then they opened up with a massive gunfire, and we lost 152 men in the first twenty-four hours. I saw people getting killed left, right and centre. It was a real tragedy, that. The Germans must have had massive casualties as well, because they arranged a ceasefire so we could both collect our wounded, and we were able to pick up our wounded lads and our dead.

Karl Von Hase
German Staff Officer

On the 20th July 1944, there was an attempt to assassinate Hitler at Rastenberg. My father's brother, General Paul Von Hase, the Kommandant of Berlin, was involved in the plot. At first, it was thought that Hitler had been killed but then they found out that he was still alive and the whole thing collapsed. All those active in the plot were arrested and my uncle was hanged on 8th August. At the time, a move was introduced that if a member of your family was involved in an act of disloyalty, you were not trusted any more and you had to share in their disgrace. Stauffenberg's children suffered in this way. I was forced to leave Italy, where I was Operations Officer of a Corps that was defending the Adriatic coastline. I was sent home and interrogated by General Maisel, the same general who was later to give Rommel his poison. He asked me what I felt about the plot and whether I knew anything about it. I knew that my uncle was not a partisan of Hitler but I didn't know that he was involved in the plot and it was difficult to know what to say. If he hadn't liked my answers, then I would have lost my life. I said I was against the plot but that I didn't believe that the plotters had acted out of dishonourable motives. I said they must have felt that it was a way to help Germany. Maisel was ice-cold and businesslike. He didn't raise his voice. After that, I was sent to an artillery training camp in Pomerania.

Gunter Von Waskowski
German officer, heavy artillery regiment

After the Hitler assassination attempt in July, suddenly we had to abandon our military greeting and use the Hitler salute – which annoyed us, because we were not completely Hitler followers at that time. Then we were moved from the Pas de Calais at the end of July up to Le Havre to cross the Seine, and we were involved in Hitler's idea to cut the Americans off after they broke through at Avranches – but that was a failure. Our whole unit moved – mostly at night because during the day you couldn't move – you'd be cut to pieces. Our offensive stopped. We couldn't get any further. There were mainly American troops against us. We were able to get some success with our 88 Panzer tanks, but in general, after three or four days we were retreating.

Frederick Winterbotham
Secret Intelligence Service
It was established that Rommel had taken part in the July plot to assassinate Hitler. We didn't know anything about that at the time but he was sent home to recover from his wounds and it caught up with him. According to the information given by his family, he was visited by two generals and offered the choice of going back with them to Berlin or taking his own life. It was a pathetic story, this man who had done more for the German Army than most, to be taken out, put into a motor car and given a pill to take. Which he did. That was hushed up and he was given a state funeral, fitting for a great general.

Major Peter Martin
2nd Battalion, Cheshire Regiment
On the 4th August, I learned that Villers-Bocage had been captured, two months after we were supposed to have captured the place on D+1. For the first time since D-Day, the whole company was relieved and went into a rest area, where we stayed for a couple of days.

Private Fritz Jeltsch
5th Company, 214 Regiment, German Army
After Normandy, in early August 1944, our position came under fire. We were surrounded, they were shooting from every direction, and almost everyone in my unit died. It was awful.

I remember one of my mates was running just in front of me, and we were attacked again. He was hit and he fell on me, so I got hold of him and dragged him to one side. An ambulance came along, and I was crying out to this first-aid man, 'Can I put him in?' and he said to me, 'It's too late. You can't do anything for him any more. Save yourself.' So I left him and ran into a field to join the other few survivors. I couldn't do anything about it, but it's laid on my conscience for years.

Major Cyril Brain
GHQ Liaison, 'Phantom' Regiment

The Germans fought doggedly and efficiently to try and stop us closing what was to be known as the 'Gap' at Falaise in August 1944, because this was their way back to Germany if they had to withdraw. About a week later we got support from the Royal Air Force. The raid consisted of about 800 aircraft, and at three o'clock one afternoon on a beautiful day the first wave came over and dropped its bombs where the Germans were, but the second wave unloaded their bombs on us. This was a catastrophic mistake.

The Poles and the Canadian troops took a pasting, with about 150 losing their lives. This was a most peculiar and sad day, because when we were helping units who had been hit, an ambulance carrying wounded was attacked by a Spitfire and rolled over into a ditch, a burning mass. I can't think of any excuse for it unless it was a Spitfire stolen by the Germans on some other front.

Private Eric Collins
1st Battalion, East Lancashire Regiment

The day after the bombing of the Canadians by the RAF, we started off through the Falaise Gap, and at either side were devastated Tiger tanks and horses that had drawn the gun-wagons blown up like balloons. What people tend to forget is that the German Army was largely supplied by horse-drawn supply columns, so it was horses and carts, and dead horses, and dead men and dead equipment – an absolute horror. The appalling smell and stench – it was a terrible sight to see.

Flight Sergeant Allen Billham
609 Squadron, RAF

The Falaise Gap is difficult to explain. There are a lot of roads, valleys leading up to the exit to the gap like the little roads on the Yorkshire Dales. They were full of German petrol lorries, tanks and all sorts of supply vehicles. They had made their attack and got blunted. The Americans came round from the south and the British, Canadian and Polish came round from the north, and started nipping. The Germans just weren't allowed to retreat at first and when they were allowed to retreat, it was too late. During daylight hours, nothing moved, because if it moved, it got shot at.

Ernst Eberling
German pilot, Kampfgeschwader 53
On the 19th August 1944 we had to fly from Paris to supply the trapped German troops in the Falaise Gap. We were supposed to drop our supplies between a triangle of three fires, but when we got there, there were fires all over, so the first night we didn't know what to do. However, the drop the next night was better. It was dangerous and we suffered many losses from the Allied night fighters.

Corporal Reginald Cutter
British fitter/driver, 425 Battery, 107 Medium Regiment,
Royal Artillery
The Germans were surrounded all round on three sides at the Falaise Gap. A gap had been left for them to escape, but they just wouldn't give in. So we went on shelling, from morning to night, and the bombers did their stint all day and night. Our guns were starting to get worn out because we'd used an enormous amount of ammunition – a ton. About 75,000 Germans eventually came out of there, and I've never seen such a bedraggled lot in all my life. They were absolutely shell-shocked with the punishment they'd taken, but at the same time, they'd put up a pretty strong resistance.

We eventually saw the scenes of devastation that our guns had caused. There seemed nothing left standing.

Flight Sergeant Allen Billham
609 Squadron, RAF
The Germans certainly fought their own corner during the week of the Falaise Gap. Whereas the British convoy would stretch over two miles and have the regulation fifty yards between each vehicle, the Germans believed in putting everything close together and having flak all the way round and in the middle of them. Everything joined in our attack – Spitfires, Mustangs, Thunderbolts, you name it. But our Typhoons had the rockets and the 20-mm cannon, so we did most of the damage, certainly against the armoured vehicle. We never sensed during our attacks that we would not defeat the Germans. After all, they were just fighting a rearguard action.

Lieutenant William Jalland
Platoon Commander, 8th Battalion, Durham Light Infantry
The rot had started, and we chased over to the northern side of the gap where the Germans were trying to get out. It was the first place where I became aware of the

fact that the Germans were hanging their own deserters. We came across an orchard there, where half a dozen to a dozen Germans had been hanged for running away. Their feet were just a few inches off the ground, swaying gently in the wind – very moving. We'd never come across that sort of thing before.

Private Fritz Jeltsch
5th Company, 214 Regiment, German Army

After Normandy we crossed the Seine at Rouen and carried on up towards Amiens and on the 31st August, when we'd made camp, one of our lookouts was so tired that he fell asleep at his post. He suddenly cried out and we looked up – and they were all there – the Free French and the Canadian troops. Of course we had to surrender then, because we were finished. There was no hope.

Sergeant Thomas Myers
6th Battalion, Durham Light Infantry

I'd gone to the 6th Battalion not far from Amiens. We got in about seven at night with no sign of the Germans, so we went into a café and had a beer and got talking to two pretty girls. The barman said to me in broken English, 'They've been collaborating with the Germans.' I said, 'They can collaborate with whoever they want – I'm going to have that blonde tonight,' and my mate said, 'I'll have the other one.' We spent twenty-four hours there and then it became a mad rush. Jerry had started his real pull-out and it was on the trucks and away.

Flying Officer Ken Adam
609 Squadron, Second Tactical Air Force

After Falaise Gap we managed to get some leave and we went to the area. The first thing you noticed was the smell, mainly of dead animals. It was incredible – all the horses or cattle were completely rigid. Then we started seeing the bodies of the Germans we had killed. I'll never forget them. Their tanks in their retreat had driven across anything in their path and it was grotesque, ghastly. I actually managed to win a German Volkswagen, one of these staff cars, but I didn't have the courage to get the two bodies out of the car. I left that to a New Zealander to do. So we had a German VW with our flight for seven or eight months but we could never get rid of the smell – the sweet smell of death.

Major Peter Martin
2nd Battalion, Cheshire Regiment
On the 30th August we heard the news that 11th Armoured Division had captured Amiens, so we went in there next day. At first the civilians were wary, but then when they realised they were being liberated, there were tremendous celebrations.

We took up a position on a nearby bridge and about five o'clock in the evening a long convoy of German soldiers came into view just across the river. They continued to march right across our front without seeing us. We could hardly believe that such a target existed, so we opened fire. It was a massacre really – but for the soldiers who had been waiting for a target like that all the way through the war, it was an absolute gift.

Corporal Terence Jefferson
9th Parachute Battalion
When the American Armoured and the French 2nd Armoured Division entered Paris on the 25th August there were scenes of jubilation. I don't think I was sober for four days, I had a lovely time. There were thousands of people in the streets, bags of hugging, lots of kissing, lots of bottles of wine. Bottles of brandy seemed to appear from nowhere. I went for a walk to the Place de la Concorde, then to the Hotel de Ville. There I saw another fellow with a red beret on. 'Who are you?' I asked. 'Who are you?' he asked back. He turned out to be a war correspondent for the *Daily Mail*. He'd dropped with the airborne and then moved on with the Americans. I told him that I'd escaped from a nearby German hospital and that there were still about 200 Allied wounded there and he said, 'Right, I'll get in touch with someone.' The following morning the Americans rolled up to the hospital and began moving everybody out.

Major Peter Martin
2nd Battalion, Cheshire Regiment
One of the DLI battalions had a tremendous party which I attended. The medical officer was well away. Later I was awoken by one of the platoon commanders. The wife of the owner of the house in which his platoon was billeted was about to give birth. The husband was asking for assistance. I dug out the MO, who said that he would come straightaway. When I asked him if he was fit, he replied that he would 'get the little bugger out even if he had to use a corkscrew'. All went well and the mother announced that the child would be called Philippe Libération.

Major Peter Carrington
2nd Armoured Battalion, Grenadier Guards
David Fraser and I were given forty-eight hours' leave to spend swimming on the beach at Arromanches. We decided that this would be rather boring. The Americans and French were liberating Paris, so we drove there in a couple of Jeeps. We drove around to the Ritz – the Germans were going out of the back as we drove up and booked in. The Hotel was quite unmoved by what they appeared to regard as a perfectly ordinary occurrence – one lot of visitors leaving and another lot coming in.

Major Peter Martin
2nd Battalion, Cheshire Regiment
When we arrived in Brussels, we were to be there for four days. We drove there up exactly the same route as we had in 1940, through Tournai. The next evening I told the troop commanders to go off and have a really good time. I would hold the fort. They and most of the soldiers went off. At about 2200 hours, I was woken by a dispatch rider from 151 Brigade HQ with a complete change of orders. We were to move out at 0700 hours the next morning to the Albert Canal. Out of my usual five officers and 140 soldiers, I had myself, one officer and 30 soldiers. All the rest were out on the tiles in Brussels, doing goodness knows what, goodness knows where. We sent all over the place scouting for them. The platoon commanders came in at 0300 hours. Somehow we got away at 0700 hours but it was a terrific blow to morale. You thought you were going to have a rest and suddenly you're not. It's much more shattering that way.

Company Sergeant-Major William Brown
8th Battalion, Durham Light Infantry
On the 8th September, we were about to have three days' rest when we were ordered to cross the Albert Canal that night. Assault boats were there to meet us. These were collapsible wood and canvas boats and heavy to carry down the bank. We could see boats sinking and blokes getting shot by German machine guns. Later, I was standing talking to a section commander in a sunken road when the enemy opened up with a machine gun. It looked like flashing lights going past me. I fell into the sunken road. About three men were killed and my guts were oozing out. I said to a young officer 'Give us your hand. Grip it as tight as you can.' He took my hand. I was conscious all the time. I thought, 'If I lose consciousness, I will die.' Stretcher bearers came and they put about four field dressings on me and carried me down the road. The German machine guns could

have opened up on us, but they didn't. At the RAP I was given morphia. They wrote on my brow the time administered. The MO said it was definitely a Blighty one.

Major Peter Martin
2nd Battalion, Cheshire Regiment

As the mist began to clear on the morning of the 9th September, the enemy tanks started to take a toll of our tanks and transport. Our anti-tank guns were having no effect on the well-concealed German armour although a German commander who stood up in the hatch of his tank, shouting in English, 'I want to die for Hitler!' had his wish fulfilled by one of my platoons. As the mist continued to lift, Du Pré, one of my platoon commanders, spotted a Tiger 100 yards away, facing in the opposite direction. He crawled to a nearby Sherman and directed its fire into the Tiger, brewing it up. This seemed to mark the turn of the battle.

The enemy may have sensed that they were in a very sticky position and began to withdraw. As soon as their tanks came out of hiding, they were good targets for our anti-tank guns and Vickers. By about 1400 hours, the enemy were all accounted for – hardly a man, gun or tank escaped. I found a young German hiding in a barn. I was very angry as one of my best soldiers, Private Price, had been killed during the night, just outside this barn, and I felt this young man was partly responsible. Price had been with me right through the war. I was hopping mad, pointing my finger at this chap, shouting at him in fury. He was wounded. He said he was only seventeen and had been in the army just three months. His friends had stripped him of everything of value, his watch and money. I took him prisoner but I was so angry that I was hardly in control.

ARNHEM

The success of operation Market Garden, relied on airborne troops landing and taking five Rhine bridges in sequence – the last, at Arnhem, being assigned to the British 1st Airborne Division. Simultaneously, the British XXX Corps would drive through along a road linking the bridges and join the men at Arnhem. The Paras – by definition a lightly armed force relying on surprise to storm and take their objectives – desperately needed the support of ground troops to hold out at Arnhem, where German tanks quickly closed in. The first airborne landing was made in daylight on the 17th September – and achieved a degree of surprise – but a second landing found the German defenders on the alert and casualties were heavy.

Strong enemy defences prevented XXX Corps from arriving to support the Paras in Arnhem, where they were pinned down in fierce fighting for three days and four nights.

Major Ian Toler
Glider Pilot Regiment

There were endless delays and cancellations leading up to Operation Market Garden – order and counter-order and the consequent disorder were the order of the day. We spent the whole of one day loading and unloading our gliders – when the order changed for the sixth time that day, we just sat back and laughed. It was a good job we had some sense of humour. But we really were getting almost apathetic – we couldn't believe that it would ever come off.

Major Tony Hibbert
Headquarters, 1st Parachute Brigade

Having rocketed down from Grantham to Moor Park once or twice a week to attend briefing sessions by General Browning on a series of operations which were all cancelled, we were given the details on the 6th September of the 15th operation in this series – Operation Comet. This involved 1st British Airborne Division taking on all the tasks which three divisions failed to complete ten days later. On its own, 1st Parachute Brigade had the task of capturing and holding Arnhem. I wish to God Comet had gone ahead. It could have worked – at that stage the Germans were still demoralised, still on the run and hadn't had time to regroup and reorganise.

But Comet was cancelled. On the 10th September, the original D-Day for Comet, we were briefed for Operation Market Garden – a rehash of Comet – but with three divisions instead of one, and with the whole of 1st British Airborne Division and Polish Parachute Brigade taking on the task of capturing Arnhem Bridge and holding it for forty-eight hours. There was a considerable gung-ho spirit and I'm sure that if somebody had offered to drop us in the middle of Berlin we'd have been as happy as sandboys. I believe Browning shared this over-optimism and was not as careful as he should have been when planning the Arnhem operation. Brian Urquhart, Browning's intelligence officer, came to see me after the briefing. He'd received confirmed reports that the 9th and 10th Panzer Divisions were in the Arnhem area, but Browning dismissed these and a doctor suggested that Urquhart was under stress and should rest. The operational plan was gravely flawed.

Insufficient planes were allocated and of these something like thirty were taken to land the Corps Headquarters with Browning, south-east of Nijmegen, where they failed to influence the battle in any way. By dropping there he succeeded in putting himself out of communication with everyone in the critical first five days, and removing those planes from the 1st Division meant that we had to drop in three separate waves, which ensured that the division could be taken out in bits by the Germans. A fatal flaw. The next disastrous decision was the refusal of the Air Force to drop the 1st Division anywhere near the bridge, on the basis of faulty intelligence which suggested that there were anti-aircraft guns on the bridge. Urquhart didn't have the experience needed to overrule both Browning and the Air Force. These and other errors were leading to an epic cock-up.

Corporal Ray Sherriff
3rd Parachute Battalion
We were at Spalding before going to Arnhem and we were all confined to barracks for quite a long time. There were about sixteen alerts during that time, so the chaps were getting fed up with being confined to barracks. Now you could nip off into Spalding – there were lots of pubs there – and at one stage the nipping off got so bad that the RSM said he wanted two NCOs to go round these pubs and get the men back. So another NCO and I were detailed to go round together. We looked through the blackouts and in one particular pub we saw two of our chaps with a couple of females. I said, 'Right, we'd better get in here and get rid of those.' So we went in and sent the blokes off and then we went after these two females. We walked all the way back with them and they said, 'Come in.'

My mate went to another house up the street, and I went with this particular one and she got me some egg and chips, and a cup of cocoa. Then, we went upstairs. Trouble was, I was all kitted up in full para gear. I had my smock with all the big pouches, grenades, my jacket, then a string vest and big boots. I finally got this lot off and got into bed when all of a sudden there was a knock on the front door and I said, 'Who the hell?' 'It's probably my husband,' she said. I asked what to do. She said, 'Don't worry, he'll be drunk and he'll want something to eat, so when you hear us down there, just get dressed and nip out the front door.' I got dressed and stuffed most of the things in my pockets, put my boots on, no socks. It was a moonlit night. I looked and there was a lovely patch of freshly dug soft soil below the window. I didn't fancy going down the stairs, because I might meet the husband coming up so out I went . . . did a lovely landing.

Just as I was getting up, someone put their hand on my back. I thought it was her husband so I swung round and hit him. It was only my mate, who'd come to get me! He'd gone back to camp and had found out that we were on the move, at two o'clock. He had a bike, so I sat on the cross-bar and he rode us back to camp. Just as we were going past the orderly room, who should walk out but the RSM Lord. Of course, he didn't have time to do a lot then because everybody was on the move and we had to go and pick up our 'chutes from the hut, but he said, 'I shall want to see you after this operation.'

Private James Sims
2nd Parachute Battalion
I shouldn't have been on Arnhem, only for a trick of fate. There were three of us – a fellow called 'Brum' Davies, myself and a young Geordie, we were all only 19 – and Colonel Frost said, 'You're too young to go in the battle, but if you follow the Second Army with the baggage train, you'll see something of what war is all about. When we're victorious you'll meet up with us north of Arnhem.' At the last minute, however, three old sweats went absent thinking it was just another false alarm and they couldn't be found. They went round the fleshpots of Nottingham shouting their names out through loud-hailers, trying to get them to surface, but they didn't want to know. So we got roped in and had to go.

Lieutenant-Colonel John Frost
2nd Parachute Battalion
In the briefing at Brigade HQ, near Grantham, on the 15th September, Brigadier Lathbury's orders were that the 2nd Parachute Battalion was to take the three bridges over the Rhine – first the railway bridge, which was outside the town, then a pontoon bridge, and finally the main road bridge. I was to have some part of my force south of the main bridge, but the bulk on the north side. By the time we had this bridge, of course, we hoped that the rest of the brigade would have got into Arnhem and would be holding a perimeter north of the bridge.

I did think that having to take three bridges was asking rather a lot and I wasn't at all happy at having my force split by the river. I would have preferred if we had been given the task of taking the north ends of the bridges and somebody else the southern ends, by dropping south of the river.

It was not an early take-off so we had time for a leisurely breakfast. In the mess everything was unhurried. One had the feeling that everything would go well. Outside it was a perfect day – clear, fine and cloudless. I checked

Men of the 1st Airborne Division sit laden with their kit prior to take-off for Arnhem, 17 September 1944. Their task to take and hold the bridge over the Rhine at Arnhem – it proved to be a bridge too far.

everything with my batman, Wicks, and arranged for my shotgun and golf clubs to follow later in the staff car. As we moved down the drive the resident pheasants and partridges seemed indifferent, almost as though they knew that we would never be able to trouble them at any future date.

We took off from Saltby to do battle for a bridge that Montgomery urgently required. I was very optimistic because the German army had taken a tremendous hiding in Normandy and all the information was that they were a beaten force, retreating more or less in disorder back to behind the Siegfried Line into Germany, so I was expecting a fairly easy battle. We knew that XXX Corps was coming up to cross over the bridges after we'd taken them. They were fresh, they had been rested, re-equipped, and one could see absolutely no reason why the thing shouldn't go according to plan. As for us, we always had a few miscreants who absented themselves, but they had a sort of grapevine which seemed to tell them, wherever they were, that an operation was pending, so they ought to turn up. In fact, one party of men arrived at Saltby in a taxi from London – morale was terrific. On the plane we read the Sunday papers, ate our sandwiches and smoked. Then, as we got over Holland, as the number one, I stood in the door to make quite certain that we drop exactly where we expected, and we did. I had a perfect landing.

Captain Frank King
11th Parachute Battalion

With five minutes to go before the jump, the crew chief should have been busy rechecking all our equipment. He was a nice young American encased in nylon body armour, but at that moment he made me angry because he was lounging in his seat, a picture of contented idleness. 'Bloody Air Force,' I thought, and shouted at him. There was no reaction. It was only then that I noticed a large and growing pool of blood beneath his seat. He was dead, shot through the floor of the plane.

Private James Sims
2nd Parachute Battalion

We started off into the town – everyone thought it was a sort of walkover really, because we had been told we wouldn't meet much resistance, only line-of-communication troops and second-rate German personnel, which I don't think exist!

One thing that did hold us up a bit was the Dutch people greeting us and giving us drinks, tomatoes, flowers and saying, 'We've waited four years for you!' From a window a really beautiful dark-haired girl looked down at me and whispered 'Goodbye,' which gave me a shiver. I could have done without that. As we moved on, we passed an SS police barracks with several men dead outside. Slumped across a machine gun were two bodies in Luftwaffe blue. They were a boy and girl about my age. She was lying beside him with the ammunition belt threaded through her fingers, her blonde hair streaked with blood.

Lieutenant Edward Newport
1st Battalion, Border Regiment

When we landed it was quite extraordinary – the Dutch, who thought the war was ending, were out on the streets in force. We kept saying to them very politely, 'It's nice to see you, yes – but don't think this is the end of it. We're expecting trouble.' They couldn't understand why we were so polite compared with the Germans. We would knock on the door. When the lady came to the door, we'd say, 'We are terribly sorry, but we want to use your upstairs bedroom. Do you think you could move out your valuables, or stack them at one end, and we'll remove the curtains.' The Germans would just put a gun straight through the window.

Private John Stanleigh
21 Independent Parachute Company

We weren't far from GHQ dropping zone, when Major Wilson, our commanding officer, spotted some Germans. One of them was firing at him, so he walked up to them and started to shout at them. 'What the bloody hell do you think you're doing, firing at British officers?' And the Germans put their weapons down. They were rather elderly German troops, I must admit, but I still thought that was tremendously courageous. Major Wilson had won an MC at Cambrai in the First World War. He never even pulled his revolver, he just used psychological pressure and the Germans were frightened of him.

Lieutenant-Colonel John Frost
2nd Parachute Battalion

Before we got to Oosterbeek, where the railway bridge was, we did meet pockets of resistance which we dealt with quickly, without deploying, because once one diverges from the main objective, people get lost, so I was determined to try and keep everybody as close into column as I could. One of the measures we took was to bring one of the anti-tank guns, which was normally at the rear of the column, up to the front to cover the main road. This was very effective against prowling enemy armoured cars.

Operation Market Garden, 17 September 1944. Heavily loaded down, British paratroops dropped outside Arnhem get refreshments from welcoming Dutch locals. Private Hill, centre with helmet, carries part of a three-inch mortar and two mortar bombs in his pack.

When we got up to the railway bridge, C Company, debouched from the column and under the cover of machine-gun and mortar-fire got on to the bridge fairly quickly without much trouble. But when the leading platoon was about half-way across, the bridge was blown up in their faces and they had to come back. The basic mistake of dropping airborne troops on the far side of a river, when you want them on both sides, now became apparent. Airborne troops were invented to land behind the enemy and not to cross obstacles in the face of intense fire.

Once we got to the main bridge it was getting dark, so we quickly occupied buildings which dominated the north end and its approaches. Having established our position, our main aim was to get across the bridge to the far side. A platoon of A Company started to move across. It was a horribly dangerous thing to do, even in the half light. As they started to move forward they were met by withering fire from a pillbox and an armoured fighting vehicle sited on the bridge. It was obvious that there was no future in a direct approach. Robin Vlasto's platoon 'mouseholed' through a number of buildings with PIAT bombs and then put in an attack on the pillbox with a flame-thrower. The north end of the bridge was now clear, but just as we were about to make another attempt to cross, lorries drove up from the other side. We brought them to a halt near the burning pillbox – which caused the lorries to catch fire. The Germans inside now became our prisoners. The heat from the burning lorries was so intense no further approach could be made that night.

With the bridge blocked, I wanted to see if one of the other companies, who still hadn't emerged in my area, could get across the river. So I sent my chief engineer, George Murray, back to where the pontoon bridge had been to see if there was any way of getting across. He came back and reported that it was not possible, for no suitable barge or boat could be found. That made me all the more certain that there was no way of our getting across to the far side of the river. I then determined to make as tight a perimeter as we could to hold that north end, until XXX Corps came up from the south.

Private James Sims
2nd Parachute Battalion
It was about teatime, but quite dark. I was sharing a slit trench with this chap who had been at Dunkirk, Narvik, and God knows where – he'd been everywhere. His name was 'Slapsie', after Slapsie Maxy Rosenbloom. We had a bit of army slab cake between us and I was fed up with digging. We were exhausted, but he said, 'Tomorrow morning it won't seem half deep enough, keep digging.' I said, 'Well, how are we going to get out of the damn thing?' it

was getting so deep. I slept all through that night and when I woke up Slapsie was sitting there, looking at me, full of admiration. He said, 'Be careful – but take a look over the top.' When I looked there were dead Germans carpeting the road. I said, 'Where have they come from?' He said, 'They attacked during the night – I couldn't wake you so I had to stand on you to defend the position. You slept through it all!' Slapsie thought I was a cool customer and I began to get this completely undeserved reputation for being cool under fire.

Major Chris Perrin-Brown
1st Parachute Battalion

As we fought our way through our casualties were heavy. Nobody is in such dire need of companionship as a dead man, so you'd see lads undoing their chin-straps and sitting down to comfort their dead pals. This meant that their section corporals were continuously re-entering houses to root them out and chivvy them away from the dead mate, and to keep them moving. The sergeants, in the meantime, were searching for their missing corporals, while the platoon commanders were trying to continue the war.

Corporal Ray Sherriff
3rd Parachute Battalion

At one point I was blinded – I lost all bearing. I was being bundled about from one place to another. In one house a medic said to me, 'Would you like a biscuit?' so I said, 'Yes.' I ate one of them but I didn't have sufficient saliva to swallow it – I couldn't get it down. It must have been two days or more since I had swallowed anything at all, so he said, 'Would you like some jam on it?' I thought that might make it better, so off he went and came back with two biscuits covered in jam, which I ate. It wasn't long after that I was violently sick and I couldn't understand why. I put it down to shock. Much later, a bloke said to me. 'Do you know why you were sick? When we first went in there, we brought a German in who'd had both his legs blown off, and we put him in this bed with white sheets. When he died, we had to throw him out of a window as we couldn't go outside. And on the bed there was all this blood in the shape of a cross where his legs had been, so we added to it with strawberry jam to make it into a clear red cross on the white sheet, and we hung it out the window.' When I'd said I wanted jam, they'd gone and taken it off the sheet. I haven't touched strawberry jam since.

Lieutenant-Colonel John Frost
2nd Parachute Battalion

By dawn on the Monday, I felt quite happy about our situation at the north end of the bridge. I was confidently expecting the rest of the 1st Parachute Brigade, and XXX Corps would be up with us in twenty-four hours. Not very long after first light, a column of enemy armoured cars and half-tracks began to cross the bridge. This turned out to be the reconnaissance squadron of the 9th SS Panzer Division – which really surprised me because we'd been given no information about the presence of such troops in the area. Things were not so good after all. Although three vehicles got through our anti-tank weapons, crews soon found their range and destroyed seven.

By this time we had about fifty men killed or wounded. We kept the wounded in the cellars beneath the main government building. I now wanted to concentrate as much as I could of the rest of my own battalion, because I realised that things weren't going very well for the rest of the brigade. I managed to get a message to Douglas Crawley of B Company to leave what remained of the pontoon bridge. He came up and strengthened the positions by the head of the main bridge, but I could get no word at all from C Company, who were now in the area of the German headquarters which was in the western part of the town.

Then gradually the enemy pressure increased all through the Monday and Tuesday, so that by late Wednesday we were in a pretty bad state. We were running out of ammunition and there was no replenishment whatever. When you're fighting at close quarters, one thing you have to have is ammunition. I gave the order to fire only when absolutely certain of having a kill, but that allowed the Germans time to improve their position. We did get a certain amount of support from our own light regiment who were at Oosterbeek, three or four miles away, but that was the sum total of the support.

On Tuesday afternoon I was able to speak to General Urquhart on the radio. He had been incommunicado because he had gone to see what was happening to the 1st Brigade and had got bottled up in a house and was unable to take any part in the battle for that first day and a half. He wasn't able to hold out very much hope of relief. I told him about our shortage of ammunition, but I couldn't say too much because the Germans would have been listening in and if we started whining they would have moved in even quicker.

As the German attack continued with 40 mm flak guns, the buildings one by one caught fire. Because they were largely built of wood, they went on smouldering for a considerable time, so there was no refuge in the rubble, as there can be in buildings which are largely made of stone. There was no means of extinguishing the flames – they became no-man's-land. But we still kept the Germans off the bridge. Every time they tried, our mortars, artillery and machine-guns hit them hard. We eked out our forty-eight-hour packs and found some apples and juicy pears. We also had to find food to give our German prisoners. They had to be watched carefully, because water was a problem and twice we caught them turning on a tap and leaving it running full blast.

Water was not the only problem. The Germans had now brought up a 150 mm gun, which fired a shell weighing 100 pounds from point-blank range. Every hit seemed to pulverise the masonry and scared us out of our wits. It was lucky for us that our mortars scored a direct hit on the ammunition close by the gun, killing the crew and disabling the gun. All day the Germans pounded away at us, and by now I was beginning to be very concerned about our wounded. Water had run out and many needed to be evacuated. During the day the Germans sent back to us, under a white flag of truce, one of our sappers, Stan Halliwell, who had been captured. He told me the Germans had sent him on trust to ask if I would meet the German commander under the bridge to discuss surrender terms. I said to him, 'That's complete nonsense, there's no question of that.' He then said, 'Well, sir, what shall I do – do I have to go back and tell them that, or can I stay and fight?' I told him to stay and fight and that they'd get the message anyway!

Corporal Stan Halliwell
1st Parachute Squadron, Royal Engineers
About thirty yards in front of us was a German tank with another close by. I thought it was empty, so my mate Hicks and I ran towards it. As I got within 15 yards I saw one of its small guns traverse. I ducked down and Hicks, who was right behind, was killed. I don't know why, but I thought the safest place to hide was underneath the German tank. As I lay under it, panting, I could hear the radio, in German, talking to the other tank. Then he opened up with his main armament and nearly blew my eardrums. As if that wasn't bad enough, he began to start the tank. Then one of our lads hit it with a PIAT. I thought, 'Christ, I've had enough of this!' I crawled out and put my hands up, and was taken prisoner. The Germans sent me back to Colonel Frost with a message. I agreed to go but at every corner I came to, some bugger fired at me. Eventually I found Colonel Frost and delivered the message. He said, 'Well, if you go back, tell them to go to hell.' So I thought, 'I'm not going back to tell them that,' so I stayed.

Private James Sims
2nd Parachute Battalion
There was a Welshman with us who was a sniper. He waited practically the whole morning to get this German, who was in a church behind a grille. He waited with his rifle trained on this spot, and never moved, and eventually the German either wanted to relieve himself or had cramp and got up on one knee, and he caught him. A bit later, after a German attack, an SS man was left in the road. He was badly wounded yet he pulled himself, hand over hand, right across the road to the pavement, to where he had only to put one hand out and he'd have been in his own lines. This Welsh sniper just put a bullet through the back of his head. That upset me – not only me, it upset quite a few of us. Nobody likes snipers – and I said, 'What the hell did you do that for? He was out of the battle.' The Welshman said, 'Well, he was the enemy, he was a German wasn't he?'

I went into another part of the house, where there was a bed piled with beautiful silk underwear and stockings, and as I ran these through my hands I wondered if I'd ever feel the soft skin of a woman again. When I looked into the corner of the room there was one of our lads laid out. He'd been hit full in the face by a sniper's bullet. Someone had put a handkerchief over it. Only a few weeks ago I'd falsely signed him a sleeping-out pass so that he could see his girlfriend.

Major Tony Hibbert
Headquarters, 1st Parachute Brigade
Suddenly from a house about 250 yards up the road emerged a very dishevelled-looking woman pushing a brand-new, immaculate pram, presumably with a baby in it. With her free hand she was waving frantically and I could see she was screaming hysterically as she weaved her way through the rubble. The small-arms fire around her stopped instantly, but the heavy guns continued. Miraculously she survived and when she got to about 100 yards from our HQ, one of our platoons managed to get a Dutch-speaker to call her over and we got her under cover. The poor woman had completely lost her mind.

Corporal Danny Morgans
1st Parachute Battalion
We literally had to wreck a beautiful house. First the windows had to be smashed, so the glass couldn't be blown in on us. Then the furniture was piled into barricades inside the room. Everything that was watertight, from the bath to buckets, vases and jugs, had to be filled with water, as the Germans were

Major Tony Hibbert seen here in the uniform of the Royal Artillery in front of a Lagonda that he bought for £35. In his battery was Pat Porteous who won a VC at Dieppe. Hibbert volunteered for No 2 (Parachute Commando) and dropped with the 1st Parachute Brigade as their Brigade Major at Arnhem where he won the MC.

using incendiary ammunition to burn us out. Very soon the place was an organised shambles. Suddenly the old gentleman who owned the place appeared in his wrecked lounge. He was carrying a tray with glasses and a bottle of Advocaat. He solemnly filled up the glasses and handed them round to the men who'd just wrecked his home. I apologised for what we had done and he replied, 'It is not you, my son, it is the war.' And he returned to his cellar. To this day, if I am taking a drink and get sentimental, I call for an Advocaat and think of that marvellous Dutch gentleman.

Lieutenant-Colonel John Frost
2nd Parachute Battalion

Towards evening, heavy tanks appeared, incredibly menacing and sinister in the half-light. Their guns swung from target to target, their shells bursting through our walls. Dust and debris was everywhere and the acrid smoke and smell of burning, combined with the intense noise, bemused us. But we had to stand our ground in order to meet any infantry advance.

Then our gunners brought a six-pounder round to the front and, combined with a bold move by the PIAT crews, we repelled their attack. Twenty yards behind us in the schoolhouse Major Hibbert, the brigade major, and the rest of the brigade staff had to sit it out, sniping whenever they had a chance.

The last onslaught had left us weary. Arnhem was burning. It was as daylight in the streets, a terrible enamelled, metallic daylight. However, that night was more peaceful. But at dawn the attack began again. This was our third day of holding on under continuous enemy pressure. It was all the more demanding on our patience in that it followed on after the exhilarating journey from England, our early successful thrust into Arnhem, and the high expectations of reinforcement from XXX Corps.

It was during this attack that I was wounded by mortar-fire – not badly, but extremely painfully, in both legs. After a time I was given morphia and taken down to the cellars. Freddie Gough assumed overall command at the bridge, but he used to come and refer any problems to me. We discussed doing a sortie and going northwards, but I felt it was much more important that we should stay in position, at the north end of the bridge, for as long as possible so as to give maximum help to anybody trying to cross from the south. So, even if we were left with no ammunition at all, we might have been able to do something to help them. There was, however, no way we could possibly move, we were absolutely sealed in by a ring of enemy infantry and armour.

On the final evening the Brigade HQ caught fire, but there was no water. Jimmie Logan, my head doctor, came to see me and said, 'I'm afraid there is no hope of putting the flames out. Unless something else is done your 200 wounded are going to be burnt alive, including you, sir.' We'd almost ceased to be a fighting force because of lack of ammunition. The doctor then asked if he could try and make contact with the Germans so as to evacuate the wounded. The Germans agreed to a truce. Then everybody, including the SS, laboured with might and main, to get everybody out of the building, which by this time was blazing fiercely. After they'd got almost the last man out, the building collapsed. Then our men dug positions in back gardens, hoping to be able to continue resistance somehow, but when the morning came greatly superior numbers of German soldiers completely overwhelmed each group in turn. I was taken to St Elizabeth Hospital but I knew that as soon as possible the Germans would evacuate us further. I'd taken off my badges of rank and hoped that I would be able to escape as a private soldier, but early next morning we were put into ambulances and driven right into Germany. The Germans, and particularly the SS, were complimentary about the way we had fought the battle, but my bitterness was unassuaged. No enemy had beaten us before, and no body of men could have fought more courageously and tenaciously than the officers and men of the 1st Parachute Brigade.

Lieutenant Edward Newport
1st Battalion, Border Regiment
The end was really quite an anti climax. I came round the side of a building and as I did so, there, straight in front of me, was a German patrol of seven men. They stopped and I stopped, we both looked at each other, and I slowly raised my hands. That was the end of my war.

Major Geoffrey Powell
C Company, 156th Parachute Battalion
We had very detailed orders on how to pull out. We left in groups and we had glider pilots as guides to lead us to the river. The way was marked with white tape and Bofors on the opposite bank fired over our heads to give us the line. We held on to the airborne smock of the man in front. The intelligence officer led, I was in the rear. About halfway to the river, we hit a German position and my column got split. I arrived at the river with fifteen men. There were no boats. We crouched under the bank up to our knees in water.

There were a few people there from other units. A sergeant, hysterical with fear, made a lot of noise. I did something I'd never done before, I hit him on the mouth. That finished the noise. We moved along the river, hoping to pick up a boat. We could see some people starting to swim but none of my party did. We passed one boat with the crew dead around it. Then we met another boat with a Canadian crew and outboard. In we piled. I was the last. The coxswain said, 'We can't take any more.' My chaps said, 'You're taking this bugger,' and pulled me in. When we got to the other side, we ran for the large embankment just inland. I remember the feeling of relief as we climbed up and over – we were out of this battle.

Private John Stanleigh
21 Independent Parachute Company
We didn't really think that we'd have to retreat. We felt we'd done well on our particular front, so it came as quite a surprise. As we got away, we marched down to the river. I was marching next to a bloke who was wearing a German helmet. 'Why are you taking that home?' I asked. 'Vass' he seemed to reply. I looked at him and the penny dropped. 'Are you German?' 'Yes.' 'What are you doing in this column?' 'I've had enough of this war, thank you. I want to be a prisoner.' So he got evacuated on the boat along with the rest of us.

Major Tony Hibbert
Headquarters, 1st Parachute Brigade
The war correspondent Tony Cotterill and I settled into a coal-shed which was so small that we hoped it would seem an unlikely place for anyone to look. Unfortunately someone hiding near us fell asleep and started to snore so loudly that the Germans started ferreting around. Soon Tony and I were hauled out, covered in coal dust, feeling very angry and foolish. They marched us off to the cathedral square where a depressing sight met our eyes. About 20 officers and 130 other ranks were being guarded by a large number of unfriendly SS guards. This probably represented most of the survivors from the bridge. It was a great shock – we'd felt sure some of them would have got away.

That evening we were told we would be moved to another location; anyone breaking ranks would be shot. Freddie Gough put us through a quarter of an hour's parade drill before we set off. Let's show these bastards what real soldiers look like. This boosted morale and restored our self-confidence, which had been a bit shaken by the events of the last day. We marched very smartly, and as we went along we gave the local Dutch the Victory sign. This infuriated our German guards and they threatened to shoot us if we did it again – which we did whenever possible. We hoped by irritating them that we might get a chance to slip away, but there were too many of them around. They marched us to a small house on the outskirts of Arnhem and shoved us into a tiny room. It was here that Tony Deane-Drummond found a cupboard and we reversed the lock and hid him in there with a few bits of bread and a jam-jar of water to keep him going.

Major Tony Deane-Drummond
1st Airborne Division
On the evening of the 22nd, the Germans came round taking all names, so to avoid this I began hiding in a cupboard. There was no room to sit down, of course, so I started the drill that was to become almost automatic over the next fortnight. First I put my weight on one leg, then the other; then I leaned on one shoulder and then on the other. I could sleep all right, but sometimes my knees would buckle beneath me and bang against the door. Every bone in my body ached and the lack of food, water and rest made me quite lightheaded. To make matters worse, the day after I got into the cupboard, the Germans started using the room as an interrogation centre, with the table right up against my cupboard. It was quite bizarre – only half an inch of wood lay between me and the rest of the world outside. I heard every prisoner being interrogated and I was quite surprised by the responses of many of our men. The Germans would ask quite innocuous questions about families, that sort of thing, and then would sneak in a question about something of military importance. Most people told them a few non-military facts, but two men didn't hesitate to pass on everything they knew.

Major Tony Hibbert
1st Parachute Brigade
A convoy of lorries soon arrived to take us to prisoner-of-war camp in Germany and this was our best chance to escape. I was in the last group to leave – our lorry was a three-tonner, open, with sideboards about three feet high and thirty of us, mostly officers, were crammed into it, along with two old Luftwaffe guards armed with pistols and rifles. There was a third guard with a Schmeisser on the front mudguard. The lorry tore off at about 60 mph, which was obviously intended to prevent us hopping off in transit. We continued to give the V sign to the Dutch as well as the odd German, and every time we did this, the corporal on the mudguard lost his temper and stopped the lorry to tell us he'd shoot us if we did it again. But we carried on playing the fool, because every time we stopped it took some time for the lorry to build up speed again, and this was the opportunity we were waiting for.

We stopped for a third time for the usual tirade and I winked to Denis Mumford that we'd make a jump for it when the lorry got going again. I asked

Pat Barnett next to me to keep the nearest guard busy and pulled myself over the side as the lorry started, the guard shouting, '*Nein, nein!*' I hit the road fairly hard but nothing seemed broken though there seemed a lot of blood flowing. Denis was caught by the corporal's machine gun as he climbed over a wall, while I made a dash for the nearest side-turning, zigzagging to avoid the bullets and crashing straight through the wooden fence at the end, Donald-Duck style. Then I zipped through half a dozen gardens and decided to go to ground until it got dark. I covered myself with logs in a small garden hut and listened to the weapons still firing in the streets and the shouts of the search party. The noise eventually died down and, after a long time, I heard the lorry move off. My plan was to get well outside the town and approach a small farmhouse and try to find out where I was, get news of our troops and how to contact the underground.

After I'd gone what I thought was about two or three miles, I found a small isolated farmhouse. I pulled hard at the bell and tapped on the window and eventually a small circular window in the wall slid open and a very suspicious man stuck his head out and shone a torch on me. I felt conspicuous in the torchlight and retreated hastily behind a bush while trying to convince him in German, French and English that I was a British soldier and would be very grateful for their help. I was wearing a groundsheet and my face was covered in blood and bruises and dirt so the glimpse he'd had of me can't have been very reassuring. It soon became clear I wasn't getting through and I left. I heard later that he thought I was a German deserter. When he heard the next day that I was a bona fide Englishman he burst into tears and spent the rest of the day bicycling about looking for me.

On the night of the escape, I was in charge of a group of 60 who were due to rendezvous in a hut in the middle of the forest. We changed into uniform in the hut and collected and cleaned our weapons.

Exactly at midnight, the assault boats came and took us over. On the other side we were ferried away by jeeps along a road parallel to the water. I volunteered to sit right on the front bonnet to guide the driver as, of course, there were no lights. We were going fairly fast when the driver went slap into another jeep coming from the opposite direction. I moved my legs and feet at some considerable speed or they would have been chopped off at the knee. As it was, I just raised them in time, did a triple somersault, landed in the road and bust my leg, and spent the next three months in hospital. So a thoroughly unsatisfactory battle ended in a thoroughly unsatisfying anticlimax.

Captain Jan Lorys
1st Polish Parachute Brigade
For many years a feeling of frustration – a feeling that we didn't really manage to beat the Germans – was to haunt many of us . . . me definitely. We were so full of vigour. The whole Western Front was marching forward, but instead of going forward, we were stopped. We did what we could – we couldn't have done much more. It was the brigade's first operation – its first battle. The soldiers behaved very well and we did make an impact on the battle. We secured and held the south side of the river and by doing so we enabled the remnants of the 1st Airborne to be evacuated from the north. We were very sorry that we didn't win the battle, but we are still proud.

Private James Sims
2nd Parachute Battalion
One morning in Stalag XIB, I saw RSM Lord of the 3rd Battalion coming towards me. He was tall, slim and immaculate in battledress, with red beret exactly an inch above the eye. His badges and buckles shone like jewels and his black boots were like glass. I automatically adjusted my collar, which was undone, and put my beret on straight. I had never met the RSM. 'What battalion are you from?' he asked. I told him the 2nd Battalion. He asked me about the other wounded men and his expression hardened. Then suddenly he gripped me by the shoulder and said, 'Don't let them get you down lad,' and then he was gone.

RSM Lord always treated German officers and NCOs correctly, but did not bother to disguise his contempt for them, referring sarcastically to the Germans as 'the detaining power'. His task in Stalag XIB was a very difficult one. The Airborne accepted him without question, as did also any Guardsmen, but there were men from almost every unit in the British Army, as well as some Canadians, Australians and New Zealanders. Some of them felt that now they were prisoners they should no longer come under army discipline.

Enforcing discipline was extremely difficult, as a man could not be confined to camp, or his pay stopped. Extra duties would have been no punishment, as boredom was our main problem and most of us would have volunteered for any extra work if we could have got it. For the most part the RSM had to rely on the good sense of the men, plus threats of post-war punishment. He did not hesitate to make an example of anyone who transgressed, and I remember that when one soldier refused to wash, the RSM had him stood up in a sink stark naked, and buckets of cold water were thrown over him whilst two NCOs scrubbed him down fore and aft with yard brooms, and it was below zero.

The RSM had made an office out of Red Cross packing cases, and on his door was a notice which said, 'British RSM. Knock and wait.' A German warrant officer was in front of me and he walked into the RSM's office. I heard a scuffle and the RSM shouting, 'Can't you bloody well read?' then the German warrant officer came hurtling out to land flat on his back. His cap was tossed out behind him, and the door slammed shut. As the German was armed, I feared the worst, but he got up, dusted himself down, grinned and walked to the door and knocked. The RSM shouted, 'Come in', and that was that. This incident more than any other, as far as I was concerned, illustrated how good RSM Lord was at understanding the enemy. There was nothing the average German understood better than a good kick up the arse from someone in authority.

RSM Lord had been wounded in the right arm at Arnhem and when his arm was better he told us he had decided that he would salute any German officer he saw. He said, 'In future, when I see a German officer I shall draw myself to my full height, look him straight in the eyes and I shall salute in the correct fashion. However, gentlemen, as I do this I shall say to myself in a firm voice, "Bollocks!"' We thought this was wonderful. From that moment on, we were saluting every German officer we could find – I tell you, we were looking for them. They were as pleased as Punch – they thought we'd really come round to their way of thinking. That one word 'bollocks' summed it all up. Now we began to believe in ourselves again. We needed food, medical help, warmth, but above all we needed hope and that's what J.C. Lord gave us – hope.

THE ADVANCE TO GERMANY

After the setback of the Arnhem campaign, the Allies regrouped to continue the advance towards their ultimate targets of the Rhine and Berlin

Sergeant Harold Harper
426 Battery, 107 Medium Regiment, Royal Artillery

We were pulled back from our advance in November to free the island of Walcheren. That was a tricky business. It was a question of survival more than anything, because it was deep winter of course, and the roads were in a disastrous state, so keeping on the roads was as important as getting into position.

We had a bit of a tussle at Walcheren, I was back with the guns, and all we

Fighting eventually boiled down to the attrition of house-to-house street fighting, particularly in the Oosterbeek area, where airborne troops are seen clearing a house.

were doing was firing. All those islands were still inhabited by the Germans, so we had to clear them up, but from then on one could sense that the war was drifting to an end, that it was in the bag so to speak.

Sergeant Kenneth Kennett
No. 4 Commando
I was in the first LCA to land at Flushing in the Walcheren area. It was important because its capture would allow the Allies to start using Antwerp as a port. Soon after the barrage lifted, our boat touched down. We scrambled out and up the greasy mole – there was no fire. The Intelligence Officer turned and shook hands with me, saying, 'My God man, we're lucky!'

Sergeant Irving Portman
No. 4 Commando
While the rest of the Commando went on into Flushing, my troop cleared a boatyard in which there were three pillboxes in a row. We chucked in grenades and the Jerries came out like rabbits. The troop went on winkling them out ahead of us, sending the prisoners back to just three of us until we had a hundred and twenty to look after. We had some trouble from a sniper in a crane cabin, so the troop commander manned an anti-aircraft gun on the roof of one of the captured pillboxes. He got the sniper with his first shot.

Sergeant Frederick Weston
No. 41 Royal Marine Commando
We crossed to Walcheren in Buffalos – craft the Canadians used which were like tanks with no tops. We were in the open, unlike D-Day, so we saw everything as we went in. It was very heavily defended, we manned gunboats to take these on and we also had rocket ships that shot off scores of shots at a time. We'd also been told that there could be fixed flame-throwers on this part of the beach, so that was something to look forward to. We managed to get on alright and got into the village there, and saw their strongpoint at the base of a lighthouse. We got cover in an old house and found the old hands in there were getting a brew of tea going. As we were pretty wet and miserable at the time, we had a quick cup of tea.

We had kind of a forced march to get to their artillery and take these batteries. It was at this point that I realised I had dysentery, so I wasn't very palatable to my mates.

Unfortunately our troop commander was killed when we reached their strongpoint. It was a very sad occasion for us, it seemed like they were giving themselves up and then one man decided not to, and that was the end of our troop commander. It made us all very angry.

Captain John Graham
Argyll and Sutherland Highlanders

We went to the Peel country, south of Helmond in Holland at the end of October and stayed there, closing up the river Maas. There were mines everywhere, all the buildings were booby-trapped and it never stopped raining. The communications were just farm tracks, which became a morass. It was a struggle against nature as well as the enemy. It was bloody.

We had in two or three months the same experience as the infantry in the First World War endured for years. Some people got trench foot. But the medical support and things like the excellent self-heating soup made life better, as did the mail.

Everybody has a breaking point. It is the job of the commander to watch out for it and send that person back for a rest. A kip in a barn, a good square meal and the batteries are recharged. Divisions started setting up rest-centres to which people could be sent to recuperate.

Major Peter Martin
2nd Battalion, Cheshire Regiment

I spent the winter on 'The Island' – the Nijmegen Bridgehead between the rivers Waal and Rhine. It was very monotonous there and very wet. The slit trenches were filled with water. We had to get empty 44-gallon oil drums for people to stand in to keep themselves dry. The people in the local farm were very friendly and very upset to hear that we were to leave before Christmas. We were told this was because they were fattening up their cat to give us in lieu of a Christmas turkey. For that reason I was quite glad we did leave.

Sergeant George Teal
Tank Commander, Guards Armoured Division

At Nijmegen in Holland, I was billeted with a couple called Abramson. They were Jews, and it was strange that they'd not been gobbled up. The Dutch were dealing with their collaborators and next door to the Abramsons' house was a young lass, about nineteen years old. Some people dragged her out of the house and stripped her off and began to shave her – her head and everything else. And they were going to tar and feather her. Mrs Abramson asked me to go and stop them. I told her I couldn't. I said, 'We've had orders. This has been happening all the way across France and Belgium. The women that have been sleeping with Germans have all been tarred and feathered.' Mrs Abramson said, 'She's a lovely girl and he was a nice German and it was love.' I told her I couldn't interfere but she begged me so I asked some of the lads to help me. We confronted the Dutchman in charge, 'Leave her!' The Dutchman came up to me and put his face right up close and said, 'You'll be moving on and then we'll be coming back for her. You don't know what this occupation's been like. The British will never understand. But we know.'

Hans Behrens
9th Panzer Division
After Arnhem we had regrouped on the western side of the Rhine and just before the Ardennes offensive in December 1944, we stocked up – or tried to – and in due course, we were given the advance command. We did not have sufficient of anything. It was incredible that on a shoestring we managed to progress so far.

V BOMBS

On 13 June the Germans launched the first V-1 bomb, nicknamed 'doodlebugs'. It a small, jet-powered pilotless plane carrying a ton of explosives which would detonate on contact. The 'V' stood for *Vergeltungswaffe* – reprisal weapon – and its deployment brought a new terror to the civilian population of Britain, where RAF squadrons were quickly mobilised to shoot them down before they could land. The V-2, its more powerful succssor, was a prototype ballistic missile with a range of over 200 miles, capable of flattening a large building. From 7 September, this caused widespread fear – after D-Day, Britons had been lulled into a false sense of security.

John Brasier
Child in Stevenage
One Sunday morning in 1944, I was doing a Sunday paper round when I heard a noise which I later understood to be a V-1 doodlebug. I ran into a side of a house and pressed myself against the wall. Dogs were barking – I had no idea what it was. I had no idea that it was a pilotless vehicle with a bomb in it. It was a cigar-shaped thing with a fin and a flame belching out of the back and a terrible humming noise. To see it so low, literally a hundred feet up in the air – I'll never forget it as long as I live.

Wing Commander Roland Beamont
Tempest Wing, RAF

On the 16th June we heard a noise like a motorbike roaring through the night sky. It was the first of the V-1s, and we were ordered to stand by with a whole wing of Tempests at dawn. From that moment, we were totally engaged in defence against V-1s. The Tempest proved to be the fastest fighter by a long margin, and the most capable, because it had a very good gun platform. It could fire 20 mm cannon very accurately. We were able to shoot down so many of the things in the first few weeks, that on my recommendation, an area along the south coast from Eastbourne to Dover was restricted to Tempests, a squadron of Spitfire XIVs, and a wing of Mustang P51s. All other fighter aeroplanes, including the slower marks of Spitfire, were kept out of the area. Over the period from the 16th June to the end of July the Newchurch Tempest wing shot down over 600 V-1s.

Terrence McEwan
Schoolchild living in London

You'd hear the V-1 cut out and when it didn't hit you, your attitude was, 'Oh good, I'm all right.' It was a very selfish attitude we all had. I suppose one blocked out imagination in those days. On one occasion when we were in the shelter, we heard a V-1 cut out and my mother put a blanket over our heads to stop it hitting us. I'm not sure it would have helped much, but we never thought these weapons would turn the war in the German favour. It didn't ever dawn on me that we would lose.

Ellen Harris
Reuters reporter in Houses of Parliament

In 1944 Parliament had decided to sit in Church House opposite Westminster School. I was walking from Dean's Yard to Westminster Station when a doodlebug came over. The doodlebugs would cut out then come backwards and drop. I was terrified but I didn't want to show it. Would I run? No fear! Nobody else was running – I wasn't going to run. If a single person had thrown himself down into the gutter, I'd have followed but no-one did. Not one.

Eleanor Hudson
Volunteer canteen driver in London

I was driving a canteen van when the flying bombs began. I remember when one very nasty bomb came down at the corner of Earls Court Road and Kensington High Street, half destroying a whole block of flats called Troy

Roland Beamont was credited with five 'kills' during the Battle of Britain, then after work as a test pilot, went on to lead the RAF's Tempest Wing, formed to combat Hitler's final terror weapon, the V-1 rocket bomb. Beamont alone shot down thirty-two V-1s before they could wreak havoc on the ground.

Court and a Lyons Corner House. As a lot of choked men dug away at the wreckage, trying to pull out survivors, I was busy making tea for them all. Suddenly, a young American soldier jumped into the back of my van and said, 'Oh ma'am, please let me help, let me wash the cups.' He was white as a sheet but he insisted, so we let him do the washing-up. After a while his colour improved and he said, 'I heard the explosion and I started pulling dead people out of the building and I felt so sick, so terrible. And then I saw your little kitchen and I jumped in. It felt like home. You were the nearest thing to having my mom with me.'

Ernst Eberling
German officer pilot, Kampfgeschwader 53
Because there were no launch sites left in France and Belgium, the V-1 rockets were struggling to reach central London, so in October we began to fly with them. The main problem with them was the wind. If we didn't judge the wind right, we missed London. Also, many of our V-1s got shot down by English flak. We had to climb to 500 metres before we could let go of the V-1, that is, if the English fighters didn't get us. It was dangerous for us because the light when we launched the V-1 would reveal the bomber. By the time the V-1 came in, we still had a little hope we could win the war, but not much, as the Allied air power was so superior.

Myrtle Solomon
Civilian in London
The doodlebugs were pretty frightening, but the V-2s were terrifying. Perhaps we were tired by that point in the war, but we were much more scared than when the bombs were raining down on us during the Blitz. I was longing for the end by then.

Ronald McGill
Telegram delivery boy in London
I was a 14-year-old telegraph boy in London. I grew up very, very quickly because my job was basically delivering death telegrams. The girls in the instrument room used to say to us, 'This is a priority. It's death.' When we came down the road, we used to see the curtains go – they'd twitch – because we were feared. People knew our uniforms and they were scared of us. We were told to knock on either side of the house you were delivering to – it was better for a neighbour to break the news, I suppose. I remember one occasion, delivering a death telegram to a house near Hammersmith Bridge. I saw the

curtain twitch as I knocked on either side and the lady in question came out. 'That's for me, isn't it?' she said. 'Yes,' I said and she just fainted. She fell on the ground. Her two little kiddies ran out and saw their mother lying there. What was I supposed to do? I was fourteen. I knew nothing. She hadn't even opened the telegram. I managed to get another neighbour to come along and we pulled her into the house. The lady woke up and she and the neighbour opened the telegram. It was her husband – he'd been killed. I just stood there. I didn't know what to do. When I got home that night, I told my mother and she cried as well.

THE ARDENNES

By mid-December the Allies had reached the forests of the Ardennes in northern France, and Hitler, detecting a weakly held sector of the Allied line, ordered a do-or-die attack. The available strength of the Allies and the last-ditch nature of the German attack left the eventual outcome in little doubt. However, the suddenness of the assault by 12 infantry divisions and some 700 tanks and 2,000 field guns put serious pressure on the thinly spread Allied forces of around 2,000 men and one armoured division, who were defending 100 miles of front. US troops, tired from their gruelling advance, were taken by surprise, but the Americans fought on under siege for vital days until reinforcements could be directed to their support. Fighter bombers were grounded due to bad winter conditions at the start of the attack – soon dubbed 'The Battle of the Bulge'. On 23 December, however, the weather changed and, with a sharp freeze to harden the ground and a clearing of the skies, the US 9th Air Force was able to join the attack and the Germans were quickly overcome. Hitler's best troops had been sacrificed, and there remained little strength with which to defend the German Reich.

General Anthony McAuliffe
US 101 Airborne Division
On the 22nd December 1944, the German commander ridiculously demanded surrender of Bastogne. I just replied, 'Nuts,' for I knew that one word best expressed the feelings of the Division. The wounded were wonderful. No word can best describe their cheerful acceptance of a tough situation. On Christmas Day, the Germans launched their biggest attack with infantry and tanks in large numbers from the west of Bastogne and the rear of

the position. Prisoners later said that their officers had told them that Bastogne was to be a Christmas present for the Führer. On 26th December at 5 p.m., we made contact with friendly troops. Through it all, no-one doubted that we would hold the town under any attack the Germans could put on.

Hans Behrens
9th Panzer Division

I remember Christmas – we were at our most westerly point between Bastogne and St Hubert in the Ardennes. The turning point for me about the folly and the terror war instils, was that Bastogne was taken several times, to and fro, and one of those times we were coming down a hill and on the left side was a Sherman tank with its turret open. I don't know why, but I got out my vehicle and looked down inside in this tank. What I saw there was a young man absolutely charred black and one clean hole in the side of the turret. At that moment I realised that this man could be me and that he had a mother and a father. It became hard to carry on.

Sergeant Thomas Broom
571 Squadron, RAF

When the Ardennes battle was going on, they wanted the supply lines blocked. They selected a series of railway tunnels for the raid which was to be on New Year's Day 1945 at half-past eight. I was in the mess, having a pint the night before. We knew the operation might come along because we'd done a couple of low-level practices. I got a tap on the shoulder. 'That's your lot tonight. We're taking off at half six in the morning.' I didn't listen, I had three more pints before I went to bed and then we were up at three, had our briefing and we took off at half-past six. It was the first time 4,000-pound bombs had been dropped at low level. We flew to our target, dropped the bomb and went back to have a look. We picked up some enemy fighters, but we lost them over the hills of the Ardennes and then flew low-level back to the base and got back to our New Year celebrations.

Major Jack Watson
13th Parachute Battalion

Our battalion received an order to move to Pondrome, to attack a village called Bure, and then secure another village, Grupont. These were the furthest points reached in the German offensive. My task was to attack Bure to secure the high ground. We were formed up ready to go in at 1300 hours. It was a bloody cold day, still snowing heavily, and even going through the wood to the start line was very difficult because the snow was as much as three or four feet deep in some places.

We looked down on this silent and peaceful village. The Germans knew we were there – they were waiting for us, and as soon as we started to break cover, I looked up and I could see about a foot above my head the branches of the trees being shattered by intense machine-gun fire and mortaring. They obviously had the guns on fixed lines and they pinned us down before we even got off the start line. This was the first time I'd led a company attack and within minutes I'd lost about one third of my men. I could hear the men on my left-hand platoon shouting for our medics. We were held up for about fifteen minutes because of the dead and wounded around us but we had to get moving. We were about 400 yards from Bure, and so as soon as I could I got my company together and gave the order to move. We had to get under the firing and into the village as soon as possible. On the way down I lost more men, including my batman. One man took a bullet in his body, which ignited the phosphorus bombs he was carrying. He was screaming at me to shoot him.

We secured the first few houses, but it was difficult finding out just what was going on. I pulled in my platoon commanders to establish that they were secure and to start movement forward. It was eerie. We would be in one house, myself on the ground floor and my signalman telling me that there were Germans upstairs, and at other times they would be downstairs and we upstairs. It was a most unusual battle.

Our numbers were getting very depleted as we moved forward from house to house. I eventually got to the village crossroads by the old church, but by that time their 60-ton Tiger tanks had started to come in on us. It was the first time I had seen Tigers, and now here they were taking pot-shots, demolishing the houses. I moved from one side of the road to the other, deliberately drawing fire. A tank fired at me, and the next thing I knew the wall behind me was collapsing. But a PIAT team came running out, got within fifty yards of the tank, opened fire and smashed the tank's tracks. It went on like this all day – they counter-attacked but we managed to hold them.

It became difficult to keep the men awake – after all, they were tired and there was no hot food. All through our first night they were shelling and firing at us, and we were firing back. When we told HQ we had German tanks in the area they decided to bring in our own tanks in support, but our Shermans were no match for the Tigers. By the end of the battle 16 Shermans had been blown up. We were reinforced by a company from the Ox and Bucks, commanded by Major Granville, and by that time I was down to about one platoon in strength. The Ox and Bucks went forward, but they were not out there very long before they were forced back into our positions.

At one point in the battle Sergeant Scott, RAMC, went forward in an ambulance to pick up casualties. A German Tiger, which had been fighting us all day, rolled forward alongside him, and the commander seeing him unafraid said, 'Take the casualties away this time, but don't come forward again, it is not safe.' Even Sergeant Scott knew when to take a good hint!

Over the following day we suffered five more counter-attacks supported by Tiger tanks, trying to blast us out of the village. We held these attacks and then it all went very quiet, though the Germans left one Tiger behind as an irritant. It was time at last to secure the other half of the village. Together with C Company and the Ox and Bucks, we went from house to house, ferreting the Germans out. It was very much hand-to-hand fighting. By about nine o'clock on the evening of the 5th January, we had the whole village in our hands with my company eliminating the last enemy post. We took up defensive positions, but that same night we were told to withdraw. The 7th Battalion had come in from a different direction, met with little resistance and taken Grupont. It meant that we did not have to go any farther. So very early on the morning of the 6th, just after midnight, I got all my company together and we withdrew to Tellin – very wet, very tired, unshaven. The battalion lost about 68 men killed and about half of them were from my company. They were buried in a field in Bure by our padre.

Hans Behrens
9th Panzer Division

Things started to turn very bad for us in the Ardennes. We suffered great losses. It was very, very cold. Food was becoming difficult, so was fuel, and I remember not having washed for three weeks. I must have stunk. I was eventually captured in February. I remember I was sending a message from the back of my tank when the door opened and there was an American with his sub-machine gun.

Herbert Holewa
German paratrooper

I had been taken prisoner by the Americans at the end of 1944 and we were soon put aboard a landing ship and sent to Southampton. We were taken from there to Kempton Park. We all had tickets round our necks and mine read 'PP' which meant 'Protected Personnel'. We were interviewed quite often. This colonel, a Norwegian who spoke perfect German, said, 'Why don't you go on the wireless and speak to the German troops.' I said, 'Sir, when Hitler is dead – yes. While he is still alive – no.' This was because I had sworn my allegiance and I had to keep it. We were then sent to Crewe Hall and then to Camp 183 on the Scottish border. In that camp, the commandant had apparently found out that British prisoners of war received no heating during the day. So, tit for tat, the British wouldn't heat our camp. We revolted by showing passive resistance – we refused to do anything, so then we were sent to Camp 22. That was excellent. It was a 'Nazi' camp – which meant that it was full of paratroopers, U-boat men, SS officers and pilots. Three thousand people in all. We had a fantastic choir, which used to sing German *Lieder*. It was marvellous there.

THE FAR EAST

Jungle fighting was just as intense and still tested the Allied forces to their limits, but when the Japanese launched a full-scale offensive on eastern India in March 1944, the British-Indian forces had gained in strength and experience as was shown at Sangshak. The British Fourteenth Army fought the Japanese to a standstill at Kohima and Imphal. If they had fallen, then India would have been open to the Japanese forces. The Japanese were outfought and had outrun their supply lines – they had to fall back. With an assault led by General Slim across the Chindwin into Arakan, and an attack in northern Burma by the Chindits led by the charismatic Wingate, and Chinese units, the tide had turned decisively against the Japanese.

SANGSHAK

Captain 'Dicky' Richards
50th Indian Parachute Brigade
The original composition of our 50th Indian Parachute Brigade embraced 151 British, 152 Indian and 153 Gurkha Para Battalions, together with its complement of Engineers, Signals and Medical units. Volunteers came from almost every regiment and corps, in both the British and Indian Armies, practically regardless of caste or creed. Many were professionals, and others were wartime soldiers, from many different walks of life, but with one thing in common – an urgent desire to get to grips with the enemy.

Our commander, Brigadier M.R.J. 'Tim' Hope Thomson – an imaginative planner – persuaded GHQ India to send us on a 'jungle warfare exercise in a threatened area', which meant the Assam–Burma border to the east of Kohima and Imphal, down to the line of the river Chindwin. It sounded challenging and our spirits rose. A few weeks later we set up camp near Kohima and were briefed by Major General Ouvry Roberts. He emphasised that it was thought that the expected main Japanese thrust against India could only develop from well south of Imphal, since it seemed highly improbable that a major attack could be mounted from the east. There were several thickly jungle-clad mountain ridges, rising up to 3,000 or 4,000 feet, which ran north to south, and also the Chindwin River – which an attacker would have to cross. Certainly the terrain looked almost impenetrable by a force of any size. He then gave us a vast area of this mountainous jungle, on the east side of Kohima and Imphal, measuring about 80 by 50 miles, which we were to patrol on foot with animal transport only. Our orders were to keep the area clear of Japanese patrols and infiltrating agents.

It was an exciting challenge and since we were expected to 'live off the country', some of us had even brought fishing rods and shotguns. The first to move south was 152 Indian Para Battalion, to set up patrol bases some 20 miles east of Sangshak. It was breathtaking country, but progress anywhere was slow because of the narrow mule tracks and footpaths, almost vertical in places. One false move by man or mule could result in a 1,000-foot plunge down the 'khudside'. At the beginning of March, reports of one- or two-man Japanese patrols, stealthily moving between clumps of bamboo, began to filter in. It was what we had been warned to expect. But at 8 a.m. on the 20th March, a message came from 152 Battalion saying that C Company, under Major Fuller, was under attack from two Japanese battalions beyond Sheldon's Corner near the Chindwin. They had no wire or other defence stores, so would soon be in grave difficulties. The other three companies of 152 Battalion were deployed too far apart to give mutual support, so C Company were on their own. By 10.35 a.m. they were overrun and had heavy casualties – other companies were ordered to give support and an appeal was made for supplies of Dannert wire to be dropped by air. Without barbed wire they hadn't a hope in hell of keeping the massive attack at bay – but none arrived, and despite gallant attempts to relieve them, all but a few of C Company were killed that day.

Only the day, before the deputy commander of 23rd Division Headquarters had put out a signal to all brigade and 'box' commanders, telling them that 'the Japs have embarked on a foolhardy ambitious plan for the capture of Imphal, and may be expected to "infiltrate" any day'. Infiltrate my foot! This was the start of a major offensive by two divisions of Japanese who had got safely across the Chindwin and were heading our way, with only our para brigade between them and Imphal with its Headquarters, airfields and massive store dumps practically undefended – and we were widely dispersed as it was, completely without defence stores.

Headquarters had decided that we should form a 'strong box', a self-contained base, in the village of Sangshak. This was a small Naga village on a piece of high ground, tactically very well-sited. There with artillery and mortar batteries one could at least delay, the Japanese advance on Imphal and even Kohima. We moved up from the Sheldon's Corner area whilst still under fire from the enemy. The men of 152 Battalion marched a wearisome ten miles on their flat feet, carrying as much as 70 pounds of equipment per man through the mountainous terrain to Sangshak. At the head of the column marched Lieutenant-Colonel Paul 'Hoppy' Hopkinson and Lieutenant Alan Cowell. Hoppy refused my offer of a lift although he was tired – he would continue marching with the rest of his men to the end of the road, he said.

Captain F.G. Nield
153 Gurkha Parachute Battalion

The day after we arrived in Sangshak, the 22nd March, we started to dig in earnest; 152 Battalion were expected in that evening. To speed our actions, we watched the Japanese appearing from over the hill down the road from Ukhrul. It was unbelievable – we might have been watching a play from the dress circle. We had the 15th Battery of the 9th Indian Mountain Regiment with us, commanded by Major Lock – a typical mountain gunner if ever there was one. He was a large burly fellow, with the appearance of a rugger player, wearing the most ridiculous little fore-and-aft forage cap and puffing contentedly at a pipe. He was in no hurry and waited until the whole length of the road was full of Japs before he let them have it. We saw the little white puffs bursting all along that road. Lock beamed – his only regret was that the guns had no shrapnel. He said that it was the best day's shoot of his life.

All night long the attacks came in – and all night long the wounded passed through the regimental post where I was medical officer. There was little that we could do except stop any bleeding, give morphia and then evacuate them during lulls to the 80th Para Field Ambulance in a little dip about 200 yards away in the centre of the perimeter.

During the day we began to realise the seriousness of our position as the reports of the casualties came in. The machine-gun company had suffered very heavily – all shot through the head while sitting up firing from their exposed positions.

We were only partially heartened by finding a large number of Japanese dead in front of our positions. What funny little men they looked – in the bright light of day it was more as if we were taking part in some strange Wellsian fantasy than fighting for our lives against these yellow hordes.

Captain 'Dicky' Richards
50th Indian Parachute Brigade

Major John Ball, the brigade machine-gun company commander, asked me to help pull in some bodies which were just below the church, on the enemy side, and exposed to their fire. I made a grappling hook out of a decapitated wireless aerial and some line, hoping that with any luck the corpses could be hooked in from a distance, even under fire. We got up to the eastern edge of the church without attracting any fire, but whilst we were scanning the dead through binoculars, a Japanese machine-gun opened up and started traversing. Bullet holes started to appear in a line from the far end of the whitewashed mud and wattle wall, about 18 inches from ground level. For a moment I froze, then John shrieked, 'Down!', the spell broke, and we flung ourselves face downwards, flat on the ground. The fire passed over us with only an inch or two to spare, going to and fro for some minutes. John called for some mortar fire which shut them up long enough for us to pull in a few bodies and get clear.

It was a worthwhile expedition – one of the dead Japanese officers had some very interesting maps on him, showing the plan and intended routes for the attacks by the Japanese 15th and 31st Divisions on Imphal and Kohima – a priceless find, which was taken back to Headquarters at Imphal by two men.

From the maps it was quite obvious that our position at Sangshak would have to be eliminated if the Japanese were to carry on according to plan. We were inspired by a message from the corps commander based on the captured maps, saying that the holding of Sangshak was vital to the main plan, and that plans for the reinforcement of the brigade were in progress, but that it could not be carried out for some time. This caused much optimism all round, despite the fact that we were almost on our knees from lack of sleep alone, as well as shortage of food and water.

Major Harry Butchard
153 Gurkha Parachute Battalion

Despite intensive training, most of us had never been in action before, and we weren't used to the dangers of moving about the position at night. More than one man was accidentally shot because he failed to hear the whispered challenge – he was taken for an infiltrating Jap. The Japs were doing their best to undermine our confidence – in front of the Gurkha trenches they spoke Gurkhali, outside the Indian position, Urdu, and during lulls in the firing and general pandemonium, you'd even hear the enemy addressing you by name and rank.

It was all very eerie. By day, conditions on the plateau soon became pretty grim – bodies lying about, human and animal, decomposing rapidly. Snipers were a constant nightmare – one morning I was speaking to two officers of 152 Battalion, and when I returned that way a few minutes later, I found them both lying dead, in exactly the same place – shot through the head. The Field Ambulance area, packed with wounded, dead and dying men, was very vulnerable to small-arms fire, but the senior medical officer was convinced that the bullets were coming from this vast, thickly leaved tree above the hospital. You could easily picture a slant-eyed Jap strapped to a branch up there, aiming at us as we walked about below. There was sort of grim humour about this situation, which was finally resolved by a Gurkha with a kukri in his teeth who climbed up the tree, covered by two or three riflemen and the intelligence officer. Nothing was found up the tree, but that feeling of being watched remained.

Captain 'Dicky' Richards
50th Indian Parachute Brigade
Supply drops were a serious problem at Sangshak. The mountainous nature of the ground and the low-lying cloud made air supply hazardous, even if you could identify the target upon which to drop the supplies. Naturally, at base, if supplies were dispatched, they assumed that they had arrived, but communications were so bad that at times they had no idea that two-thirds of them had arrived or fallen elsewhere or got into Japanese hands.

We continued to fight by day and night. The position became utterly gruesome and macabre. The perimeter was littered with corpses which could not be buried and there were mule carcasses everywhere. Some went into the cooking pot, but others very quickly rotted in that climate – and there were Japanese bodies, our own bodies, and excreta everywhere. It was impossible to construct properly dug-down trenches, dysentery became rife and the situation was almost intolerable. We were getting weaker by the hour – our men were getting killed off one after the other, we were running out of ammunition and food and some men were almost delirious after many days without sleep. Some of us would drop off for a few minutes in mid-conversation. The situation was desperate, and by the 25th March, none of us expected to get out alive. But somehow that didn't seem to mean anything, either – we just went on, relentlessly. I never heard a single man complain.

Shortly before dawn on the 26th, the Japanese actually penetrated our position in the Church area, and set up machine guns in the trenches which had been occupied by the brave men of 152 and 153 Battalions. Things got incredibly intense – they were now only 100 yards from Brigade Headquarters and we'd run out of grenades. But our men became even more ferocious and daring. Every man was fighting for his life and there seemed no limit to their endurance – everyone, everywhere, was pleading for more ammunition and grenades. By 0730 hours the situation was desperate, but the brigadier was determined to regain complete control of the Church area. He sent a party from the Brigade Defence Platoon on a frontal counter-attack. This was led by young Lieutenant Robin de la Haye, nicknamed the 'Red Shadow' by the men because of his habit of doing the rounds at night wearing exquisite Jermyn Street red silk pyjamas under his webbing equipment. Robin and his men made a spirited attack but were cut to pieces by enemy fire from West Hill. Again and again we counter-attacked, now led by Lieutenant-Colonel Hopkinson, later by Colonel Abbott – but each time we were beaten back. At last, at 0930 hours, Major Jimmy Roberts with his A Company of 153 Battalion was successful and restored the situation, accompanied by deafening blasts from our own howitzers firing over open sights.

Just before six that evening there was a shout from one of the Brigade HQ signallers for everyone to keep quiet – a message was coming through from Major General Roberts. His shout was so urgent and excited that everyone fell silent. The signaller listened hard to the crackling set and scribbled on his pad, talking into his handset. It seemed to go on for ever. Then he suddenly shouted into the microphone, 'You can stuff your bloody thoughts, General! What about the bloody reinforcements?' He was beside himself with rage as he handed over the message. It read, 'FIGHT YOUR WAY OUT, GO SOUTH THEN WEST. AIR AND TRANSPORT ON THE LOOKOUT' and ended with the words, 'GOOD LUCK. OUR THOUGHTS ARE WITH YOU.' This had prompted the signaller's reply. Our reactions resembled a 'Bateman' cartoon. For a moment we were horrified by his audacity, but seconds later broke the tension with spontaneous laughter – and that was a sound not heard at Sangshak for quite some long time.

A conference of unit commanders was called and, as night was about to close in, we heard the familiar sound of the air-supply Dakotas in the distance. Our initial euphoria at this last-minute chance of survival was soon dampened by the enormous problems of evacuating the seriously injured, who would have to be carried, and the walking wounded, bearing in mind the sheer mountainous jungle slopes between us and Imphal. I cursed when I found that the bulk of our supply drop had fallen straight into the hands of the Japanese. As the night darkened, the Japs lit fires and sounded overjoyed at this unexpected bonus. Brigade Commander Tim Hope Thomson decided that there should not be any movement before 2230 hours that night. Units were to give top priority to pairing off walking wounded with their comrades, using every able-bodied man to help carry and protect the stretcher-cases. Our greatest concern was the plight of the wounded – many were within an hour or two of death and others so serious that death would occur if they were moved. It was the worst dilemma to face any man and we were stunned by the selfless courage of our Indian Medical Services senior officer, Lieutenant-Colonel 'Bobby' Davis, who pleaded to be allowed to remain behind, after the evacuation, to tend to the dying men who could not be moved, and anyone else who might not have been found in the utter shambles we were to leave behind.

Tim Hope Thomson gave it much deep thought, but knew that on past records of the Japanese, neither the gallant doctor nor his patients would have any chance of survival. We should try and take those who were considered to be mortally wounded, no matter how slim their chances of survival appeared to be. At Brigade HQ our cook, Swami, excelled himself, keeping his cauldron on the boil well into the evening. We were amused to see him adopting the role of a Brahmin high priest, which was hardly his status, giving dispensation to the Hindu to accept the possibility of corned beef within the cauldron, and the Muslim not to reject the infamous American-made 'soya link' sausage and gallons of rum included in the pot!

As the 2230 hours start-time approached, tension mounted. That evening Japanese fire had been limited to sporadic shots and a few bursts, but we wondered whether they would strike. If they did, our chances for survival would have been slim – but they didn't. Colonel Abbott ordered me to channel the few remaining exhausted men of 152 Indian Para Battalion through the 4th/5th Maratha Light Infantry position, which was the safest of the lot. The former had taken a terrible hammering with over 350 killed. Few had properly eaten or rested for well over a week and they were now practically without ammunition or grenades, or senior ranks to guide them, with a tortuous journey facing them through the Jap-infested jungle to Imphal.

As the break-out got under way, I felt surprised at the quietness and orderliness as parties with makeshift bamboo stretchers and walking wounded vanished from sight into the jungle below. It was a painful and heart-rending experience, particularly for the medical men, whom I saw patching up and attending to anyone showing any signs of life.

Nearly a week later I arrived back at HQ 23rd Indian Division in Imphal. We had survived walking into an armed Japanese supply column heading for Sangshak by throwing ourselves or rolling into the thick elephant grass and lying 'doggo', whilst they passed within feet of some of us – we had no grenades and hardly a round between us. Days later whilst intelligence officers were debriefing us, I had a quiet cup of tea with Ouvry Roberts, whom I knew well. He left me in no doubt about the value of the stand which we had made. He said that the brigade, with its attached units, fighting under the most appalling conditions, had undoubtedly saved both Kohima and Imphal from the danger of being immediately overrun by the Japanese spearhead troops. This was later to be confirmed in a Special Order of the Day by General 'Bill' Slim himself.

As we were taking our leave, I asked him off the record whether he had heard the British signaller's comments on his personal message – 'You can stuff bloody your thoughts, General!' His reply was just an enigmatic smile.

THE BATTLE FOR KOHIMA

Lieutenant-Colonel Gerald Cree
2nd Battalion, West Yorkshire Regiment
As the Japanese launched their main assault on Kohima, we were ordered back towards Dimapur to hold the road. This was a most foolish thing to do. The road was jam-packed with vehicles trying to get out of Kohima and others trying to get in. If I had split the battalion into four detachments over 40 miles of road, I'd have had no control over them, couldn't have affected the battle at all, and would have been mopped up in detail. I disobeyed, and we went back to Milestone 10 and settled there for the night. Suddenly the general appeared. I thought, now I'm for it. However he didn't mind at all. I explained what I felt and he agreed, and said, 'Tomorrow go back to Kohima and help defend it.' So back we went and took up positions around the place and prepared for a long siege. I occupied the matron's quarters in the former hospital. We found a harmonium there, which greatly pleased our padre.

After a couple of days orders came that the West Yorks were to move to Imphal, and transport was being sent for us. Colonel Richards was rather dismayed, being left naked again without anybody to defend him, except the odds and sods of the convalescent depot. I couldn't have been more pleased.

In the heart of the Jungle, a British mortar team works in the heat and ear-shattering din of the battle around Imphal and Kohima.

The vehicles arrived. We piled on to them, and went down the road to Imphal like scalded cats. We were the last people to get through.

Major John Winstanley
4th Battalion, Royal West Kent Regiment

The 4th Royal West Kents, the Assam Rifles and odds and sods defended Kohima against an entire Jap Division in a 14-day siege. The perimeter shrank and shrank until it only included the Tennis Court and Garrison Hill where the final stand took place. At first B Company were only observers on Kuki Picket. After five days we were ordered to relieve A Company on the Tennis Court. On the other side the ground fell away – that's where the Japs were, only fifty yards away. The battle took place on the Tennis Court – we shot them and grenaded them on the Tennis Court. We held that Tennis Court against desperate attacks for five days. One of the reasons we held them was because I had instant contact by radio with the guns, and the Japs never seemed to learn how to surprise us. They used to shout in English as they formed up, 'Give up!' which gave us warning each time an attack was coming in. One would judge just the right moment to call down gun- and mortar-fire to catch them as they were launching the attack, and every time they approached us they were decimated. They were not acting intelligently and did the same old stupid thing again and again.

We had experienced the Japs in the Arakan – we knew they bayoneted the wounded and prisoners and we didn't respect them. They had renounced any right to be regarded as human, and we thought of them as vermin to be exterminated. That was important. We were aroused and fought well. Also our backs were to the wall and we were going to sell our lives as expensively as we could. But we wondered how long we could hang on – not that we had any other option.

Throughout this period, we had no idea we were confronted by a whole Jap division and outnumbered by ten to one. We had no thought of surrender at any level – we were too seasoned soldiers for that. We couldn't taunt the Japanese back as we couldn't speak their language, but there were some JIFs, Indians fighting for the Japanese on the other side, and we taunted them in English. We took a steady toll of casualties – mainly from snipers. Showing yourself in daylight resulted in being shot by a sniper. They also used their battalion guns in the direct-fire role, in morning and evening. This caused mayhem among the wounded lying in open slit trenches on Garrison Hill, so that many were killed or re-wounded. We heard that 2 Div were being flown in to relieve us, and we could hear the sound of firing to our north, as the division fought its way down to us. But it seemed to take ages. After five days I was relieved on the Tennis Court by the Assam Regiment and moved to Hospital Spur. The Tennis Court position held, but we were in a filthy state.

Major Francis Boshell
1st Battalion, Royal Berkshire Regiment

We took over from the 4th Royal West Kents who had had a terrible time. To begin with I took over an area overlooking the Tennis Court, although only my left forward platoon could see the Court. The Dorsets were responsible for the position closest to the court itself. The lie of the land made it impossible to move by day because of Japanese snipers. We were in Kohima for three weeks and we were attacked every single night. On the worst night they started at 1900 hours and the last attack came in at 0400 hours the following morning. They came in waves – it was like a pigeon-shoot. Most nights they overran part of the battalion position, so we had to mount counter-attacks. When part of my right-hand forward platoon was overrun, we winkled them out with the bayonet. I lost two platoon commanders, but good sergeants took over. Water was short and restricted to about one pint per man per day. So we stopped shaving. Air supply was the key, but the steep terrain and narrow ridges meant that some of the drops went to the Japs.

Company Sergeant-Major Martin McLane
2nd Battalion, Durham Light Infantry

I was woken by shouts from my company commander, Major Stock. Green phosphorus was pouring into one end of the trench. I was covered in the stuff – which causes deep, penetrating burns. I was rubbing the stuff off me with earth, then the Japs came in yelling and shouting. They were in among us and just ten yards away there was a fearsome looking man waving a sword. But we did for him. When the position was finally cleared, my company commander, the runners and the signallers were all dead. A shell had landed right in the shell hole they were standing in.

Major Alexander Wilson
2nd Battalion, Durham Light Infantry

General Grover reckoned that the fighting on Garrison Hill at Kohima was worse than the Somme, where he had fought in the First World War. The 2nd Battalion DLI had more casualties there than anyone else. In my three companies there were four officers left. Of the original 136 men in A company, only 60 were left. The pioneer and carrier platoons also lost many

As the tide turned against the Japanese in the battle for Imphal and Kohima, men of the Dorsetshire Regiment sign their names on Japanese flags captured at Nippon Ridge.

killed and wounded. The fighting was hand-to-hand. Men were kept going by training, regimental pride and the will to survive.

Lieutenant Sam Horner
2nd Battalion, Royal Norfolk Regiment

We were ordered to march to the south of Kohima to cut the Imphal Road. This involved cutting a trail over a 7,000-foot ridge. The physical hammering we took is difficult to understand. The heat, humidity, altitude and the slope of almost every foot of ground combined to knock hell out of the stoutest constitution. You gasp for air, which doesn't seem to come, you drag your legs upwards till they seem reduced to the strength of matchsticks, and all the time the sweat is pouring off you. Then you feel your heart pounding so violently you think it must burst its cage – it sounds as loud as a drum, even above the swearing and cursing going on around you. So you stop, horrified to be prodded by the man behind you or cursed by an officer in front. Eventually, long after everything tells you that you should have died of heart failure, you reach what you imagine is the top of the hill – to find it is a false crest, and the path still lies upwards. And when you finally get to the top, there is a hellish climb down. You forget the Japs, you forget time, you forget hunger and thirst. All you can think of is the next halt.

Sergeant William Robinson
2nd Battalion, Royal Norfolk Regiment

At Oaks Hill, Kohima, Colonel Scott lined us up with Bren guns. He was ill at the time with malaria, and all he had was his pistol and his cud stick. His famous words were, 'Right-ho boys, let's go.' The instructions were to fire at everything, spraying up and down, some up and forward of course, because there was a bunker there. Up to that time I hadn't seen a Japanese at all, but hidden in this semi-clearing with low bushes, several got up and started running away. They didn't get far because the firepower was terrific – about twelve Bren guns. The bunker was taken.

Sergeant Bert 'Winkie' Fitt
2nd Battalion, Royal Norfolk Regiment

We went straight into the attack and took the position at Oaks Hill, Kohima, with the bayonet. I used this Bren gun for the remainder of the attack, running with it, using it from the hip. The Japanese positions were facing outwards, so they had to come into the open if they wanted to fight us, and that suited us. We wanted them in the open so we could see what was going on. We tore down this Ridge as fast as we could. About halfway down, I saw what looked to me like a flat piece of ground, and I thought it was a bunker facing the other way. I jumped on to this and I found myself looking straight down the muzzle of a mountain field-gun. I threw a grenade in. Three Japs jumped out, and my runner, Swinscoe, shot the first one. He twizzled him like a rabbit – a marvellous shot. We took the other two prisoner and I left them to be guarded by one of my soldiers.

Colonel Scott came up and I told him about the prisoners. 'Where are they?' he asked. I told him they were being brought up by one of the chaps. 'Good,' he said. Well, up came this fellow without the prisoners so I asked him where they were. 'Back up the track.' 'What do you mean? They'll be gone.' 'Never,' he replied, 'they won't go anywhere. Remember my brother got bayoneted in hospital? Well I bayoneted both of them.' When I told the CO that we hadn't got the prisoners, he flew at me and said, 'Bring the person who let them escape to me.' I said, 'They didn't escape, sir. His brother had been bayoneted in bed in hospital – so he bayoneted the prisoners.' Colonel Scott looked at me and said 'Well, that's saved me cutting their bloody throats.'

Private Dick Fiddament
2nd Battalion, Royal Norfolk Regiment
Suddenly Colonel Scott comes along. There we are, crouched down in our holes. Scott says to us, 'Come on you chaps, there's no need to be afraid, you are better than those little yellow bastards.'

Sergeant Bert 'Winkie' Fitt
2nd Battalion, Royal Norfolk Regiment
Colonel Scott wasn't a man who just went and got in a dug-out and stayed there. Oh no, he went round his positions to make sure that everything was covered and he spoke to people as he went round. He was a great soldier – one of the finest soldiers you could ever meet. I always said that he should have had the VC. When he got scalped, he shook his fist at the Japanese. He said, 'The biggest bloke on the damn position and you couldn't get me. If you were in my bloody battalion, I'd take away your proficiency pay.'

Second Lieutenant Maurice Franses
2nd Battalion, Royal Norfolk Regiment
Colonel Scott had always been a keen cricketer, and when he threw his grenades he reminded me of a medium bowler, lobbing. He was being seen, it was a big help to us all – it certainly was a big help to me. After a few minutes of this, a

Japanese grenade came down towards Robert Scott and I think he decided to kick it away. He misjudged it slightly and it went off and brought him down.

Company Sergeant-Major Walter Gilding
2nd Battalion, Royal Norfolk Regiment

I saw Scott go down and the stretcher bearers come to try to pick him up. They cut his trousers open to put a field dressing on his wounds. This uncovered his bottom and through all the noise that was going on, I could hear Scott shouting 'Cover my bloody arse up!'

Sergeant Bert 'Winkie' Fitt
2nd Battalion, Royal Norfolk Regiment

We were ordered to make another attempt to take the Norfolk bunker. Our plan was to attack it from the front. It consisted of about seven or eight bunkers. My platoon was spearhead in the centre with 12 Platoon on the right. It was a frontal attack at dawn, and we had to climb a hill with very little cover. The trees had been so shelled that their branches had been stripped bare. Captain Randle came up and lay beside me. He said, 'I've seen all the horrible things that's happened to me in my past.' I said, 'So have I.' I think he had an idea that he wouldn't come out of that attack. We moved and got about half-way to the base of the hill. Captain Randle staggered twice before we ever got to the bottom, that told me he had been hit fairly heavily in the upper part of his body. I shouted to him to go down and leave it to me, you could see that he had already lost blood. He said, 'No you take the left-hand bunker, I'm going to take this right-hand one.' There were two light machine-gun posts and they were carving up the company terrible. I got mine by coming up underneath and before they could spin a gun on me I had a grenade in the bunker.

After four seconds it went up with a great noise. I knew that anyone in the bunker was either dead or knocked out. I immediately spun right because I thought I could have got to where Captain Randle was before anything happened. I saw him at the bunker entrance. He had a grenade he was going to throw into the bunker. I just stood there, I couldn't do a thing. If he had held on for about three minutes, I'd have got on top of the bunker and knocked it out. But he had been hit again at point-blank range. As he was going down, he threw his grenade into the bunker and sealed the entrance with his own body, so that nobody could shoot from it. He killed all the occupants. I thought, 'That's the end of Captain Randle.'

At the next bunker, a Japanese soldier rushed out. He knew if he stayed there he was going to get a grenade in, so he came out of the back door, which was behind me. I didn't see him when he fired. He got me through the side of my face. It felt like being hit by a clenched fist but it didn't hurt as much as a really good punch in a fight. I spat out a handful of teeth, spun round, and he was a few paces away, facing me. He had a rifle and bayonet. I pressed the trigger but I'd got no ammunition. As he came towards me, I felt it was either him or me. I was an instructor in unarmed combat, so. I let him come and threw the light machine-gun in his face.

Before he hit the ground I had my hand round his windpipe and I literally tried to tear it out. It wouldn't come – if I could have got his windpipe out, I would have twisted it round his neck. We were tossing over on the ground. I managed to get his bayonet off his rifle and finished him with that. I stood up and had a call from 12 Platoon telling me they were pinned down from another bunker. I asked them where it was and when they told me, I threw a grenade. It went over the top, and a chap who could see shouted a correction. I threw a second grenade, it hit the ground short but bounced in, killing the occupants. There were still more bunkers. One of my corporals spotted another bunker slightly over the crest. He started going for it. I yelled at him to stop, but he continued for four or five paces and was shot down.

Captain Dickie Davies
2nd Battalion, Royal Norfolk Regiment

You couldn't throw grenades at the bunkers, so you made a hole in the top with your bayonet, and dropped the grenades in. I picked up a Sten gun, thinking I'd carry that instead of a rifle. Four Japanese got out of one of the bunkers and ran down the hill, I pressed the trigger and nothing happened. They always jammed – a useless weapon. I threw it at them. We were in captured slit trenches that evening. In front of the trenches were tins with stones in them that the Japs used as a form of early warning. We heard the tins rattling and the Japs shouting, 'Are you there Tommy?' hoping we would shout back. It was horrible, I was very scared. We were soaking wet, we had no cover. The main bunker was full of Jap dead. We had been sent up some bully beef and my batman said, 'Let's have it.' He got his hankie out, it was filthy, and put it over the bare tummy of a dead Japanese. He pulled the warm bully beef out with his finger, put it on a biscuit, saying, 'Here you are, sir.' I couldn't eat it – I was sick.

Sergeant Henry Cook
2nd Battalion, Dorsetshire Regiment
People behave differently in action from their normal behaviour. One chap, Corporal Day, normally a mild-mannered man who wouldn't hurt a fly, stood on the top of a little trench at Kohima, shouting and cursing the Japanese – he was in another world.

Lieutenant Lintorn Highlett
2nd Battalion, Dorsetshire Regiment
The Japanese were magnificent in defeat. Every army in the world talks about holding positions to the last man. Virtually no other army, including the Germans, ever did – but the Japs did. Their positions were well sited and they had a good eye for the ground. They relied on rushing and shouting in the attack. We thought they were formidable fighting insects and savages. We took few prisoners – about one or two in the whole war. We wanted prisoners, but wounded men would have a primed grenade under them, so stretcher bearers were very careful.

THE BATTLE FOR IMPHAL

Corporal Arthur Freer
3rd Carabiniers
During the Japanese advance on Imphal, the Japs took Nungshigum Hill. We mounted an attack to take it back. We lost our squadron leader, shot through the head while standing in the open turret, directing our fire. In the attack, as we got closer, the Japs ran out of the bunkers, and up to the sides of the tanks carrying sticky bombs attached to a bamboo rod. They stuck the bomb on the side of the tank and as they ran off, they pulled the pin – hoping that it would blow the tank to pieces. We managed to deter them from sticking them on by firing machine guns along the side of the tank. I fired the front Browning, which could not traverse but only elevate or depress. If I could have traversed it I could have killed a lot more Japs.

We learned afterwards that there were 250 Japanese bodies found. Our squadron leader was hit by a bullet under the chin and it came out of the top of his steel helmet. Under his body we found a grenade, which he had been about to throw, without a handle, and we had had it in the tank with us amongst all that ammo, and we couldn't understand why it hadn't exploded. We found out later that it was a dud fuse.

That night Colonel Younger came round to our tank, bubbling with the success. Although he had lost some of his bright young men, he looked upon this as one of the risks of war. I was new to it. He had fought with the 7th Hussars in North Africa and in Burma in the retreat. Here each squadron of the Carabiniers fought individually. The next day we had a lot of work oiling guns, replenishing ammo and cleaning up the tanks. The tracks were clogged with bits of Japanese uniforms, bones and bits of flesh.

Major Dinesh Misra
5th Battalion, Rajputana Rifles

We were trying to take Lone Tree Hill from the Japanese. I mounted a frontal attack with two companies. I told my men that speed was of the utmost importance as the Japanese were in the middle of preparing positions. We got to within 30 yards of the objective and were grenaded back. We withdrew and took up a defensive position, spending all night there.

Next morning, the RAF Liaison Officer arrived and asked what he could do to help. We were so close to target that any shots from artillery would risk dropping on us. During shelling the Japanese would withdraw down the reverse slope, and come back when the artillery stopped. I said to the RAF Liaison Officer, 'You bring in air strikes in a north-south direction. When your aircraft have dropped their bombs, don't let them go away. Get them to turn round and attack in dummy runs while we advance.' The aircraft did this, and during the dummy runs we got on to the top of the hill without any firing. I told the company commanders, 'Get your LMGs out in front, facing the direction which enemy would come from.'

After about ten minutes, the Japanese appeared. We let them come within thirty yards and opened up with everything. They dropped like flies. The survivors withdrew. By then it was getting dark. I told the company commanders to expect a counter-attack about two hours after dark. Sure enough it came. Everything opened up. We beat it off, but we had taken a few casualties. I knew that in the early morning there would be a final counter-attack. It came, and in the hand-to-hand fighting we had more casualties. I felt hatred for the Japanese and was determined to kill them. We were shouting our battle cries, and the Japs shouted *Banzai*. The Japanese withdrew and I knew we had won. There was a tremendous feeling of joy and relief. We counted about 150 Jap dead. The Hill became known as Rajputana Hill.

Lieutenant James Evans
1st Battalion, 4th Gurkha Rifles

Returning in the evening from a patrol, I was fired at by one of our own sentries. 'It's Evans Sahib!' I shouted to stop him. The Japs must have heard this because later that night, when the Gurkhas opened up on a Jap patrol, one of the Japs called out 'Evans Sahib!' The Gurkhas were not taken in and they carried on firing.

Corporal Arthur Freer
3rd Carabiniers

We were sent to Bishenpur where we were in action almost every day. It was paddy on both sides of the road, and on one side was the Logtak Lake. The Japs would fortify the villages with bunkers and use the bunds as defensive positions. At night, having half cleared a village, we would remain guarded by a platoon of the Bombay Grenadiers. All of us had the runs. There was a latrine at Bishenpur, a four-seater, always occupied, so you would have to go elsewhere. It was a communal meeting place, and you would chat and have a cigarette. It stank. The MO ordered that it was to be covered with oil daily to seal it off. This was OK until we were short of oil, but we had plenty of high-octane petrol, because the tanks had aero engines, and someone put that down. Someone lit a cigarette, dropped the match, and up went the petrol burning the backsides of the four men sitting there.

Prickly heat drove you mad. The best way to relieve it was to stand out in the rain. The thing I remember most is being stuck in the tank day and night when I had the runs. There were three of us with the runs at the time, and I was the worst. To sleep in the tank you sit in your seat. To crap you got the 75 mm gunner, who was standing on the escape hatch on the other side of the tank, to move to your seat, and you lifted the hatch and crapped on the ground a few feet below. You then got the driver to move the tank a bit away from the stench. Put the lid back again. Nobody slept. We all stank to high heaven, we were all unwashed. There was always a revolting stench in the tank. At dawn you stood to, the tank guard would move away, and we would go into action again. It could go on for three days and nights at a time.

One morning I crossed a road, saw a stagnant pond with thick green water, and I was just scraping this away to try to get some clean water when a jeep pulled up and the CO got out. He had come from Imphal, having driven through a Japanese roadblock. His uniform was immaculate, brasses shining and I stood in front of him like a scarecrow. He asked me what I was doing, so I told him. He asked me where the Major was, I said, 'He's in the next pond looking for water.' He came back and inspected us two hours later. We had changed into our spare jungle greens by then.

Captain John Randle
7th Battalion, 10th Baluch Regiment

On the Silchar track at Imphal, conditions were rather like the Western Front. We were dug in, the positions were wired and the Japs were only about 50–60 yards away. Everyone was mixed up. For about three weeks there was very intensive fighting. The scrub was thicker than in the Chin Hills and very wet. It was a very hard infantry slog. The Japs attacked, then we counter-attacked. Positions changed hands several times. It was the most close fighting I ever saw in Burma. Japanese attacks tended to come up and close the last few yards with bayonets. In a counter-attack we gave enemy positions a really good pasting, then fought our way in, clearing enemy positions with grenades, Tommy guns – Gurkhas with kukris, and our chaps used a bayonet. Casualties were high in this period but we had no morale problems. We felt we were winning. We had far more artillery than the Japs, and the RAF were in evidence all the time. Rations came up. The wounded were taken out by the American Field Service. There were none of the uncertainties of the retreat.

Major Alexander Wilson
Durham Light Infantry

We met the Imphal garrison coming north. We were clearing road blocks quicker than the Japs thought we could. The Japs would blow the little culvert between two ridges, and sit on the other side – there were no bunkers but foxholes, and they fought hard. The technique was to fix them in the front and climb above them, and outflank them. The Japs were getting short of men. Artillery support was very important. Sometimes the guns fired direct over open sights. The Jap artillery was very sparse – they were an army in disarray . . . but it didn't mean they didn't fight.

THE SECOND CHINDIT EXPEDITION

Flight Lieutenant Arthur Gill
84 Squadron, RAF

Major-General Orde Wingate was a strange man – he had a temper – but when talking to him, he was an extremely charming, rather shy, small man. I liked him a lot. He was a brilliant tactician – but he wasn't everybody's cup of tea. He didn't get on too well with even Lord Louis Mountbatten, because he was very outspoken and determined in what he thought was right and proper.

He was very strict with his troops, but they would follow him anywhere. They respected him as a leader and as a fighter and as a soldier. There was the story of how he used to walk around with an alarm clock dangling from his belt and ticking away to remind people that time was passing and wasn't to be wasted. I remember flying with him Christmas morning. We visited one of his columns during the training period at Gwalior, and he was greeted by the column commander. Instead of replying, 'Happy Christmas', he said, 'I thought I gave instructions that no camp was to be sited within two miles of water. You will up sticks now and move.' That was Christmas morning, whilst lunch was being prepared.

Sergeant Harold Atkins
2nd Battalion, Queen's Royal Regiment (West Surrey)
Each time I saw Wingate, he looked a rather scruffy individual for a very senior officer. He used to wear an old sort of topee – the old-fashioned topee – and it seemed to sit well down on his ears. He had his customary beard and his khaki drill was normally crumpled. He wasn't a big, imposing figure at all, so the first appearances didn't impress one really.

Captain James Dell
2nd Battalion, Queen's Royal Regiment (West Surrey)
In pouring rain the Second Chindit Expedition started. It took us a whole day to get the column up the first mountainside – it was as steep as the roof of a house. The sappers had cut steps in zigzags, but they crumbled before half the column had passed. In places the slope was so steep that the mules had to be unloaded and their loads passed up hand-to-hand. It rained all the time. At least we in the leading column got to the top by nightfall. We bedded down on the saturated ground. It was very cold, and we slept in pairs to try to keep warm. We had been issued with super-light-weight blankets, which became so saturated, the next morning they were all abandoned because they were so heavy. Despite the rain and saturated ground, we were short of water – but we could hear the streams thousands of feet below. I had to indent for an airdrop of water in order to have enough for the mules.

Sergeant Harold Atkins
2nd Battalion, Queen's Royal Regiment (West Surrey)

Our plan was to attack Indaw from the south, with the Leicesters coming in from the north. But unfortunately things went wrong. Because of the long journey south, our arrival at a place called the Miza Chaung was spotted and we had to set off from there very quickly. We made for the start line for the coordinated attack on Indaw. We arrived at this place at the end of the first day. The commanding officer decided that we would bivouac here. Now this was rather a lengthy process and in the Far East, darkness falls very, very quickly. There's no twilight period. We hadn't got into a secure bivouac when darkness was completely upon us. People were milling around – we were trying to establish where everybody was. People had offloaded their packs, got them on to the ground, put their weapons up against a tree which was going to be their base for the night, and were interested in getting their brew and their evening meal going before they got their heads down for the night – when all of a sudden, one could hear the roar of engines. It was half a dozen lorryloads of Japs – and they drove slap, bang into the middle of our bivouac.

They were out of their lorries in no time, and bullets were flying here, there and everywhere. Grenades were going off. There was screaming and shouting – a terrible night. Some people were close to their weapons, others weren't, and they lost direction because of the shooting and meleeing that was going on. I hadn't even had time to get my pack off. We hastily took some cover along the top of what turned out to be the banks of a wadi down below us. We were just waiting for things to develop. Eventually, we got across this wadi, which was very deep. We lost several men crossing it – they just went down and were never seen again. We went on for about a mile or two away from that bridgehead, leaving the Japs in possession of our original bivouac area, and lay up quietly until daybreak, when we were able to assess the damage that was done.

It was discovered that we had something like 70 men missing. We'd lost nearly every mule and almost all our wireless and medical equipment. As we moved on, we had to cross the railway line running from Katha up into Indaw. We were about to go across it when we heard a train chuffing and chugging its way along this railway line. Now, I don't think I've seen four or five hundred men disappear into the jungle so quickly as our column did. After the last ambush, we were not sufficiently organised to get involved in another melee, so we lay there and watched this train loaded with Japs, chug-chugging right the way up into Indaw. We continued the journey into the hills and made our way back towards Aberdeen. On the journey, we lost two chaps. We'd halted in the hills and decided to go searching for water. We found it and found our way back – except for two chaps who simply disappeared. Nobody knew where they went – what happened to them – and they were never heard of or seen again.

Captain Richard Rhodes-James
1st Battalion, 6th Gurkha Rifles
Although the Second Chindit Expedition did have an effect, it was not cost-effective to achieve this with six brigades. The 77th Brigade achieved great things, the other brigades did not. Two or three brigades would have been enough to commit to the LRP task, and Slim could have used the other three more brigades to much better effect in the main battle. When people find out I was in Burma, they often ask if I was a Chindit. The romantic stories of the Chindits are often the only thing people remember about the Burma campaign. At times you see and hear in the media that Wingate turned the tide of the war in Burma. I think it was turned at Kohima and Imphal by the Fourteenth Army.

1945

They had terrible sunken eyes and they put their
hands out to try and touch us as we went past them into the camp.
It was a complete shock to us. We didn't have the faintest idea.

After the war ended, I was surprised that I wasn't all that elated.
I just felt a slightly lost feeling – relieved a little bit that one was safe now – but
not very happy . . . One day I saw one of our corporals digging up the road in
Chancery Lane when I was walking to the Law Society. We talked and I was
glad to see him. I think he was glad to see me. But there was really nothing to say.
It was all gone.

Germany was under invasion, Allied forces were advancing towards Berlin, and the end of the conflict in Europe was only a matter of time. On the night of 13/14 February Dresden was destroyed by Allied bombs, soon Berlin was surrounded and Hitler committed suicide on 30 April. On 7 May, Germany surrendered. Following the German capitulation and the death of Hitler, the next concern for the Allies was to restore order in the ruins of the Reich and round up the Nazi leadership to be tried for war crimes.

However, in the Far East, although the British had largely secured Burma by spring, there was still strong Japanese resistance in the Pacific islands. America wielded the ultimate weapon and unleashed the devastation of the atomic bomb on Japan – and within days the war was over.

THE FALL OF GERMANY

As the Russians advanced toward Berlin, the Allies moved in from the west. There was a sense of relief among the German population in western Germany that they were in the Anglo-American sector and not the Russian area of 'liberation'. In the east there were many instances where the invading troops took the opportunity to exact revenge for atrocities committed in their own homeland.

The victorious Allied progress through Germany was punctuated with the discovery of the concentration camps. The troops sent to liberate the inmates became aware of the horror of Hitler's 'Final Solution'.

DRESDEN

Air Vice-Marshal Donald Bennett
Commander Pathfinder Force, RAF
Dresden is a name that has long been produced to make out that we went to the trouble to bomb women and children. We bombed Dresden because it was a prime target on that night. We were called during the day by the Russians, who particularly called for a raid on Dresden with everything we'd got, because troops were pouring through Dresden. There were something like 80,000 at the time on their way to the Russian front, less than a hundred miles away. The Russians were being held up by these troop reinforcements. Could we help? So at short notice, we were put on to Dresden, which we bombed perfectly normally. The fact that it caught fire rather easily was the Germans' fault. They had no air-raid precautions and they didn't believe in building anything other than wooden residences in Dresden. They also happened to have the German civil service in Dresden, more than anywhere else. They'd moved them out of Berlin for safety – so we did some heavy bombing.

Karin Busch
German schoolgirl in Dresden
Before the 13th February 1945, there had not been any air activity over Dresden. We had warning exercises but that was all. It was considered a safe city and we believed that culture-loving people would never destroy a jewel like Dresden. We felt safe in that knowledge. A few anti-aircraft guns had been placed around Dresden but a few nights before the raid, they were removed. No shelters had been built in Dresden. The only defence measure was to provide buckets of sand.

My father and brother were both at home on leave and my mother had broken into her food rationing cards and bought a lot of food and then, the following evening, the bombing started. At about half-past nine I was sitting sewing a bag for a friend when I heard a roaring noise. I didn't know what it was – we had no warning at all. In case of an air raid, you were supposed to receive a pre-warning and then a full warning but now we heard the full warning and suddenly the town was lit up by flares in the shape of Christmas trees all over the sky. Then hell broke loose. It was terrible, absolutely terrible.

We ran into the cellar. My mother grabbed two Japanese lacquer boxes – one had food in it and the other had all our documents – and we ran down. My father and brother, who were both in uniform, began organising people and telling them what to do. It was very hot and we heard all this noise going on when suddenly a bomb fell into the cellar. It didn't go off, but total pandemonium broke out and we tried to climb out. I tried to help my mother out, I held her and tried to force her through but as I did, I lost my grip on her and she disappeared.

Outside, I was hit by an inferno of wind and firestorm. It was like looking into a huge burning oven. I saw my twin brother sitting down, holding his eyes. He couldn't see, so I held him and together we were swept along by the storm. Flames were licking all around us and somehow we found ourselves by the River Elbe. I could see phosphorus dancing on the water, so for people throwing themselves into the river to get away from the fire, there was no escape. There were bodies everywhere and the gasmasks that people were wearing were melting into their faces. The massive throng of people was moving aimlessly and we started looking for a cellar to hide in, but in every cellar we looked into, we saw people sitting dead because the fires had sucked the oxygen out and suffocated them. I have no idea how long the hell lasted – time had no meaning when all this was going on.

I looked around and I saw the whole city in ruins. Everything, all the beautiful churches, everything was destroyed. We stood on Marshallstraße with its huge houses – now a mass of rubble with a few chimney stacks standing out. When I called out to someone I thought I knew, one of these chimneystacks fell down just from the echo of my voice. My brother had lost his sight from the heat. One eye recovered later but the other did not.

We found our father and older brother by calling out their names and together we went back to the cellar where we had first taken shelter. Inside, I saw a pile of ashes in the shape of a person. You know when you put wood into a furnace and it burns and becomes red hot and it keeps its shape with an inner glow but when you touch it, it disintegrates? That's what this was – the shape of a person but nothing left of the body. I didn't know who it was but then I saw a pair of earrings in the ashes. I knew the earrings. It was my mother.

CROSSING THE RHINE

The Ardennes offensive left Germany with little military strength with which to defend against the Allied invasion. Through February and March, Allied troops spread out along the length of the west bank of the Rhine in preparation for massed crossings.

On 7 March the Americans seized the bridge at Remagen, and General Patton's Third Army crossed the river to the south on 22/23 March, followed the next day by a British crossing, led by Montgomery to the north. Operation Varsity was the largest airborne action of the war, and with this sledgehammer blow, Germany's ultimate defeat was only a matter of time. Once in the heartland of Germany, the Allies found a shattered landscape and a people exhausted by the attrition of bombing – for them the end of the war could not come soon enough.

Brigadier James Hill
3rd Parachute Brigade
The largest and most successful airborne operation in history took place at ten o'clock on a glorious sunny morning on the 24th March 1945. That day, the Allied Airborne Corps formed a spearhead for the British and American armies that breached the formidable enemy defences on the banks of the River Rhine at Wesel.

Private James Bramwell
224 Parachute Field Ambulance, RAMC
Codenamed Varsity-Plunder, you can't imagine a more unfortunate name. We called it Varsity Blunder. There was no mystery about it – it was all in the newspapers with headlines shouting about the imminent drop. It was like a sporting event with BBC commentators waiting to send the news back to London. We were to drop in daylight, right on top of the enemy, which was news to us. When Brigadier Hill briefed the brigade, there was no hint of the horrors to come.

'No doubt you will find some Germans when you reach the ground, but you can take it from me they will be bloody frightened. Just imagine the reactions of the wretched Germans cowering in their slit trenches, when lo and behold, wave after wave of you bloodthirsty gentlemen come cascading down from the sky. What would you do in their place? But let there be no misunderstanding. If anybody does shoot at you, you will ignore him completely. You're job is to hasten to the RV and not to amuse yourself by returning his fire. And if I find any of you gentlemen going to ground, I'll come round personally and kick his bottom. If you happen to hear a few stray bullets, you needn't think they're intended for you. That, gentlemen, is a form of egotism.'

This briefing had a tonic effect. It gave exactly the right tone and in such a delightful turn of phrase.

Sergeant Dan Hartigan
1st Canadian Parachute Battalion
As we flew inland from the coast at about 1,200 feet I looked down to see a strange countryside. What I saw wasn't just a western European winter landscape, but ravaged terrain. The vegetation cover was so sparse and looked a somewhat burgundy tinge – mud oozing through turf. I'd never seen anything like it. It was quite surreal. For a few miles along the flight path and stretching towards the French coast on the Channel, as far as the eye could see, were hundreds of thousands of crater rings. There were so many it appeared almost incomprehensible. Yet there they were, sullen on the surface of this ravaged landscape. We had heard of no heavy-artillery attacks in this area, certainly nothing of this concentration of fury. Then it dawned on us quietly that we were flying over the World War I battlefields. It was a sobering sight, which filled us with melancholy for the suffering which must have gone on down there. Yet here we were 26 years after that last war ended, going to fight the same enemy. It took some time to come back to reality.

Flight Lieutenant Malcolm Guthrie
296 Squadron, RAF, 38 Group, 2nd Tactical Air Force
The job of flying the aircraft with a glider on was very much simpler than the job the glider crews had in actually controlling their glider while they were being towed. On take-off, one had to hook up and then inch forward very carefully until you got a taut rope. It necessitated an extremely long take-off. The glider was airborne at about 60 or 70 knots, long before the aircraft was, and that assisted in bringing the tail up. The glider went to what was called the 'high tow' position – that was above the aircraft – and stayed there during take-off and generally during flight. So, on take-off, the glider would become airborne, the tail would come up – but the aircraft appeared to linger for an awfully long time at well below take off speed. Then, the other problem was engine overheating. You had to watch the engine temperatures very carefully because you were flogging them at full-rated boost for almost twice as long as you would in a normal take-off. On top of that, if you had the slightest drop in

power, you had to make a pretty rapid decision whether to cast off the glider. We had an intercom cable running down the centre of the towrope, so the tug was in communication with the glider. The most spectacular casualty I saw was when I happened to be looking on the port quarter at a Halifax towing a Hamilcar glider at the moment the Hamilcar caught a direct hit on the tail. It blew the tail off the glider and I remember seeing the glider sag – but for an instant it remained on tow. During that instant, the tank that was in the glider, rolled out. I saw the tank falling and the glider breaking up. The Halifax was also hit and within moments the whole starboard wing was ablaze. The wing folded very quickly and the aircraft just rolled over and went down.

Major Tod Sweeney
2nd Battalion, Oxfordshire and Buckinghamshire Light Infantry

Quartermaster Bill Allsop shouldn't have been flying into action – he was quite old, about forty, but the commanding officer wanted him there. As his glider was coming in to land, he saw first the left-hand pilot slump over his joystick and then the right-hand pilot do the same. They had both been shot, and the glider was hurtling down to the ground. So he pushed one of them aside, and had a guess at what he should do. He sat down and as the glider plunged towards earth, he pulled the joystick back. He had no idea how to apply the brake or the rudder or anything else, but at least he straightened the glider out and it landed and ran on before coming safely to rest.

He spent the rest of the day sat in our headquarters without saying a single word. He was in shock – absolutely devastated by what had happened. The commanding officer had a sense of humour and put him in for a Distinguished Flying Cross. He didn't get it.

Corporal Doug Morrison
1st Canadian Parachute Battalion

As soon as I dropped with the rest of the Canadians I set up my Vickers near the south-west corner of a field close to the drop zone. There was a farmhouse about 200 yards to our front, and for most of the afternoon it was occupied by the Jerries. A glider came down in front of the house and as the troops jumped out, the Jerries picked off the first three or four. Although we fired away with our Vickers, they were out of the line of fire.

The remainder of the men inside the glider stayed there, but were subjected to a steady stream of fire from the farmhouse. The thin shell of the glider didn't give them any protection. I sent a runner to our rear, where we had a three-inch mortar position, to ask them to lay down smoke between the glider and the farmhouse to give the men in the glider some protection. But after ten minutes we still hadn't got any smoke and the situation was now pretty desperate. Then without a word to anyone, Corporal Chambers jumped up and took off across the open field towards the glider. He was under fire from the time he began his dash, was knocked down once, but got up and kept going until he reached the glider. He took out a smoke-grenade, pulled the pin and tried to throw it over the glider towards the farmhouse. Unfortunately, the phosphorus-grenade didn't clear the wing and rolled back down close to him and exploded. It spewed molten phosphorus all over him. He had a fair amount on his face and in his hair. His helmet had fallen off when he was hit and went down on his run out to the glider. We could see him rolling around on the ground, scooping up handfuls of earth and putting it on his face and hair to extinguish the phosphorus burning him.

I felt helpless, because all I could do was keep firing at the house, but I couldn't hit the enemy troops who kept up a steady stream of fire on the glider. Suddenly, Charlie Clarke jumped up and raced towards the glider. He was hit before he was halfway there, but he too got up and managed to make it to the partial protection of the fuselage. Just then the mortar platoon finally laid down smoke between the glider and the farmhouse, so a number of us went out and brought back everyone, including John Chambers and Charlie Clarke who were handed over to the medics. Clarke soon died, but Chambers recovered.

Captain Richard Smith
2nd Battalion, Oxfordshire and Buckinghamshire Light Infantry
I'll never forget that day. It was the 24th March 1945 and I was in a headquarters glider, which carried a great deal of equipment and a few men.

When we took off it was a lovely morning, and we had a perfect flight up to the Rhine itself because Monty's armies had reached the Rhine, so we had control of the land below us. But as soon as we crossed the Rhine – and our purpose was to attack the gun emplacements about 11 miles the other side of the Rhine to prevent them from shelling the Rhine crossing which was to take place that day – we met the most incredible flak which was supposed to have been neutralised beforehand by the RAF.

When we eventually came near to the landing zone and Hamelken railway station, which was to be our RV, we experienced really heavy flak and the front of the aircraft was hit by a shell. The first pilot was wounded in the shoulder, and then the rear of the aircraft was struck. I heard one or two of the signallers screaming. Much more ominous was the fact that the jeep started to catch fire. It was smouldering and we had full petrol tanks on board, and all this three-inch mortar ammunition in the trailer behind. Suddenly, I felt a loud explosion and a tug on my side. The second pilot said, 'I think we should put this thing down very quickly, sir.' I told him to get down asap. We had a smooth approach and bumped along the field. The only problem was that, by this time, the glider was well on fire. Also, we were being shot at by small-arms fire. I distinctly remember hearing the bullets ping off the bonnet of the jeep.

I got up and hauled the door up, and to my relief, found an empty German slit trench about five yards away. I dived into that, hotly followed by the signals sergeant. By the time I realised where we were, the two pilots had scrambled out on the other side of the glider and had run into a farmhouse, ten yards from them. Unfortunately the signallers in the back were trapped, and they were burned to death. We could hear them screaming, but there was nothing we could do.

The glider was blazing furiously and the ammunition inside was exploding, so it was extremely dangerous to put your head above ground. At this juncture, a German tank, preceded by two motorcyclists, came screaming down the road. There was a German officer standing up in the cupola and he saw the glider blazing a matter of a few yards from him – so he came to a halt. His motorcyclist dived into the ditch and then, to my astonishment, he gave an order which I could hear quite distinctly. The gun of the tank swung round and fired straight into the nose of the glider, which was almost disintegrating with the fire. He then saw me and the signals sergeant standing up. I remember having a faint desire to surrender. I put my right hand up, which had a revolver, and waved it at him. He shouted an order, and the tank's gun swung round, and it was obviously going to shoot at us. So I shouted to the sergeant to get down. We both went down at the bottom of the trench, and the gun of the tank couldn't depress itself low enough to shoot at us. It was too near, and the shot went over the slit trench and landed on the ground behind us – the blast was tremendous.

I looked up to find that the German officer had shouted another order – looked at me, waved his hand and drove off with his motorcyclist in an endeavour to get away from the landing zone. By this time I'd had enough, so I shouted to the medical sergeant to get out of the trench and run to the farmhouse – which we did. How many times we were fired at, I just don't know, but we would have beaten all records for the sprint. We charged into the courtyard of the farmhouse, only to be confronted by a solitary German paratrooper – the First Parachute Division was defending that area. We bumped into him and I remember feeling absolutely no fear at that time. The poor fellow was unarmed, and we got him on the ground. The sergeant said, 'Get off him, sir,' and fired his sten gun into the German. This was a Saturday morning, and the paratrooper was unarmed and it seemed that he was at the farmhouse to see his girlfriend, because at that moment, a young girl appeared from an underground shelter in the courtyard, saw her boyfriend lying dead on the floor and went absolutely berserk and charged at us. We had considerable difficulty in bundling her down into the same underground shelter – where we locked her in.

We then thought it was time to find out whether there was anybody in the farmhouse, because although I'd seen the glider pilots disappearing that way, I wasn't sure that they were in there. So we searched the farmhouse and found nothing until we came to a trapdoor in the kitchen. I lifted the trapdoor up and I went down the stairs to find the two glider pilots lying behind some bags of potatoes, with their Sten guns over the top of the bags. One of them said to me that he would have shot me had he not recognised my gaiters. We then found some champagne in the cellar and we drank that – which made us feel much better.

I went out on to the road and there met Huw Wheldon, later of television fame, who was commanding a company of Ulster Rifles and Devons, who were literally lying in rows on the ground, doing some sort of ostrich trick. Then I proceeded down the railway track to Hamelken railway station. There I saw our commanding officer, who was moving with surprising agility, being chased by a 20 mm gun, which was spattering the walls of the railway station just behind him. It was rather like a Wild West scene.

The regiment had lost 101 dead on the landing zone, and 356 wounded – along with a lot of our ammunition, mortars and light anti-tank guns. What was left of the regiment was placed in defensive positions, and by the evening, the Germans had recovered from the shock of the landing and had started to become aggressive. They must have realised that we were weak. One of our platoons was overrun – we had to blow up the bridge at Ringenburg because the tanks were trying to rush through us. Altogether we had a rather unpleasant twenty-four hours. Next evening, Monty's 21st Army Group arrived and we handed over our positions to them.

Corporal Derek Glaister
The Parachute Battalion

When we got to the Rhine, myself and ten others came down near a farmhouse which had an 88 mm gun just outside it. Just before my feet touched the ground a bullet smashed through my left elbow, so I lay on my stomach and pretended to be dead. I saw nine of the others come down – some into trees. The Germans shot them as they hung there helpless – it was a sickening sight. I was in big trouble. I am left-handed and my left arm was useless. But when five Germans came towards me I got my Sten gun in my right hand and as they got close I fired and I think killed them all. Then I made for the farmhouse, hoping to get some help – but as I peered round a corner I saw German rifles poking out of every window. I tried to give myself some cover by throwing a smoke bomb, but just as I was making for the nearest ditch, a German SS officer came up and shot me in the back from ten yards with a Luger pistol. I spun round and fell down, and this officer grabbed my left arm and shoved it through the straps of my webbing, then he took hold of my water bottle, flung it in the ditch and looted whatever he could. I was worried that he'd finish me off with my knife but I had the presence of mind to lie on it and when he'd gone I got hold of it and threw it in the ditch. I lay there feeling pretty rough – my left arm was like a great black pudding by then, all swollen up – and watched those poor fellows swinging in the trees. Then one of our gliders came over, but the 88 mm cracked it open like an egg and the jeep, gun, blokes all fell out. Point-blank range – they couldn't miss at 50 feet.

Towards the evening I was still lying there, in one hell of a bloody mess. I was finding it difficult to breathe because the second bullet had touched my lungs. Then a couple of captured airborne soldiers came by – a glider pilot and Lance Corporal Butler from my own battalion – and they asked their German escort if they could pick me up. So they gave me a shot of morphine, which helped, and put me in this wheelbarrow. They carted me along in this farm wheelbarrow along a bumpy old road, until the Germans took them away for interrogation and I was wheeled on to a big mansion near Hamelken. At dusk a German lorry came along and two Jerries picked me up like a sack of spuds and dumped me in the back of the truck on top of some dead blokes sewn up in sacks. They must have thought I was dead. That was the first time I fainted – my wounds had opened up and were bleeding again.

I came to in a German toilet with my head near the pan. That was where all my troubles started. Two orderlies took me into an operating theatre and pulled my clothes off, which was very painful. They'd just been operating on some chap and they slithered me straight on to the aluminium table which was still covered in his blood. Then they put an ether mask over my face and out I went. I woke up five days later, my arm in a Nazi salute in plaster and paper bandages all around my back. No medicines or antibiotics. My back had opened up again as the stitches had come apart, so I was carried off to be restitched. When we got to the top of some massive stairs I was tipped off – deliberately I'm sure. I landed at the bottom on my head, breaking my nose and smashing the plaster. There was a hell of a row about it and those orderlies didn't appear again. They stitched me all up again and put another plaster on, still in a Nazi salute. Then they had a go at my nose with no anaesthetic. They probed about pulling bits of bone out but they went too close to my eye and damaged it so I've got permanent pain and double vision from that.

I lay in that hospital until the British arrived. They flew me over to the RAF Hospital at Wroughton and sent for my wife and parents as they didn't expect me to live. My father was also in hospital at the time, having his leg amputated as a result of World War I. When my mother and wife came into the ward they walked right past my bed – they didn't recognise me. I had pneumonia by then, so they put in a tube to drain off the fluid and sent me by ambulance to an orthopaedic unit. The tube came out in the ambulance, so they just pushed it in again, nearly choking me when it reached my lungs. When at last they got around to getting the German plaster off, one of the nurses fainted; the stench was bad enough, but the plaster was full of maggots, put in by the German doctor to eat the dead flesh. No wonder it itched. A surgeon took one look at my arm and said, 'Off' just like that. But there was a lady doctor, Miss Wagstaff, who said she'd like to have a go at saving it, since I was left-handed. The surgeon said it would take years and still might not work, but they tried. It took three years in hospital and 55 operations to get me where I am now, which is 80 per cent disabled.

Captain John McKerchar
5th Reconnaissance Regiment

We crossed the Rhine just south of the Dutch border and it was an extraordinary sight. It was on a long pontoon bridge with Bailey construction girders all running across the Rhine – a wonderful engineering feat. We were going through all this flat farmland – you saw all these broken gliders which had ferried the troops across, all the parachutes hanging in the trees. You saw hundreds of livestock, swollen, on their backs with their legs in the air.

We went quickly because we wanted to catch up with the war. Those were our orders. We stopped that first night in beautiful woodland. Our orders were that we were not to fraternise or to despoil the land in any way. The strict order also went out that we weren't supposed to kill chickens, but as we were sitting in this farmhouse having dinner one night, we heard a bang. One of the lads had shot a chicken and it caused an almighty row.

Far more of a concern was the fact that during a patrol a few days later, our leading armoured car got brewed up. A bazooka went through it and set fire to the petrol. The whole thing went up, blazing terribly, and the men inside were trapped. Somehow, they'd left the wireless on and the switch was depressed so the whole terrible scene of these chaps struggling to get out and burning to death was played out on the radio. It was quite dreadful.

Corporal Eric Lord
5th Battalion, Coldstream Guards

Once we were across the Rhine and progressing through Germany, we came across lots of Germans fleeing. Once, we passed a convoy of horses and carts and a young girl was sitting on top of one cart with all her possessions on the cart behind her. She stared at me with a look of cold hatred. I knew a bit of German so I called at her, '*Denken sie an . . .*' to tell her to remember Poland and France and Russia and the terrible things the Germans had done. She carried on staring at me, full of hate.

Major Peter Carrington
2nd Armoured Battalion, Grenadier Guards

The Germans were very, very good soldiers to the last. After the Rhine crossing, we had 15th Panzer Grenadier Division in front of us, fighting a rearguard action all the way to the very end of the war, in circumstances in Germany when they must have known that they were going to lose the war and had very little hope. Yet they fought absolutely magnificently with great courage and skill. Looking back, I did at this time commit a war crime. We commandeered a house, and left tanks and jeeps by the house. I woke up in the morning to see the son of the house putting sticks of explosive under my jeep. I considered that an unfriendly act so I came down and said to the people in the house, 'You have half an hour to take everything out of your house, and then I'll burn it down.' After half an hour, I asked my CSM to put jerry cans of petrol all round the house and I threw in a match. The match went out and we let the son of the house go. The fact is that I did not feel sorry for the Germans. They had proved enormously inconvenient and this was the sixth year of the war. I don't think we behaved badly. We behaved rather well. We helped ourselves to one or two things which we shouldn't have. I found a marvellous Mercedes, which in the jargon of those days, I 'liberated'. The Divisional Commander saw me with it and said, 'Where did you get that?' When I told him I had liberated it, he said, 'That's the most disgraceful thing I've ever heard. Send it immediately to Div HQ.' The next day I saw him riding in it.

Corporal Eric Lord
5th Battalion, Coldstream Guards
As we moved forward, the tanks would lead the way for so long and then the infantry would take over. There were some very strong points of resistance from the Germans. They were fighting for their homeland. Some of our chaps were saying, 'Why don't the silly bastards give up?' but they had no intention of giving up. I nearly came to grief in one German town. Our platoon was detailed to make an attack from the flank on foot. We entered from the suburbs and unfortunately, I found that I was leading the way. Dashing across the road with my Sten gun, I occupied the entrance to the house and as I wasn't fired on, I gave the OK for the rest of the platoon to follow me. I went upstairs to look for a vantage point but when I came down again, just one of the guardsmen was still there. The others had moved off, he said, so we waited together by a low wall at the side of the house. A minute later we saw some of our own tanks coming towards us at a distance and at that precise moment, a sixth sense came into play and I yelled at the guardsman to get down. We ducked behind the wall and literally a second later, the masonry came alive as a hail of bullets hit the wall. We'd have been neatly cut in half if I hadn't yelled. Goodness knows why I did. Never mind the Germans, it was easy enough to be killed by your own side.

Captain John McKerchar
5th Reconnaissance Regiment
We came to a farm area which looked suspicious. Before we went any further, I shot one of our cannon shells through the farmhouse window. Immediately, a white flag came out. There were three Germans inside with a bazooka – an anti-tank weapon rather like a sort of club with a mace at the end. When we got inside the farmhouse, one of my sergeants found another bazooka. He was infuriated and smashed it against a tree. The thing blew up and wounded him badly. Emotions did run rather high at the time. A bit further on we found a village which had been 'fortified' by German troops. They'd knocked holes from one house to the next and made the village into a little fortress where they were able to move undetected between houses. In the battle for that village, our colonel lost an eye and ended up being decorated – with the MC, I think. I didn't get an MC. On the other hand, I didn't lose an eye either.

Sergeant George Teal
Tank Commander, Coldstream Guards, Guards Armoured Division
We avoided Hamburg and stopped outside a town called Rotenburg, where we could see the Jerries walking about looking at us at the end of the road. Eventually, we moved in. My officer told me to take a row of houses, so I went in one house and said, 'Get all the civvies out. We're taking over this row of houses,' but inside the house was a man and a woman with a blind little girl. I think she'd been born blind and that melted my heart, so I said to the woman, 'Your husband better get out but you can stay in the cellar and keep out of sight of the officers.' She was terrified – she thought we were going to do her.

Eventually she calmed down and a couple of days later there was a knock on the door and a young lad in German uniform was stood there, about 15 or 16 years old, and he was her son. He'd been taken prisoner in Denmark by the British who'd kicked him off his backside and said, 'Go home!' and he'd walked back from Denmark. His mother was delighted, but when he came in and took his jacket and shirt off, he was alive with bloody lice – like all the German soldiers, because they didn't have DDT. So I said, 'Go outside!' and his mother said, 'No,' but I said, 'No, he has to. Lice cause typhus!' We stripped him bollock-naked, poor lad, burnt his uniform and dusted him with DDT from head foot. He had little scratch marks over his entire body. Covered in them.

Corporal Terry Boyne
A Squadron, 2nd Fife and Forfar Yeomanry
As we advanced through Germany, we arrived at Lübeck – which was an open city – about the last one to fall. Hundreds of Germans were handing themselves in to us because the Russians were on the other side and they chose us over them. They were coming in all sorts of vehicles to surrender – horses and carts – even a fire engine on one occasion. They were marching in and throwing their arms down. There were also released and escaped British ex-prisoners of war wandering around. As we were advancing, the Germans were marching them back and some were escaping or being left behind. They were flitting about, arming themselves and looking for their ex-guards to take some revenge. A lot of these chaps had been captured in 1940 and they didn't even recognise our uniforms. Once, when I'd left my tank and I was going back to my squadron, I turned round to see four chaps running towards me, waving their arms and hollering. They were RAF men who'd slipped out of a group that was being marched back from a prison camp. They'd climbed up to hide in the trees and they'd seen us arrive, but they couldn't recognise our

uniforms so they spent hours trying to listen out for our voices to work out who we were.

Many people got into the warehouses around Lübeck which held a lot of brandy and goodies. Tanks would back into the warehouses and the doors would just fall open. Once in the middle of a very noisy action, the co-driver of my tank suddenly called out, 'Won't be a minute,' and he dived out of the Comet tanks and ran out towards a shop. High on the shop's shelves were a load of bottles and he grabbed a few, stuck them under his arm and dived back into the tank headfirst. 'Look what I got!' he said and we moved off again. When the action was over, we opened one of these bottles and it was full of vinegar. All that effort for vinegar. People weren't really getting drunk at this stage, but it was nice to have it in stock because the end was in sight.

Bombardier Martin Addington
Royal Artillery, attached to Marine Commando
I can remember one town we went through. As soon as they saw our green berets, they shouted out, 'Churchill's butchers!' and slammed the doors and windows and bars. They were scared of us. They thought we were like the SS, I think. They must have heard terrible rumours about the Commandos. We'd been through so much, we just took it. One particular incident I'll never forget. One of our mates got mail – which was very rare – he got mail from home to say that his whole family had been bombed and killed. Well, that sent him berserk. They shouldn't have given him the letter – but not knowing, they should have opened it first. The first thing he did was to burst into a house. We followed him. He burst in on this family, lined them all up in a bedroom and held them at gun-point. Then he went through their belongings shouting, 'You've got this! My wife never had this! What's this? My kids never had this!'

Frederick Riches
Ambulance Driver, Royal Army Service Corps
I drove a small ambulance and the orderly was sitting at the side of me. He said to me, 'Coo Fred, what a blooming smell!' This was any amount of different smells all mixed into one. It was really horrible and we put our handkerchiefs across our faces. As we drove on, it finally started to ease off and three miles down the road we stopped in a field, where an officer came towards us and saw our handkerchiefs out. 'What you passed just now is a concentration camp.'

416

THE CAMPS

Sergeant Alan Brewster
58th Light Anti-Aircraft Regiment, Royal Artillery
We came up to these marvellous wrought-iron gates, which the Germans opened for us to let us in. I think they'd been disarmed by now, they didn't have any rifles, and we drove in and these inmates, all in their striped uniforms, looked up at us. They were lying around on the ground. They had terrible sunken eyes and they put their hands out to try and touch us as we went past. It was a complete shock to us. We didn't have the faintest idea.

I walked to the main building and I heard this thudding noise. I recognised it from my days in a band. It was someone putting a bass drum on the ground. I wondered where the devil it was coming from. I kept on walking and I came across all these men in their striped uniforms, lined up in front of the main building with musical instruments and they started playing 'God Save the King'. I stood stiffly to attention. Some of the inmates who were lying dying on the ground struggled to their feet, they were helping each other up and they stood to attention too. And then a couple of the inmates who were in better health ran amongst the others, taking off their caps. It was an amazing sight. At the end of the anthem, they slowly sank down to the ground again.

Bombardier Martin Addington
Royal Artillery attached to Marine Commando
There was an utter silence when we went in and saw these poor creatures crawling about and scratching. Those who had the strength ran up to you asking for food or a cigarette, with flea-bitten rags on them. They were like, if you can imagine, a skeleton with a bit of skin on, that's all. They were all ages – men, women, kids. We couldn't speak to them. We were too choked to speak.

Corporal Frederick Riches
Ambulance Driver, Royal Army Service Corps
We saw what the Germans were doing to the inmates – we thought why didn't they just shoot them in the first place? For a start, there were no regular meals. All the Germans used to do was fetch a tip truck with turnips in it and upend it and let the inmates fight amongst themselves. We watched them doing it when we first got in. We saw Kramer, the chief, and Irma Grese, the second-in-command, giving the turnips away. As people were fighting to get to them, Kramer and Grese were pushing some away and letting others get them. And this is what we were *allowed* to see. Before Kramer and Grese were taken away,

we made them eat the same way. We put turnips at one end of the camp for them and made them go and get them. 'Oh, we're not going to eat them!' they said. 'Sorry,' we said, 'you've got to. You let other people eat them. Now it's your turn.' 'We're prisoners of war,' they said, 'we want proper food.' 'No,' we said, 'you get what we give you, same as you treated the others.'

David Bradford
British volunteer medical student at Belsen

A lot of them were starving. They hadn't had solid food for a long time and the only thing you could give them was fluid to get them used to it. A lot of them had been in the camp for a number of years but I think the reason why Belsen was so bad was that as the British advanced from the West and the Russians advanced from the East, many inmates were being brought into this part of Germany and so the numbers were swollen by people from other camps. At Bergen, which was the military establishment in the next village to Belsen, there was a room which was full of watches which had been taken from the inmates. There was another room full of human hair because they were nearly all shaved – their hair was cut off before they were incinerated. There was another room full of other trinkets. It was beyond imagination. In our little hutted hospital, we had a family come in – two brothers and a sister all under twenty. The girl had been looking after her two brothers but then one of the brothers died and she clung on to him. She clung on and she wouldn't let go and eventually several of us had to drag her off his body so that we could take his corpse outside.

Leslie Clarke
British volunteer medical student at Belsen

Every morning at Belsen, you had to go through a hut where you were covered in DDT. Literally covered. Hats off, blow it in your hair, up your sleeves and down your trousers. They were worried we would get lice, which they believed spread typhus. After you'd been sprayed, you walked on, you saw a dusty array of wooden huts, separated down the middle by a sort of dirt track, barbed wire keeping people where they were supposed to be. Then you saw this vast mass of people shuffling. Nobody seemed to lift their feet – nobody seemed to have the strength. From time to time, you came across people who were obviously dead. Everyone was emaciated. The smell was unmistakable. I can't describe it, but it was quite unmistakable.

Marjorie Ashbery
British member of the Friends' Relief Service
The inmates from Belsen were sent through a procedure known as 'The Human Laundry'. Ambulances brought them into one end of this great building where their clothes were taken off, they were shaved of all their hair and bathed. Then they came out at the other end and were taken to an area we called Harrods where they were clothed if they were well enough. If not, they were taken in clean ambulances to the hospital area. Some were put into beds, others on to the ground on straw mattresses. They were so thin. I remember once a doctor called me over as he was examining an inmate. He told me to put my hand on the man's stomach. I did and I could feel his spine through his stomach.

John Dixey
British volunteer medical student at Belsen
There were enormous open graves at Belsen and standing in them were German guards who were being ordered to straighten out the bodies and lay them in rows as they were bulldozed in. It's a powerful image, but it wasn't as horrifying as you might reasonably expect it to be, because it was on such an enormous scale. I've often thought about this over the years. If it had been several hundred bodies, one might have been really, desperately upset and affected by it mentally and psychologically. But no – it was on such a huge scale it was rather like trying to count the stars. There were thousands and thousands and thousands of dead bodies and how could you relate to them as people? You couldn't consider them to be your aunt or your mother or your brother because there were just too many.

Sergeant Alan Brewster
58th Light Anti-Aircraft Regiment, Royal Artillery
The arrangement was that five days after we got to Belsen, all the German soldiers who had been left behind would be taken back to their own lines. They were mainly older soldiers who had been left behind to make sure that the prisoners didn't get out into the fatherland and start spreading diseases. But we didn't know how we were going to get these soldiers back to their front line because our front line had gone way past the River Elbe. We also had lots of Germans coming towards us giving themselves up. There wasn't much point taking the other ones back to their lines. So, when the time came to take them to their lines, we stopped in this lane to let them relieve themselves and they came out of the trucks and ran straight across the fields. Nobody

BU4002

As Allied troops drove through Germany, they discovered the horror of the Nazi concentration camps. At Belsen, a British soldier talks to English-born Louis Bonerguer, who was captured and interned after parachuting into Germany to work under cover in 1941.

stopped them. I don't know where they went to after that. We were only too pleased to see the back of them.

The inmates got a bit naughty with some of these German soldiers who were left behind. The soldiers had been disarmed and at night time you could hear these screams in the distance. On one occasion, in the middle of the night, there was a banging on our door and a big strapping German officer stumbled in, wearing only a pair of trousers. His back was absolutely black and blue – it looked as though he'd been hit with an iron bar. Some of the prisoners must still have had some strength and they'd caught him out and he was in a mess. Ironically, he'd come to us for help.

Captain Philip Stein
2nd Battalion, Glasgow Highlanders

I can remember being absolutely enraged by the reluctance of prosperous well-fed German families, even to give up a blanket for the concentration-camp survivors. I remember trying to talk to one or two Germans there, and everyone protested they didn't know about the camp. You could smell the bloody place, and like most Germans during the war, they turned their heads away. OK, they were frightened – but they didn't want to know.

I certainly felt, when I saw some of the people coming out of the camp, that I wouldn't particularly want to intervene if they decided to beat or hang any of their old guards.

Captain Richard Smith
2nd Battalion, Oxfordshire and Buckinghamshire Light Infantry

The first thing I saw was a whole collection of German guards, stripped to the waist, barefooted, with no belts, carrying corpses from the pits where they'd been flung into a newly-formed burial ground on the other side of the road. The Germans were being beaten by the British guards with their rifle butts. I went into the headquarters established by the provost who was in charge of the camp, and the major who was there said, quite honestly, 'I have no control over my troops.'

We were taken in to see the camp commandant, Kramer, who was known as 'the Beast of Belsen', and that woman Irma Grese. He was eventually hanged. The woman had obviously been given a beating. It was the most extraordinary few hours and I've never forgotten it.

It has to change your attitude to the Germans. I remember a day or two later, in Celle, in the market square, the British authorities had taken these photographs of Belsen and had put them up on the notice boards to show the population what had been going on under their very noses. An old woman was looking at these photographs – she'd come out to get a few potatoes or whatever it was. She didn't know I was behind her, and when she was looking at these photographs showing the corpses in these communal graves and skeletons, and God knows what, she said, 'Ah – propaganda.' I just seized her by the back of the neck, pushed her face into the photographs and said it wasn't propaganda. I lost my temper. Yes, you're bound to be affected by things like that. You can't possibly escape being affected. The thing that everybody asked was how on earth could a massive camp of that type be fed and watered without the population nearby knowing? It's almost unbelievable. But when you asked any German, they said they didn't know what was going on. It was a stock answer.

Herbert Holewa
German paratrooper, prisoner of the British

Whilst I was a prisoner of war, held by the British at Market Rasen, we were shown films of the atrocities that had been taking place in concentration camps. People say that as Germans, we must have known what had been going on. We did not. I remember from years before, a chap I knew had been sent to a concentration camp and when he came back, I asked him about it. He said, 'We got up in the morning, had morning sport, then we had breakfast, then schooling, then we had lunch, then a rest,' and so on. He was obviously afraid to tell the truth. If he'd told us then he'd have been sent back again and he'd never have come out. People who knew did not speak – to preserve their own lives. It's diabolical but that's how it was. We knew of the existence of concentration camps – we knew of Dachau and Bergen-Belsen. In '41 and '42 I was in an army camp at Bergen with a fantastic barracks and a cinema but there were no rumours going around about the conditions at the concentration camp. None. None. None. So when the British authorities told us about what happened . . . when we were shown the films . . . we could not believe it was true.

Clare Parker
Inmate, Mauthausen concentration camp

For us, liberation was just these American soldiers who had no food on them, who found us accidentally. They were driving past and they saw these people through the gate. As they had nothing on them, they didn't know what to do, you know. The only thing they had on them was cigarettes and so they gave us each a cigarette and we tried to eat them, I didn't know what they were. I was a child – I just didn't know.

LIBERATION AND OCCUPATION

Captain John MacAuslan
Intelligence Officer, 5th Reconnaissance Regiment
As we moved on we entered Neustadt and it was a most extraordinary sight. There were a lot of drunk Russians looting and burning the town. They were prisoners who had been freed by the Allies and they'd found a liquor store. It was chaos – total chaos. The main square was full of drunken Russians, terrified Germans and houses on fire. Then we found the concentration camp and that was horrific. I don't know how many people were in it – several thousand – and a great many of them hadn't had any food or water for eight days. They were totally dehydrated and when they walked – those that did walk – they were like marionettes in those dreadful costumes they had to wear – pyjamas with a bluish thick stripe and white in between. They were a lot of walking skulls. We tried to feed them and we also had to prevent them from leaving the camp. We tried to get them to organise themselves and tell us what they wanted. We got them to drink and made soup for them. None of the Germans would help at all.

The hospital refused point blank to take any of the concentration camp prisoners – until we made them do it. The most horrifying place in Neustadt was the beach. The Germans had barges into which they'd packed prisoners. They then took the ladders away and machine-gunned them. These barges were packed with women and children who had been shot. And there were several hundred little children who had been clubbed. The bodies lay in front of us. Little children with their heads caved in. They were tied back to back with cords through their mouths and beaten to death. And not by the SS. These children had been murdered by ordinary German marines. A little later, we stopped at a little manor house owned by a German – a sort of minor squire – and he said to me, 'Come and look at my books.' I told him I wouldn't understand them. He said, 'I'll translate them for you. I've got Goethe and Dickens.' He was obviously being friendly but I said no. He asked why not and I said because of what I'd seen at the Neustadt camp. I asked him, 'Did you know what went on?' He said, 'Yes. Not in detail but in fact we did. But I had a wife and two small children and they would have been sent to a camp if I'd done anything. Do you think you would have done anything?' That, of course, is a very difficult question to answer. 'I don't know,' I said.

Private James Bramwell
224 Parachute Field Ambulance, RAMC
In Wismar on the Baltic coast we took over a Luftwaffe hospital. Our greatest problem was trying to stop the Russians from attacking the German nurses.

Helene Leach
Resident of Dresden
We could hear the firing of the guns for a day or two and we were hoping that the Americans would occupy Dresden because they were not very far away at all – but they just stopped dead still. In the meantime, the Russians came nearer and nearer. It was about two o'clock in the afternoon when the first Russians came in by tank. They seemed all right. They looked quite normal apart from being a bit dirty. But after a few hours, when the infantry moved in, well, I'd never seen anything like it, especially when they'd had all the wine and spirits they found in the cellar of the hotel where I worked.

We knew there'd be a problem, so we'd warned our boss to get rid of the alcohol. We'd even volunteered to work the whole night through dumping it in the river – but he wanted to hang on to it. He thought he'd be able to sell it. But as soon as the Russians arrived, they asked him for the key to the cellar. He told them he didn't know where it was. 'No problem,' they said and they bashed the door in with their bayonets. Then it really started. You've never seen anything like it. They drank out of the bottles and in no time most of them were absolutely rotten drunk. Everything was smashed up – barrels of fish and sauerkraut tipped all over the hotel – you name it. The hotel was swimming in brine and alcohol. Then they started looking for women – and that's when the nightmare really began. They first helped themselves to their own Russian girls who were working in the hotel – they were mostly fifteen or sixteen years old but that didn't matter. All the French girls and a couple of Belgian girls ran together to where we thought we were safe. The Russians were saying, 'It doesn't matter, French or what, women are women.' Some women living nearby the hotel were raped six or seven times.

Waltraudt Williams
Civilian in Berlin
By the 26th April – my birthday – the fighting was getting nearer and nearer to Berlin. We were beginning to hear it and we also heard of street fights over areas we knew by name that made us realise it was only a matter of time. Little bands of German soldiers and SS and tanks were trying to join together to continue the fight or perhaps to get away from it. I knew some who were

trying to escape and they were asking for civilian clothes – which we gave them. By this time, we had no water and had not had a thing to eat for ten days and all we could do was sit in our cellar and wait. It wasn't safe to be in the house as the Russian planes were strafing.

I remember a German army lorry standing right outside where we lived. An elderly German lady who was one of the tenants had spent all night praying on her knees and she rushed into the house shouting, 'Meat! Meat! They've brought us meat! I've seen it in the lorry outside!' Some of us went out to look and we saw her meat. It was a lorry full of dead soldiers and what she'd thought was meat was the blood dripping through the floorboards of the lorry. At the time, we felt that Berlin should surrender but we knew they wouldn't. Goebbels has been quoted as saying, 'When we bang the door behind us, the whole world will hear.' We knew that wasn't an empty threat – that they could carry it out, they could finish us all. They tried to turn all sorts of people into soldiers – they gave men over seventy Belgian rifles and they issued children with the Panzerfaust. That's a terrible weapon for a child to carry on his shoulder and be sent to immobilise tanks. The Russians made good their promise to get to Berlin on 1st May, but they didn't reach us until the next day. Some of us had ideas of ending it all, but I was too much of a coward.

My Uncle Arthur came to find out whether we were still alive just after the Russians had set fire to our house. We had no way of putting the fire out, so Arthur herded us along the road to his house where there was food to be had – not much, but a little. The Russians seemed largely oblivious to the plight of the civilian population, perhaps because their own people had had far worse. Whatever food they found, they ruined deliberately. They filled bath tubs with edible food and defecated all over it. They didn't want us to have it because they didn't think we were entitled to it.

Helen Bauch
British civilian married to German physicist in Charlottenburg, Berlin
When the British troops arrived in Berlin, we heard through our secret radio in the cellar that they were coming to our part, Charlottenburg – so I put my British flag in my flowerpots and waited. I was a British woman, married to a German, and I'd spent the war in Berlin. I said to my husband, 'The British are coming and we can start to live again.' And then on Sunday morning, there was a knock on the door. I couldn't believe what I saw. It was two British officers who'd seen my British flag. You can't imagine the salvation I felt. I said, 'Good heavens, I'm so pleased to see you but I can't offer you anything. I have no tea or coffee.' They said, 'We're the advance troop. We've just come

to find billets for the army coming up behind us and we're looking around for buildings that are still standing. We have to go because we must look around and see what we can find. We'll be in touch.' They went out and that moment a German woman came running in and said, 'Mrs Bauch, those British soldiers have left a big notice on the door. What does it say?' And this notice said, 'This property has been requisitioned. Everybody to be out by 10 o'clock tomorrow morning, taking with you only what you can carry.'

I couldn't believe it. We'd been holding our breath and marking time all these years and now they'd arrived and they're throwing us out on to the street. That night we took our bicycles and went to see what the British authorities could do about it. I was wearing a British flag around my arm and I said, 'I'm British. I'd like to speak to the officer in charge of billeting,' and the British soldier pointed at my husband and asked, 'Who's he?' 'My husband,' I said. 'Is he British?' 'No.' 'Well then he can't come in.'

So I was led in alone and I was so impressed – two British officers stood up. That never happened in Nazi Germany. If you went into any German office, you were bawled at. But this was civilisation. It was heaven. The officer asked my purpose. I said, 'I'm British and I've waited all these years for the British to arrive and they've arrived now and put me on to the street with two small children.' He said, 'You knew you'd lose your British nationality when you married a German.' 'Yes,' I said, 'but when you're eighteen and you fall in love you don't think about nationality or politics. In any case I am probably more British than the royal family.'

At the end of it all, he said that as a British woman, he would allow me to take all my furniture and possessions out, but he said that they really did need my building for the Signals Division. We came home at midnight and started to pack. At ten o'clock the next morning, two army lorries arrived and the soldiers came in and packed everything. Fifteen hundred books, bookcases, beds, they packed it all. And they were so friendly. I couldn't believe it. And then the colonel ordered a nearby property that had been owned by Nazis to be requisitioned to me. It was a house round the corner that had belonged to one of the directors of Telefunken, who was someone we knew, so I went to his house and his wife was there. She was crying and she said, 'The Russians came at midnight last night and took my husband. They just rammed in the door and he's gone.' And she thought we had heard this news and had come to commiserate with her. We said we hadn't heard. The Russians were doing this. They knew the British were coming into this sector and they had taken all the eminent people out quickly – scientists and people they could use – before the British moved into the territory.

After hearing all this from her, I showed her the note that her house had been requisitioned and that I was to take occupation of it. I decided that I couldn't do that to her so I went back to the colonel and said that I couldn't take the house. I told him that it was difficult for the British to realise but not everyone who was a member of the Nazi Party was an ardent fascist. It was true. If you held any prominent position, you were obliged by law to be a member of the party. The colonel was very understanding and gave us another address belonging to the chairman of the Sunlight Soap Company. He seemed happy to go to a flat round the corner whilst we took over his villa. Which is what happened.

Major 'Tod' Sweeney
2nd Battalion, Oxfordshire and Buckinghamshire Light Infantry
We had marched all the way through Germany to the Baltic. We literally marched the entire way and I suppose we had a little battle about every ten miles when we were in the lead. Then we received instructions to get up to the Baltic as quickly as possible to cut off the Russians heading for Denmark. So for the last day of our war, instead of fighting our way along we commandeered any vehicle we could get hold of, off-loaded all our stores from the jeeps and trailers and just motored along to our objective.

All afternoon, coming past us, down the other side of the road was the German army in perfect formation, marching with their rifles properly carried, their tanks, their guns, their womenfolk and so on, getting away from the Russians. We were not taking the slightest notice of each other and yet two days before we'd been fighting. They didn't acknowledge us at all. They just kept on going. The 40 miles from just beyond the Elbe to Wismar and Lake Schwerin we covered in that one day. Within twenty-four hours of our arrival the Russians turned up.

I was deputed to take a party of our men over to the Russians to have a celebration. There were forty or fifty of us, and we went to their Brigade Headquarters, but of course we had terrible language problems, and our interpreter and theirs had to speak German to each other. We stood around and these tough-looking Russians with shaved heads came up and started showing us the collections of watches they had all the way up their arms.

The Russians cleared out a couple of houses and brought in German women to lay the table with linen tablecloths and glasses, and then we were all invited in. The senior officers and brigadier sat down and we had the British and Russian officers seated alternately around the round table, and then out in the rest of the house were the private soldiers –

Russian/British/Russian/British – all seated around. There were toasts to Stalin, Churchill and Roosevelt and we gradually got more and more drunk. By the end of two or three hours we were all well gone. All the soldiers, Russian and British, had their arms on each other's shoulders and were singing. One or two of our men became a bit difficult and wanted to kiss the Russian women, so I thought we'd better get away before they had their heads chopped off – if a chap was in too bad condition we called for stretcher bearers and took him off to his billet.

About five days later we went back across the Elbe. The Germans who had been stopped and put into camps were horrified we were going because they would be left in the Russian zone. A lot of them were trying to get away to cross the river with us.

Sergeant George Teal
Tank Commander, Coldstream Guards, Guards Armoured Division

As soon as the armistice was signed, thousands of German soldiers appeared, lining the roads. Our officer said, 'Keep your guns loaded and your fingers on the trigger. First sign of trouble, we'll mow the bastards down.' We were itchy-fingered because there was so many of them. At Cuxhaven Airfield, we had to take the surrender of the German 6th Parachute Regiment and they came marching in, wearing brand-new uniforms with flags flying, swords out. Someone wanted to present arms to them but our CO, Colonel Gooch, wouldn't allow it. They halted and their commanding officer came forward and handed over his sword and put his hand out. Colonel Gooch said, 'This has not been a football match,' and refused to shake hands.

Corporal Eric Lord
5th Battalion, Coldstream Guards

When the war ended we were issued with some rum, but there was no grand celebration. There should have been a great sense of relief. We should have had somebody to organise something. We should have had somebody to tell us to raise our mugs to the PBI – the Poor Bloody Infantry – but no-one did. I just sat there, trying to collect my thoughts, and all I could think was, 'Well that's the end of that. I don't have to dig any more slit trenches or hear the sound of the multi-barrel mortar again.'

Sergeant Alan Brewster
58th Light Anti-Aircraft Regiment, Royal Artillery

I was in Belsen on the day the war ended. I got my pass and travelled to Osnabrück, the first staging place from Belsen. I got there, managed to clamber up the stairs, got into a bunk bed and the following morning, I couldn't move. They had to come and lift me out. A Scottish doctor came to see me and told me that I had rheumatic fever. I caught it from Belsen. They took me by ambulance to a big country house. I lay on a bed with no pillows, stiff as a board. I was fed through a teapot, through the spout. And I could hear the doctors and nurses having a good time because it was VE Day. I was very cross because I was missing it all.

VE DAY

David Bradford
Medical student in Belsen

When VE Day arrived in Belsen, a lot of the inmates didn't seem to take it in at all. I think they probably couldn't see any future. What was VE Day to them? If they managed to live – well, that would be alright – but even then, what did they have to look forward to? The prospect of returning to their ruined home towns in Poland and Czechoslovakia to find their families and friends all dead.

Rolf Weinberg
Officer, French Army

I remember the day of victory. We were lodged in the Hotel l'Opéra in Paris. On that day the order came that at three o'clock in the afternoon de Gaulle would speak to us, and he came out of the Opéra together with Lily Pons, the well-known soprano, and there was an enormous multitude of people. He said Hitler was dead and that the war in Europe had ended. France was free again. It was such a moment that I fainted out of emotion. I was picked up and carried to my hotel room and a wonderful nurse was holding my hand and she said, 'You should be enjoying yourself with the others. Don't lie here. Come down and we'll have some champagne.' I said, 'You're right in a way. But for me this is not the time for a fiesta because I'm thinking of all my comrades and all of those who have been killed by this damn Nazi regime. I'm just glad that I had the chance to help to wipe the regime out.'

Ellen Harris
Reuters reporter in Parliament

I shall never forget it. I couldn't move – I couldn't do anything, whatever had happened. Although we'd known this was coming, the House of Commons itself just went into one great roar of cheers, papers went up in the air, I just sat and the tears were rolling down – it was relief after all this long time. And this kept up, the roaring and cheering and shouting for some time. And then the Speaker dissolved the House.

I came home quite early in the day and I said to my husband, 'What are we going to do?' He said, 'What do you mean, what are we going to do?' 'Well, this is a most momentous day, we can't stay home.' 'Can't we?' he said, rather surprised. 'We must go up the West End somewhere.' 'Where? It'll be so crowded.' 'Never mind let's be in the crowd.' So we went to Whitehall, Charing Cross. We got through gradually. I was underneath the Ministry of Health Balcony – thousands upon thousands of people packed tight. They shouted and shouted for Churchill. Nobody was quite certain where he was but he came out on that balcony and he threw his arms out. He said, 'God bless you all,' and said a few words. He praised them for their fortitude – they had won the war, he said. He thanked them all – it was short and sweet but lovely for the Londoners. And he finished up once more, 'God bless you all!' The cheers – it was a wonder the clouds didn't come down. It was a really most momentous occasion.

Lilias Walker
Teenager in Hull

I remember the announcement being made on the radio that, at such and such a time, the war would be over. Where people had got stuff from I don't know where, but immediately there were bonfires and everybody drew back their curtains and turned on all their lights. Every single light in the house was on because, of course, no lights had been allowed during the war.

Lady Anne Chichester
British civilian who worked with Red Cross in London

When VE Day came, there were the most amazing celebrations and a cousin of mine and a couple of boyfriends went out to Piccadilly Circus. The whole of Piccadilly was solid with people and they managed to produce flags and streamers and all the cars were hooting and everybody was singing. There was a great deal of drink around, but I never remember feeling frightened. We all moved down in a seething mass to Buckingham Palace and we all stood outside and some lights came on and this was very exciting because having had the blackout we weren't used to seeing the lights come on and everybody called and called, 'We want the King,' and out on to the balcony came the King and Queen. Everybody went absolutely hysterical.

Christabel Leighton-Porter
Model for Daily Mirror *cartoon character 'Jane'. Performed in revues throughout the war*

On VE Day I was playing the Kilburn Empire and I had to change my act very quickly so I decided to turn the finale into a semi-nude 'Rule Britannia'. I'd got hold of a big Union Jack and the local fire brigade lent me a brass fireman's hat to wear. After the show, the whole lot of us went up west to Piccadilly where everybody was going mad. It was absolutely wonderful and we stayed up all night. I went into the Savoy Hotel – you could go absolutely anywhere that night. I met so many boys that I'd met in the forces who were on leave in London. One chap, a New Zealander, with his legs in plaster, was sitting on the bonnet of a car and I went and sat there with him and we danced on the roofs of the cars and that went on for a whole week. I don't think any of us went to bed for a week. But we still did our show every night.

Sylvia Townson
Civilian in London

We had a party on VE Day. They must have closed off Fernhead Street because they had a bonfire in the middle of the road. There was lots of food because everyone gave something towards it off their coupons. I remember my father entered me for the talent contest. I belted out 'You are my Sunshine'. I came second.

Petty Officer Ronald Duquemin
Depth Charge operator, aboard HMS Mermaid

When VE Day was announced, we were anchored outside Liverpool and we all said we'd go ashore and get drunk, but instead we had to go and round up these German submarines that had surrendered. The submarines were still in the Atlantic and they had to fly a big black flag, and so we went fifteen or twenty miles out from Liverpool and escorted them in. We were still nervous that they might fire on us. The only Germans I saw were on the conning tower and we flashed a signal to them and they followed us back to port.

Sergeant Charles Pratt
Mortar Company, 1st Battalion, Middlesex Regiment

On VE Day, I was lucky. I was on leave at home in Portsmouth. I'd already met a Portsmouth girl and we celebrated together until about five o'clock in the morning. I was a bit nervous even though I was 21 because I had a strict father. I tell you, if you were in uniform, you couldn't move. You were pulled in everywhere. The best thing to do was either to stay indoors or find some civilian clothes to put on, because if you walked about in a military uniform, you just couldn't move. Parties developed all over the place. If you were down in town, you were cordially invited to have a drink and the pubs didn't close for a week. The police went blind for seven days.

Peter Bennett
Child in Godalming

On VE Day, we broke into school and stole a shirt off one of the footballers and put it on the flagpole in the local recreation ground as a form of celebration. We had VE Day parties on the village green – bonfires and later on, the following year, we got a letter from King George VI – thanking the boys and girls for coping so well during the war and reminding us what our older brothers and sisters had done for us – which was a nice thought.

I remember having oranges during VE parties – but I was sick after eating the orange peel, having no idea that wasn't what you did.

Major Peter Martin
2nd Battalion, Cheshire Regiment

On the day the war ended, I felt an incredible sense of anticlimax. From the age of 19, the German war had always been there – and suddenly it disappeared. I couldn't see much point in existence any more. My whole reason for being had suddenly gone. I can remember weeping that night and I don't think I was the only person in the Division.

Sergeant George Teal
Tank Commander, Coldstream Guards, Guards Armoured Division

After the armistice, we moved on to Hamburg. Montgomery told us that we were now off to Japan and we all muttered, 'Testicles!' under our breath. We didn't want to be off nowhere. We handed our tanks over and we became infantry again and we went to Bad Godesberg, a beautiful spa town on the Rhine, that had only once been bombed. I was billeted with a woman called Frau Suttemeister. She was an old lady whose husband had been killed during the bombing and whose sons had been killed fighting in Russia. In spite of all that she treated me like her own son.

Herbert Holewa
German paratrooper, prisoner of British

I spent the end of the war in a British prisoner of war camp. At the beginning of August 1945, our camp speaker went from hut to hut, telling us that the war was over and that Germany was decimated. He told us to pop a letter into the War Office, which would allow me to work. On the 11th August, we were put on a train and brought down to Market Rasen and were put into Working Camp 256. For the first couple of weeks, we didn't do any work but after that we started to go out in work parties to do jobs for farmers. On our third day there, we saw a forest fire on the opposite side of the road. We jumped over the three barbed wire fences to try to put it out, but after a while the fire service came and told us that they would take care of it. So they marched us back into the camp and they counted us and they counted us and they counted us again. No one had run away. The next day, they took up the three barbed wire fences and replaced them with a single wire. We were told that if we wanted to go out of the camp, we could use the gate. That was their way of thanking us and showing us that they trusted us.

After that, I remained in Britain. On the 3rd June 1946, I was billeted next door to the Brown Cow pub in Nettleham. I worked for a contractor and I built a garage. In 1947, I worked on a farm near Lincoln and in April 1949, I moved near to Doncaster. The following year, I met the woman I was to marry, a beautiful English nurse, and I have lived in this country ever since.

THE FAR EAST

BURMA

Early in 1945 the 14th Army continued its advance not in the jungle, but in the open plains of Upper Burma. In March Mandalay fell and Slim conducted a successful crossing of the Irrawaddy before heading south to Arakan. The Japanese proved a formidable enemy in denfence and there was much fierce fighting before Rangoon was taken on 3 May.

In the shell of bombed-out houses in East India Dock Road, East London, locals line the streets to greet the King and Queen as they share the celebration of VE Day.

In the heart of London's West End, in Piccadilly Circus, VE Day revellers celebrate the end of the war in Europe. Even if hard times were ahead, this was a time to join in a national outpouring of joy and relief.

Corporal Arthur Freer
Radio operator, B Squadron, 3rd Carabiniers
As the Japanese retreated, we advanced. We headed towards Shwebo through teak forest and jungle. Nothing happened until we started to get into thicker jungle. There were signs that we were catching up on the Japs. We saw food that had been left behind. I asked the squadron leader, 'Shouldn't we net in on the sets to talk to the infantry?' but he didn't do anything about it. Then we came under small arms fire from a Jap roadblock so he got out of the tank to speak to the infantry CO. That was the last we ever heard of him until a troop leader, Captain Swann, eventually called us, telling us that he was badly wounded. I took off my headset and climbed into the turret to take command of the tank. I put my head out, and I felt a heavy bang on my head, and woke up on the floor of the turret. My head was hurting, there was no blood, but a lump the size of an egg. The sniper's bullet had hit the turret outside, chipping off something which hit me, but I got away with it. I ordered the turret gunner to spray the trees above us and around. Captain Swann came on the air and said he was taking command of the squadron, and he asked me why I was firing. I told him I was trying to spray the sniper. He told me to leave him alone, the infantry would sort him. We were told to bypass the Japs and press on. The next day we burst through a Jap cookhouse, smashing a huge pot of boiling rice which burst all over the tank. We were hungry and the rice smelt delicious, but we couldn't stop. By now we were out of the jungle and smashed through the Jap roadblocks. Each day another battalion, from 2 Div, took over the lead.

Lieutenant Michael Marshall
4th Battalion, 5th Royal Gurkha Rifles
We got the word that the advance into Burma was to take place. We went from Tamu to Kalewa, down Kabaw valley, and news came that we were to march down Gangaw Valley at night as the whole movement of the division was to be kept secret. The Gangaw Valley we found to be one of the most unhealthy places in Burma. It was very hot even at night – dry and dusty. We marched 300–400 miles, which took the whole of January 1945. Marches generally started at 2200 hours and lasted for 11–12 hours. It was tiring for the British officers because Gurkhas have short legs and march at between two and three miles an hour, whereas the British Army marches at between three and four miles an hour. So it takes longer. By the time we had finished this march one could say that everyone was fit.

Corporal Arthur Freer
Radio operator, B Squadron, 3rd Carabiniers

We entered Shwebo from the north, taking a war correspondent in our tank. He had been the last British person to leave Shwebo. We came to a gateway where there was a dry moat crossed by a bridge. There was no sign of life, but there were Jap bunkers on the other side of the moat. The leading tank crossed and those behind him noticed wires leading from the bridge over the moat to the bunkers. Everybody was told to halt, and our sapper officer went forward and found some 500 kg bombs fixed for setting off by men in the bunkers, but they had been abandoned because we had sprayed the bunkers first. We went into the town, which was dead, with a few chickens running around, but no Burmese or Japs. The war correspondent produced a report which he showed me, and the only thing I could recognise were the names and addresses of the tank crew. The rest of the report was from his imagination.

Captain Frederick Rowley
5th Battalion, 10th Baluch Regiment

The advance continued as we crossed the Irrawaddy River. It was the longest swim I ever had. I was charged by my divisional commander to take my rifle company across the Irrawaddy, four miles higher than where the main crossing was to be, and we had to swim it. I had some Indian sappers who helped us build bamboo rafts to carry our weapons and kit. We also took our 18 mules. When we came to look at the Irrawaddy at close quarters it was quite a fast-flowing river, and we had to work out how far we had to start upstream to hit the bank on the other side where we wanted to be.

I took one platoon to start with, and I got across reasonably all right. I was able to signal the rest of the company to come, plus the mules. Mules are very good swimmers and we crossed dressed except for our boots. All the mules got across. I was very relieved because a mule swept away down the Irrawaddy would have given away the fact that we were there to the Japs. In fact they did not know we were there for several hours. I moved downstream to where the main crossing was to be. We joined the main bridgehead. I had a few hours rest and was summoned to Divisional HQ, to our commander Pete Rees, who said to me, 'I want you to get Pear Hill, and hold it.'

I went back and sorted out my company. We left the bridgehead, which was quite risky because the Japs had surrounded us and were potting at us, and I didn't want to get too close to where they were. I got out with my company in single file along the riverbank. Several hundred yards along, we got to the bottom of Pear Hill. I left my company at the bottom, and climbed with my Subedar Major, my orderly and my signaller. I wanted to recce and see what was up there. It was lightly wooded, very rugged, and I tried to keep as quiet as possible. At the top, there was no sign of the enemy. I turned to my Subedar Major and told him to bring the rest of the Company up. Like an idiot I had taken all my equipment off including my revolver, and suddenly I found myself looking straight at a Jap observation post position close by. I shouted to my men. The Subedar shouted 'Sahib!' A Japanese officer rushed at me with sword raised to slice my head off. He got to within three yards of me, when my Subedar Major shot him. We killed the observation post party – all of them.

I told the Subedar Major to get the company up as fast as possible, and I laid them out ready for an onslaught which we knew without question would come. I sat on a rock feeling the most appalling anguish. I was not religious at that time. But I sat saying, 'Lord Jesus what is wrong?' And I listened, the most important thing when you pray is to listen, and this is what staggered me. I got a message, not a voice, but a message, and it said, 'You're not on the top of the hill.' I thought oh my God. I walked forward. We were short of the top by about eighty yards. And there were the Jap emplacements, totally empty. I shouted to my chaps, 'Get up! Advance at once!' and we secured the place. And in due course the Japs belted us. But it would have been a massacre if we had been in the original place. We held the hill even though the Japs threw artillery at it.

Corporal Arthur Freer
Radio operator, B Squadron, 3rd Carabiniers

After Shwebo, we had a few more actions in villages in the area between the Irrawaddy and Chindwin Rivers. The tanks were wearing out, and we had tracks dropped to us by air, which we fitted within hours. Food was also dropped by air. It was announced that Christmas Day 1944 would be held on the 15th January 1945. The cooks produced some chickens and we had Christmas pudding. After that it was sorting out roadblocks again.

On one occasion we were clearing a village with a company of Royal Scots. The tanks were in the lead. I saw two Japs jump into a slit trench just ahead. The squadron leader told me to guide the driver to it. I opened my little port, just as a grenade landed beside the trench, about five feet away from my port. It was the squadron leader who had thrown the grenade. It killed the Japanese, but a splinter from the grenade had cut the wire that ran under the tank wing to the wireless aerial. The set wouldn't work. So the squadron leader ordered me out to repair it. I asked him to turn the tank sideways to give me cover.

I climbed out and with a pair of pliers, and jackknife, I looked under, found the two wires, repaired them, but not before I got a tremendous electric shock, because the Squadron Leader had started transmitting, using me as an aerial. The fighting continued and we had tiffin on the move, eating cold baked beans out of the tin. We then went back to the slit we had attacked earlier and from the Jap's bodies took the papers out of their pockets. Just then machine guns opened up and rounds cut up the ground around us. I recognised the sound of a tank Browning. We all threw ourselves to the ground. I said, 'It's one of our tanks, sir.' 'Well go and stop it,' he said.

That's when I broke the world 100-yard record. I jumped into our tank and picked up my headset to hear a troop leader say, 'I still think there's some movement there, give them another burst or two.' I said over the radio, 'Able 5, were you firing your Maggie?' 'Yes,' he said, 'I'm engaging some Japanese, over.' 'Cease firing.' I said. 'Why, over?' 'You are firing on number 9 and his crew, over.' There was a horrible hush, then, 'Wilco out.' The CO had been listening and chipped in, 'I want a report on the situation within minutes. Out.' After that, we were told we were going to cross the Irrawaddy and go on to Mandalay.

Lieutenant Peter Noakes
1st Battalion, Northamptonshire Regiment
My company was the reserve company for crossing the Irrawaddy. The attack, at night, was by 1 and 3 Companies. When number 3 got into their boats to go, the boats sank. The company commander ordered his men out and on shore. The CO was fed up and ordered me to get my boys into boats that were made available. We set off like a crocodile of rubber dinghies with an outboard motor on the front one, which kept on conking out. We were met by machine-gun and mortar-fire which was not very effective.

A couple of nights before we crossed, a young officer was sent out to the far bank in a rubber boat and told to fix an Aldis lamp with a red filter as a guide to us. The Irrawaddy current is quite fast, so navigation across at night is difficult. The red lamp was a brilliant idea. The RAF were asked to send their noisiest plane to patrol up and down the river to cover the sound of the crossing. This also seemed to work.

We waded ashore, and dug in on the beachhead. Two days later the whole battalion was across. After a few days, it was decided to extend the bridgehead, and my company was sent to a chaung, a tributary of the Irrawaddy, which was used as an observation post by Jap artillery. We turfed them out, dug in and we were shelled every day.

The area was all elephant grass, which crackles as you walk through it. The Japs attacked one night. They didn't come through the elephant grass, but up the chaung. Fortunately we heard them because they are such great chatterers. They brought up Bangalore torpedoes made of bamboo, with which they attempted to crawl up to the wire. But we never allowed them to get close enough to do that. We found a lot of Jap dead near the wire. I found one dead officer, called Lieutenant Yamamoto, beautifully dressed with a sword, which I still have. We advanced across open country, and saw no Japs until we got behind Mandalay. The Japs were evacuating the city, and we ambushed a party of them. We found a Jap who was Head Clerk of Army HQ in Mandalay, carrying a case of documents, which we passed back. We shot him, and he crawled away. We heard him moaning so I told one of my platoon commanders, 'Put him out of his misery.' As he approached, the Jap shot himself anyway.

Lieutenant-Colonel Hugh Pettigrew
GSO 1 to Major-General 'Punch' Cowan, 17th Division
As we moved forward, Punch Cowan had a real rush of blood to the head, because he cut straight across country with the whole of Div HQ. It was highly exhilarating, the whole lot in jeeps, signals trucks etc. driving over fields, and leaping over bunds. We reached a road just as it was getting dark, cut back along it to regain the main road to Meiktila. Cowan told me to get on and find rest areas for the brigades that night. I said to Punch Cowan, 'You remember we had a good saying on the Frontier, "you must make camp two hours before dark", and I reckon this applies here.' We had carried the lessons over from the past.

Major John Randle
7th Battalion, 10th Baluch Regiment
We came upon a scene from hell with flames and screams. It was a Japanese base hospital full of wounded and sick, in a filthy state, smelling ghastly. We came across it as we cleared the western section of Meiktila. We were under strict orders not to hurt the Burmese.

One of my patrols came across a bunch of Japs having it off with some Burmese girls. The girls ran in one direction, the Japs in another. We shot the Japs. Then we found more of them in a bunker with more Burmese girls. We managed to get the Burmese girls out before my chaps threw in some phosphorus grenades and burned the Japs to death.

Captain Frederick Rowley
5th Battalion, 10th Baluch Regiment
When we went into Fort Dufferin in Mandalay, we went in prepared because we didn't trust the Japs. We crossed the moat and climbed over the rubble into what had been a prison courtyard. We knew there was a prison where we entered, but we didn't know that it was empty and that the doors locked from outside, so we could not get out. I had to use a machine gun to blow the lock away. We were going along gingerly, when we heard and saw a figure about fifty yards away. As it got closer, it didn't look like a Japanese. I shouted a challenge, and he turned out to be an American from Shwebo who had just driven in his jeep to look for souvenirs. He said, 'The gates were open, I came in. I'm on leave. I'm on holiday.'

Sergeant Stanley Wood
2nd Battalion, Durham Light Infantry
In the middle of a riverbed we saw a pile of fresh straw which we were about to cross. I contacted the tank commander through the tank telephone, and suggested he give the heap a burst with his machine gun. This was lucky, because no sooner had he blasted at the straw, than a Japanese jumped out of the hole. When we got there, he was dead, cross-legged in the hole, with a huge shell between his legs. He had a stone with which to hit the detonator when the tank went over the top.

Lieutenant Dominic 'Nicky' Neill
Intelligence Officer, 3rd Battalion, 2nd Gurkha Rifles
With orders to procure a Japanese captive, we patrolled the village of Lambagunaon in the Arakan. As we were moving through the northern part, the villagers said the Japs were occupying the south. We took up a position overlooking a strip of paddy between the two halves of the village. From there we saw three Japs stand up from behind a small mound 75 yards away. We watched them fascinated as we had never had the chance to study Japs at leisure before. We made the most of this opportunity and then we killed them.

The next day, we learned from villagers that a Japanese patrol was approaching the base. There were nine of them, bunched up in single file, with rifles with fixed bayonets slung on their shoulders. They were moving idly and talking among themselves. I was surprised at such laxity. It was very unusual. I grinned at the soldier alongside me and he grinned back. When the Japs were about seventy-five yards away, a long burst of Bren fire shattered the silence. Excitement had obviously got the better of the left-hand section's gunner. The

Japs took cover behind the bund like lightning. Everybody fired without any control orders from me. The sight of our enemy pinned down in front of us drove us berserk. We fired and fired until the barrels of our weapons became red hot, raking the bund. I had fired nearly three out of my five magazines, and hit nothing before changing to single shots. I saw one Jap trying to crawl away so I fired quickly two or three times. I saw hits on the wet shirt on his back. A wet rump poked up for a moment, and I fired three quick shots at that. One of them hit and the Jap was flung backwards into the flooded paddy.

As I hit him with another shot, I remembered that our mission was to take a prisoner, and if I didn't act soon, all candidates for the POW cage would be dead. I screamed above the din to the left-hand section to give me covering fire and ordered the section with me to cease fire, fix swords, draw kukris and charge. Over the bund we leapt, and plunged into the water of the rice field, yelling blue murder. I could see the strike of the shots from the supporting section hitting the field ahead.

Suddenly two enemy broke cover and tried to make a dash for it. I fired at one – too short – magazine empty. I knelt and guiltily changed magazines, switched to automatic, determined to kill the Jap. The other fleeing enemy stopped and flung up his hands in surrender. I was not gaining on the other man, my chest was heaving, my Tommy gun muzzle was going up and down, my eyes full of sweat. I fired three bursts and could see the rounds hitting the man's back, flicking away pieces of shirt and flesh. I had not realised the hitting power of a .45-inch bullet before. The Jap shot forward like a rag doll hit with a sledgehammer. I went over to him and took his rifle. I told my men to check the remaining seven bodies for signs of life, and that I wanted to search each one for documents. The Japs were great ones for keeping diaries, which disclosed useful information.

I started on the body of the man I had been chasing. His documents told me that he was a private of the 143rd Regiment. He was about my age – we had come a long way from our respective homes to meet under such violent circumstances in a flooded field on the remote coast of Arakan. In his wallet there was a photo of a young girl and his two tiny children. In the years since, I have often thought of the young woman I made a widow and the children I made fatherless. Then I think what he would have done to me had our positions been reversed.

I walked back to where our prisoner was standing among the dead and the reddening rice water. We were exposed and asking for trouble to remain long. At that moment I saw the Jap infantry doubling over the paddy some 800 yards away. The full enormity of my failure to control fire earlier struck me.

Gurkha soldiers cross the Irrawaddy in 1945. Throughout the war in the Far East, the Gurkhas earned a reputation for toughness, total loyalty and courage in the face of the enemy. During the course of the war, ten Gurkhas were awarded the VC for their extraordinary bravery and self-sacrifice.

Had we had ammunition we could have stayed to fight and give the Japs a bloody nose. As it was we might have to fight to hold the beach while waiting for the steamer. In the meantime we had no alternative but to get out of Ponra as soon as possible. A few days later we learned that our prisoner was an Indian fighting with the Japanese, which was disappointing.

One of my worst moments was on Snowdon East, when after a raid on a Jap position. I came across my friend's body among the men he had led in an attack three days earlier.

All their bodies were shiny, translucent black, and bloated like a Michelin man. I came across a corpse only two yards from the entrance to a bunker. I saw a yellow lead pencil sticking out of his pocket. This was Steve Stephenson's hallmark. Steve had been killed attacking the bunker. I gingerly turned him over. He had been hit by an LMG burst and his entrails were hanging out. He was still wearing his signet ring, and I thought I would take it from him so it could be handed it to his widow. With great care I started the awful task of taking the ring off Steve's decomposing finger. I got it partly off, when skin and ring fell into his exposed entrails. I was nearly sick on the spot. With the ring out of sight within Steve's poor body, I had neither the heart nor the courage to delve inside to find and recover the ring. I decided it would remain with Steve.

Major-General Hugh Stockwell
82nd West African Division

When I took over as Commander, I found the 82nd West African Division to be rather a luxury organisation. It was my responsibility to win the battle with the 82nd Division. I picked out an RSM from the 3rd Nigeria Regiment, who had been awarded the Iron Cross fighting for the Germans in West Africa in the First World War. He stayed with me as a personal RSM for a year and a half. He advised me on the Africans and through him I could find out what they thought of their British officers. He was tremendous, I got him a DCM, and he must be about the only soldier to wear an Iron Cross and a DCM.

Captain Dominic 'Nicky' Neill
3rd Battalion, 2nd Gurkha Rifles

During our assault on Snowdon Ridge in the Arakan, the unexpected happened. One soldier gave us the true leadership we had lacked hitherto. Number 5 Platoon's left section commander, Lance Naik Chamar Singh Gurung, rose to his feet and yelling obscenities to the Japs above him, started clambering through the broken tree trunks and up the hill, in the face of showers of grenades and heavy rifle- and machine-gun fire. Urged on by the screams of encouragement from the men of his platoon, he ran on up, spraying the hill with his Tommy gun. Changing magazines as he ran, he was hit by goodness knows how many enemy bullets as he reached the first enemy trench. But he stumbled on, squeezing the trigger of his Tommy gun, falling dead across the lip of the Jap trench.

He was the first man on Snowdon East that afternoon. His gallant conduct and inspiration turned what might have been defeat into victory. His action triggered off a series of other actions. Rifleman Bhanbhagta Gurung, the second-in-command of a section, stood up and killed a tree sniper, and inspired by Naik Chamar Singh Gurung's bravery, he yelled to those near him to follow, and started to run towards the top of the hill. Others rose and charged with a tremendous roar. The Japs met this attack with showers of grenades and rapid fire. The MMGs on Whistle cut down soldiers, and once again they wavered in the face of this murderous fire, and went to ground – this time only twenty yards from the Jap forward trenches.

This however proved to be no repeat of the first time. Without waiting for orders, Bhanbhagta Gurung dashed forward alone and attacked the nearest enemy foxhole just above him. Throwing two grenades, he killed the two occupants. Without hesitation, he rushed to the next trench and bayoneted the Jap in it to death. The leading platoons rose up and fell upon the Jap defenders of Snowdon East, and the battle lasted until the last Jap soldier had been killed or had run off. Bhanbhagta Gurung then attacked a lone machine gun in a bunker. By now out of grenades, he flung in two white phosphorus grenades, and two Jap soldiers came out with their clothes on fire, to be cut down by Bhanbhagta Gurung with his kukri. A remaining Jap, despite grievous wounds from burning phosphorus, continued to fire, whereupon Bhanbhagta Gurung crawled inside the bunker, where he beat out the Jap gunner's brains with a rock, capturing the machine gun. For his action, he was awarded the Victoria Cross.

Lieutenant Ian Fraser
Pilot of midget submarine, RN
We were towed by S-class submarines to the Strait of Singapore. Then we took over from the passage crew and were towed for about another twelve hours before slipping about 35 miles from the entrance to the Strait. There was an old British boom across the entrance, but when I got to it the gate was open, so we went through. Then we had 11 miles up the Strait to get to the cruiser, *Takao*. Navigationally it was a bit worrying as there was nothing to get a fix on and we had to guess our course, more or less. Eventually I saw the

cruiser through the periscope about a mile away, so I let each of the crew have a look – Kiwi Smith, Leading Seaman Jamie Magennis who was the diver, and Charlie Reid who was steering.

The *Takao* was lying in very shallow water – 11–17 feet at high water and just three feet at low water. It would have been impossible for us to get under her, except that there was a five-foot depression in the sea bed, 500 feet wide and 150 feet long, over which the *Takao* was lying. The plan was to skim across the shallows, slip down into this depression and under the cruiser's hull. But I really didn't think it would be possible.

About 400 yards from the ship I put the periscope up to have a look around and saw a Japanese liberty boat with about 40 men aboard only ten feet away. They were so close I could see their lips moving. We went deep immediately, but I'll never know why they didn't spot us.

Then we scraped along the seabed towards the ship with only ten feet of water above our heads. We were hoping to go down into the dip at any moment, but suddenly there was an almighty crash as we bashed straight into the side of the ship. I felt sure the Japs must have felt the crash.

We were all sweating hard by this time, especially Magennis in his diving suit. After a breather we started the motor but the boat wouldn't budge. We were stuck – either in an anchor cable or jammed under the ship's curved bows. It took ten terrible minutes of straining at full power forward and back to free us. Then we came out 1,000 yards from the ship, turned around, and started a second attack.

This time we slipped down into the hole and under the *Takao's* keel. I looked through the periscope and saw that the hull was only a foot over our heads and covered in thick weed. Magennis could hardly squeeze himself out of the hatch. Then we had to wait while he laid the mines. He seemed to take forever and each time he made a noise I thought the Japs would be bound to hear it. He was only gone thirty minutes but it seemed like thirty days. I was very anxious to get away as it was already nearly four hours after high water. But all we could do was watch him through the night periscope and drink pints of orange juice. It was sweltering down there.

At last he got back, as we worked, he told us what a terrible struggle he'd had, fixing the mines. He'd had to cut away the thick weed and scrape away a thick layer of barnacles before the magnets on the mines would stick to the hull. He had stuck on six. He was exhausted.

The port charge fell away from the boat all right, but the starboard charge would not budge. The tide was falling so quickly that I decided we should get the hell out from under the ship and then free the starboard charge. So we set

David Russell was captured when the Japanese overran the air base in Sumatra and, after a spell in the Bandoeng Camp, suffered a gruelling sea journey to Japan, where he was sent to work in a copper mine.

the motor at half speed ahead, but the boat wouldn't budge an inch, even at full speed. I was in a flat spin. I was sure the *Takao* had settled on top of us in the falling tide and we'd be stuck there for good.

For half an hour we went full speed astern and full ahead, with no success. I made a mental plan to abandon ship before the charges went off in six hours' time. But just as I was despairing, we felt a movement, and the XE3 climbed out from under the ship. It was such an incredible relief to see daylight through the periscope.

Now we were sitting less than twenty feet down in perfectly clear water. Anybody looking over the side of the *Takao* would have thought, 'What's that bloody great rock down there?' I offered to go out in a diving suit and release the starboard charge, but Magennis insisted he could do it. So out he went with a bloody great spanner and for a couple of minutes he made a hell of a noise freeing the charge. They were the most anxious minutes of my life. All the time I was cursing him, cursing Captain Fell, and, more than anything, cursing myself for having volunteered for this madness. In the end the charge fell away and Magennis got back into the hatch. We were all exhausted but at last we could go. 'Home, James,' I said, 'and don't spare the horses!'

PRISONERS OF THE JAPANESE

Flight Sergeant David Russell
RAF, taken prisoner of war

We were taken prisoner by the Japanese in 1942 and sent to an established prison camp in Java where there were 600 Dutch. The Dutch women were still free, but because the men had joined the home guard, they were all in the camp.

After we'd been there about two weeks three Dutchmen were caught climbing back over the wire at night, having visited their wives. A few days later we were all taken on to this football field where they had dug three graves. A Japanese sergeant-major got us all on parade, arranged on three sides of a square, staggered, so that nobody could miss what was going to happen. Eventually these poor creatures were led out, hands tied behind their backs, bleeding profusely from cuts and bruises all over them, staggering as the Japanese prodded them. One was placed opposite each grave. Two ranks of Japanese soldiers, none over 17 years of age, seemed to be the firing squad. A black Dutch chap standing beside me translated the sentence read out in Malayan by a Japanese officer. He said, 'They are going to kill them, but they are not going to shoot them. They are to die by thrusting.'

While all this was going on, the Japanese officer lit a cigarette in a tortoiseshell holder, put his hands in his riding breeches' pockets and stood beside the three victims, really enjoying the scene. Then he signalled and three young Japanese left the ranks. One stood opposite each prisoner with a fixed bayonet. The officer looked to see if we were all watching, threw away his cigarette, took out another and put it in his holder. The three Dutch guys refused to be bandaged. The Japs thumped them with their rifle butts and they had to submit to the bandage. They were standing each in front of his grave.

The Japanese officer made his men practise bayonet drill on these men – forward, retreat, forward, retreat, forward and then a lunge. Eventually they lunged for the stomach and the three men fell on the ground kicking. They kept thrusting at them and threw the men still kicking into the graves. By then my mouth was just dry.

After that we were marched into Bandoeng, a very big camp which was highly organised. I became the camp librarian under the aegis of Colonel van der Post, who was quite a character. He got all the talent together and started a school – a gunner called Rees, who was a lecturer in French, started giving French lessons; another guy was teaching Italian, and another Russian. My navigator friend, Ken Wibley, started Russian in prison camp and later became Senior Lecturer in Russian at Bangor University. Van der Post spoke Japanese, but he was getting information from all sources by pretending he didn't understand a word of it. He was a great morale-builder – he would come round the sergeants' lines and say 'Morniiing!', singing it out as if life was just perfect. He was charming and very inspirational. He'd been fighting guerrilla warfare against the Italians. He was well built and strong, because he had been out in the jungle so long. He loved cowboy stories – open-air spaces got him away from the close environment of a prison camp.

I had quite a reasonable life for four or five months and then they decided to take us to Japan. We had five days on a ship to Singapore and another 28 days on a ship battened down. We lost quite a number of people on that trip. There were burials every day at sea with canvas bags overboard. It was a terrible journey. We couldn't lie down. We slept sitting up, back to back. There were rats everywhere, running over your face at night. Feeding was very difficult. They would bring a big wooden barrel full of mushy rice to the top of the gangway. The mess tins had our names on them and were passed hand over hand. When we landed I was eventually moved to a place called Ikuno, where I became a copper miner. Most of my friends were there.

The Japanese soldiers wouldn't come down the mine – it was only us and

As the british advance on Mandalay, troops patrol the ruins and temples of the Burmese town of Bahe.

the civilian miners. Our job was to get great big heavy buggies and fill them with copper ore. My abiding memory is of starvation. The food was just minimum. We were trying to do a ten-hour shift in the mines on a few grains of rice a day. It was unpolished rice, full of weevils just scraped off the floor of some store. We stole like mad. I became a very accomplished thief. In summertime the Japanese gave us little cotton shorts, which was all we wore, and you could see everybody's ribs. We were burnt black from working outside. On one day a week we worked in the gardens outside the camp, but weren't allowed to touch the produce. They grew magnificent crops of oranges, plums, breadfruit, eggfruit and rice. Sometimes they let us take the white radish tops which we put into the soup. There was no soil. They grew everything on sand covered with manure, which we supplied. They had these huge concrete pits behind each billet, for latrines. They gave you a long pole with a big tin on the end of it and you filled the wooden barrels with loose shit – everyone had diarrhoea and dysentery, and you had this pole which you placed in hoops attached to the top of the barrel and you carried the honeypots out to the plants and you fertilised them.

It sounds odd but our morale was high. We lived on hope. We were getting information, and that was important for morale. We had a fellow called Arthur Brady who taught himself Japanese. We stole newspapers and he was able to translate a lot of it. We knew when Germany packed up because first of all the Japanese put us all on parade at 3 a.m. and beat the hell out of us. We knew something big had happened. We were delighted. Arthur got hold of a paper, and was able to translate the word Eisenhower. We thought he was a bloody German. We'd never heard of him.

We had no library when we went to the mines. We'd each taken one book. Some fellows took the Bible. I took *The Essays of Elia*. Those were the only books we had. It was an odd funny thing in the mining camp, books became in such short supply that you took pages 1–50 of, say, *The Murder of Roger Ackroyd* and you gave it to somebody else. So you'd get guys coming round the billets saying, 'Anybody got pages 145–190 of such and such a book?' We read books by instalments. I managed to keep mine. No one wanted to read it.

After the end of the war in Europe we thought maybe the Japanese would go easy. But they didn't. They were getting all sorts of propaganda. The women were out practising bayonet drill, the kids were out practising throwing hand-grenades – pieces of rock – on the sand outside the camp, and the newspapers were full of how to defend the country against the American invader. The Jap guards were saying, 'The Americans come, you die!' They cut down on the food because they were beginning to starve themselves. And they kept reminding us of what they were going to do to us. It was terrifying.

But there was one big act of kindness that happened to me after the German capitulation. I was working down the mine and Taff and I had just been given a beating for not working hard enough. We discovered that, in addition to the pit props, if you got a great big piece of copper ore into the buggy, that filled up quite a big space. I lifted this huge piece, and as I got to the edge of the buggy my stomach muscles just collapsed and the thing dropped over the edge and cut the end of my finger off. I was bleeding like a stuck pig and Taff was flapping around saying, 'You're going to die!'

He went and fetched the Japanese foreman. The Japanese didn't think you were sick until there was blood all over the place. So he saw the blood and got on the blower to the surface and down came the Japanese sergeant we called the King of Jazz, because he used pomade on his hair. He saw the blood and marched me back to camp two solid bloody miles with me leaving a river of blood behind me. We had two doctors in that camp. Harold Knox wanted to know why I hadn't brought the end of my finger, because he could have sewn it back on. He could only put a tourniquet round my arm, because he had no anaesthetic. The little bone was sticking up and had to come off. It wasn't pleasant because the nail-bed was still intact and he had to get the nail to go over the end of the bone. He did it. But he had to cut the end of the bone with a pair of scissors, and I nearly went through the roof. After that a Japanese did my work for me for a solid month, wouldn't let me lift a thing. People won't believe that of the Japanese.

Marine Peter Dunstan
Royal Marine, taken prisoner at Singapore
In the camp, we lived in huts made of bamboo which we had to build ourselves. Just a bamboo platform eighteen inches off the ground and a palm-leaved roof over the top. No sides, so the mosquitoes had a whale of a time. No blankets, except what you owned yourself. No clothes or food utensils were issued. So it was a pint mug of rice in the morning, then we were marched out of the camp and on to the railway before dawn. At midday they would let us stop for some more rice, then we carried on working until it was dark and we were marched back to the camp. For three months I never saw the camp I was living in. If it poured with rain, you carried on working, boiling sunshine or monsoon, you just carried on. We liked the monsoon because we had a bath.

It was a struggle to survive. We had nicknames for all the Japs. One little swine was known as Silver Bullet because he had a bullet on his belt. At this particular cutting the chaps were working on bosun's swings, drilling the rocks for dynamiting. Silver Bullet would stand right on the edge of the cliff and if he thought you weren't working hard enough he would throw a rock at you. One day he slipped and landed in the river about two hundred feet below. It was very strange, how he slipped. There was another one called the Mad Mongol. He was a Korean and the Koreans were worse than the Japanese. I was going to the toilet one night and I didn't bow or salute and he knocked the hell out of me. But it was a question of suspended animation. You just avoided any trouble that you could. I only got bashed twice in three-and-a-half years – I was lucky, I kept out of it.

Sergeant Clifford Bailey
Rifle Brigade, taken prisoner by Japanese in 1942
What they called 'Wampo' was quite a pleasant period, and we organised several camp concerts. The Japs would really encourage these camp concerts to take place. They saw it was good for morale, and they would come along and clap and enjoy the singing and whatever took place. We had one chap that played a trumpet, and he gave little recitals of various popular and classical music on his trumpet. Another chap out of the Gordons, he would play his bagpipes and various instruments would emerge. We had quite a pleasant little evening from time to time.

We knew we were building a railway which would bring military supplies and troops up on to the Burma front, and of course everything was done to slow up the progress of the railway. When we were building the embankment, the Japs would disappear, and go and lie under the trees out of the sunshine, and leave us to our devices, so what we used to do when we were unobserved, we would bring from the jungle lengths of dry bamboo. Dry bamboo is very light and you can carry a 60-foot length of dry bamboo which had all the water right out of it – it's like carrying a massive length of straw which had no weight to it. So a lot of dry bamboo went into the building of the embankment, which made our work much easer as we were able to complete that section of the embankment in record time, because we were given so many metres of embankment to complete. We later realised that we were making a rod for our own back by completing the work quickly, because when we'd finished the required length, instead of going back to camp, they said, 'Right, now you can do an extra stretch.'

The word went out from Tokyo to speed up the work to get it done on schedule. Sick men were sent out to work – men virtually died carrying stones and ballast to the embankment. It was a period when you went out to work in the morning and you didn't know what time you'd get back at night. You

Ian Fraser, VC. On 31 July 1945, Fraser piloted a midget submarine eighty miles through mined waters to place a charge under a Japanese heavy cruiser. Although at one point stuck under the vessel, he persisted, freed his craft and returned to record a successful attack. Leading Seaman Magennis, his diver, who planted the mines, was also awarded the VC.

could be working from soon after light in the morning till the early hours of the following morning to complete various sections of work. Work went on under the light of bamboo fires and the whole scene was incredible, with these bamboo fires and flares, and men toiling away – hundreds of men carrying baskets of stones and earth to build up the embankment. But eventually the 'speedo' came to an end. There were a lot of deaths, but the railway was joined up and finished in October of '43. The Japs had a celebration. I think we were given a spoonful of sugar each, and a banana. They insisted that we held a parade and a church service to commemorate all those who had died building the railway. This was quite an impressive ceremony, because all of us standing on that parade had seen a lot of our friends die, and had had to dig their graves and help bury them – and we realised that we were jolly lucky to be alive.

If things were going particularly badly for them, you knew it by the Japs' attitude. They'd take it out on us. The day that Germany surrendered, we didn't know. This wasn't confirmed until after we'd been released. But on this particular day in May, we came back from the iron foundry, and instead of being dismissed on the parade ground, to go and get a wash and have your food, we were kept on parade and we were told that we must march round and round the yard – and we must sing. We did that for about two hours. It didn't matter what you sang, but you had to sing – and if you didn't, if you faltered a bit, or you weren't singing, you had guards around with bamboo canes or pick handles, and they would rap you across the legs. It wasn't until long after that we realised that that was the day that Germany had surrendered, and the Japs knew they were on their own.

Sergeant Terry Brooks
Royal Marines, taken prisoner at Singapore

One day we were on parade, Tenko, five o'clock in the evening. I heard aircraft. Somebody said, 'Look up,' and I looked up and there were 27 Liberators coming over, very low. I could see the bomb doors open and all the bombs as they fell. They went for the bridge, bang, bang, bang and I thought, 'God that one was near,' and I looked over and saw that our Number One hut was blazing. I dragged one lad out but for three days after that we were digging bodies out. We lost about 19 men in that raid. A short while later they wanted a party to build airstrips further down the isthmus and I was one of them. We marched 200 miles barefoot. It took us a fortnight. By this time I was pretty low. I think I was in a daze. I was down to six stone seven. The lads used to carry me to work because if you didn't work you didn't get any rations. I went blind for three months. It was frightening. That was the worst time. The lads used to go out and collect wild peanuts for me, which was the only way to treat the disease. Somebody got me on to a truck back to the main hospital. I laugh when you call it a hospital camp – you went there to die. There were Scottish doctors, Australian doctors, but hardly any drugs at all. But I didn't think I was going to die – it never occurred to me.

Lieutenant Ian Fraser
Pilot of midget submarine, RN

When I'd rested up and written my patrol report, we were on deck watching a film. The film suddenly stopped and the captain said, 'I've stopped the film, gentlemen, because the return to Singapore has been delayed. They've dropped a bomb on Hiroshima.' I thought, 'Thank Christ, it's been delayed.' Then, lo and behold, five or six days later they dropped the second nuclear bomb and the war was finished. So we didn't have to go back.

Later on that year I was awarded a VC. On my way back home they asked if I'd like to go to Singapore to see the *Takao*. So I went with a Japanese interpreter who took me on board the hulk. He opened the hatch and I could see that the whole ship had been blown to bits. It had virtually no bottom. Jamie Magennis, who was also awarded a VC, and I went together to Buckingham Palace to collect our awards. Our wives came too. I've no idea what King George said to me; all I can remember is that he talked with a lisp.

THE ATOM BOMB

As the Americans fought from island to island in the Pacific and launched bombing raids on Tokyo and other industrial cities, plans were made for the invasion of Japan in 1946. However, American casualties on the islands of Iwo Jima and Okinawa had been heavy, and a prolonged campaign would only add to this toll. Seeing Japan under pressure in Burma, China and at home, it was decided to try to end the war with one mighty blow.

On 6 August, a B-29 bomber, 'Enola Gay', piloted by Colonel Paul Tibbets, took off from Tinian in the Marianas Islands and dropped an atomic bomb on Hiroshima. The strike left an estimated 66,000 Japanese dead and 69,000 gravely injured. Japan, however, made no move, so on 9 August a second bomb was dropped on Nagasaki, where an estimated 39,000 died. Reeling from this second attack, Japan surrendered on 14 August. The war was over.

The atomic bomb dropped by the United States on Hiroshima, 6 August 1945,
heralded the end of the war in the Far East. In the devastated city, little remained
standing. The bomb had proved the ultimate weapon.

Geoffrey Sherring

Civilian radio operator with Merchant Navy, POW in Nagasaki

The day the bomb was dropped was beautiful to start with, with very little cloud. It was for this reason that the secondary target, which was Nagasaki, was selected by the bombers after they'd got over their primary target. They'd gone to the primary target and found it covered with cloud, and had therefore gone hurrying south to Nagasaki to give us the benefit of the bomb. We had a practically clear sky and a nice southerly breeze, but our foremen at the works had been terrified by the news that had been spreading throughout Japan about atomic bombing.

We didn't know this, of course. We knew that they were very, very air-raid-conscious. We went down to the foundry where we had an air-raid warning, but it was a customary air-raid warning. We heard it and were immediately taken back to the camp because we had, by this time, begun digging trenches in our encampment as air-raid shelters. We went down into the shelters and when the 'raiders passed' signal was given, we all fell in and marched down to the foundry again – where, to our surprise, we found nobody. There were no foremen or work people there to take over from us. What had happened, of course, was that they'd all left their place of work and gone away, having heard about the atomic bombing of Hiroshima. We weren't to know this at the time. So we were all marched back to camp again.

I was working with an Australian whose name was Bernard O'Keefe. I said to him, 'There's nobody about – let's nip in there and have a smoke.' This we did, and it must have been a couple of minutes to eleven. I had a burning glass, and we each had a cigarette end somewhere about us, so we set alight our cigarettes with the sunlight, and retreated back into the trench, which was roofed, to smoke in peace. The atomic bomb went off whilst we were in there. Bernie said to me, 'I can hear a car on the road.' I said, 'Don't be ridiculous – there's no petrol in Japan, let alone cars – it must be an aeroplane.' He said, 'I'm going out to have a look.'

He began crawling away from me towards the hole in the roof of the trench that he could get out of. As he did so, and I was looking after him, I saw the flash from the bomb – which was exactly like the sort of bluish light that you get from an electrical welding operation. It was very blue, and it came in exactly the opposite direction from the sun's rays – it completely eclipsed them. It was this thin, blue blazing light, shining down a square hole in front of Bernie, who hadn't, fortunately, reached the hole – or he would have been burned too. Then we heard the vibration and shaking, which wasn't a bang by any means. It was a continuous shaking of the whole air and earth about it. It was separated by several seconds from the flash, because we were not directly underneath the bomb – we were about 1,100 yards away.

Then this thundering, rolling, shaking came along, and everywhere went completely dark. What had happened was the shock wave had rolled over us, lifting as it went, all the earth and dust around us and blowing the building flat at the same time. So when we came out, in a matter of seconds, we came out into a choking brown fog. This fog lasted for quite a while before the south-westerly breeze blew it back up the city. As it did so, we had a shower of most peculiar rain. It was in very, very large droplets, about as big as grapes, and it was almost entirely mud – just thick blobs of mud falling from the sky.

It didn't take us long to realise that there was something seriously amiss, because the camp had collapsed and there wasn't a building standing anywhere near us. We could see further than we'd ever seen before across the city, which was all in a heap. Most of the buildings had been made of wood and some of them nearer to the site of the bomb had already been set on fire and it was spreading. I ran to a storehouse nearby and the Japanese in charge of this must have been standing in the doorway, because his skin was completely burnt off him, and he had fallen on the ground. He was a distressing sight, with a lot of his insides hanging out. I was trying to make him comfortable but all the skin came off his arms on to my hands, just like thin wet rubber. He, of course, was in great pain, and shouting for a stretcher – which I couldn't provide for him so I left him.

On a horse and cart we made our way out of the town in a westward direction, up into the hills. By early to mid-afternoon, we had made ourselves as comfortable as we could on a terrace overlooking the city, and thought we should stay there for a while. But the houses, each of which was on its own terrace, had begun to burn from the bottom upwards. We exhorted the Japanese who lived in the house on the end of the terrace we were sitting on to move their stuff before their house was burnt down. Nothing would induce them to go. Absolutely nothing.

I said, 'Come on lads – we've got to do something.' So we all dashed into this house and collected everything we could take out – for instance drawers with all their contents – and passed them from hand to hand out on to the field. The Japanese were pitifully grateful about this, but they would never go in to help themselves. I got the feeling they felt this was almost a supernatural occurrence, and that they couldn't do anything about it.

We were feeling very tired from our exertions and hoping nothing more would happen, when a Japanese soldier came along. He had his rifle and still had his bayonet fixed. He told us that the bulk of our prisoners were on the opposite side of the city – over on the other side, occupying a similar hillside position to ourselves. He pointed out that they had no stores, food or blankets – nothing. I was very impressed by the way he went about his duties in the middle of all this terrible chaos, so I got three Dutch East India men and we put buckets on thick bamboo poles, and we loaded these up with tinned food of various kinds and we folded blankets on to the poles, and carrying these burdens, we set off into the burning city.

It was very impressive to move down these roads, and in many cases we had to wait until the flames had blown aside until we could run like mad to get past the fire. We went straight into the middle of the city where we saw a tram that was still on its rails, but with absolutely no woodwork left – just the metal chassis of the tram sitting on the rails. I remember at one point lighting a cigarette from a nearby wooden pole. Most of Japan's services – telephone, electricity and everything like that, was carried overhead, so there were huge numbers of poles and quite a lot of these had begun to burn at the top, and were burning steadily downwards. The one that I lit my cigarette from was just about head-height, and I remember going to it the following morning and finding it was in a five-foot cavity in the ground. It had burned its way steadily down all through the night and there was a little heap of ashes in the bottom of this five-foot cylindrical hole.

The dead were lying everywhere. In the first few days, when we were actually sleeping in the city, my little corner of brickwork was also occupied by a Japanese woman whose husband's corpse was with her – and she'd covered it over with straw matting, but gradually it became distended and smelly. She didn't want to hand it over until the police more or less wrestled it from her. This problem of corpses became very severe, so we gathered all the timber we could find, that had been used in the construction of houses, and put it in long rows down the middle of the concrete road, and then we stacked the corpses neatly on top of this pile of timber. We were left with rows of corpses a hundred yards long. The police chalked the identity of the corpse on the pavement beside the body. Then, as we left in the afternoon, we set fire to the timber, and the following morning the whole thing had burned out. The calcified skeletons were lying in a row on the road with their names beside them. They were then able to be picked up with chopsticks and put into their little wooden boxes with their name on. The box was about as big as a seven-pound tea chest.

It was interesting to remember that within three or four hours of the bomb going off, we – that is to say my Dutch comrades and myself – had worked out what it was, how it was, and where it was. On a wooden building which was a very small one, and didn't completely collapse, a new nail had been driven into the woodwork. The building itself was in the full light that fell from the bomb, and therefore it was burned like toast to a crisp – but the shadow of the nail fell down the building in such a way as to make it look like a white knitting needle with a big head. If you laid a straight edge from that big head to the nail's head, you could look up it and see where the light came from, that had fallen on this nail, so it was quite possible, with two or three markers like that, to come to the conclusion the bomb had gone off above the baseball stadium about 1,500 feet high.

We also knew by the size of it, that one single bomb, delivered by one single aeroplane, could only contain that kind of energy if the atom had been split – so we instantly assumed this was done by the splitting of the atom. We were right.

There were shadows of all kinds. Wherever anything had been sheltered and the light from the bomb had not actually been allowed to fall upon it, the surfaces were quite different from the places that had been irradiated. The heat must have been intense. Everything that was made of ordinary wood crisped and roasted before it actually caught fire. For instance, our camp fence turned a dark brown. The rice crop had been green in the fields – but by the end of the afternoon it had turned brown and ripened prematurely. All the trees went autumn-coloured, and the leaves fell off them – those that didn't actually catch fire.

All these effects on the natural order of things about us were fascinating to see. For example, kites were always hovering over Nagasaki – big brown birds of the buzzard type – very big birds. A number of them must have been hovering when the bomb fell, because I came across two or three of them, walking about in the city with no feathers on. Their feathers had been burnt off them in mid-air, and they'd collapsed to the ground. They were wandering around on foot. Horrifying sight. It impressed me more than the sight of the Japanese and their sufferings, because, after all, the Japanese had scarcely endeared themselves to me. I felt they deserved it.

THE END OF THE WAR . . . AND ITS AFTERMATH

Hostilities were over – but it took time for troops around the world to get home. Some continued to serve in occupied Germany and the Far East, but for many who returned home, life would never be the same. Those who were seriously injured faced a life crippled and dependent on others for their survival. After the widespread joy of VE and VJ days, there was for many a sense of anticlimax. The post-war world to which they had returned was very different from the one which they had left.

Sergeant Martin McLane
2nd Battalion, Durham Light Infantry, Burma

One day I was in the sergeant's mess to make sure that it was neat and tidy prior to a parade. Everything had to be spick and span ready for anybody coming like a brigadier or a general, to have a quick look around the depot. I turned the wireless on – we had a little Nuffield battery set – and they started talking about two bombs that had been dropped. I was amazed. I was a man used to explosives. I couldn't imagine a bomb of such size. Well, we weren't going to take the whole of Burma at the rate we had been going, a yard at a time, stage by stage. We were going to lose an awful lot of good servicemen at that rate and we were also going to take a lot of time – years – to conquer Burma and India. But with this happening, it seemed as if the end of the war was immediately in sight.

Major John Randle
7th Battalion, 10th Baluch Regiment

We thought it would go on and on. We were wearing a bit thin by then. I had been in Burma from the beginning. If my CO had said you have earned a rest, even before we went back in early 1945, I would have taken it. But I would never have asked for it. Couldn't put your hand up and say I've had enough. The prospect of fighting on across Burma, Siam and China didn't appeal. When I heard about the bomb, my company was defending a gun box. We were on the banks of the Sittang with the rain pissing down. We had some captured Jap MGs and fired a terrific *feu de joie*. The gunners fired star shell. Brigade HQ asked what we were firing at.

We were ordered to arrange the surrender of the Japanese 18th Division. The CO was on leave and I was the acting second-in-command. The CO, adjutant and I sent in a message to the camp where the Japs were, and when we arrived a whole crowd with fixed bayonets rushed up, and I thought we were going to be killed. It turned out to be a quarter guard. Only one chap could speak English, a Chicago University-trained fellow. We took the view that this was not the time for arrogant behaviour, and we would teach them how to treat defeated people. We told them all to hand in their weapons at the railway station. They agreed, and asked about their swords. They wanted to hand them in personally and not be dumped with the rest of the weapons. We told them that at the end, each officer would hand his sword in individually to officers. The Divisional Commander would hand his in to our Brigade Commander. Each Jap officer came up, saluted, unsheathed his sword, and handed it over. We had six or seven crack Tommy-gunners standing by with one up the spout and safety-catch off in case some Jap officer decided to go to his death hacking off the head of a British officer. After that, the Japs did fatigues for us. We had a cricket match and they rolled the pitch. I have to admit I came to admire the Japs, for the way they behaved, they were neither obsequious nor arrogant – just well disciplined.

Masao Hirakubo
Japanese officer, 3rd Battalion, 31st Mountain Gun Regiment
We were taught to kill ourselves by hand-grenade rather than to surrender. Actually, I heard the noise of hand-grenades going off all over the jungle. If I had been cornered and I could see no way to escape, then I would have killed myself. One of my divisional classmates killed himself in the jungle at Kohima because he felt sick and he couldn't allow his orderly to support him. He couldn't allow the position to continue where his orderly was helping him every day. But on the evening of the 15th August, I heard from Divisional Headquarters the Emperor's broadcast of surrender. I had a feeling of having lost everything. I thought the war could go on. We felt that even though we were preparing for the next battle, Japan itself had decided to finish. We found ourselves crying.

Within a week, many things happened in Japanese units in Burma. As far as my group was concerned, I made a speech to the soldiers on how we should behave. I said that we had lost the war and that meant that our generation had lost the war. We had spoilt the whole country of Japan that had been constructed by the previous generations. So we could not pass it on to the next generation unless we could recover it, at least to some degree. So we should go back to Japan and work more, even harder, to compensate the people who died in the war, so we must work harder to make Japan recover. Until that time, I said that in relation to the British army, we must keep our pride and that no man could live without belonging to a nation. So we had to go back to Japan.

Not every unit did as we did, though. It depended on the commanders – some platoons escaped in the night with provisions and arms to the mountains, saying that they would continue to fight or that they would wait there for the next war to break out. We did not try to escape. The disarmament of our regiment was only done in the middle of October. I was in charge of handing weapons over to the British. In our camp, the British gave us rice, dried potato and corned beef, so we had to collect fruit and vegetables for ourselves. We were sent to the British camp to work, for repairing of roads, painting and so on, once a week. In the camp, I taught English and we played sports and games and each company competed in putting on theatre performances. Compared to the time of fighting, it was a very easy life. There was no mistreatment of Japanese prisoners. The only problem was that our gums were bloody because we were not getting enough vitamin C. We asked the British supply officer to provide more fruits and on the following day, we were given fruit and the problem seemed to stop. But even now, my gums are spoilt and I lost all my teeth years ago.

Sergeant Clifford Bailey
Rifle Brigade, taken prisoner by Japanese at fall of Singapore
We noticed rather a sullen and indifferent attitude by the Jap guards and the civilian population, and we thought that, obviously, something's up. On the third day of this sort of uneasy calm, the work party wasn't called out. So as the morning went on, Captain Poat-Hunt decided to go to the Japanese camp commandant, which was a Lieutenant Watanabe, and ask him what was taking place. He rather bluffed it out – he gave him the usual courtesies and he took a chance. He said, 'You know that the war is over. I know the war's over, and the men know the war's over. What are you going to do about it?' And the man was a bit nonplussed. He didn't quite know how to answer him. He said, 'I cannot give you any information. I'm out of touch with Tokyo.' And as far as he was concerned, the interview was at an end. Another two days went by – still no news from the Japs, or any change in attitude. They just had this sort of sullen indifference, and left us alone. Food was issued as normal.

Out of the blue, came a lone Grumman Avenger, and it flew round and round the camp and dropped a canister. In the canister – rather small canister – were packs of Chesterfield and Camel cigarettes and a newsletter gave details of the squadron and of the task force which was lying off Japan, and it said that the war had finished on the 15th August – and the war had been brought to an end because of the dropping of the two atomic bombs. We were to stay put until we heard from either the Japanese or the Allied authorities. Two days or so later one lone B-29 came over low and went round and round the town, and we were spotted. They then proceeded to drop in the outlying areas, away from the town, four 50-gallon oil drums, welded together on eight parachutes – red, white and blue parachutes. The Japanese were told that when these drums were landed, they had to be collected and brought into the camp.

In those drums were vast supplies of food, medical supplies and clothing, and these were opened up, all this taken to the stores and issued to us. The food was issued to us rather carefully, because they didn't want any people to go mad. We were completely transformed – we had been dressed in rags. But from then on, we were clean and dressed in American Army uniforms, and had a good supply of food. The Japs just left us alone, simply disappeared. Overnight, they left the guardroom, and we were virtually left alone in the camp. All their arms and ammunition were left behind. It was rather curious and quite understandable that, when it was decided that we would mount guard on the camp, there was immediate clamour to be allowed to go on guard. I mean, during normal army service, that's the last thing you want to do – you just didn't want to go on guard. You don't want to miss your night's sleep – you don't want to stand outside with your rifle – but men fell over themselves. They just wanted to be first in the queue.

Flight Sergeant David Russell
Prisoner of the Japanese

The day the Japs surrendered was a very interesting morning. I got my barrack out as usual, at 6.30 in the morning, with the boys lined up in fours, and no Japs came to take the count! They never failed before. Dead on time you had to be there! We hung around wondering what the hell was going on. Eventually we sat down – normally the last thing we should have done. Then we saw one of the Japanese sergeants emerging from the Guard Room and his head was bowed. He looked around a bit disconsolately then went back in. Everybody was wondering what was going on. We thought the Yanks had landed and the Japs were going to kill us. The uncertainty frightened the life out of me. Then the sliding window of the cookhouse was suddenly rammed aside and there was Kinsella, the cook, and his eyes were staring, and he shouted, 'The fucking war's over! The fucking war's over!' For the following two weeks we hung around, speculating about what would happen and foraging for food.

Sergeant Terry Brooks
Royal Marines, prisoner of the Japanese

But then came the day when I was standing at the door of the hut and the Japanese were marching along, changing their reliefs. There was something funny about them, I couldn't quite place it. So I decided not to come to attention – but they didn't notice. I thought, 'You bastards, it's over.' The next

Although painfully thin, the inmates of a Japanese prisoner-of-war camp raise a smile for a photographer with the liberating Allied troops.

minute the British officers came and said, 'It is over.' We all sang 'God Save the King,' and 'Abide with Me'. Then we heard explosions all over the place. The Japanese soldiers and Korean privates and corporals were committing hara-kiri by blowing themselves to pieces. All the Japs we hated were dead.

Sergeant Thomas Woodhouse
Royal Corps of Signals

After years as a prisoner of the Japanese, we embarked on the cruiser, the *Mobile*, after a hot bath on the quayside. There was all the food you wanted – in small doses, cigarettes, soap, changes of clothing, even a row of beads for Catholics. It was a lovely ship, together with big hefty American marines to help you up the gangplank if you wanted. He would carry your kit for you. It was a wonderful feeling. I had a big kitbag full of stuff but I didn't want him to carry it. 'No thanks, old son,' I said. 'I walked into this bloody country and I'll walk out of it, and lucky I've made it without falling on my chinstrap.' That first night, there was a film show on board and there was a band playing. I can remember the tune – 'Sentimental Journey'. I couldn't settle to sleep so I sat on the upper deck, smoking all night. By the next morning I'd started to readjust and I've never had any hang-ups since.

Sergeant Clifford Bailey
Rifle Brigade, released from Japanese prisoner of war camp

On the ship coming home from the Far East, we had virtually nothing to do – just pass away our leisure hours – and there was a cinema on board. It was showing *Going My Way* with Bing Crosby. I think we saw that two or three times each. One night, we were queuing to see it when a brash young naval boy of about eighteen, nineteen, not a medal on his chest, turned round in the queue and saw one of our sergeants standing there. This was a sergeant who'd seen quite a lot of service in the Far East. He'd gone out in 1937 and his tour of duty had almost finished when war broke out and it had prevented him from coming back. So he hadn't been in the UK for eight years. We'd now been issued with medal ribbons and the young boy said to the sergeant 'I suppose that yellow stripe down the middle of the Pacific Star is for Hong Kong and Singapore.' The sergeant just hit him straight between the eyes and we had a job to restrain him. After that we began to wonder if that was the sort of reception we'd get when we got back home. Had people seen the loss of Hong Kong and Singapore as an incident in which the British Army hadn't been shown to be any good?

Corporal Jack Sharpe
1st Battalion, Leicestershire Regiment, prisoner of war of the Japanese at Outram Road Jail

In solitary confinement, every hour during the night the sentry would bang on the door and I would have to call 'yes' in Japanese, so long periods of sleep were impossible. Then for something to do they would just beat me up. I had a bucket for a toilet, three bowls of rice a day and a mug of dirty water. There was nothing for me to do but dream of home and my mother and hang on to the insult from the court martial. After 14 months I was let out. The Japs cut my hair and beard and put me in another cell.

During the day we prisoners cut grass and worked on rope-making, but all the time the guards would just beat us. So many were dying. If they weren't dying they were executed. We had no doctor. The Japs began to worry about the reputation of the place and started moving some prisoners to Changi Jail, which had some medical facilities. They wanted to move me but I refused. I was so determined to walk out of Outram Road Jail a free man. My friends pleaded with me to go but I wouldn't. In the end I was the longest survivor in that jail. During that time I got scurvy, which made my eyes like balls of fire, all matter coming out. My mouth was all swollen and red raw. I could barely swallow. Then I got scabies, which killed so many. I was covered in scabs from head to foot. There was no treatment. Mother Nature or death took over. I kept saying, 'Keep going, keep going,' and months later the scabs disappeared. So many around me were starving to death or simply giving up.

The only time I faltered was when my best friend died. I couldn't see the sense in going on. But I had to. In May 1945 we heard about the end of the war in Europe so I was determined to stay alive. Then in August the American bombers arrived and blasted Singapore. Two days after the raid the Japs surrendered.

When the camp was relieved the lads picked me up like a conquering hero. As I was being carried out I saw the sign over the gate and I asked the lads to put me down. I was determined to walk for freedom. I managed a few steps, got outside and then the lads had to pick me up again. I had weighed eleven stone when I was captured – I was now only four.

I'd contracted dysentery and was unconscious for 48 hours in Changi. When I came round I saw the padre so I thought I was in heaven. Later, a really thoughtful NCO came into the ward and called me outside to sit on the verandah. He gave me 38 letters, all from my mother. She had never believed I was dead and had written to me every month for more than three years. Reading them I just wept and wept. I thought of my dear mother and all the

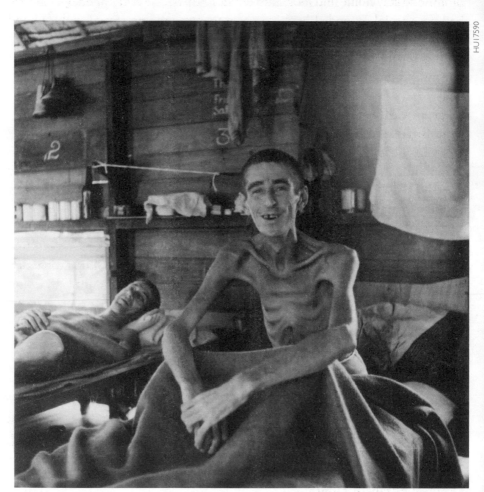

Defiant and very much alive, weighing only four stone, Jack Sharpe lived to fulfil his promise to his Japanese captors. He survived illness, starvation and solitary confinement yet still managed to take the few faltering steps to leave Outram Road Jail. His was an extraordinary triumph – a testament to his determination and unshakable belief in the eventual outcome of the war.

pain she had been through. That was the first time I'd allowed myself to cry. After a few weeks' rest I was flown to Bangalore to recover.

One day in Bangalore, I was sitting on my bed and feeling a bit low – and heard footsteps. I looked up and there was my older brother, Jess. I'd made him promise to stay home and look after our mother, but he had joined up. Now he had got special extended leave to come to find me. He stayed with me and taught me to walk again as he had done when I was a child. All the same, it was a year before I was fit enough to go back to England. There at long last I saw my mother.

Sergeant Clifford Bailey
Rifle Brigade, released prisoner of of the Japanese

After I got back to England, I went home. I arrived at my house and I walked in, and it was quite an emotional experience, actually, because I'd been away since '41. My father had been reasonably fit when I left – now he was virtually bedridden with a chronic heart condition. He was being looked after by a cousin of mine who had made her home with us through the war, because my mother had died in 1940. She greeted me at the door – very emotional. She said, 'Oh, you know, be careful of your father – not too much shock.' She said, 'He's been very ill.' One of the rooms had been converted into a bedsitting room for him, because he couldn't go up the stairs. And I went in, and he greeted me calmly. He looked at me – he said, 'I knew you'd come back.' We talked well into the early hours of the morning, and eventually, about three o'clock in the morning I suppose, I went to bed.

That was quite an experience, because up to that time, I'd been with a crowd of people, so I'd never been completely on my own. To go into that bedroom and close the door . . . all the thoughts came flooding back then, you know, the preceding years. It was the first time you could stop and really come to terms with yourself and find out what it was all about.

Dorothy Elizabeth Hont
Women's Land Army

When we knew my brother was going to come home, and all the neighbours had found out, the children painted, 'Welcome Home Les, Five Years POW', across the middle of the road, and it was there for years, because they did it with white paint. It was there 'til they tarmacked the road. The lady who lived across the road – she's dead now – she brought her piano out on to the green, and she came over with a basket with a quarter of tea, a pound of sugar, half a pound of marge, a couple of slices of bacon, and a little bottle of brandy – very kind.

Strangely, my mother had been to some friends in Cumbria a couple of weeks prior to getting notice Leslie was coming home, and there was a farm cowman. He said, 'Have you had any eggs, Mrs Hont, of late?' She said, 'Oh, eggs! They're magic – we don't see them.' So he went round all the farms during the week, and whoever could spare two or three, he built it up until he had five dozen eggs, and put them, well packed, in a box. Mother brought them home, and she had to stand in the guard's van, because it was crowded with servicemen, and she was terrified.

She used all these eggs to feed him, and he had nothing but eggs and brandy for about a week. When the doctor came to see him, he said, 'You've probably saved his life, because a young man two doors down, who was only two years a prisoner, he died through overfeeding.' They fed him ice cream, tinned fruit – all kinds of things their son had brought from abroad in the navy. His stomach had reduced to such a small size, he couldn't take it, and he died – whereas my brother survived. He had dysentery but when he'd recovered we had this party in the road. We had dancing and singing, and everybody contributed something for eating. All mother's china cups got broken – everybody wanted to wash and dry up, and all her best china got broken.

Sylvia Taylor
Child in Hook, Surrey

After the war, everyone was so very happy, elated and relieved. We didn't know what was coming because we didn't remember what was before the war. We thought we would have sweets, heating and coal.

Terrence McEwan
Schoolchild living in London

My respect for women went down somewhat as a result of the war. I was only a boy but I'd watched a lot of Americans and French sailors walking them down East Ham High Street. They used to congregate at the Black and White Milk Bar and I used to see all these young ladies that I knew quite well – some of them married – mixing with these American and French sailors and it left me quite disillusioned.

Patricia Crampton
British translator at Nuremberg Trials and at subsequent trials

I went to work as a translator at the Nuremberg Trials. While I was there, we were always free to go into the courtroom. On one occasion, we all went into court for the sentence of a man called Oswald Pohl, who had been in charge of the labour and concentration camps and who had been making fun of the judges throughout his trial in every possible way. On that last day, the judge was foolish enough to ask him to raise his hand to take the oath. How Pohl sneered because he was manacled, as the judge knew perfectly well. He just wasn't thinking. Pohl claimed to have been personally responsible for signing the documents that led to the deaths of six million people. After sentence was pronounced, he rose to his feet and said that he would do it again. And then he bowed to the judge. As if to say, 'You wait. You next . . .'

I was involved in the 'Doctors Trial'. That was about the experiments conducted by doctors using Jews and 'undesirables' as guinea pigs. I was translating the depositions of people who had come out alive. Some very well annotated records survived. One aspect that I never really got over was the fact that alongside the doctors were people who were carrying out this behaviour for no legitimate purpose. The insertion of mice into women's vaginas, the repeated breakings of children and adults' legs to assess the different healing capacities of different ages. There were people who were actually enjoying carrying out these experiments and there were no lengths to which they would not go. I remember, when I got back to England, my cousin asked me what I thought of the Germans now. I said, 'There but for the grace of God.' He said, 'You can't mean that!' but I'd seen that all sorts of people had been involved with these experiments. They weren't just Nazis, members of the party, there were all sorts of people, many saving their own skins by being involved. There but for the grace of God. Unfortunately, in England, people seemed to think that this was not a proper job for me to have done. I was lucky with my parents. They knew, like me, that it was hugely important. But no one else wanted to hear anything about it at all.

Hedy Epstein
German, worked at Nuremberg Trials for US War Department

During a recess in his trial at Nuremberg, I stood in front of Goering. I didn't say anything. I just stared at him. It obviously made him feel uncomfortable as he didn't know who I was. I was a German Jewish girl who had escaped to Britain on the Kindertransport in 1939, but I had been given an American uniform to wear during the trial so he probably didn't suspect that I spoke German. He said to his defence lawyer in German, 'Who is this little one? What does she want?' and the lawyer answered, 'I don't know who she is but she obviously works for the prosecution and I don't know what she wants. Don't say anything, don't do anything.' I'm thinking, you know, here is Hermann Goering, whom not very long ago I would have feared mortally, and here am I – and he's afraid of me.

Patricia Crampton
British translator at Nuremberg Trials

Whilst I was working in Nuremberg, there was a rule that we were not to eat at German restaurants – not because of a rule against fraternising – but so that we wouldn't take the German people's rations when we were more than adequately fed. Actually, we didn't get a lot of fresh food. Most of our food was American, which was shipped over. It wasn't terribly good for us as a matter of fact. In the British zone there was still a rule against fraternisation. I used to get in awful trouble over it. I began developing a growing circle of friends in Munich and Heidelberg and we ate a lot of German rations but we were able to supply whisky and above all the currency – cigarettes. There was nothing you couldn't buy with cigarettes, you could buy your train tickets and you knew the price of everything in cigarettes.

When I look at my letters home – every letter is telling my mother that some marvellous material has arrived at the PX (the NAAFI) and asking her if she'd like some. She could make a suit for my sister. Would my cousin like nightdress material? What about shoes? I was able to send chocolate. It was England that had won the war and was undergoing such austerity and yet I had everything I needed. I used to go back home on leaves with crates of china. In England, everybody had been reduced to this revolting thick utility china and I could take whole services for my mother and aunt and grandmother. I was able to adopt 'the new look'. I was able to have my clothes made by a German dressmaker, I wore navy blue nylons and black nylons. The excitement!

A lot of currency exchanging went on. People were exchanging vast amounts of currency. A lot of people were getting currency that the poor devils in the internment camps, which contained refugees in huge numbers – often people released from the concentration camps – had managed to hang on to. So they would hand over money that they needed in order to arrange travel and they would get cheated by people who offered to exchange it into other currencies. The other thing I remember in that context is drugs. I'd never heard of them in England. When it was realised how high up the drug ring went, the American inquiry was stopped abruptly.

I remember once I was on a train, and I'd been speaking German to the conductor, when a Nazi started speaking in the carriage about how unfortunate it was that the war had been lost. I listened to this man with great interest and he was quite unaware that I was not an ordinary young German woman, until I spoke to someone beside me in English. At that point the man spat on the floor with great violence and left the carriage. Interestingly, I later came across a lot of that sort of talk when I was in Switzerland. I used to hear a lot of very cosy chats between the Swiss and the 'new businessmen' who had been Nazis about what a pity it was that the wrong people had won.

Margaret Gore
Air Transport Auxilliary
I think that in Britain, the black market had undermined people's honesty, and I think as a society, we were much less honest afterwards. I think it all started because we did scrounge petrol and nylons, and extra butter and so on. I think it all started in the war.

Major Corrie Halliday
11th Hussars
After the war there were times when I was so depressed that I came close to suicide. It wasn't so much that I was fed up with having survived the war or that I felt bad that some of my friends had been killed and I hadn't. It was the future. I'd had six years taken away from me. Whereas before the war there was a future – if I didn't like the bank I was working in at the time then I was free to change direction, but by the end of the war I'd got round to asking what good has the last six years done me? Why am I here? Where am I going from here?

I had no anchor in life and I was restless. I couldn't sit down and read a book – I'd done enough of that in a prison camp. So I decided that I'd do a labouring job that exhausted me completely so that I could put the mental strains and stresses in the background. And I moved out to New Zealand to become a sheep farmer. And it worked.

Flight Lieutenant Frank Ziegler
609 Squadron, RAF
The end of the war took away the purpose that for years had united young men of a dozen different countries in friendship and mutual loyalty. Flying together and fighting together, it had been a way of life and fulfilment that few would ever experience again, even if for so many others, it had been a way of death.

Corporal Patricia Coulson
RAF, administration
After the men came back from the Far East, they were given their Post Office books. We received a letter from a mother. Briefly, it read, 'My son who is living with me, has been given his Post Office book. Could you please give me authority to draw out the money to look after him? He has returned minus his

arms and legs.' He was 23 years old. This sums it all up. However much I may not remember of the past as I grow older, these things I saw and heard during this period of my life will always be with me.

Captain John MacAuslan
Intelligence Officer, 5th Reconnaissance Regiment

After the war ended, I was surprised that I wasn't all that elated. I just felt a slightly lost feeling – relieved a little bit that one was safe now – but not very happy. I didn't know what to do. I knew I'd have to be a solicitor but I didn't want to be a solicitor. What I knew about was all finished. I'd only had one leave at home in two years and I hadn't enjoyed it very much. It was rather depressing with blackouts and bad food and one thing and another. And now, what I'd known for such a long time vanished and there was nothing to take its place. One day I saw one of our corporals digging up the road in Chancery Lane when I was walking over to the Law Society. We talked and I was glad to see him. I think he was glad to see me. But there was really nothing to say. It was all gone.

Index of Contributors

Page numbers in *italic* refer to photographs

General Index

Page numbers in *italic* refer to photographs
Other italicised entries indicate names of ships and other vessels